The navy blue of the heavens is broken up by wisps of strato-cumulus from behind which peep myriad stars, dimmed in the brightness of the moon which casts a silver swathe across the ocean almost to her door. On the far side of the strait she can see white waves breaking soundlessly upon the dark rocks of Eisdalsa's southern shoreline. The tide is high enough tonight to crash over crumbling sea walls into the old discarded quarries which encircle the island.

Beyond Eisdalsa the strange triangular silhouettes of the Islands of the Sea stretch westwards toward the New World, encouraging yet more of the beleaguered islanders to set sail for other lands.

Millicent breathes deeply in the fresh clean air and thanks Providence for allowing her to dwell in this peaceful place.

Shivering involuntarily in a sudden gust of cooler air she turns to go in. At the same moment, a heavy cloud moves across the face of the moon and leaves the world in darkness . . .

Where the Wild Thyme Grows

Mary Withall

CORONET BOOKS
Hodder and Stoughton

First published in Great Britain in 1997 by Hodder and Stoughton
First published in paperback in 1997 by Hodder and Stoughton
A division of Hodder Headline PLC
A Coronet Paperback

10 9 8 7 6 5 4 3

British Library Cataloguing in Publication Data

Withall, Mary
Where the Wild Thyme Grows
1. English fiction – 20th century
I. Title
823.9´14 [F]

ISBN 0 340 64054 5

Printed and bound in Great Britain by
Mackays of Chatham PLC, Chatham, Kent

Hodder and Stoughton
A division of Hodder Headline PLC
338 Euston Road
London NW1 3BH

For Petre

Acknowledgements

In the writing of the Eisdalsa Trilogy, my thanks are due to the Curator of the Easdale Island Folk Museum, Jean Adams, for allowing me unlimited access to records of the slate-quarrying industry and the community which it sustained; also to Pam Moore, of the Museum of the Goldfields, Kalgoorlie, Western Austrailia.

Mary Withall
Easdale Island, Argyll, February 1996

The Beaton Family

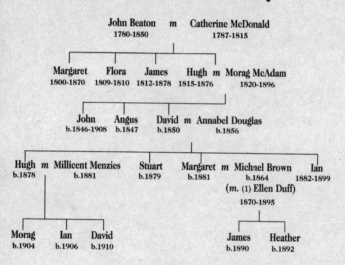

John Beaton *m* Catherine McDonald
1780-1850 · 1787-1815

Margaret 1800-1870 · Flora 1809-1810 · James 1812-1878 · Hugh *m* Morag McAdam 1815-1876 · 1820-1896

John b.1846-1908 · Angus b.1847 · David *m* Annabel Douglas b.1850 · b.1856

Hugh *m* Millicent Menzies b.1878 · b.1881 · Stuart b.1879 · Margaret *m* Michael Brown b.1881 · b.1864 · Ian 1882-1899
(*m.* (1) Ellen Duff) 1870-1895

Morag b.1904 · Ian b.1906 · David b.1910 · James b.1890 · Heather b.1892

The McGillivray Family

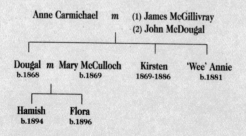

Anne Carmichael *m* (1) James McGillivray
(2) John McDougal

Dougal *m* Mary McCulloch b.1868 · b.1869 · Kirsten 1869-1886 · 'Wee' Annie b.1881

Hamish b.1894 · Flora b.1896

Preface

Eisdalsa 1913

It is midnight, and a full January moon bathes the island and the sea around it in a mystical white light. The sharp, ragged outlines of scarred rocks are softened and rounded by the shadows, and despite the season the breeze is gentle as it whispers around the walls of the whitewashed cottages which cling to the edge of the quiet harbour.

The heavy door to the old Volunteers' Drill Hall hangs from its one remaining hinge and swings drunkenly in a stronger gust of wind, complaining wheezily to have been left so neglected.

Between the ferry landing and the first of the cottages, the deserted schoolhouse stands sentinel. From rafters which once rang with the chanting of young voices hang fishing nets and sails, while ropes and spars, rods and creels, litter the floor. In the shadow of the school, the teacher's bothy stares blindly out upon the deserted houses. For a moment it seems that there might be someone within, as a ragged piece of white curtain flutters behind a cracked window pane, but no one has occupied this house since Katherine McLean closed the schoolhouse door behind the last of the children, and went to concentrate her energies upon her garden at Johnstones on Seileach.

The cottages around the green are all in darkness. Closer inspection will show that some have no windows and others have lost slates from the steeply pitched roofs. Here and there a door stands open, too swollen by the autumn rain ever to close again.

A pair of boots beside a door, a heap of coal, a pile of driftwood neatly stacked, indicate the cottages which are still occupied. Their inhabitants, too old to be burning the midnight oil, huddle in their beds for warmth . . . it is cheaper than burning precious fuel.

On the far side of the harbour, the house of the last quarry master, William Whylie, has been taken over by the McPhersons whose prodigious family fills the spacious dwelling to capacity. Here, alone, there are signs of recent industry. Spread before the house, in various stages of construction, are vessels of every size. Some are small rowing boats such as those which ferry the inhabitants of Eisdalsa across the strait to the village on Seileach each day. Others are fishing smacks used by those West Coast fishermen who earn their meagre living from the treacherous waters. The hull of a thirty-foot ketch, standing in the stocks, seems to dwarf even this, the largest house on the island. The enterprising McPherson brothers have turned the depression in the slate industry to their own advantage, by expanding their boat-building business in a spot ideally situated for the purpose.

On this side of the harbour there is only one other house: the cottage belonging to Margaret Brown, daughter of Dr David Beaton.

There is a light in the window. Margaret's mother, Annabel, sits alone beside the dying fire and dreams of the days when the island was alive with people, when hammers rang from dawn until dusk and the pumps which drained the deep quarries were never still. She dreams also of her former life at Tigh na Broch, and wonders where her son, Stuart, is tonight. David insisted upon his becoming a surgeon, but Stuart, just as determined a character as his father, won his own way in the end. He is somewhere on the high seas . . . a surgeon, certainly, but also a sailor. Even her husband has had to admit that Stuart looks wonderful in his smart naval uniform!

David must be at Dunoon tonight, preparing for another foray into the mountains, to visit some school or other. She hopes he is happy with his new job, that he feels it is worth these long weeks of separation. She has no desire to leave Eisdalsa and accompany him to Glasgow, particularly as he will be travelling about the country for most of the time. Once the medical inspection scheme is set up, she trusts he will have more time to spend at home. She really must exert herself over the question of finding a new house. They had considered Connel to be a handy place . . .

Across the water on the larger island of Seileach many of the cottages are deserted also but, as on Eisdalsa, there are still some signs of occupancy.

The telephone bell rings in Meg Roberts's tiny post office. She emerges from the bedroom next door in her diaphanous white nightdress and puts through a call to Tigh na Broch. She waits for young Dr Hugh to pick up the receiver, listens to his calm measured tones as he tells a distraught husband that he is on his way, and nods to herself with satisfaction. She had known that Bessy McArdle's baby would be born tonight. There was something about the way she was carrying herself when she came into the shop this morning. The poor doctor will have a long drive over the brae to the Ballahuan estate. It is fortunate that it is such a clear night.

She pulls out the plug when she hears Hugh Beaton put down his receiver, switches the set to standby, and creeps back to her bed.

At the end of the village street the substantial manse built for their minister by the parishioners of Eisdalsa lies in darkness. Old John McCulloch, unable to sleep, remembers his dear Ellen – he has been a widower for nearly twenty-five years – and wonders if his daughter Mary is already on the high seas, on her way to a new life in Australia.

They had wanted him to go with them, Mary and her husband, Dougal McGillivray. He was tempted to accept, especially when he found that Dougal's mother Anne intended to accompany them with her new husband, John McDougal. But the old folks here abouts cannot do without their minister. There has already been too much change. They need some element of stability in their lives, something which only he can provide.

Beyond the manse lies the Seileach school, struggling to stay open with fewer than twenty pupils mustered from the two islands of Eisdalsa and Seileach. One young schoolmaster in his first post is sufficient for this school which once employed two teachers and two pupils, in the days when Farquar Ogilvie was the principal and Elizabeth Duncan his assistant, in charge of the school on Eisdalsa Island.

Along the shore road which links the village with the rest of the island of Seileach, Tigh na Broch, the family home of the Beaton doctors nestles beneath the crags of Caisteal an Spuilleadair. The lights are on in the ground-floor surgery and there is evidence of activity in the stables, now a garage housing the doctor's Model T Ford. As Hugh Beaton backs the motor out on to the driveway his wife, Millicent, runs from the house carrying his medical bag. She kisses him lightly on the cheek and watches as he makes his way along the drive and turns left, on to the shore road. The acetylene headlamps, scarcely necessary in the bright moonlight, pick out the rocks beside the narrow track cut into the side of the hill, allowing her to follow his progress until he disappears around the corner at the head of Smiddy Brae.

For a few moments she surveys the scene, relishing the quiet of the balmy night. The navy blue of the heavens is broken up by wisps of strato-cumulus from behind which peep myriad stars, dimmed by the brightness of the moon which casts a silver swathe across the ocean almost to her door. On the far side of the strait she can see white waves breaking soundlessly upon the dark rocks of Eisdalsa's southern shoreline. The tide is high enough tonight to crash over crumbling sea walls into the old discarded quarries which encircle the island.

Beyond Eisdalsa the strange triangular silhouettes of the Islands of the Sea stretch out towards the New World, forever persuading the beleagered islanders to go seek their fortunes in the west.

Millicent breathes deeply of the fresh clean air and thanks providence for allowing her to dwell in this peaceful place.

Shivering involuntarily in a sudden gust of cooler air, she turns to go in. At the same moment, a heavy cloud moves across the face of the moon and leaves the world in darkness.

Part I

1913

Chapter 1

The iron wheels of the train rattled over another complex set of points, shaking at least one of the dozing occupants of the gloomy compartment into wakefulness. The black and white Border collie pricked her ears and surveyed her surroundings with pensive brown eyes.

The floor, although relatively free from litter, was covered with a fine film of dust, smelling of sulphur and coal-tar fumes. The bitch shifted her muzzle until it rested on the foot of her sleeping master. In this position the offensive smells were overlain by the more familiar tang of polished leather and Highland tweed. She lifted her nose, hoping to catch the longed-for scent of heather and salt spray through the partly open window. Disappointed, she lowered her head again and replaced it on her master's boot.

At the sudden increase of weight on his foot, Jack McDougal shifted uneasily, snorted abruptly and then sank back into slumber.

Their journey by rail from Glasgow to London had seemed endless. There was little comfort for second-class passengers travelling overnight; no sleeping cars or hot meals for those to whom every penny would be precious in the months to come. Little wonder, therefore, that the party from Argyll was exhausted on this, the last lap of their journey to Tilbury.

Anne McDougal stretched her arms, careful not to wake her husband. Her movement was sufficient to disturb the dog, however. She slunk between the legs of the other passengers and rested her heavy head on the woman's lap. Absently, Anne ruffled the soft fur, scratching the collie behind her ears.

'Hush, lass,' she murmured. 'We'll soon be there.'

Satisfied that all was well, the dog settled at Anne's feet and resumed her silent vigil.

Anne glanced at her husband's face, old and grey-looking in the early-morning light. She wondered, again, if it had been fair to expect John McDougal, now in his sixty-seventh year, to set out upon this great adventure so late in life. He had certainly seemed eager enough at the time. It was clear to all who had observed the elderly widower during the first months of his second marriage, that John McDougal was a new man since the Widow McGillivray had taken him in tow!

There will be plenty of time for resting on the long sea voyage, Anne assured herself. Nevertheless, she could not help feeling concern at the sight of those deep shadows resting beneath John's sunken eyelids, his pallor intensified by twenty-four hour's growth of black stubble.

She shifted her shoulders against the unyielding padding of the sparsely furnished carriage. The seats were narrow, forcing the sleeping passengers to rest in an unnaturally upright position. Her granddaughter's head had slipped sideways on to her brother's shoulder, her hat tilted, drunkenly. Anne smiled. Flora had been adamant that she should wear her best bonnet for the journey. Her raven black locks, piled forward on to her brow in the latest, although to Anne's mind too adult, style, hung in wisps over her ears.

Flora's brother, Hamish McGillivray, was wrought in his grandfather's image. Anne's first husband, Jamie, had been a large, rawboned individual with a shock of flaming red hair, a bushy Highlander's beard, and piercingly clear grey eyes. He had been a gentle giant, however, his voice carrying the soft intonations of the Outer Hebridean island where he had been born.

At the age of eighteen, his grandson resembled him in every respect save the beard. So much so that occasionally, in an unguarded moment, Anne had been so startled by the likeness as to imagine that it was her former husband's ghost she was seeing.

When Hamish spoke, however, it was with the mixed accents of the slate quarries of Argyll, where he had been raised, and the

Glasgow school to which he had won a scholarship. There was no hint of the quiet, musical tones which one associated with those from the islands of his ancestors.

For a time Anne allowed her thoughts to dwell on those last sad days on the island. Competition for foreign imports had reduced the price of slate to such a degree that it was no longer economic to quarry it. A fickle building industry now preferred to use clay tiles, while the product of the Eisdalsa quarries, the slate which for centuries had been used to roof castle and cathedral, country mansion and cottar's bothy, accumulated on the quayside. The men, paid only when the slate they had made was sold, had been forced to call upon the parish for support in order to feed their starving families.

Her son Dougal had been rather more fortunate than the other quarrymen. A beneficent laird had provided the funds for his education, and with a degree in engineering from the Royal School of Mines, he was equipped to work anywhere in the world. Dougal had William Whylie to thank for arranging this new appointment in the gold fields – the last generous gesture which the quarry master had been able to make on their behalf before his retirement.

Anne, torn between her love for her family and her attachment to her homeland, had had her decision made for her when old friends Elizabeth and William Whylie had announced their departure for a new life in the Borders. For Anne, Eisdalsa could never be the same without them, while for John McDougal and his son, too many unhappy memories and too much shame was attached to the island where both his daughters had borne illegitimate children.

Martha's child Iain, had grown into a fine boy of whom his grandfather could be justly proud but his mentally retarded younger daughter, Ellen, had murdered her baby when it was born and had been committed for life to an institution for the criminally insane.

Since the day they had taken Ellen from Inverary Jail to that terrible place on the outskirts of Edinburgh, he had not been able to lift his head in public. His first wife, Katrina had died of grief soon after, and he might well have followed had it not been for Anne McGillivray.

Mary McGillivray woke suddenly. She blinked in the dawn light that had begun to creep through the smeared glass, and rubbed her eyes.

'Are we nearly there, do you think, Ma?' she asked, stifling a yawn.

'We have been following the river for a long while,' her mother-in-law replied. 'The last stop was a place called Barking Creek,' she added, but the name meant nothing to either of them.

'I can see cranes.' Mary pointed from her position facing downstream of the River Thames.

'There have been many already,' said Anne. 'Every village seems to have its own dock.'

Soon a much larger conurbation came into view. Here vessels varying in size, but many considerably bigger than anything the two women had encountered on the West Coast of Scotland, were manoeuvring in the river. Some were leaving dock, others just about to tie up. Amazed at this amount of activity, Mary shook her husband.

'Look, Dougal,' she cried. 'Do you see the great port we are coming in to? Will one of these be our ship, do you think?'

He stretched, yawned, and gazed sleepily in the direction she indicated. Then he laughed.

'This looks like Rainham village,' he said. 'We are still some way from Tilbury. As for the ships – why, they are merely coasters, small cargo vessels. I trust that the S. S. *Geraldtown* will be a little larger and a deal more modern than these!'

Mary sat back and concentrated on the sepia print of a sea-front with pier which faced her across the carriage. Two such illustrations decorated either wall of the compartment. Between each pair of pictures hung a small mirror. These might have been quite an asset had they not been so covered in grime as to distort any reflection. Flora, disturbed by the talking, opened her eyes, drew away from her brother and began to fiddle with her hat. Catching sight of the mirror, she stood up, steadying herself by holding on to the luggage rack as the carriage swayed. She observed her image with dismay.

'What a mess!' she exclaimed, and tentatively wiped an already soiled glove across the surface, the better to survey the ravages after their night of travelling. She removed her hat, a confection of squashed velvet lavishly decorated with ribbons and silk flowers, and exposed a straggling coiffure. This latest fashion she had been permitted to wear only since her sixteenth birthday, a week or two before. How much simpler its dressing would have been now, she realised, if she had still worn her hair in its former, thick dark braids.

Valiantly she struggled with the elaborate arrangement until, teased mercilessly by her brother, now also awake, she pulled the hat firmly back on to her head and fixed it securely with long pins.

'Never mind, lass,' said her grandmother mildly. 'Once we are aboard ship you will have all the time in the world to primp.'

'Yes, indeed,' agreed Hamish, cringing at the thought of such frivolous feminine activity. 'Six weeks at the very least!'

'Oh, but I do so want to make a good first impression on the other passengers,' complained Flora, who would perhaps have stood up and repeated her efforts had not her mother put out a restraining hand.

'See here,' Mary interrupted, 'we are coming into another station.' Then, in a voice filled with awe, 'Oh my, can this one be our ship?'

They all crowded to the side of the carriage in order to gain their first view of the *Geraldtown*, the vessel which was to carry them to their new life in Western Australia.

'Now you see what I mean by big,' declared Dougal, as they gazed in wonderment at the imposing structure alongside which the train had come to a halt. The giant hull, lined with gleaming portholes, blocked out everything else, including the daylight. Towering high above the station roof, the black and red funnels belched smoke – a signal that the preparations for departure were well underway. There were two smartly painted gangways by which passengers were already boarding.

The McDougals and the McGillivrays descended from the

carriage and joined the queue of people filing past the customs and emigration officers. All about them there was a kind of orderly turmoil. Each member of the party felt a rising sense of anticipation.

Vicky, the collie bitch, whined in uncharacteristic fashion, and Jack bent down to whisper words of comfort in her ear. Whether she was confused and frightened by the crowds, or whether she sensed that she was soon to be separated from her master, he did not know. It would not be the first time she had exhibited such acute intuition. Once on board Jack was going to have to part with her. Livestock, even dogs, must be confined to the cargo deck. He was very anxious about Vicky's reaction to the separation. He had never been out of her sight since she was six weeks old.

Passage to Australia in the first decades of the twentieth century was encouraged by an Australian government seeking to populate its vast, empty territories with Europeans, particularly those of British stock. By making the fare sufficiently modest to accommodate the pockets of skilled artisans, working-class people of good character, they hoped to be able to keep out the threatening hordes of the eastern races hammering on their door, begging admission to the new lands of the Commonwealth.

Applications for immigration into Australia had been made some months before. There had been no difficulty for Dougal McGillivray and his family; he was going out to a job to which he had already been officially appointed. His son, Hamish, was of the age and calibre most needed. He had recently completed an apprenticeship with a firm of electrical engineers and would have no difficulty finding employment. There might have been a few eyebrows raised at John McDougal's age, but in view of the fact that Jack was accompanying his parent, and that John had the proceeds from the sale of his croft on Eisdalsa to invest in his new country, any objections were finally waived.

Their papers in order, the party was free to board the *Geraldtown* by the second-class gangway.

Stewards awaited the eager passengers as they stepped down on to the deck, anxious to have them all safely stowed in their allotted cabins before the ship sailed. The men were escorted to

C deck and the women one flight up, to D deck. In second class, passengers were expected to share a cabin between four – an arrangement with which the four men were quite content. The three women, however, wondered dubiously who their travelling companion would be. It would be most tiresome if the stranger was not an agreeable sort of person.

Anne and Mary, claiming priority because of age, selected the lower bunks. Flora, happily ensconced upon the tier above her mother, declared, 'Suppose she is older than you, Mama? She might insist that you remove yourself!'

'Nothing will make me shift now that I am settled,' Mary protested, and as though to take full possession of the space, she deliberately arranged her toiletries upon the tiny shelf behind her head.

They did not have to wait long. Within a few minutes there was a sharp rap on the door. A small, swarthy steward in immaculate white uniform entered bearing innumerable bags, and a somewhat battered hatbox. The three women viewed these with dismay. Each of them had been most particular about bringing only the most essential items into the cabin, the main bulk of their belongings having been sent ahead for storage in the hold. The newcomer's luggage took up most of the available floor space.

There was a brief exchange in the corridor outside, and then their companion for the voyage stepped into the cabin.

She was a youngish woman of perhaps twenty-five or thirty. Her complexion being fresh and rosy, it was difficult to be precise about her age. Her face was unadorned by the creams and powders so commonly in use, and there was no hint of artificial colour on her lips and cheeks. For this Mary was thankful. Flora was sufficiently taken up with all these modern foibles already. She had no need of a tutor!

The stranger's fair hair was scraped back from her face and screwed into an unattractive bun. Her dress, although of good woollen cloth, was a drab brown colour that did nothing to enhance her somewhat plain features.

The newcomer looked about her expectantly, eyes adjusting to the dim light in the cabin. On registering the pleasant smiles of the three Scotswomen, her face lit up instantly. The transformation was amazing.

Bright blue eyes, widely set, sparkled in what little sunlight there was, and the hint of crow's feet at their corners, curving upwards attractively, suggested that this was someone accustomed to smiling most of the time. A perfect row of brilliant white teeth was exposed by her wide, unaffected grin.

'Oh, good!' she cried. 'I feared that I might find myself in disagreeable company but here you are . . . three more welcoming faces I could not have hoped to encounter.'

It was difficult in such cramped quarters for the ladies to observe the normal proprieties of handshaking, but Mary stood up and took the proffered hand.

'Let me introduce you,' she said. 'This is my mother-in-law, Anne McDougal.' Anne smiled and nodded, unable to reach out to take the stranger's hand. 'My daughter, Flora,' Mary continued. 'And I am Mary McGillivray.'

The young woman raised an eyebrow at this, recognising the difference in the names. 'My mother-in-law has recently re-married,' Mary hastened to explain.

'And I,' announced the newcomer, 'am Jean Parsons, lately of the village of Chiddingstone, in Kent.'

'Well, Miss Parsons,' said Mary, 'as you can see, we have already arranged ourselves according to our own preference. I trust that you will not mind taking the upper berth?'

'Indeed not,' declared Jean, confirming it by flinging the jacket which she had been carrying over her arm on to the bunk indicated.

'Please do not think me impudent for saying so,' she continued, 'but you all come from Scotland, do you not?'

'From Argyll,' Anne assented. 'We are from the parish of Kilbrendan, on the West Coast.'

'From a small island called Eisdalsa,' Flora chipped in.

'I too am from a small village,' Jean told them. 'How glad I am not to be travelling with townsfolk. They can be so pushy.' She broke into a peal of infectious laughter which set them all off.

had it. Yet I knew just how it would look. I knew where every piece of furniture would stand.'

Margaret put her arm about the little girl's shoulders.

'I am so glad that you recognise it,' she said. 'When I was not much older than you are now, my grandmama would allow me to come and stay with her for a few days at a time, just the two of us . . . and old Sheilagh, of course.'

Morag knew all about the Beatons' servant who had lived with them as housekeeper, nursemaid and friend, when even Grandpa David was a boy.

'What was she like . . . old Sheilagh, I mean?'

Margaret perched on the arm of the chair.

Above their heads they could hear the sound of cupboards opening and closing, and the patter of feet as Ian ran hither and thither, exploring the loft rooms, now cleared and tidily furnished.

'Sheilagh was a true islander,' Margaret explained. 'She came from the Isle of Skye.' She recalled with a pang of regret those sharp eyes which never missed anything, and the soft, unwrinkled rosy cheeks on that round, smiling old face. She could still hear the steady clicking of knitting needles, and the little grunt which marked disapproval of something which one of her charges had said or done.

'It was Sheilagh who told me many of the old folk tales which I put into my book, and Granny Morag too, of course . . . she had a store of old remedies and predictions, but Sheilagh's tales were the best!'

Both Morag and Ian had absorbed Margaret's stories from the cradle, and one of Morag's most precious possessions was the copy of her aunt's book of *Highland Folk Tales*, lovingly inscribed.

The conversation was interrupted abruptly when Ian came down the stairs two at a time and would probably have fallen had not Margaret leapt forward to catch him.

'It's all clear upstairs,' he cried excitedly. 'There are two bedrooms, each with a little bed in it. Who will sleep there, Auntie?'

'Anyone who comes to stay,' was her reply. She gathered him

into her arms, despite his great age. 'You, if you want to,' she went on, 'and if your mama will let you.'

'Oh, can we? Can we stay with you, Auntie?' he pleaded.

'May we,' Morag corrected him, primly.

Ignoring his sister, the boy persisted, 'Can we stay here with you, Auntie, on our own, I mean?'

'You may stay sometimes when Uncle Michael and I come for weekends. We may even be here for longer in the summer, when he has a holiday. Uncle Stuart will use it too, when he is on leave, and so will some of our friends from the city.'

'Can . . .' he caught Morag's eye '. . . may I sleep in one of the beds upstairs?' he begged.

'Well, as a matter of fact . . .' she took hold of Ian's hand and led him over to the wooden panelling beside the range '. . . I thought that you and Davy might like to sleep in here.' She slid back the panelling to reveal a bed, barely five feet long but wide enough to take two slim youngsters side by side.

'Ooh, a box bed,' the boy exclaimed delightedly. 'I've never slept in a box bed. Why haven't we seen this before?'

'Because,' Morag observed dryly, 'Grandpa's bookcase was standing in front of it.'

Ian would not be satisfied until he had been allowed to creep inside and pull the sliding door to after him.

'Well, goodness me,' observed Millicent Beaton from the doorway, 'that is the first time I have seen Ian go to bed without argument!'

She staggered under her load and Margaret went forward to help her. In one hand Millicent carried a bag of groceries and under the other arm David Beaton Junior, a plump little two-year-old.

'I have brought us some tea,' said Millicent. 'I knew you would not have bothered with anything to eat.'

Margaret took the baby and sat him down on the rug before the range. In two seconds he was on his feet and over at the box bed, clamouring to be let in beside his brother.

Morag, unbidden, had disappeared into the narrow scullery and was carefully unloading the contents of her mother's bag.

They chatted and giggled as they struggled to find places to put everything in the confined space. Very soon compromises had been arrived at, allocations agreed, and the cabin began to look quite tidy.

'Comfortable,' declared Jean approvingly as she settled back against the pillows of her elevated perch, hugging her knees in girlish fashion as she struggled to gain a view through the porthole.

Anne wondered how the menfolk would be managing down below, but decided against going to organise them. Men had their own peculiar methods of living in close confinement and would no doubt work out an amicable solution among themselves. Putting aside all thoughts of housewifely duties for the time being, she smiled with satisfaction as she remarked, 'I can see that this voyage is going to be a complete rest!'

From outside there came the unmistakable sounds of an imminent departure. Flora tried to see what was happening through the porthole, and announced that the gangplank had been removed and that she could see the gap between ship and shore steadily widening.

'Oh, Mama,' she cried, 'can we go up on deck to wave goodbye to England?'

'You go along, my dear,' Mary replied. 'I shall stay here with Grandmama and rest a little.' She felt instinctively that, like herself, Anne had made her farewells to her native land when they had been ferried across the narrow channel between Eisdalsa Island and Seileach, to catch the steamer for Glasgow. Was it really only a week ago?

The steamer, which had carried them through the Sound of Lorn and south to Crinan, had offered them their final view of home. They had no tears left to shed for this grubby port of Tilbury, on London's river.

'I think I'll join you, if I may?' declared Jean.

'Oh, would you, Miss Parsons?' Flora replied, delighted. 'I am not sure I could find this cabin again on my own.'

'Of course,' said their new friend. 'And that's enough of this Miss Parsons nonsense. Just call me Jean!'

The door closed with a thump. Anne and Mary exchanged exasperated looks, and then laughed.

'It will be good for Flora to have a friend,' commented Mary. 'Miss Parsons seems an agreeable enough person, don't you think?'

Anne nodded absently. She had taken from her handbag a crumpled envelope from which she extracted an obviously much-read letter.

20 Old Ford Road, Bow
23 January, 1913

My Dearest Mama,
I am so pleased that things are going well for you all at home. It cannot be long now before you set out upon your great adventure. I know that you would be happy to have me join you, but I do hope you will understand that, for the time being at any rate, I feel that I am needed here. If in due course my work for the WSPU is finished, then I might well come out to Australia to join you. I am given to understand that there are opportunities for women lawyers to obtain employment in that country.

Please understand that it is not any lack of family feeling which keeps me here, but only the certain knowledge that ours is a just cause, one for which those of us who are best equipped, through education and privilege, must fight the hardest.

I will not come to the boat to see you off. We are neither of us good at partings, are we? I know that dear John will take good care of you.

Pray for our speedy success.
You will be always in my thoughts.
Your loving daughter,
Annie

Mary watched her mother-in-law fold the letter and replace it in the envelope.

'You really must not worry, Ma,' she said. 'Annie is a big girl. She can take care of herself!'

'But we shall be so far away . . . if anything happens . . . you know.'

They were both well aware of the trouble which the Suffragettes had been getting into in the past few months. The activities of the Women's Social and Political Union occupied the front pages of every newspaper. There had been suggestions of long terms of imprisonment for civil disorder, and the WSPU was proposing that those who were imprisoned should make their protest known by means of hunger strikes.

Anne shuddered at the thought of her girl being locked up. Tears welled in her eyes, and Mary went and sat beside her. Wordlessly, they clung together as the shouts and singing of passengers and their friends on the dock were drowned by the ship's siren announcing their departure.

Jean and Flora forced their way to the ship's side, and hung over the railing. Bunting of every colour fluttered in the breeze, lending an air of festivity to the occasion. As passengers crowded the shoreward side of the deck, to get a last view of loved ones, a military band which had formed up on the quay played 'Will Ye No Come Back Again?'. Scarcely had Jean and Flora begun to join in the familiar tune than it changed to 'Auld Lang Syne'. The singing was taken up all around them. English, Irish and Welsh voices blended with those of the Scots aboard, to sing the familiar words. Flora McGillivray, clinging desperately to her imprudent headgear, was surprised that this mighty throng actually knew a song so beloved in her own homeland. She joined in with gusto.

Beside her, Jean Parsons sang lustily. Then, glancing at each other, the two young women were suddenly choked with emotion. Each noted the tears in the other's eyes, and they clung together in a moment of mutual sadness at parting from the country of their birth. Who knew if they would ever see these shores again?

The *Geraldtown* was soon well out into the river, bearing down towards the estuary on the ebbing tide.

Slowly the deck began to clear, and Jean and Flora were able to move more freely, and to observe those passengers who, like themselves, were reluctant to go below to their cabins.

Suddenly Flora spotted her brother standing beside the rail with John McDougal and her father, and insisted upon introducing her newfound friend to the rest of the party from Argyll.

'Hamish – Hamish!' she cried, to attract his attention.

'Oh, lor',' Hamish observed as his sister approached. 'See what a ragbag of an acquaintance our Flora has found for herself.'

John McDougal, who was less inclined to make snap judgements about his fellow human beings, turned slowly to greet his step-granddaughter and was immediately struck by the friendly smile and straightforward, honest gaze of her companion.

'Grandfather,' said Flora, slipping her arm comfortably beneath that of her grandmother's new husband, 'this is Miss Parsons who is to share our cabin with us for the voyage. Jean, this is John McDougal.'

Jean shook the old man's hand warmly.

'Pleased to meet you.' She bobbed her knee with old-world courtesy, thereby enchanting John. Hamish was unimpressed. Surely his sister did not intend to make a friend of an English woman?

'My father, Dougal McGillivray,' Flora continued. Again Jean made her bob, and Dougal shook her hand, giving her a friendly greeting.

'Welcome aboard, Miss Parsons,' he grinned.

'And this is Hamish,' Flora went on, undeterred by her brother's ill-disguised distaste.

As a young child Hamish McGillivray had been something of a disappointment to both his parents. He had shown little enthusiasm for academic study and when he went missing from classes, which was often, he was most likely to be found tinkering with some discarded piece of machinery in the smithy or operating the treadle of the lathe for Mr McPherson the joiner.

Had his grandfather been alive to see it, James McGillivray would have recognised in the boy something of that same inquisitive, inventive spirit which had governed his own progress from tea boy and foreman's runner to gang boss, before his accident had rendered him unfit for anything but an office job.

Hamish's parents, having both worked their way through college by winning scholarships had hoped that their son would follow a similar path and were sorely disappointed when Hamish announced that the new power source, electricity, held untold opportunities for a practical man and that he wanted to become an electrician.

Dougal had found a place for Hamish with one of Glasgow's leading installation engineers, who were at that time beginning to electrify the tramways and some of the city's most prestigious buildings.

In an environment which suited him, Hamish had soon begun to shine among his contemporaries, and encouraged by the apprentice master he began to study at night school. Here, where mathematics and physics could be applied to his everyday work, he not only found his studies to be absorbing but was surprised at the ease with which he could remember the information when there was a purpose to it.

At the end of five years, Hamish had returned home with a certificate in his pocket from the City and Guilds of London Institute, and a gold medal for gaining the highest marks in electrical engineering in the country.

Away from home at such a young age, and living amongst a group of boys brought up on the streets of Glasgow, Hamish might well have been bullied and led astray by his street-wise companions. On the contrary, it had soon become clear to him that the rigours of life on the West Coast coupled with his Grandfather's legacy of a tall and muscular frame, had prepared him admirably for fighting his battles for supremacy in the factory yard. His superior strength and intellect were quickly recognised not only by his employers but also by his contemporaries. Within a few weeks of joining the apprentice boys he had become the leader of the dormitory.

On the whole Hamish was pretty tolerant of his fellow men. He did not suffer fools gladly, but he was always ready to lend a hand to the underdog where he felt that help was deserved, and he was staunchly loyal to his friends, his family and his country. He was fiercely Scottish and suspicious of foreigners – in particular, the English.

Hamish's knowledge of Scottish history had been gained, not in the schoolroom which he had abhorred, but on the terraces of Hampden Park football ground and in the pubs after the match. So far as Hamish was concerned the English were all tyrants as was shown by the behaviour of Edward the First and King Billy. They had drained Scotland of her resources and heaped intolerable taxation on her people. English landlords had driven crofters from their homes to seek a better life overseas. The English were loud-spoken, arrogant and stupid and they talked in a peculiar way as if their mouths were full of marbles . . .

At the Evening Institute he had rubbed shoulders with all manner of people of different origins and learned to appreciate their various good points. His encounters with the senior management of the firm he had worked for, and with such people as William Whylie, the Cornish quarry master at Eisdalsa, may have begun to soften his attitude somewhat in recent months, but Flora needn't think that he was going to befriend this dowdy looking English governess just to satisfy her whims.

If Jean noticed anything remiss in the boy's behaviour, she gave no sign. Flora chattered away happily about her expectations of what life would be like in Australia, explaining to her new friend all about her father's appointment as a mining engineer and how her grandparents planned to set up a farm nearby, so that the whole family could stay close together.

From time to time John or Dougal interposed with a mild comment when Flora became too carried away. The effect of it all was to make Jean feel very much alone in the world and envious of the close ties which bound this Scottish family.

Jean would have proceeded to tell them something of her own plans for the future, but at this point they were joined by yet another member of the party.

Jack McDougal, having satisfied himself that his collie was comfortably settled in her kennel down below, had come to seek out his travelling companions. A naturally shy person, and still a bachelor in his early forties, he hesitated when he saw a strange woman in the company. Indeed, he might well have held back and slipped away quietly had not a merry peal of laughter, coming from the very object of his embarrassment, attracted him.

'Jack!' his father beckoned. 'Come and meet the young lady who is to share the voyage with our womenfolk. Miss Parsons, this is my son, Jack.'

Shyly, he put out his hand and murmured, 'Good day to you, ma'am.'

'Oh, please, do call me Jean,' the young woman requested, spiritedly. 'And I shall call you Jack, if I may?'

Jack had turned a brilliant shade of red. Disconcerted by her close proximity, he stuck one finger into the stiff white collar which seemed suddenly to be choking him, and drew it round the back of his neck.

'Oh, my,' exclaimed Miss Parsons. 'How warm and uncomfortable you look. Surely it is not necessary for the gentlemen to dress so formally aboard ship?'

'Indeed, I hope not,' John McDougal chuckled. 'With your permission, ma'am, we will wear our shirts without collars tomorrow.'

Flora, who had a great fondness for both the men in her grandmother's new family, now stepped forward and took Jack's arm.

'What about poor Vicky, Jack? Have you seen where they have put her?'

Flora understood how he hated to be separated from his dog. He had been most distressed to learn that she could not spend the voyage in the cabin with him. The girl was relieved to see him smile in answer to her question.

'Och,' he declared, 'she has a fine sleeping kennel and a good run all to herself. Already she has won the heart of the mulatto fellow who has charge of the animals – and just to make her feel at home there is a small flock of pedigree Cheviots keeping her company.'

'That's wonderful,' observed Flora. 'When may we go to visit her?'

'The man said to go and give her a wee walk every morning and evening,' Jack replied. 'You may come with me sometimes, if you like.' Then, surprising even himself, he turned to Jean. 'Perhaps you would care to visit the animals, ma'am? There are cows, pigs, and all manner of fowls being transported.'

'I most certainly would,' she replied. 'I come of farming stock myself, you know!'

He did not, but the information seemed to please him inordinately.

Glancing from one to the other, the youthful Flora thought she detected a certain attraction between these two. She did so hope that she was right. It seemed cruelly unfair that her grandmother's stepson should have no woman of his own. In the eyes of the romantic sixteen-year-old, it was unthinkable that anyone should go unmarried for so long!

'Your service!' Hamish called, as he surrendered his quoit to his partner.

'Oh, damn!' exclaimed Tom Pain as his aim went wide and the pair on the far side of the net whooped with delight.

Hamish turned around, annoyed to see the reason for his partner's loss of concentration.

'What are you doing there, Flora?' he demanded crossly. 'You're putting Tom off his stroke.'

'I can sit here and watch if I like.' She pouted. 'You don't own the whole deck.'

'I've had enough anyway,' declared Tom, wiping his sleeve across his brow. 'Why don't you play a game of singles?' he suggested to Hamish. 'While I take your sister down for a drink.'

Flora smiled triumphantly over her shoulder at her brother as the cheerful Londoner took hold of her elbow and guided her towards the gangway.

Tom was not exactly handsome, not by the standards of the heroes in the cheap novels with which Flora passed her leisure hours, but he had a kind face, with brown eyes like those of a cocker spaniel and chestnut-coloured hair which curled over his forehead and behind his ears in a most engaging manner. He was of stocky build, probably three or four inches shorter than her brother, and he was strong. His shoulder muscles, developed during the months he had spent as a stevedore in London's dockyards, rippled beneath his cotton shirt. The silky gingerish hairs which covered his sun-browned arms tickled her cheek excitingly as he handed her down the narrow stairway to the lower deck.

The two Smythe sisters were seated in a corner of the saloon. Flora noted with satisfaction their envious glances in her direction as Tom seated her in chivalrous fashion before going to the bar to order their drinks.

'For the young lady, a long cool lemonade,' he told the barman, glancing across at Flora for her approval, 'and a cold beer for me, if you please.'

He carried the drinks to the table, calling out some pleasantry to the Smythe sisters. Flora, in seventh heaven herself, was magnanimous in her acceptance of his attention to the other girls. She could afford to be generous, after all, she was the one he was sitting with. She was the one for whom he had bought a lemonade.

'They tell me there is to be a dance tonight in the main ball-room,' Tom observed as he despatched half a pint of beer in a single swallow. The game had made him thirsty.

'I believe so,' Flora replied nonchalantly, every nerve tingling with anticipation.

'Will you go?' he asked lightly.

'I might,' she replied, knowing full well that nothing could keep her away.

'I'll call for you at about seven, then . . . if you like?' he suggested. Flora could not believe that this was happening to her. A real beau, her very first . . . and not even a lad of her own age, like those wretched boys who had tormented her at school, but a grown man. She glowed with pleasure.

After a while they rose to go their separate ways. As Flora passed ahead of him, easing herself around the table where the Smythe sisters still sat, Tom leant over the back of one of the chairs and said something to them. They both listened intently, and then Rosie laughed.

'That sounds fun,' she cried.

'Don't forget to save at least one dance apiece for me!' Tom called back over his shoulder.

'As many as you like,' giggled Rosie.

Flora would have liked to have shared the joke, but was far too reticent to ask what he had said to the girls. Was it quite proper for one's boyfriend to speak quite so freely with other girls? she wondered. Determined not to show how jealous she was, she avoided making any comment about the exchange, thanked him politely for the drink and made her way to her cabin.

Chapter 2

Annabel Beaton wandered along the shoreline, retrieving the odd pieces of driftwood which seemed to gather in this west-facing bay. She supposed that it must be some quirk of the currents which swirled and eddied around the tiny island that brought everything to rest in this one spot. She broke up the remains of a shattered fish box and placed the pieces in her basket. Stencilled on the longer side were the words 'Gillies of Oban'. She wondered how long it had taken for the box, no doubt discarded by some inept handler on the quay some miles to the north, to reach Eisdalsa. She smiled to herself when she considered what stories her Margaret might weave about the adventures of such a piece of flotsam.

She had reached the eastern end of the beach. Before her there rose a barrier of whinstone rock, part of that spine of hard volcanic material that bisected the island from north-east to south-west. She must either climb over the boulders, or struggle up the steep scree of waste slate left from the quarrying activities which had now all but ceased on the island.

Choosing the whinstone route, she scrambled upwards, placing the half-filled basket just above her at every step, until at last she was able to sit astride the highest point of the barrier and look down into the still waters which filled the discarded quarry at its foot.

Exposed now to the full force of the chill February breeze, Annabel decided that this was no place to sit and daydream. She clambered down to the rim of the quarry and made her way cautiously, around the edge towards the great wall which the Eisdalsa masons had constructed a century before to keep back

25

the sea. She noted with dismay that in places the vertically set stone slabs, which were held in place by dint of their own weight and the mason's art, had been forced out of line, and in some places gaps were beginning to open along the top of the wall. Without the regular maintenance of former days, the quarry would soon be open to the sea.

At least we shall have fish coming in, she thought to herself, and where there are fish, seals will follow.

Since she had come to live in Margaret's house on the island, for much of her time quite alone, she had taken to making early-morning forays along the beach to collect the driftwood and to observe the wildlife. She knew where the sea otters had their holt and upon which sea-smoothed rocks the female seals deposited their young whilst they went searching for food. She could recognise a variety of sea birds by their appearance and their calls, and had begun to record the wild flowers that grew in profusion across the deserted landscape.

She had reached the far end of the wall now and was making her way through rough heather and across hummocks of freshly sprouting wild thyme. Those tender green shoots would become swathes of delicate purple flowers in a month or so. When she reached the main path which skirted the base of the hill, she was startled by a noise which she had come to believe might never again be heard in this place: the steady clip-clip of a slater's zax.

Beyond the pathway, between it and the hill, was a quarry – shallow by Eisdalsa standards, no more than a hundred feet in depth. It was one of the few which had no water collecting in its bottom, and was named the Klondike because it had been opened in 1896, the year of the Canadian Gold Rush. On the quarry floor squatted a gnome-like figure, his head bent over his work so that his big round bonnet of faded tartan quite hid his face. On one side he had gathered to him a pile of half-finished or damaged slates, discarded in more profitable times, while upon his other side stood a steadily growing pile of neatly finished roofing slates. Small by commercial standards, these undersized tiles would never the less make a sound covering for some poor cottar's roof.

'Good day to you, Wullie Prentice,' Annabel called to the old man. She had known him in earlier days as a strapping fellow, an inveterate bachelor with an eye for the ladies. The thick bright auburn locks were grizzled now, and the lithe body shrivelled and bowed by rheumatism, but when he lifted his gaze to identify the speaker, there was that same teasing grin and bright sparkle in Wullie's grey eyes that had turned many a lassie's head in former years.

'It iss good to see you out and about so early in the day, Mistress Beaton, so it iss,' he called in his soft, lilting Highland tones. 'And how iss the good doctor?'

'Still finding his feet in his new job, Wullie,' she replied, and approached closer to the quarry's edge.

'I am so glad to see someone is still cutting the slates,' Annabel observed, remembering the days not so very long ago when the whole island was given over to the winning of slate, and when each day was marked out by the sounding of the quarry bell, warning of blasting or indicating the end of working.

'It iss for old Widow McFadden's roof, Mrs Beaton,' he explained. 'The Factor has agreed that I may glean what slates I can from the site and use them for the repairs.'

'That's a splendid idea, Wullie,' she called back. 'Come along for a piece and a cup of tea later on. I have a few wee repairs that you might be able to fix in my daughter's house.'

There was little enough to occupy the few elderly folk left living on Eisdalsa. The young men and women had gone away to find work in the Lowlands; some had even gone across the seas, following the example of her friend Anne McDougal and her family. No doubt they would begin to send money home to help their relatives once they had established themselves, but in the meantime the old folks were having a pretty thin time of it.

Acknowledging the invitation, Wullie gave her a cheerful wave and she moved off along the path, catching her stockings on the straggling briars. Beneath a tangle of blackthorn and wild fuchsia, she spied a clump of celandines glowing bright yellow in the shadows. In a week or two from now, this bank would be carpeted in primroses.

As if to confirm the promise of spring, a little jenny wren began to sing stridently from the thicket beneath the escarpment.

Only last September, she and Anne had gathered brambles from these hedges beside the path. Where was she now? Annabel wondered. Anne's going, so soon after the departure of Elizabeth and William Whylie, had left a great yawning chasm in Annabel's existence. With David away also, she felt deserted and very lonely.

'Life must go on!' she told herself, shrugging off this moment of sadness. Maybe things would improve soon. This evening she would write a letter to Anne. Arriving in a strange country on the other side of the world, she would be sure to welcome a letter from home.

As she approached her house Annabel caught sight of her son Hugh striding towards her across the green.

'Just in time for a cup of tea!' she called, and waited to give him a peck on the cheek before slipping before him into the cottage.

'There's a telephone message from Pa,' the young Dr Beaton told his mother. 'He says that if you will meet him at Margaret's house tomorrow afternoon, he would like to take you to see a place he has heard about in Connel.'

Immediately she was all agitation. Really it was too bad of David to spring such surprises on her. 'How does he expect me to arrange transport to Oban at such short notice?' she demanded.

'It so happens that I have a meeting at the hospital in the morning.' Hugh smiled at her anxious frown. 'You can ride into town with me.'

'Everything happens so suddenly these days,' his mother argued, plaintively. 'Everyone is in such a hurry. I blame it on that wretched telephone.'

Her son laughed aloud at this. 'One can't stand in the path of progress, Mama . . . not even you!'

'And what about Margaret, pray?' Annabel demanded querulously. 'Does she appreciate that her parents will be descending upon her household, presumably for luncheon?'

'All arranged, Ma. Father had already made arrangements with her before passing his message on to you.'

There he was, at it again, arranging everyone's lives for them. As she bustled about in the tiny kitchen Annabel recalled other times when David had assumed total control of his family's personal affairs.

It had been his earlier collaboration with Elizabeth, now Mrs Whylie, in attempting to improve the health of her Eisdalsa pupils, which had inspired his plan for the regular medical inspection of all schoolchildren. Maintaining that a healthy start in life would ensure a more robust adulthood, he had set about proving to the authorities the benefits to be gained from monitoring the state of children's health during their time at school. Having at last captured the attention of the Chief Medical Officer, and having obtained Council approval for his scheme, it was inevitable that David should have been offered the prestigious appointment of Schools Medical Officer for the County of Argyll.

Even as she had painstakingly copied out his plan in a legible hand, Annabel had known that this appointment was going to bring about the total disruption of her comfortable existence. This she might have accepted, had her husband shown even the slightest interest in her own reaction to the proposed alteration to their lives. As it was, she had learnt of his decision to take up the new post by being asked to rewrite his acceptance letter. Not once had he discussed with her the consequences of the changes they would be obliged to make, so that when he had announced that he had found an apartment for them in Dumbarton, close to the County Offices, she had refused to accompany him.

She would live in Margaret's cottage on Eisdalsa, she had declared. He might visit her there whenever he was in the district, but she had no intention of going to live in the town.

David had been stunned by her refusal. Even now she had to laugh to herself at his expression of utter bewilderment when she did not go along with his proposal.

The rift might have been irreversible had David not capitulated at the last minute, agreeing that once he had established the framework of his new organisation, they would buy a house in a place, not too far away from Hugh and Margaret, with good communications to all parts of the country.

Angrily, Annabel poured boiling water into her brown earthenware teapot. Even now, after that terrible argument which had almost resulted in their parting for ever, David had not learnt his lesson!

Her annoyance was short-lived, however. After all, she mused, it only proved how anxious he was that they should be together again . . . and she herself had suggested that Connel would be the ideal place.

By the time she rejoined Hugh in the living room, she was smiling.

'What time shall we be starting out in the morning?' she demanded.

Aboard S.S. Geraldtown
Somewhere in the Indian Ocean
20 February, 1913

To Mrs Elizabeth Whylie
Solway Academy for Girls
Annan, Dumfrieshire

My Dear Elizabeth,
We shall be docking in Colombo in a few days' time and I could not forego this opportunity of writing to tell you something of our journey so far.

The ship is a marvel of man's ingenuity . . . I would never have thought that so many people and so many objects could be put so comfortably into what is, after all, a very small space! We are in the second-class accommodation where the men and women are in separate cabins in order that four persons may bunk together. This is a little trying for a pair of newly-weds like John and myself, and I am sure that Dougal and Mary feel equally deprived. We do, however, manage to arrange to have a short time alone together every day . . . the others are very understanding.

Our cabin companion is a delightful person called Jean Parsons, English, but a country girl like ourselves. Although she is nearer Mary's age than Flora's, she has befriended the girl, and since she is a governess, going to teach in

Adelaide, Mary is very happy to see the two of them spending so much time together.

Hamish has met a group of young men of his own age, all fired with enthusiasm for their new life in Australia. Most of them are bound for the towns where they believe that work is to be found. Hamish now talks constantly of the opportunities there are to be found in Sydney and even Brisbane.

As you know, I was rather worried as to how well John would stand the upheaval. Sixty-six is a great age at which to be setting out upon such an adventure. In fact, both the inactivity and the warm climate have done wonders for him. He has shed ten years in these last weeks. It was a great wrench for him to leave Eisdalsa, as it was for us all. Before we left, he visited Katrina's grave for the last time, and I could see that he was struggling with the thought that he would not be able to do so again. Fortunately, his daughter Martha was with us at the time, and she has promised to keep flowers on her mother's grave, and also on those of my Jamie and dear Kirsty. This seemed to reassure John, but I know that he still worries that he is not there to tend the plot himself.

Mary and Dougal (I suppose I shall have to get used to calling him Doug, for that is what everyone on board calls him), seem to be enjoying the voyage, although I believe that Dougal will be glad to see the end of it. He has confessed to me that he is very apprehensive as to what he will find when he eventually arrives at Kalgoorlie. He has been talking to some men who worked last year in the gold fields, and it seems that the situation at Keningo is little improvement upon that at Eisdalsa – an under-invested operation, situated four hundred miles from the company headquarters in Perth. There are rumours that the Keningo mine is on the point of closure, and that most of the able-bodied miners at the settlement have already moved on.

How is your own dear husband? It must be very strange for him to find himself almost totally surrounded by females! But what lucky girls are your pupils, to have such a splendid teacher of mathematics! Does he also instruct them in astronomy? I remember how much we all enjoyed his lectures to the Eisdalsa Technical Institute. The night skies here in the Indian Ocean are very bright and clear, but of course once we cross the equator there will be a whole new galaxy of stars to learn about. Already we can just see the southern cross lying low on the horizon to the south-east.

The young people are having great fun. There always seems to be something going on, and as you may imagine, Flora and Hamish are generally in the thick of things. At present there is a great deal of anticipation concerning preparations for the ceremony of crossing the line, which will take place a few days after we leave Colombo.

Flora seems to have grown up very suddenly. No longer a hoyden, she is now a young lady, particular about her dress and her looks. She is highly flattered by the attentions of Hamish's friends, who manage to include her in most of their activities. Mary feels that she is perhaps becoming a little too forward in her behaviour, but as I keep pointing out to her, what harm can there be in the occasional mild flirtation? Once we reach Perth, they will all go their separate ways!

Should you find time to write, I am sure that any letters addressed to the Perth office of the Keningo Mining Company will find us. We shall leave a forwarding address there. Until John and Jack have settled upon a suitable place to farm, I have no other address by which we may be reached.

My love and best wishes to you both, from your friend,
Anne McDougal

Despite her excitement at the prospect of the evening ahead, Flora was not too busy to remember her pledge to arrange a suitably romantic meeting between Jack McDougal and Jean Parsons.

So far the two had met at mealtimes, or in company with the older members of the Eisdalsa contingent. Once or twice Jean had accompanied Flora to the lower deck to join Jack when he was exercising his collie, but Flora felt certain that the two had never been alone together. Perhaps this evening's ball would be a suitable occasion?

She encountered Jack as he mounted the companion ladder from the cargo deck.

'How is Vicky this afternoon?' she enquired, brightly.

'She is getting mightily spoiled by the crew,' he declared, rather proudly. 'Several of the men seem to have adopted her. They take her titbits and give her the occasional run round the deck. She was sae spent wi' all the exercise she has had the day, she was almost too weary to accompany me! With all this attention, I am thinking that it will be difficult to get her back to work, once we land in Australia.'

'I doubt it,' laughed Flora. 'The minute she spots a straying sheep she will be off after it, you mark my words.'

'Ah, weel, mebbe you are right, lass,' he sighed. 'It will be a week or two yet, I am thinking.'

'Are you bored, having nothing to occupy you?' she demanded, spotting her opportunity.

'Och, not bored exactly,' he protested, 'but I shall not be sorry to have my feet on dry land again, and that is a fact.'

'You should join in the entertainment more,' she urged. Then, as though the thought had only just occurred to her, 'There is a dance in the ballroom this evening. Will you not go?'

'Och! Who would want to dance wi' an auld doychle like mysel'?'

'That is not true, Jack,' Flora protested. 'You are never a stupid, slovenly person. What a way to describe yourself! Anyway . . .' She hesitated momentarily. Dare she say it? Would Jean be cross with her? she wondered. Determined to fulfil her promise to herself, she continued, 'I happen to know that there is one lady who would like very much to go to the dance, if only someone would offer to partner her.'

Jack was not so indifferent to the attractions of the fair sex as Flora had supposed. There was, however, only one female person on board with whom he would want to spend an evening dancing, and she had shown no interest in him, whatsoever.

'I don't think so, lassie,' he replied, kindly. All the same he appreciated the wee girl's concern for his well-being.

'Oh, that is a pity,' said Flora archly, 'Jean will be so disappointed not to be asked.'

'Is it Miss Parsons who wishes an invitation to the dance?' he asked, surprised and suddenly interested.

'But of course!' the girl replied. 'Mind you, she will only go if *you* ask her. She is very much attracted to you, Jack.'

'What?' he demanded. 'What's that you say? Has she spoken about me?'

Even Flora had not reckoned on such a positive response from her dour uncle. She backed off a little. 'Well,' she replied, 'Jean always speaks most highly of your knowledge of farming matters. She says that in conversation upon the subject, you talk more sense than all the other gentlemen put together. And of course . . .' she knew this to be her master stroke '. . . she dotes upon Vicky!' Anyone who was attracted to Jack in the slightest degree must, inevitably, love his dog also.

'I'll mebbe see how she feels about it then,' Jack said, and wandered off deep in thought, leaving Flora wondering whether she had been right to assume that Jean would welcome an invitation to the ball.

She stole a glance at her watch, and let out an unladylike squeal of alarm. It was nearly tea-time and she had given no thought at all to what she herself was going to wear to the dance!

The dancing had begun conventionally enough, the young people demonstrating their energy and precision in executing not only the quickstep but also a new dance from America called the tango. The older passengers had contented themselves with an occasional sedate waltz or even the more daring and very modern foxtrot.

The evening was in danger of becoming rather too tame until Rory MacGreggor appeared with his pipes and John McDougal hurried off to find his fiddle. Nothing then would satisfy the Scots amongst them but they should dance 'The Dashing White Sergeant' followed by an eightsome reel.

The gentle, reticent, softly spoken Jack McDougal had turned into a wild Highlander upon hearing the first skirl of the pipes. His nimble feet seemed scarcely to touch the floor as he performed one intricate movement after another. Without asking her permission, he had swept Jean into the dance, and despite her complete ignorance of the measures, she had followed his steps like a shadow.

Jack could see that his partner was overheated, and clearly in need of some fresh air. When the music stopped at last, and the musicians crowded to the bar, he led Jean out on to the promenade deck.

For some moments they stood beside the rail, watching the fluorescent waves sweeping along the side of the vessel and forming into a straight white wake which stretched behind them into the velvet darkness of the tropic night.

'It's been a lovely day,' sighed Jean.

'Are you happy?' Jack gazed at her intently.

'I never knew it was possible to be as happy as this,' she murmured.

'There were nights like this on Eisdalsa,' he murmured. 'Sometimes, even in the middle of winter, there would be a calm spell with clear skies, and the stars sae bright you felt you could reach out and pluck them.'

'It sounds such a wonderful place,' she sighed, 'I cannot imagine how you can bear to leave it.'

''Twas a case of necessity, just,' he replied. 'The quarries had closed and all the families were leaving the island. We could hae gone on farming our wee croft, I suppose, but without a population to feed, it would have meant selling our produce elsewhere, and transport is verra expensive. We might hae gone on wi' it, had not my faither married Anne McGillivray. When Dougal and Mary decided to emigrate, Anne persuaded Pa that they should go with them. I could see that there was nae future for me on Eisdalsa Island, so when they invited me to join them, I jumped at the chance.'

'You are lucky to be going as one big family,' Jean mused. 'It is a very lonely prospect for someone who has put aside all ties and travels alone.'

'Do you leave a family behind in England?' he asked. 'If you were happy there, what made you want to leave?'

'It's a sad little story,' she told him. 'Are you sure you want to hear it?'

Jack studied her face carefully for the first time. For the moment the bright blue eyes held a hint of sadness. Suddenly he felt an overwhelming desire to fold her in his arms . . . to protect her from all the harsh realities of a life which so clearly troubled her. Restraining his natural instinct, however, he removed his jacket and placed it over her shoulders as a substitute for his own embrace.

Wordlessly she accepted the gesture, leaning back against him and gazing into space. She spoke as though in a dream, recalling the events that had brought her here.

'I grew up on my uncle's farm, near Edenbridge,' she began. 'My father died when I was a babe in arms. When my mother died shortly after, my uncle and aunt cared for me as though I was their own daughter.

'There were four of us children. My cousins – two boys, Paul and Thomas, and a girl, Miranda – accepted me as their sister. When we grew older, first the boys and then Miranda left home to earn their living.

'I went to school in Tonbridge and was by all accounts a model pupil from the word go. When I was due to leave, my teacher asked my guardians if I might become her pupil teacher, and I was formally apprenticed. I continued to live at the farm, and when my aunt became ill last spring I undertook more and more of her housekeeping duties until, when she eventually died, I gave up the schoolwork and acted as my uncle's housekeeper.

'At first he sat about the house all day, grieving, and then one day, quite out of the blue, he announced that he was to marry again.

'From the start his new wife made it very clear that I was no longer welcome. I think my uncle might have tried to persuade me to stay on, but even he could see that there was no way we could all three continue living in the same house.

'Thinking it best to make the break as quickly as possible, I answered an advertisement for a governess to take charge of two small children in Adelaide, South Australia.'

For the first time Jack really gave some thought to what would be happening at the end of the voyage. It had never crossed his mind that Jean might not leave the ship with them when she docked at Freemantle.

'Will you stay in Adelaide for long?' he demanded. 'Have you no thoughts of travelling to other parts?'

'My new employer has paid my fare,' she explained. 'I shall be obliged to work for her for at least a year, or be forced to pay back the money.' She saw his crestfallen expression and continued more encouragingly, 'Once I have worked out my contract, I shall be free to take whatever employment suits me best.'

Jack, ever cautious, refrained from opening his heart, but he hoped . . . oh, how he hoped . . . that he was to be a part of the new beginning which she sought. 'Would you ever consider returning to farming?' he asked.

The still night air was suddenly rent by the loud bellowing of cows on the lower deck. 'We might be back in Kent,' mused Jean. A sudden thought struck her and she gave a little laugh.

'What?' he asked.

'Nothing really,' she replied vaguely. 'I just had a vision of my uncle's new wife scrubbing out the dairy and milking the cows. I am sure that she never expected to do such work herself when she entrapped the poor dear man.'

Her tinkling laughter made Jack turn his head. He joined in with her laughter, wishing to be part of the joke.

'It is your ability always to see the funny side of everything which makes me . . . like you so much,' he declared.

'Do you . . . do you really?' she asked, softly.

He made no reply for some minutes.

'Jean . . .' He spoke abruptly, painfully aware of the lack of finesse in his approach. 'I hae never before believed that a woman could be important to me. I was aye too concerned about the welfare of my family, my farm and my animals to consider anyone else. Now, suddenly, I ken that all my plans, all my hopes for the future, are tied up with thoughts of you, and how you might fit in wi' 'em.'

She raised a hand as though in protest.

'No, don't stop me. Let me tell you everything, now that I've started.'

He caught both her hands in his.

'I'm no' a young man,' he insisted, 'and I have nae much to offer in the way of gentlemanly manners, but I am hard-working, sober and God-fearing. For the time being, I can offer ye neither a hame nor a living, but I promise ye that as soon as my faither and I have our new farm running smoothly, I shall come to Adelaide to look for ye.'

Again she made a move to interrupt. Again he forestalled her.

'Nae, lass,' he protested, 'I beg you to say nothing the now. If, when I come to find you, you have . . . made other arrangements . . . found yourself a good position or a man to share your life . . . I shall understand.' He paused, allowing his words to sink in. Then brightening suddenly, he concluded, 'But should you find your new life to be less than you hoped for, perhaps you will be willing to come and share mine?'

For a moment Jean hesitated. Had he asked her outright to marry him, she knew she would have accepted his proposal. Might she perhaps have lived to regret her decision?

He was right to suggest that she must first sample the new life she had planned for herself. She did, after all, owe an obligation to her employer to work out her year's contract.

Dear, thoughtful, person that he was, Jack had made it easy for her. She could try her luck in Adelaide, and still hope to see him again. The period of their separation would give them both time for reflection. Shipboard romances were commonly thought to be transitory episodes, to be put aside when both parties had their feet firmly on dry land.

He pulled her to him and gave her a rather clumsy little kiss on the forehead. She melted within his embrace, lifting her face to him for a second – longer this time, and on the lips.

'A year seems a very long time,' Jack murmured. His fingers wandered through her hair until he found the sensitive spot at the nape of her neck.

Jean gave a little gasp of pleasure, and in an instant he had pressed his mouth to hers, his inquisitive tongue forcing a passage between her parted lips. Suddenly she pushed him away and with a strained little laugh she said, 'Oh, once you have your land and your sheep, and your dog the year will go by in no time!' 'The air is rather chilly,' she continued, lightly, 'and listen, is that singing coming from the ballroom?'

Clear and sweet as a mountain stream Anne McDougal's voice reached out to call them in: ' "Oh where, oh where, has my Highland laddie gone?" '

Chapter 3

~

On the last night at sea the passengers seemed more subdued than they had been throughout the trip. It was a time for reflection rather than celebration. Their small world, created by the circumstances of the long sea voyage, was about to come to an end. For many of them the future was hazy and filled with doubts and misgivings. They were about to confront the realities of living in an alien land, amongst new people who might not necessarily welcome them.

News from the homes they had so recently left was not good. With so much opportunity for talking, there had been endless discussions about the prospect of a war in Europe, sooner or later. To the young men among them, this was a challenge, a promise of adventure even greater than that of settling in a new country. They might be leaving Britain because they were disillusioned with what she had to offer them in peacetime, but when she found herself in trouble, not one among them would refuse to take up arms in defence of his homeland.

All over the ship, in the saloon, on the deck, and passing up and down the companion ways, there were hurried exchanges of addresses, with promises to keep in touch. Warm friendships, which had sustained the participants throughout the lengthy journey, were about to be broken, and not a few young hearts would suffer the agonies of parting when the ship arrived in Fremantle.

For Flora McGillivray the voyage had provided an opportunity to grow up. She seemed to have condensed her entire adolescence into a period of a few weeks. She had enjoyed the first stirrings of adolescent love, and when Tom Pain had shown her clearly that he did not share these feelings, had endured the pain of rejection. If she had boarded the ship a schoolgirl, she would disembark as a young woman, ready to face whatever the future would bring.

Hamish too had learnt something from his companions on board the *Geraldtown*. While he still found it difficult to forgive Tom Pain for being an Englishman, he admired the Londoner's wit and sparkle, envying his easy manner with complete strangers, particularly young women. For his own part, he was quite prepared to be entertained by the Smythe sisters, but had no intention of making any commitment to either of them, nor yet to any other female if he could avoid it. His ambitions for the next few years did not include the acquisition of encumbrances such as a wife and family.

While Tom could not agree with Hamish's attitude towards the girls of their acquaintance, he valued most highly the young Scot's engineering training and experience. He recognised in Hamish an incisive grasp of the economics of industry. He was a man who, as a potential business partner, could prove a tremendous asset. Tom was determined to keep in contact with his new friend. Someday they might be very useful to each other!

It was Tom's conviction that Australia was a huge untapped potential market for the internal combustion engine which had persuaded him to leave England. Already, in Britain, the competition between manufacturers of motor vehicles was becoming so fierce that it was difficult for a lone individual to break into the market.

'Believe me,' Tom had explained, at one of their late-night sessions in the saloon, 'the car and the lorry will transform Australia in a way that the horse and the railways can never hope to do. The distance a horse can travel is limited by his food and water supply, and except in the largest towns, the railways are restricted to a single line running between states, linking the capital cities.

'But where there are motor vehicles,' he continued, warming to his subject,' there must be petrol filling stations, workshops where repairs can be effected, centres from which vehicles can be sold and serviced. I propose to open one such filling station and once it is operating successfully, I shall open another, and another, until there is a chain of Pain's Service Stations across the whole continent.'

Hamish was intrigued. He admired the young man's initiative, and recognised the sense of his argument, but an enterprise of this nature required capital investment. He suspected that Tom Pain had only meagre resources.

'If I had the money, I would like to come in with you,' he declared. 'Maybe, when I have worked for a time at my own trade, I shall be able to save enough to buy into your business. Would you have me?'

'At the moment I would say yes to anyone willing to invest in my idea,' Tom assured him. 'Later on, of course, it might depend upon the agreement of my other partners, if there are any.'

'Then at least let us keep in contact,' Hamish agreed. 'You never know, I might surprise everyone with my own ideas for the provision of electric power to isolated communities. When I have made my fortune from my schemes, I will come and seek you out!'

On a calm, warm day in early April, two fussy little tugs nudged the *Geraldtown* in towards the quay. They had arrived at Freemantle, the port for Western Australia's capital city, Perth.

There was a haze over the surface of the glassy sea, and the blinding sun fought a way through it, appearing at first as a round ball of fire on the horizon, then climbing rapidly into the sky.

Suddenly the haze disappeared and the landscape lay plain before them.

The McDougals and McGillivrays clung to the rails, scanning the limits of their horizon for any indication of the kind of place they had come to.

At first sight they might well have been disappointed.

The harbour was wide, the shoreline flat. Towering into the sky on all sides, the dockyard cranes formed the only protuberances on an otherwise barren landscape.

Little by little they were able to distinguish white buildings on the starboard quarter, a few trees and the movement of vehicles along the shoreline. Their first port of call in Australia was not, after all, deserted.

Disembarkation procedures seemed to take an age. As one delay followed another, individual members of the party became annoyed or frustrated.

Although it was the end of the Australian summer the sun was still hot when, at noon, Jack was finally allowed to release Vicky from her prison on the cargo deck and bring her ashore to join the rest of the party.

Jean Parsons, with a four-berth cabin all to herself, was to remain on board until the ship reached Adelaide. Jack took his leave of her before going to collect his dog. They clung together for some minutes before she said softly: 'Time to go, Jack,' and pushed him gently away from her. 'I won't come on deck to wave goodbye.'

'I'll write to the address you gave me,' he assured her, 'just as soon as we have settled somewhere permanent.' Then he added, hastily, 'It might take a little time, we shall probably be a long way from any post office. You must not worry if you don't hear for a week or two.'

'I shall watch for every post,' she assured him. 'Just don't let me wait too long.'

Chapter 4

Margaret Brown dragged her father's old leather trunk down the last of the steps and sat upon it with a sigh. She cast a glance around the crowded living room, wondering where she should begin.

Her mother too viewed the jumble of her possessions with some dismay.

'It all came over from Tigh na Broch,' Annabel declared, optimistically, 'so presumably it will now pack away for transportation to Connel!' The two women set about wrapping china and glass ornaments in paper and burying them among the neatly folded clothing in the bottom of the trunk. Photographs in silver frames lay side by side with Angus Beaton's watercolour sketches of the district, and one of Margaret's own early attempts to emulate her uncle's work. The piles of books which had littered the floor were soon distributed between the cases, and cushions piled on top. By the time Wullie Prentice and Baldie Campbell, the ferryman, appeared on the scene, there were enough packing cases filled ready for them to begin transporting to the boat.

When David had first shown her the house in Connel, Annabel had been forced to admit that it was absolutely perfect for them. The moment that she had alighted from David's Argyll Tourer and stepped up to the front door of the old stone house, she had known that she was going to like it.

The original structure might well have dated back to the '45, and was a typical fortified house of that period. It comprised a tall rectangular building with a round tower at one side, to which had been added a number of extensions during the early part of the last century. These additions gave the entire building an air of having been thrown together without any proper plan. It was not however the external appearance of the house so much as its location that had appealed to Annabel.

Perched upon an outcrop of volcanic rock, it commanded an extensive view over Loch Etive and on a fine day one might see as far as the hills of Mull in the west, and eastward to the mountains of Glen Coe. A narrow causeway linked the house and its policies with the main road so that, to all intents and purposes, they would still be living on an island.

While it would never replace Eisdalsa in her heart, Annabel felt that Creag an Tuirc was a place where she could be happy.

David unlocked the heavy, iron-studded main door and led her into the hall. From the style of decoration, and the black and white of the tiled floor, it was immediately obvious that this was a later addition to the original house. Double doors opened into a large living room, beautifully proportioned as only Georgian architects knew how, having great windows from floor to ceiling, facing westwards along the length of the loch towards the sea. Annabel clasped her hands in delight and ran forward.

The garden fell away from a wide terrace, down to the shore of the loch. At various points there were patches of level ground which might be transformed into a series of small gardens, linked by pathways and steps. In her mind she was already turning the wild jungle before her into an orderly array of lawns and rock gardens, sheltered perhaps by some of those beautiful rhododendrons from Johnstones that Katherine McLean had promised her.

David, meanwhile, had wandered into the adjoining room where she found him carefully measuring the window bay to see if it would take his old desk which, discarded by his daughter-in-law, now languished under a pile of dust sheets in the stable at Tigh na Broch.

'This will make a splendid study,' Annabel declared, examining a second door which she found led into a small ante-room and thence back to the hall. 'Should you wish to continue to take a few private patients, this will do admirably.'

David, already three steps ahead of her, smiled indulgently and mentally placed his rather dilapidated leather armchair in the corner where it would catch the light from the window.

On the first floor they found that the three bedrooms all faced the loch; the smallest, occupying the upper floor of the tower, was rounded except on its inner wall.

'Oh,' Annabel cried in delight, 'the children will love this . . . we shall have no difficulty persuading them to come and stay here!'

The most recent addition to the house must have been the two bathrooms, one of which had been installed in what would originally have been a dressing room attached to the master bedroom. The second, smaller and rather less elaborately decorated, was intended to serve the guest bedrooms.

'You don't think this is rather too grand for us, do you?' Annabel turned anxiously to her husband. 'I mean, it's not as though we have a house full of children any more.'

'Well, no,' David agreed, 'but I can see that there may be a considerable number of visitors . . . apart from family and friends, my work involves a fair amount of entertaining, you know.'

In the weeks since he had taken up his new post she had had little opportunity to discuss this aspect of his work. She supposed that he could be right about the visitors, which led her to another point.

'I couldn't manage this great place on my own,' she told him. 'There would have to be someone living in.'

'All taken care of,' he told her, leading the way down the back stairs to the kitchen. This was a good-sized room occupying the base of the tower. It was equipped with a modern range, and hot and cold taps to the sink suggested an up-to-date heating system.

As they entered the room, a comfortable little body of a woman rose to her feet, her face wreathed in smiles.

'Annabel, this is Mrs Murchieson,' David explained. 'She acted as housekeeper for the previous occupants and has expressed a wish to be considered for the post by any new tenants.'

Taken aback by being presented with what amounted to a fait accompli, Annabel regarded the woman somewhat coldly.

'We will certainly consider your application . . . with any

others,' she replied warily. 'Always assuming that we decide to take the house.'

'Thank you, ma'am,' the woman replied, humbly.

'What accommodation is there for a servant?' Annabel enquired. Mrs Murchieson opened a door in the wall opposite the range and showed her into a light airy room which was large enough to serve as both bedroom and sitting room. A second door opened to reveal yet another bathroom. Annabel showed some surprise to find that Mrs Murchieson was quite clearly already in residence.

'The owners thought it best that someone remain to keep an eye on the house while it was unoccupied,' the woman explained.

David nodded understandingly. 'You must find it rather strange, living in a great empty place like this?' he observed.

'I must admit I shall not be sorry to see new tenants moving in,' was the reply.

'Three bathrooms!' Annabel shuddered at the thought of all that hot water. Could they really afford such a house? Of course the guest bathroom would only be used occasionally.

David gave Mrs Murchieson an encouraging grin as he followed Annabel back into the entrance hall. 'Thank you,' he said, smiling conspiratorially, 'I think we may well meet again soon.'

By the time she had stepped into the car, Annabel had quite made up her mind.

'Who is the agent for the property?' she enquired.

'As it happens, it is my own solicitor, Mr McKay of Inverary,' David told her. 'I shall be there on Thursday. What do you say . . . shall I tell him we will take the house?'

'Yes.' She nodded, happily. 'I think that Creag an Tuirc will do very well.'

'Good.' David sighed with relief. Perhaps he had been a little too sure of himself. He dared not tell Annabel that the lease, already signed, was tucked safely in his inside pocket!

Chapter 5

The railway which linked Perth with Kalgoorlie stretched in a horizontal line from west to east across the map of Australia in the school atlas which Mary held open on her knee.

She stared out of the window, attempting to see in this limitless waste of scrubland anything at all which resembled the colourful depiction of wheatbelt, cattle ranches and sheep stations contained in the book. For many years she had described to her pupils the rich farming territories of Australia, never having seen the country for herself. She questioned now, whether the author of *A New Geography for Pupils* had ever seen it either!

Jack McDougal wondered when they were going to catch their first glimpse of that 'good grass country', promised by the government agent in Perth.

'It's great country down there, south of Southern Cross,' he had assured them. 'Plenty of grass for sheep or cattle, even grain if you can find enough water. We don't call it the wheatlands for nothing.'

Well, Jack was thinking, the landscape had better show some improvement soon. We shall be pulling into Southern Cross in about an hour.

John and Anne had parted with the bulk of their combined savings as down payment on their five-thousand-acre spread. Quite unable to visualise such a vast area of land, they had had to accept the agent's assurances that it was pointless considering farming on anything smaller.

'At five shillings an acre you just can't lose,' he had asserted, 'and to experienced farmers like yourselves, the Government is willing to make a substantial loan.'

The McDougal men could not bring themselves to confess that the full extent of their Argyllshire landholding had been a few acres of arable land, and a nearby barren island where they had grazed a few sheep. They considered that if they could make a living out of fifty Scottish acres, there was no reason why they should not make a fortune out of five thousand in Australia.

The Government loan towards the purchase of the land had been essential to their plans, because it meant that they could keep back sufficient money of their own with which to buy building materials, farming equipment and stock.

John, determined to try his hand at growing a grain crop, had brought with him from Scotland seed for a first planting of barley. Jack had tried to persuade him to wait until they could find out at first hand which types of grain were best suited to the climate, but the old man had been adamant.

'If barley grows on the Western Isles, it will surely grow anywhere in the world,' he had insisted. Jack had not had the heart to disillusion his father, so two sacks of best barley seed had accompanied them aboard the *Geraldtown*.

On the map which the agent had shown them, Southern Cross had appeared to be no distance at all from the gold fields at Kalgoorlie. As the locomotive ate up mile upon mile of endless track, however, they had begun to realise just how far it was between one station and the next. Dougal and Mary would be more than a hundred miles away, the distance between Eisdalsa and Glasgow. Before they had left Scotland, to have put such a distance between the two families would have been unthinkable. Anne began to wonder if she would ever see her son again, once they parted at Southern Cross.

Doug McGillivray shifted uneasily in his sleep. He was quite exhausted by the journey, having stayed awake for most of the night, while the remainder of the party slept.

Half dozing, his thoughts sifted through the events of the week which they had spent in the city of Perth, after leaving the ship at Fremantle.

Their first impressions of the capital of Western Australia had been favourable. Splendid Victorian buildings, in a style with which they were themselves familiar, shared the main street with a mixture of Colonial styles of architecture perhaps more suited to the climate.

The city, built upon hitherto undeveloped land, had been laid out in near parallel streets, reminding Jack of some modern Scottish towns such as Helensburgh and Greenock, lacking the character of ancient cities like Edinburgh and London but places where it was infinitely easier to find one's way about!

On the outskirts of the city the buildings were less prepossessing. Somewhat flamboyant shop-fronts often disguised a timber construction to the rear, and many of the buildings were roofed in corrugated iron. The working-class population generally lived in one-roomed shacks on the edge of town.

When Mary expressed her concern about the housing conditions, Doug hastened to reassure her.

'It's a young country,' he reminded her, 'and it will take some time yet to develop fully. Someday everyone will be properly housed. The Government is committed to a long-term building programme for ordinary people.'

At the main offices of the Western Australia Mining Corporation, Doug McGillivray reported his arrival to a large-boned, flaxen-haired young woman whose skin glowed from long exposure to the intense sunlight.

'G'day,' she greeted him, smiling broadly. 'What can I do for you?'

'My name is McGillivray,' Doug told her. 'I believe that your director is expecting me?'

The girl glanced nonchalantly at a note pad lying on the desk before her, and shook her head.

'Nothing about any McGillivray here, sport,' she replied. 'What's it in connection with?'

Doug flinched at the manner of her address, but quickly recovered his composure.

'The Keningo Mine,' he replied. 'I have come to take up an appointment as assistant manager.'

'Oh, that'll be our Mr Makepeace,' she decided, and waving him to a chair, she jumped up and bustled off down the corridor, her calf-length muslin skirt serving only to emphasise the mobility of her generous figure. Coming to a halt at the far end, she rapped on the glass door of one of the offices and waited a moment before going inside. Doug heard a muffled exchange before the receptionist re-emerged, followed by a florid young man, tall enough to distract the eye away from his protruding belly and sagging jowls. His gangling limbs seemed overlong, his arms hanging almost to his knees. His hair, prematurely receding from a sharply back-sloping brow, was ginger. He gave overall an impression of a very tall orang-utan.

'Mr McGillivray.' He thrust out his huge hand and caught Doug's in a vice-like grip. 'They should have told me to expect you on the *Geraldtown*. Had I known what ship you were on, I'd have been at the dock to welcome you!'

The greeting was cordial enough, although Doug could not avoid the impression that his appearance was quite unexpected, and had caused Mr Makepeace more than a little embarrassment.

One of those overlong arms now encircled his shoulders, and he was led along the corridor to Makepeace's office.

When the polite enquiries about the voyage and Doug's first impressions of Australia threatened to monopolise the interview, he decided to come straight to the point. 'I presume that Mr McKenzie is expecting me?'

Avoiding a direct answer, Makepeace began a long resumé of the history of the company and its operation at Keningo.

'So you see, sport,' he concluded, 'the old Keningo in its heyday was one of the most productive of our mines. The size of the township will tell you how well she was doing a year or two back . . . good housing . . . a piped water supply . . . what more could anyone want?'

'Ah, yes, housing,' Doug interrupted. 'Will my accommodation be suitable for a family? I have my wife with me, and our son and daughter.'

'McKenzie had a number of kids so his place should be large enough,' Makepeace observed. 'It'll not be up to Mrs McGillivray's standards, but under a woman's hand it could be made to clean up real good.'

What did this mean? Doug wondered. Were they expected to share a house with the manager?

'Won't McKenzie have something to say about us using his accommodation?' he demanded.

'Ah, well, Doug . . . you don't mind if I call you Doug, eh? McKenzie won't have much say in the matter. Nothing at all, in fact.'

'How do you mean?' asked Doug.

'McKenzie won't be there to bother you,' Makepeace explained. 'The truth is, the old-timer took to the bottle more than somewhat since his wife up and left him last winter. A couple of months ago he fell down a shaft . . . broke both legs. He's been in Kal' Hospital ever since, and fair crook he is, according to reports.'

'So who has been in charge of the mine in his absence?' Doug enquired, with a sinking heart.

'Well . . . that's just it, mate.' Makepeace confirmed his worst fears. 'There's no one up there just now but the foreman, Jones, one or two Pommie layabouts, and a few black fellers. To be frank with you, Doug,' he admitted, apprehensively, 'nothing worthwhile has come down from Keningo for months.'

Doug recalled the warning he had received on board the *Geraldtown*. The rumours he had heard had hardly touched upon the true state of affairs.

'But earlier on you were giving me figures suggesting heavy production of ore,' he protested.

Embarrassed, Makepeace wiped a hand across his brow.

'Sure,' he agreed at last, 'those were last year's figures, before McKenzie hit the bottle hard.'

Doug glanced at the draft contract which Makepeace now handed to him. The figures which the man had just quoted were there in black and white. 'Are you proposing that under my control the mine will be expected to produce similar figures to these by the end of this year, when several months' work has already been lost?'

'You got it, sport!' Makepeace clapped him on the back in jocular fashion, serving only to increase Doug's annoyance.

'Will you have a wet?' The Australian indicated a number of beer bottles cooling in a pail of water.

'No . . . thank you.' Doug struggled to regain his composure. 'Now look here, Makepeace,' he proceeded in level tones, 'your people must be given to understand that I have come here without any experience of gold mining. I was expecting to learn the job, not to take over full control immediately.'

Makepeace shrugged his shoulders and was about to reply when Doug silenced him with a gesture.

'I have worked alongside tin and lead miners in Cornwall, and as a student I spent some time studying methods of extraction of those metals. The remainder of my experience has been in quarrying. I am no fool, you understand, and I am convinced that, given time, I shall master the requirements of your gold-mining operation at Keningo. With a totally unqualified workforce behind me, however, I can give no guarantees as to output for the remainder of this year, and I will not sign any contract which binds me to an output figure which I cannot hope to reach.' Angrily he slammed the document down on the agent's desk.

Makepeace swallowed painfully and stared for an instant at the discarded contract. He looked up to find the Scotsman glaring intently at him. Silently, he slid the document out of sight.

'Well then . . . Doug, old boy.' He paused. Doug, expecting his dismissal, wondered idly what he would do now.

Makepeace leaned back in his chair, all smiles again.

'Suppose you call round tomorrow morning, and I'll have a new agreement here for you to sign? Pay won't be much under the circumstances . . . you being as inexperienced as you say.'

Doug was quick to interrupt.

'Inexperienced in mining for gold I may be, Mr Makepeace,' he pointed out, sharply. 'Green I am not!'

He continued in a milder tone: 'I am willing to work for . . . shall we say . . . ten per cent less than McKenzie was getting? I shall, however, expect a bonus of ten per cent if my output should, after all, reach that of last year. In addition,' he paused momentarily as Makepeace seemed about to speak, 'should my output exceed that of Mr McKenzie, I will expect a bonus in proportion.'

Doug relaxed in his chair, folding his hands in his lap with an air of finality which convinced Makepeace that further argument would be fruitless.

'Very well, Doug,' he said at last, 'I will discuss your proposals with my clients, and hopefully there will be an agreement ready for signature in two days from now. Let's say Thursday, at three o'clock.'

Dougal rose, shook hands rather stiffly with the agent, and departed. Only when he was outside on the pavement did he allow himself a smile of triumph. For a moment he stood still, adjusting his eyes to the full glare of an Australian summer afternoon. Once his vision cleared, he found he was looking at a building on the opposite side of the street. **THE COMMONWEALTH BANK OF AUSTRALIA**, he read. He felt in his pocket, reassuring himself that he still carried the wallet containing his letters of credit from the Royal Bank of Scotland, then marched across the busy thoroughfare and pushed open the heavy swing doors.

When he emerged some time later he was smiling broadly. Whatever should happen now, their passage home was assured. He had deposited sufficient money for the four of them to return to Scotland if, after two or three years, they wished to go.

There was a sudden jerk, followed by a succession of thumps and wheezes as the string of carriages lumbered to a halt.

Where the train had pulled up there was a single platform about a hundred yards long, a small wooden shack, centrally situated, and a single board proclaiming that this was Southern Cross.

The McDougal contingent hurriedly gathered their belongings and stepped down on to the platform. Farther up the line the doors of the luggage brake had been flung open, and an assortment of crates, sacks and furniture was being unloaded.

The moment for separation had arrived. The McGillivrays, having passed out the McDougals' luggage, stepped down on to the platform themselves to take their leave of their kinsmen.

Anne and Mary clung to one another for a long moment.

'You will write, won't you?' Anne demanded of her daughter-in-law.

'Just as soon as we are settled,' Mary assured her. 'You will let us know what progress you are making with the farm?'

'Of course . . . oh, my dears, take care of yourselves! 'Unable to stem the flow of tears, Anne flung her arms around her son's neck beseeching him to come and visit them very soon.

'Come now, Ma,' he consoled her. 'A hundred miles is not all that far . . . not when it might have been seven thousand which separated us.'

Meanwhile Flora kissed both John and Jack affectionately, while Hamish shook each of them by the hand. He was hard put to it not to display his own emotion.

Anne and Flora clung to each other in a final embrace, while Vicky, sensing the significance of the moment, went to each of them in turn, nuzzling and licking to show her concern.

Flora had her arms around the dog and was weeping openly when the guard blew his whistle to warn them that the train was due to depart.

Piling back into the carriage, the McGillivrays waved and cried out last-minute exhortations until the station was just a small dot in the distance.

It was a forlorn little party which stood upon the platform of Southern Cross station, their worldly possessions scattered all around. There seemed to be no sign of life.

Vicky pricked her ears, lifted her muzzle, and gave an excited yelp as the familiar sound and smell of sheep reached her. Below the embankment on which they stood, they spotted a number of the animals grazing on the sparse greenery which had sprung up alongside the narrow drainage channel.

With relief, they now saw that one other living being inhabited that desolate place. A railway official, distinguishable only by his uniform cap, was leaning against the wall of the wooden hut which served as a ticket office. Apart from the paraphernalia associated with all railway stations – water tower, coal bunkers, lifting gear and stock pens – there was no evidence of a town or habitation of any kind, not even a vehicle which might take them to their destination.

Anne sat down miserably on one of the wooden crates, while the men sauntered along the platform towards the man they took to be the station master.

'G'day.' He pushed back his cap and gave the McDougals a thorough appraisal.

'How do you do?' John greeted him politely.

'We need to get into town,' explained Jack. 'Is there some form of transport we can hire?'

'Come far, have you?' enquired the other, ignoring his question. 'You're not from around these parts.'

'No,' agreed John. 'We have recently arrived from Scotland.'

The station master was not impressed.

'More Pommie bastards,' he observed, but in a tone sufficiently friendly as to cause only minor offence.

'Would there be anyone who might give us a lift into town?' Jack repeated.

'Could be.' The station master gave the question his serious consideration for a few moments. 'Name's Joe Smart,' he told them.

'McDougal . . . John McDougal, my son Jack, and this is Mrs McDougal.'

At Anne's approach the Australian's whole demeanour changed. He straightened his back, buttoned up his uniform jacket, and wiped a none too clean hand over the seat of his trousers before extending it towards her.

'Pleased to meet you, ma'am,' he greeted her enthusiastically. 'We don't see too many ladies in these parts and that's a fact!'

'Is it possible for you to suggest a means by which we can be transported into the town of Southern Cross?' Anne demanded, smiling disarmingly. 'As you can see, we have rather a lot of baggage.'

Joe was suddenly falling over himself to be helpful.

'Mick O'Flannery will be by shortly to pick up those sheep down there.' He pointed along the track. 'They came in on the morning train from Adelaide. Though what Mick wants with a mob of sheep, I don't know. His spread is no more'n a hundred acres all told.'

'Would Mr O'Flannery give us a lift, do you think?' she asked.

'Sure to, ma'am,' he told her. 'If you've no objection to sharing the wagon with a few sheep, that is?'

At the suggestion that Anne might object to the sheep, the two Scotsmen laughed.

'My mother is no stranger to farm stock,' Jack assured him. 'I am a shepherd myself!'

'Is that so?' Joe Smart asked, warming to these strangers. 'That's a fine-looking pooch you have there,' he observed, as Vicky sidled up to her master and lay down at his feet. 'She ever work with sheep at all?'

'Bred for it,' declared Jack, rubbing the collie's ears affectionately.

'Would she be able to round up that mob along the line there, do you reckon?' Joe asked. 'Truth is, they're supposed to be penned, but a bunch of the locals had a fight here last Saturday night and pulled up half the fence posts to use as weapons.' He indicated the ramshackle arrangement of dilapidated stock pens beside the track.

'I'd be glad to help,' Jack offered, obligingly. With a silent signal to his dog, he set off towards the animals which were now straddling the railway line, and occupying the ditches to either side of the track.

The collie bitch, over excited after weeks of inactivity, had to be calmed down before she could be allowed to approach the animals. With a few practice commands, Jack soon had her under control.

The sheep, alerted to the presence of the dog, huddled together in a tight bunch, protesting loudly at the intrusion. Jack counted about twenty mature ewes and a similar number of lambs scarcely a year old.

I'd have had them separated long before this, he thought, observing how the lambs, old as they were, nevertheless stayed close by their mothers in their distress. He noted amongst them a number of young rams. It was the basis of a decent flock, one which might in a year or two yield a good return.

He wondered how much these particular animals would cost? Did John have sufficient cash put by to be able to purchase them, even if they were for sale? There was a house to be built, fences to be erected, ground to be ploughed and sown for the vegetable crops which they would need to grow, to sustain themselves through the first season . . . it was unlikely that his father would agree to an outlay sufficient to buy the sheep.

Jack McDougal had never received a wage packet in his life. He had, for all his life, worked alongside his father on the family's croft, and while he had never wanted for clothing, food, or a place to lay his head, had never had any money of his own. Until now he had not thought it necessary.

Since his encounter with Jean Parsons, however, things had changed. Money had assumed a new importance in his life. Somehow he had to acquire enough to buy a railway ticket to Adelaide.

Vicky crept along at her master's heels, eyeing the sheep with her customary alertness.

'Go on, then,' he commanded, quietly.

The bitch shot away, making a wide detour around the sheep, and finally crouching in the grass on the far side.

'Bring 'em in,' was the next whistled command.

Vicky pricked her ears and rose carefully from the grass, stiff-legged, still in a half crouch. She began to weave back and forth behind the flock, gradually collecting all the animals on one side of the railway line. The beasts at the rear ran forward with startled bleats, forcing a way between the others. Then they all took up this forward movement and the entire flock began to approach Jack. Standing with his back to the railway track, the shepherd dissuaded the animals from wandering up the embankment again, while the dog kept a watchful eye out for any animal which might dare to break out on the far side of the group. She manoeuvred them expertly into the station yard and held them penned into what remained of the compound. Sinking down, her belly flat on the ground, she occupied the open end of the enclosure. With her muzzle stretched out, pointing towards the sheep, she fixed her eye on each of the ewes in turn, daring them to move.

'That has to be the sweetest bit of sheep handling I've never witnessed,' declared Joe Smart, admiringly, as Jack rejoined them outside the ticket office. 'That bitch of yours will be worth her weight in gold.'

The sound of a heavy wagon approaching cut short further comment. Drawn by a team of magnificent Suffolk Punches, a huge farm cart rolled into the station yard and came to a halt with a few well-chosen expletives from the driver. The newcomer threw the reins forward over the leading horses' heads and jumped down on to the hard standing.

He glanced over towards the cattle pen, apparently surprised to find his animals inside. Without exchanging a word with those gathered outside the station office, he strolled over to where Vicky watched over her charges, and gazed at the little bitch, reflectively.

He turned at last to the station master, quite ignoring the strangers with him.

'G'day, Joe,' he greeted him laconically.

'G'day, Mick,' Joe replied.

'Nice dawg,' commented Mick.

'Belongs to Jack here,' offered Joe. 'These are the McDougals, just arrived from Scotland,' he explained.

O'Flannery nodded briefly to John and his son then turned to the lady.

'Ma'am.' He made an attempt to raise his khaki bush hat. ''Ow much?' the carter demanded abruptly, looking from one to another of the strangers.

They were all puzzled.

'For the dawg, Mister, how much?' he repeated.

'Oh, you mean Vicky?' Jack laughed. 'She's not for sale . . . sorry!'

'I'd give you a good price, sport,' Mick persisted. 'If you ever think of selling her, I'm your man.'

'I'll remember that,' said Jack, still laughing.

Something in the tone of the conversation must have alerted the collie, for she regarded Mick O'Flannery with considerable suspicion and sought reassurance by trotting over to her master and licking his hand.

One of the ewes shifted position. In an instant the bitch resumed her vigil.

'These folks are needing a lift into town, Mick,' Joe interceded.

'Think you could help 'em out?' Then, seeing the carter hesitate for a moment, he added, 'Jack here and his dog, rounded up the mob for you while we were waiting. Don't know what you'd have done without his help.'

Silently, Mick contemplated the luggage piled on the platform.

'We–ell,' he said at last, 'if you was to get your dawg to drive the mob, I could get all your stuff on the wagon.'

'Marvellous,' replied Jack, 'how far is it?'

'No more'n a couple of miles.'

Australian miles seemed twice as long as the Scottish variety on that warm April evening. Had it not been for the breeze which blew up suddenly just as the roofs of the town came into view, Jack and Vicky would surely have expired. Anne and John, seated on the plank which served as a driving seat for the old wagon, suffered no less discomfort. However, their relief at being on their way at last, together with their possessions, far outweighed the discomfort of the journey.

Nearing the outskirts of the town, the wagon was almost upended as one of its wheels dropped into a menacing pot-hole to one side of the track.

'That Herb Kingdom!' Mick cussed at his neighbour. 'Never does anything to repair the holes.' He applied the bull-whip he carried to the flanks of the two rear horses, tickling them only. As the mighty beasts struggled to extricate the wagon from its rut. Mick explained to Anne, 'Landowners are expected to maintain the roads skirting or passing through their property. It's the only way we can get about the country. Old Herb now, he like as not goes out and digs the holes bigger, so that when people get stuck, he can charge them for dragging them out!'

Anne smiled, believing that it was a joke, but suspicious nevertheless that the accusation might have some truth in it.

It seemed unlikely that anyone would get away with playing such a joke on Mick O'Flannery, however. The Irishman was over six feet six inches in height. His beard, brown and bushy, contrasted strangely with the sparse, grey locks which encircled his nearly bald pate. His broad shoulders suggested great strength. Indeed, Anne was to discover later that Mick's exploits at lifting heavy objects were legendary. When a wagon wheel needed changing, there was no need for a jack. Mick O'Flannery would just hold up the corner of the cart while the old wheel was rolled away and a new one set in its place.

After a further half mile or so, he called the horses to a halt and indicated to Jack a ramshackle gate through which the animals should be led. Lying well back from the road stood a low building with a large wide veranda on three sides. A stand of blue gum trees provided a pool of deep shade to one side. Here a motley collection of hens and water fowl pecked in desultory fashion at the gritty soil. A dirty, nearly dry, water-hole by the gate served the property with its only supply of the precious liquid.

'This is my place,' observed Mick. 'Once Jack and I have settled the sheep in that paddock over there, I'll run you on into town.'

Grateful for the unexpected luxury of a rest in the shade, Anne and John strolled over to the water-hole, and sat down on an overturned cart. Jack and Mick, having ushered the sheep in through the gate to the paddock, leaned on it for a moment's quiet smoke, Vicky panting, at their feet.

'Will you be staying long in town?' enquired Mick as they rejoined Jack's parents.

'We've purchased some Government land in the district,' Jack told him.

'Right on,' offered Mick. 'That'll be down around Merlin's Lake, I reckon.'

'There was no mention of a lake,' Anne said excitedly. The prospect of something akin to one of the Scottish lochs on their own doorstep cheered her immensely.

Mick regarded her sagely, but said nothing. Best let her find out for herself . . . about the lake, as about so many other things. He gave the Poms no more than a couple of years. Then they'll be off, back home to Scotland, he decided.

'Your place will be thirty or forty miles south of here,' ventured Mick. They were bowling along the highway now that the sheep had been secured in the carter's paddock. 'How do you propose to get yourselves out there?'

'We had hoped we could buy a wagon?' suggested John. Mick looked very dubious.

'Not too many wagons going begging in Southern Cross,' he informed them. 'Might be able to help you out myself, though, once I've managed to get them jumbucks off my hands.'

Anne was mystified. 'Jumbucks?' she queried.

'Sheep, missus.'

'Are they not for your own farm then?' queried Jack with growing interest.

'No such luck,' said the Irishman. 'Those beasts were bought for Dan Maybe's spread, but the old feller had a stroke and died a couple of weeks ago . . . too late to stop the order, unfortunately. Reckon his poor missus has enough on her plate without being landed with a mob that size.'

'So you won't be needing the flock yourself?' Jack asked, anxiously.

'No, I'm not a proper farmer . . . don't have a large enough spread. I'm what they call a cocky, like a sort of crofter in your country. I keep a couple of cows, a few hens and ducks, grow vegetables and animal feed, and generally keep myself and the family on what we produce.'

The McDougals were silent for a while, each with their own thoughts.

'Does your farm provide you with a living?' asked John, at length.

'Nope!' was the frank reply. 'But a spot of carting and a little wheeler-dealing makes up most of the deficit. That's why I spend half my life growing oats to feed these monsters.' He tickled each horse behind the ear with his long whip. The animals changed step, but not one of them faltered.

'These sheep,' Anne ventured, very much aware of Jack's interest in the animals, 'what sort of price will Mrs Maybe take for them, do you think?'

Mick cast a quick glance in her direction. Was it possible he could get rid of the unwanted stock this easily?

'Well now,' he said, cautiously, 'the sheep don't actually belong to Mrs Maybe, not yet at any rate. The thing is, I arrange the import of livestock . . . a bit of an entrepreneur, if you like. Auctioneer, buyer . . . you name it, I do it. Understand?'

They were beginning to get the picture.

'Now then,' he continued, warming to his theme, 'if you was seriously considering starting up a bit of a sheep run, well, that there mob is as good as any you'll pick up around here.'

John McDougal was a businessman himself. 'Of course,' he suggested, 'you'll not be charging us what you would have charged Mrs Maybe, seeing that you are so keen to get them off your hands . . .'

The negotiation lasted for the remainder of the journey. By the time they had driven the length of Main Street, and pulled up outside the cheaper of the two hotels in town, the deal was done. Jack was overjoyed, hardly able to believe that his father had been turned so easily away from his dreams of an arable farm.

John McDougal, having viewed the prospects of this dry, unpromising land, had already realised that his son was correct in supposing that their living would be best made in rearing sheep. If he had appeared reluctant at first, he was merely exercising his right to make the decisions. Jack was not yet master of the McDougal domain!

Three days later, armed with a map and detailed instructions from the Land Agency office, they set out once more aboard Mick's wagon, with an additional dray following behind, carrying all manner of building materials purchased at the Southern Cross General Store, Merchants and Suppliers.

Tied to the back of the wagon was a sturdy plough horse, and a cow already in calf. Jack was to return to Mick's holding in a week or two to collect the sheep once a secure paddock had been fenced in for them. Packed into crates at the rear of the wagon were a dozen hens and a few Muscovy ducks, purchased from that ineffective road mender, Herb Kingdom.

It was not as though they were leaving behind any great centre of civilisation. The town of Southern Cross consisted of a single main street wide enough to turn a camel train – they had actually witnessed the arrival of one during their stay – and two rows of wood and corrugated-iron buildings, each providing some particular service to the community: Smiley's Tavern, Harper's Clothier, Del Doaks the Blacksmith, and Bluey's Eating House.

At one end of the street stood a wooden church and a building which might have been a schoolhouse, although there was little evidence of children attending lessons. Most of the youngsters they had come across were working, in the shops and workshops or on the smallholdings outside town.

Late in the previous century, gold had been discovered at Southern Cross. The lode had soon petered out, unfortunately, but not before the usual amenities of any mining town had been installed. The original 'exchange' had become a branch of the Commonwealth Bank; a pub, a casino, a hotel and a whorehouse had soon been introduced. The gold mines closed down but the community remained, its less savoury elements having departed for more promising fields to the east. Soon a church and a school had been constructed, while the whorehouse became a second and entirely respectable hotel. The casino, however, remained.

The McDougals had found that it was possible to obtain nearly everything they required from the town itself or from the surrounding countryside. In this respect the place differed little from their Highland home territory except that in place of a daily steamer calling at the Eisdalsa pier, there was a train three times a week in either direction.

Considerably heartened by this fact, they had set out to take possession of the land that they owned, some thirty miles to the south.

The only indication there was that they had arrived at the right place was a newly painted sign, swinging on a somewhat flimsy gate in a boundary marker which consisted of a single strand of wire stretched between posts.

COMMONWEALTH LAND AGENCY
MERLIN'S FLATS
LOT NO 28
STATE OF WESTERN AUSTRALIA

John McDougal took from his pocket a document which he showed to Mick O'Flannery.

'Bear witness, my friend,' he requested, 'that this property belongs to John McDougal.'

Solemnly Mick shook the Scot by the hand. They were both conscious of the importance of the occasion. Anne laid her hand upon the flimsy gate.

'I think we should name it properly,' she said.

'Have you any suggestion?' asked her husband.

'We will call it Kerrera Station,' she declared. 'After the island where I was born,' she explained for Mick's benefit.

They chose a site on a slightly raised piece of ground overlooking a stand of gum trees which grew beside a water-hole. Anne looked about hopefully, expecting to catch sight of Merlin's Lake, but she was disappointed. The story of a lake must be some joke reserved for ignorant Pommies, she decided, taking care not to give Mick any satisfaction by asking about it.

Here they erected a pair of tents, their living quarters until the main house could be built. Hurdles, brought with them from Southern Cross, were set up to contain the stock, while the chickens and ducks were released once Anne had scattered grain for them to eat. They would not wander far, once they had identified their source of food.

Anne went to the water-hole with a bucket and drew a pailful of the murky brown liquid. This she filtered through a piece of muslin before tasting it. It was earthy, but sweet enough. With a sigh of relief she set about preparing their first meal.

The following morning Mick O'Flannery prepared to leave.

'I'll be back at the end of the week with the rest of your stuff,' he assured them. 'Get the foundations laid for your house, and I'll try to rustle up a bit of help. You'll not get the roof on with just the two of you.' He exchanged glances with Jack, both understanding his reluctance to mention John McDougal's age. The old man would be of little help to Jack when there was any serious lifting to be done.

'That would be very kind . . . thank you,' John called after him, as the horses picked up their rhythm.

'What else are neighbours for?' yelled Mick in reply, disappearing in the clouds of dust sent up by his wagon.

It was a week later when, just before dawn, Anne was wakened by Vicky's frenzied barking. Drawing on her wrap, she roused her husband before going outside to see what had disturbed the collie.

The plot was filling rapidly with every manner of horse-drawn vehicle, piled high with timber and sheets of corrugated iron, building bricks and glazing. People of every age, from elderly grannies to babes in arms, milled about the homestead, strangely purposeful in all their movements.

As Anne tied her belt and stepped forward with a question on her lips, Mick O'Flannery appeared, demanding to know where John was hiding himself.

'He's still in his bed,' she began, mystified at this unexpected invasion. 'Wait here. I'll fetch him.'

'I'm here,' said John emerging from the tent, still buttoning his trousers.

'I don't understand,' said Anne, totally bewildered. 'What are all these people doing here?'

'I warned you,' said Mick, laughing at her bemused expression, 'they're here for the house-raising!'

After a brief discussion with John and Jack, the men set about constructing a timber building on the foundations which John had already prepared. Within the course of a single day the house had been completed, with brick chimney and corrugated iron roof. The roof was pitched in such a fashion that it extended beyond the walls and was supported upon timber pillars, to form a veranda on two sides of the house. It made an excellent porch in front, for sitting out of an evening, and additional sleeping or storage space at the rear.

While the men worked on the house, and their children scurried hither and thither, fetching and carrying for the builders, the women, with much laughter and gossip, assisted Anne in the preparation of an evening meal.

The McDougals, overwhelmed at first by the generosity of these good people, soon fell into the swing of things and worked cheerfully alongside their neighbours.

By the time the last sheet of iron had been nailed into position, the meal was ready. In the deepening twilight, men, women and children gathered around the fireside, talking, everyone hungry for the McDougals' news from 'home'. Someone began to play a mouth organ, another produced a penny whistle, and with a little persuasion from Anne, John went to collect his fiddle. Under the clear Australian sky, whose stars were as alien as the trees beneath which they sat, and the wild creatures which scurried about in the shadows, they sang the songs of their homelands.

After a while Anne became aware of more figures who had begun to gather outside the ring of firelight, squatting on their haunches and listening to the talking and singing. She started, fearing that the gathering was about to be attacked. Mick, who was sitting beside her on the ground, laid a reassuring hand on her arm.

'They're Abos, missus,' he explained, 'native Australians. Until recently this was their territory. They consider that they have a right to wander over the land, but won't interfere with you if you leave them alone. You might even get some of them to work for you . . . only thing is, if you want to get the best out of them, pay them in goods or food. If they get money they'll be off to the nearest go-down for liquor.'

Anne was scarcely reassured when she caught a glimpse of a dozen pairs of eyes reflected in the firelight.

She shivered with apprehension. John, thinking she felt cold, put his arm about her and held her close. Whatever reservations he might have had before leaving Eisdalsa, John McDougal was glad he had come. There was something so challenging and exciting about this great open landscape. He only hoped he might live to see their plans for the place fulfilled.

Chapter 6

At noon on a hot day in April the McGillivrays' hired wagon drew to a halt on the crest of a small hillock. Below where they stood, the ground fell away to a shallow depression, forming a bowl some five miles in diameter. At its centre lay the township of Keningo, huge heaps of spoil and a towering steel headframe marking the site of the mine itself.

Mary sighed. It was yet another industrial island, the customary noise and dirt set in a desert sea. Eisdalsa came sharply to mind, but there the drabness of the slate tips and the deep scars formed by the quarries were softened by the greens and yellows of heather and gorse, and brightened in summer by the occasional flash of blue from harebell and wild thyme. Here nothing relieved the monotonous beiges of the barren landscape save the occasional grey-green of a single eucalyptus tree.

Hamish, unable to conceal his disappointment, muttered, 'Oh my God!'

Their driver laid his long stock-whip across the flanks of the two great shire horses, and the heavily laden wagon moved on down the slope.

The main street was unmetalled and deeply rutted. Along each side, a motley collection of timber shacks, roofed in the ubiquitous corrugated iron, constituted the only habitation in the place.

Mary regarded the scene with pursed lips. She had anticipated that things would be fairly primitive, but never in her wildest nightmares had she envisaged anything as bad as this.

The wagon came to an abrupt halt before a long, low building with a deeply shaded veranda. Above the door a sign, barely legible for dust and flaking paint indicated that this was the: Keningo General Store, Walt Wilson, Prop.

On the veranda, stretched on a crudely fashioned deckchair, was an elderly man dressed only in canvas trousers and a greyish singlet, stained by perspiration. His broad-brimmed hat was pulled down in order to shade his eyes from the glare of the sun. From its brim, corks dangled to discourage the flies which hung around his head like a halo.

Mary, determined not to show her disappointment, raised her chin a shade higher, brushed the dust off the front of her jacket and lifted her skirts ready to descend from the wagon.

Flora and Hamish observed the scene with undisguised dismay and decided to remain on board.

In a quiet voice, Flora murmured, 'I wonder if there will be other girls to make friends with?'

Hamish was already planning to make his way back to Kalgoorlie where he had been surprised to find electric trams and street lighting already installed. There would be plenty of employment for an electrician there.

Other than the sleeping man, there was no sign of life. No washing hung from lines in the scrubby back yards, no children played in the deserted street, not even a dog's barking broke the heavy silence.

Ignoring the sleeping figure on the chair, Doug McGillivray marched into the store, the sudden movement from the outside glare into the gloomy interior blinding him for a moment.

Once his eyes adjusted to the feeble light, he was better able to distinguish his surroundings. Expecting something like Mrs McTavish's store on Eisdalsa Island – an Aladdin's cave containing all manner of items needed by a small working community – he was disturbed to note that the long counter was bare except for an elderly cash register and a set of scales.

Some opened sacks containing sugar, flour and dried beans leaned against the counter, behind which a few tins of fruit and vegetables occupied one section of a vast array of otherwise empty shelving.

At the far end of the building was a second counter where an assortment of items of male attire suggested a drapery department. A caged-off section with telephone switchboard, letter scales and other post office paraphernalia, indicated that the miserable store was also the communications centre of Keningo.

Convinced that the somnolent figure on the porch must be the proprietor, Doug went back outside to find their driver attempting to rouse the sleeper.

'G'day,' The driver shook the man by the shoulder.

The steady snoring ceased abruptly. With a sudden, loud snort he awoke.

'Whatcha want?' demanded the man, opening one eye and lifting the brim of his hat a fraction.

'How do you do?' Dougal greeted him, affably enough. 'I am looking for the house recently occupied by Mr McKenzie. Will you direct me, please?'

'No good goin' there,' came the blunt reply, ''e went to 'orspital in Kal',' he added, helpfully.

'I am aware of Mr McKenzie's whereabouts,' Doug told him, shortly. 'Just show me where his house is.'

'Watcha want it for?'

'I think that's my business, don't you?' Doug was fast losing his patience.

'Who might you be then?' His indignant tone made it obvious that the man resented being disturbed in the middle of his noonday kip by a stroppy Pom.

'My name is McGillivray, Doug McGillivray. I am the new manager of the Keningo Mine.'

Now properly awake, Walt rose to his feet.

'Now then, Mr . . .' Doug glanced at the faded sign '. . . Mr Wilson, what is your situation here?' he demanded.

Walt Wilson looked uncertain. 'Eh?'

'Do you own the store, or are you holding a franchise on behalf of the mining company?'

'Yes.'

'How do you mean, yes?' Doug demanded, scarcely able to contain his anger. 'Yes, you own it, or yes, you manage it?'

'I'm employed by the company,' the other admitted, reluctantly.

'Which, as I understand it, means you are answerable to me,' Doug enjoined. It was a statement, not a question.

Walt regarded his new boss with some trepidation. This was not a very auspicious beginning if he hoped to retain his position. He was suddenly aware of his own unkempt appearance and, removing his hat completely, attempted to slick down his mop of greasy black hair. He wiped his hands on his vest and fumbled with the buttons of his gaping flies.

'To be frank with you, Mr Wilson,' Doug continued, 'my initial impression is that your establishment falls way below the standard expected of a company store. My first task as manager will be to report to my superiors the condition of the mine workings and the village, and to give an assessment of all the company's staff.

'I would have hoped to find any operation attributable to the company running efficiently and,' he cast a glance in the direction of the open doorway, 'cleanly. Do we understand one another?'

'Yessir!' replied Walt, miserably. It had been a long time since anyone had taken the least interest in the way the store was run. 'I suppose things have got a bit slack just lately,' he agreed.

'You'll excuse me saying, Mr McGillivray . . .' Walt added hesitantly, twisting the hat between his huge fingers.

'Well?'

'The dirt is my responsibility. I can do something about that right away. Stocking the shop now, that's another matter entirely. There is so much outstanding in bills owed to the suppliers in Kalgoorlie, they won't provide any more goods until their accounts have been settled.'

'Why have they not been paid?' Doug demanded.

'The till was cleared regularly by Mr McKenzie,' came the reply. 'What he did with the money . . . well, your guess is as good as mine. He didn't pay the wholesalers' bills, that's certain.'

Doug, feeling that his point had been made, was prepared to be magnanimous. 'Very well, Mr Wilson,' he declared, 'you clean up the premises and I will look into the possibility of restoring relations with the wholesalers. Perhaps you will draw up a list of the supplies you require?'

Wilson thrust his hat on to the back of his head and stretched out a grubby hand. 'Right y'are, Mr McGillivray.' He stepped forward and offered Doug his huge dirty paw.

'Welcome to Keningo, sir . . . ma'am.' Touching his hat, he nodded in Mary's direction.

As they turned away he called after them, 'McKenzie's place . . . it's the last house on the right, beside the creek.'

'Thanks,' Doug replied, and taking Mary's hand he led her along the street, the carter and his wagon following slowly.

The house, considerably larger than those they had already passed, stood at the end of the street, well back from the road. A substantial plot of ground which surrounded the building showed evidence of some attempt at making a garden. A few miserably stunted shrubs bordered a patch of sparsely rooted grass, and from the veranda roof a pair of hanging baskets held the dried-up remains of a floral display. Alongside the plot stood a row of blue gums marking the creek Walt Wilson had mentioned. They reminded Mary of the willows of Seileach which gave that island its name.

As she waited impatiently while Doug struggled with the ill-fitting front door, she tried to visualise the house with a coat of paint on its flaking walls and the garden with its bushes watered and its lawn trimmed. Hearing the door burst open at last, she turned eagerly to find that Doug had already gone in. She followed him into the gloomy interior.

The main living room of the house was large. An assortment of crudely constructed furniture lay under a pall of thick dust which gave it a uniform greyness. Windows to front and rear were curtained in a heavy damask material which might have been any colour, and the window glass was covered in a thick film of grime, allowing only the minimum of light to penetrate.

Gingerly, Mary pushed open the first of the two doors on the right-hand wall. It swung back to reveal a large double bed, a chest of drawers and a curtained-off space, presumably intended as a wardrobe. She pursed her lips, but made no comment on what she saw. In the silence that followed, she heard a scuffling in the rafters and looked up to see a single bright eye, gazing down at her. With a little scream of terror, she backed out, slamming the door shut.

Her husband just stood there, laughing at her.

'It will be one of those lizards they call goannas,' he explained. 'Every house has them . . . they're encouraged to take up residence to keep down the flies.'

Mary shuddered.

'I think I would prefer the flies,' she declared, and stood back warily as Doug went to the second door.

It opened to reveal another bedroom containing only a bed this time. 'This one will do for Flora,' Mary decided, 'but where is Hamish to sleep?'

The answer came from her son himself. He had entered the house from the rear, through a glazed door which opened on to a second wide veranda. This closed-in porch would, he declared, make an excellent place for him to sleep since it enjoyed a cool current of air not afforded to the rooms inside the house.

In some trepidation, Mary now opened the remaining door, into the kitchen.

Her glance fell first upon the sink, piled high with dishes covered in congealed grease and mouldy food. As she approached, a swarm of black flies arose and encircled her head.

Refusing to give in to nausea, she reached across and turned on the brass tap, only half expecting any kind of a result.

With a throaty gurgle, a thin stream of brownish fluid emerged, stopped, spluttered and spat in all directions. A series of rumblings followed, as one air bubble after another forced its way along the lead pipe to freedom. When, at last, the water was transformed into a steady stream, it had lost its rusty appearance and Mary was relieved to find it quite drinkable.

'Running water!' she called out, delightedly.

Dougal joined her, his own dismay at the condition of the house dispelled by Mary's cheerful determination to make the best of the situation.

'Believe it or not,' he announced, 'we even have a bathroom, of sorts. Come out here and see what Hamish has found.'

He led Mary outside to where a shower stall had been erected, discretely hidden behind a stand of white gums and jacaranda bushes. Beside it stood a dilapidated privy, its door sagging open to reveal a rather primitive earth box arrangement capped by a somewhat ornately carved seat with hinged lid. The incongruity of this piece of elegance forced Mary to smile, despite the offensive odours escaping from the little building.

'I'll soon get it cleaned up,' Doug assured her. 'With lime and ashes down to kill the smell, it will be adequate until I can install a proper water closet.'

Remaining in the kitchen with her brother, Flora watched the stream of water pouring over the pile of dishes for a few minutes before turning off the flow.

'Where does it come from?' she asked, mystified.

'There's a pipe-line from Perth,' Hamish told her, 'the fellows on board ship told me about it.'

'But that's four hundred miles away!' said Flora. 'And mostly uphill.'

'Have you never heard of pumping stations?' demanded her brother, with a rather superior air. 'There must be dozens of them between Perth and Kalgoorlie.'

'Kitchen first,' Mary decided, as she bustled into the room with her husband on her heels. She threw Flora a dish cloth.

'When you unload the wagon,' she turned to her menfolk, 'put everything on the veranda for the present. I'd like to clean right through before we move in anything of our own.'

'What are we supposed to do with all this?' Flora demanded, picking up from the fender a flannel shirt and a pair of long-johns which had seen better days.

'Anything belonging to Mr McKenzie can go into this hamper,' her mother replied, indicating a dilapidated travelling case which stood in the corner, covered by more discarded clothing. 'I'll decide later what to do with it.'

Holding the garments at arm's length, Flora deposited them in the basket while Mary pumped up the Primus stove, filled a kettle and placed it on the burner to boil.

They ate by candlelight, a stew of tinned steak and tinned

vegetables. For pudding tinned peaches and condensed milk were followed by freshly baked bannocks and cheese.

Mary surveyed her surroundings with an air of satisfaction. The room, cleared of all evidence of the previous occupier, smelt strongly of lye soap and bleach. Curtains and other furnishings had been stripped out and lay piled in the yard awaiting the tub. Through the sparkling, newly washed windows, she could see the night sky and the swaying branches of the nearest gum trees.

There had been a certain air of excitement as the rubbish was removed, and the possibilities of their new home were revealed. Even Hamish was forced to agree that by comparison with the cottage they had left on Eisdalsa, the house was spacious, and that once Mary had worked her own particular magic, it would be very comfortable.

What life there was in the Keningo settlement stirred at cock crow. The McGillivrays, exhausted by the travelling of the day before, were still abed when the sound of horses' hooves and the rumbling of cart-wheels, together with a muffled exchange of voices, woke them.

There was a loud, insistent knocking on the front door.

Pulling on his clothes to answer it, Doug tripped over a half-empty packing case, stubbed his toe, and swore gently to himself.

He opened the screen door and stepped out on to the veranda.

The village communications system was clearly very effective. A motley collection of men, one or two women and a number of children stood before him, all curious to see the new boss.

'G'day, Mr McGillivray. Walt said you'd driven in yesterday while we was all at the mine,' explained their spokesman. 'Thought we'd best let you and your good lady settle in a bit, before introducing ourselves.'

Doug stifled a yawn. He had the distinct impression that he was not alone in that gathering in finding the hour unduly early. Some of the children, in particular, seemed a little bleary-eyed, and a few of the men looked distinctly hung over.

Doug took a deep breath of the crisp morning air and felt his brain clearing magically. He smiled at the spokesman.

'Good morning to you, Mr . . . ?'

'Dai Jones, sir, at your service!'

He was a stocky man, broad-shouldered and dark like the Welsh coalminers whom Doug had met aboard ship. His skin was pitted with ingrained coal dust which no amount of scrubbing would ever remove. He spoke in that lilting, sing-song manner which reminded Doug of the quarrymen of Llanberis, where he had first worked on leaving university.

'Pleased to meet you, Mr Jones,' he said, shaking the newcomer by the hand. He glanced over the assembled collection of men, fair-skinned and dark, elderly and middle-aged, but none of them under thirty years of age. On the outskirts of the group, half a dozen black men congregated. These were scantily clad in canvas shorts and singlets – the Aborigines whom Makepeace had mentioned.

He addressed the gathering, wishing them all, 'Good day.'

'G'day, boss,' came the answer from several quarters. Others among the crowd remained sullen and silent, reserving judgement.

'Thank you for your welcome,' he continued. 'I know that my wife joins me in looking forward to meeting all of you properly in due course. Meanwhile, I hope you will continue to take your direction from Mr Jones, and that work will carry on much as usual.'

At this there were some growls of disapproval from the outskirts of the crowd.

'I know that things have not gone well here since Mr McKenzie's accident,' Doug added hastily, 'but I would like to say how much the company appreciates the way in which you have got on with the job, despite the absence of a mine manager.'

A little flattery harmed no one, however ill-deserved. The atmosphere of menace seemed to lift a little. Doug continued with renewed confidence.

'Naturally there will have to be changes if we are to improve output to the extent demanded by my superiors, but these will come only after careful investigation of present methods, and with the agreement of all those concerned.'

This seemed to meet with their approval. Talking earnestly among themselves, the men began to move away in the direction of the mine.

Soon only Dai Jones remained.

'Will you take a seat, Mr Jones?' Doug invited, indicating a wooden bench which stood on the veranda. 'I'd offer you tea, but to tell the truth we were all fast asleep when you knocked . . . the journey, you know. And it took us a while to settle in last evening.'

'House a bit of a mess, was it?' enquired the foreman. 'Old McKenzie let the place go downhill after his missus left him.'

'I'm sure that my wife will soon have it to rights,' Doug assured him.

'Now then, Mr Jones, to business,' he continued, taking his place on the bench beside his new colleague. 'The agent tells me that there has been very little output from the mine for the last six months. Can you explain why that is?'

'We've been taking out plenty of ore,' replied the other, 'but the crushing plant needs a major overhaul, and I have had no one competent to help me dismantle the machinery.'

'Didn't you report this to the company office?' Doug demanded.

'Oh, yes,' Jones replied, 'several times. There are copies of my letters in the files.'

'And what was their response?'

'There was none.'

'Nothing at all?' Doug's heart sank. He had suspected that support from on high would be minimal; he had not anticipated that it was non-existent.

'After McKenzie's accident there was a letter telling us to expect his replacement in due course. After that . . . nothing, until a wire arrived last night announcing your arrival. By then, you were already here!'

'We'll take a look at the machinery together,' Doug assured him. 'Are there any further major problems?'

'There are plenty,' Jones replied, 'but if we can just get the crusher working, that will provide sufficient occupation for the men for the time being. As for the rest, well, you'd best see for yourself!'

He rose to his feet.

'If you'll excuse me, sir,' he said, 'I must be getting on down to the mine.'

As the Welshman turned to go, Doug called him back.

'There is one thing,' he observed, dryly. 'If I am not mistaken, a number of the men had been drinking . . . heavily.'

Jones made no attempt to deny it.

'I want you to put it about that no liquor will be sold in the company store during the working week,' Doug continued. 'They can buy whatever they want on Saturday, and sleep it off on Sunday. Drunkenness on the job will not be tolerated.' He had expected some measure of dissent from his foreman, and was therefore surprised to hear Jones agreeing with him.

'It is pleased I am to hear you say so, Mr McGillivray,' he answered. 'The mine is dangerous enough, without slovenly workmanship and carelessness due to intoxication. Do you want me to pass your message on to Walt Wilson at the store?'

'No, leave him to me. I have to see him about another matter.'

'I'll be off then, sir.' Jones stepped down on to the path. 'Will we be seeing you later, at the mine?'

'You may bet your life on it,' the new manager replied.

Mary and Flora worked their way through the rest of the building, scrubbing walls and floors, washing curtains and rugs, polishing and painting the old, mainly home-made furniture. By the end of the first week the house had been transformed.

Their activities had not gone unnoticed by the small population of women in the village. On that first morning, when Doug and Hamish had gone off up the road towards the mine workings, Flora was hanging out curtains on the line they had rigged in the back yard.

'G'day.' The voice came from beyond the high picket fence which divided their plot from next door.

Flora dropped her pegs back into the basket and moved across to see who was speaking. As she did so, two large work-reddened hands grasped the top rail, and in an instant a head appeared above the fence.

'I'm Madge Bowler,' the woman announced. 'You'll be Mr McGillivray's daughter?'

'Flora,' replied the girl, smiling.

'Pretty rough, was it?' asked the neighbour.

Flora looked puzzled.

'The house . . . in a bit of a state, I expect.' Madge heaved herself into a more comfortable position, resting her ample bosoms over the fence rail.

'Yes, it was a bit dirty,' Flora agreed.

'If anyone had said you were coming, I'd have gone in myself and tidied up a bit,' Madge commented. It was almost an accusation.

'I don't think anyone knew exactly when we were going to arrive,' Flora explained. 'Until we reached Perth, no one had told my father that Mr McKenzie was in hospital. I imagine that the house was as he left it on the day of the accident.'

'There was an Abo woman used to come in and "do" for him, if you know what I mean. I expect she packed up when she thought she wouldn't be getting paid.'

If Madge's confidence had been meant to convey some suggestion of impropriety, she saw at once that it was lost upon Flora. She would have to reserve the gossip for Mrs McGillivray.

'We shall be making a cup of tea shortly,' suggested Flora. 'Why don't you come round and meet my mother?'

'That's very kind of you, missy,' replied Madge. 'I'll just finish my own chores and then I'll join you.'

For her first visitor in their new home, Mary had produced her best tea set of bone china. Scones, baked that morning, nestled on a snowy white doily, and in a cut glass dish there was strawberry preserve, purchased in Kalgoorlie.

Madge Bowler had washed her face and changed her pinafore before calling on her new neighbour.

She was a large woman, coarse-skinned from exposure to the cruel Australian sun. Her short, straight hair was bleached almost white, although she was probably no more than forty. Her well-developed shoulders suggested that she had been used to heavy work in her youth. With lack of use, however, her arms had gone to fat, so that the soft flesh now bulged beyond her sleeveless bodice. Her legs, encased in wrinkled woollen hose, were swollen, and she walked painfully.

'I'm afraid there is no butter,' Mary apologised, seating her guest upon a wooden settle and offering her a scone. 'Perhaps you can tell me where people obtain their dairy produce?'

'You can get milk and sometimes even butter up at Jones's place, when his cows are producing. That's in the wet, you understand, when there's a bit of grass about.

'Jones? Is that Dai Jones, the mine foreman?' Mary asked, remembering her husband's description of this morning's encounter with the men.

'That's him,' agreed Madge.

Mary thought it a trifle odd that the most important figure in the mining community, save only the manager himself, should also run a farm supplying dairy produce for the township.

'Do many people have more than one job?' she asked.

'Lord, bless you, yes,' came the reply. 'They have to, to make any sort of a living. Dai Jones, for instance, came out here to farm. He only got involved with the mine when he found that there was nothing for him to do in the summer months. Once the wet sets in, he works all the hours God sends, holding down both jobs! We're just coming up to calving time now. During the summer we've had to rely on tinned butter and condensed milk from the store.'

'What do you do about fresh fruit and vegetables? Are there any to be had?' Mary enquired.

'Only what we grow ourselves,' Madge replied, 'and that's little enough. Water for the houses is restricted by meter because mainly, of course, it's for use in the mine. Most of us can't afford to use tap water for the garden . . . or only if it's already been used for something else first. Most people can't be bothered saving it. There is the creek, of course,' she continued. 'In a good wet she fills and runs like one of your mountain streams – rest of the time she's dry as a bone. Mind you, old McKenzie was forever talking about sinking a well on the plot – reckoned there's water down below.'

'Where are all the young people, Mrs Bowler?' Flora interrupted unable to contain her question a moment longer.

'Well now,' Madge eyed her sympathetically, 'there's not many your age, my dear. Those there are leave as soon as they're old enough and go to Kalgoorlie to find work. Mr Jones's girls now, they go to some fancy boarding school in the city. They left only last week at the start of the new school year.'

Miserably, Flora thanked her, disappointed by this unwelcome news.

'Who runs the school here?' Mary asked, and was rewarded with a blank stare.

'School? There ain't no school,' Madge answered. 'Families aren't encouraged to come out here, y'see,' she continued helpfully. 'It's mainly bachelors, except for the farming families.'

'How many children are there?' Mary demanded.

'Difficult to say,' was the response. 'A few on the outlying homesteads, but they rarely come here. There's maybe half a dozen white kids here in the town.'

'But I've seen any number of Aboriginal children,' Mary insisted. 'Altogether there must be sufficient numbers to necessitate a public school?'

'Abos don't count. Or at least . . .' Madge hesitated before continuing '. . . who'd allow their own youngster to sit alongside a black kid in school?' She seemed quite shocked at the notion.

Mary was astounded. Could people really be so prejudiced against the Aborigines that they would deny their own children the chance of a formal education? Something would have to be done to put things right!

Doug tested the overhead timbers with his long-handled hammer before signalling to Hamish to follow him with the light. What timber there was seemed sound enough but the had been alarmed at the outset by the widely spaced supports, particularly in the most recent workings. Clearly, his predecessor had been operating at the limits of safety for a long time. No wonder the accident rate was so alarmingly high. It also explained why so few able-bodied men stayed any length of time in the company's employ.

Cautiously, they followed the tunnel until it opened into a wide natural cavern, some thirty feet in height and perhaps the same distance across. It stretched before them, beyond their field of vision.

As Hamish turned his lamp this way and that, the beams caught a flash of white, and here and there a glimpse of sparkling minerals.

'Here,' commanded Doug, 'shine the light over here.'

As Hamish held up the lantern a thick white seam of quartz was revealed and along its edges the glint of yellow metal.

'Don't get too excited,' breathed Doug as he knocked off a piece of rock for closer examination. 'It could be iron pyrites.'

All the children growing up on Eisdalsa Island had collected the cubic pyrite crystals which distinguish Argyll slate from any other. The McGillivrays were unlikely to mistake 'fool's gold' for the real thing.

Doug chipped away at the specimen in his hand for a few minutes, then examined the shimmering metal through a jeweller's lens. Despite the poor light, he was quite convinced that what he was looking at was real gold.

He broke off a few more pieces of the rock and placed them in the haversack which Hamish had hung over his shoulder.

'I'll take that into Kalgoorlie for assay,' Doug murmured.

As they retraced their footsteps towards the main mineshaft he continued, 'I have to go and sort out this business about the supplies for the store. Maybe you'd like to come with me?'

Hamish, anxious for a change of scene, jumped at the suggestion.

'I'll be glad to,' he replied. 'Do you want me to have a word with Walt Wilson about hiring a couple of horses?'

'Good idea,' replied his father. 'I need to talk to Jones. See you at supper.'

Back in the office, Doug was quick to tackle his foreman on the question of the timber shoring.

'I'm not happy with the props you're using, Mr Jones,' he commented. 'What's the problem, shortage of timber or shortage of cash?'

'Both,' was the reply. 'Most of our timber comes from the local saw mills – good hardwood, a lot of it prime jarrah, but a while back Mr McKenzie allowed himself to be persuaded to buy a load of Swedish pine which had been taken off a cargo boat which ran aground down near Hopetoun. The timber was sodden with sea water and twisted badly as it dried out.'

'We'll have to do something quickly about reinforcing that new tunnel if we intend to open up the seam,' Doug observed. 'I'll make enquiries about supplies of timber when I go in to Kalgoorlie.'

'I want to install electric lighting throughout the mine as soon as possible,' Doug confided next day, as he and his son made the long journey back to Kalgoorlie. 'Will you help?'

Surprised and delighted to be consulted, Hamish agreed readily, and as they walked their mounts in the heat of the midday sun, the young man poured forth such a stream of information and suggestions that Doug was in danger of becoming totally confused.

Hamish knew exactly how electricity might be generated using turbines powered by steam. The water could be reused from the existing crushing mechanism. At present, once water had been used to wash the pulverised rock and separate out the gold dust, polluted by the chemicals used in the extraction it was discharged into an outflow channel, only to disappear underground after a few hundred yards.

'You'll be needing a large storage tank,' Hamish explained, 'and we'd need to install a suitable boiler to make steam for the turbine.'

'Will it no' cost a heap of money?' demanded Doug.

'The main outlay would be on the cables, insulators and light fittings,' replied his son. 'If we can just lay hands on a second-hand turbine – there may be something in Kalgoorlie – the rest, building the boiler and so on, we could manage on the site using our own men.'

'Would you be able to organise the job yourself?'

'Of course I could, Dad,' he replied confidently, excited to think that his father put this much trust in him.

Doug wanted to believe in his son's capabilities. Maybe it was time for him to be given his head.

'Just remember,' he cautioned, 'should anything go wrong, it's my job as well as yours that will be on the line. If you start it, you'll have to make the scheme work, for all our sakes.'

'It'll work, Dad . . . I know it will,' his son replied.

For the remainder of the journey he was deep in thought and when, on arrival at Kalgoorlie, his father decided that he must go first to the hospital to speak to Jock McKenzie about a small matter of unpaid grocery bills, the boy chose to make his way to the town's public library, determined to check on some of his theories.

Chapter 7

Dr David Beaton put down his pen. He yawned, stretched the arm which ached from writing, and reached for his pipe.

He ran his fingers over the carved oak decoration on his father's old desk, grateful that Hugh and Millicent had not wanted to keep it. The heavy leather armchair had also been discarded by his daughter-in-law, and stood now just where the light from the gas mantle would fall conveniently for reading. Indeed, had it not been for the persistent smell of new paint, he might still have been in his familiar study at Tigh na Broch.

Needing a breath of fresh air, the doctor pushed open a tall French window, and relished the fragrance of freshly mown grass.

He had to admit that Annabel had been right about not wishing to move to Glasgow following his new appointment. The house they had chosen was perfectly situated in a central position for his work, on a junction of major roads and with the main railway line from Oban to Glasgow easily accessible. More importantly from Annabel's point of view, they were within easy travelling distance of Margaret and Michael in Oban, and of Hugh and his family in Eisdalsa.

Margaret in particular had expressed great satisfaction at their choice. Her husband's job as superintendent of the Oban Hospital left her alone for long periods, and since her marriage she had continued to spend a great deal of time in her mother's company. They had always been very close, the only women in a household dominated by men. David realised now that it would have broken Annabel's heart to be moved too far away from her daughter.

Still childless after ten years of marriage, there seemed little hope that Margaret would ever present them with any grand-children. It was a situation which troubled and disappointed her father, but her infertility seemed to be of little concern to his daughter and in recent months even Annabel had ceased to speculate upon the matter.

All Margaret's mothering instincts had been directed towards Michael's children by his first marriage. David and Annabel too had immediately taken the two motherless waifs to their hearts. James Brown had, in due course, filled the role of David's apprentice just as Margaret's brothers had done before him. His sister, Heather, had benefited greatly from the bequest which David's mother Morag Beaten had intended for her granddaughter Margaret's education.

Even now, David flinched when he recalled the terrible scenes which had arisen as a result of his refusal to allow Morag's money to be spent on sending Margaret to university. He had handed over the legacy on his daughter's wedding day, convinced that he had been right to deny her the education which she had so craved.

She had succeeded as a writer despite her lack of an academic background, and look what had become of Margaret's friend Wee Annie McGillivray – a lot of good her education had done her! He remembered with fondness Anne McGillivray's dark-haired little tomboy of a daughter – what a pity she had grown up to become a Suffragette! Her mind filled with the nonsense doled out by those Pankhurst women, and encouraged by free-thinkers such as her mother and her teacher, Elizabeth McIntyre, Wee Annie was probably even now tramping the streets waving a green and purple banner or chaining herself to the railings outside Parliament! No, Margaret was much better off where she was.

Having no family of her own had at least given his daughter the freedom to pursue her own interests. He was immensely proud of her work – something which would have been greatly impeded had there been more children to care for. He turned to the bookcase and the special shelf, he had reserved to contain the growing number of her published writings.

He ran his hand fondly across the bindings until he came to his favourite, the volume of *Highland Folk Tales* – her first book, published shortly before her wedding day.

Taking the book down, he turned to the title page and read the dedication to his mother, Morag, and their old family retainer, Sheilagh Anderson, who had been the source of so many of the tales.

He replaced the book carefully beside a collection of adventure stories for children, and a slim volume of history: *Eisdalsa and the Slate Islands of Argyll*.

In more recent times Margaret had spent a great deal of time studying Gaelic with her ageing uncle, Angus Beaton. A well-recognised exponent of the Gaelic tongue, Angus had occupied the latter part of his life in a desperate struggle to save the ancient language from extinction. Now the two of them were collaborating in a scheme to produce a series of study books for children, to enable the schools to teach in Gaelic as well as English. Although it was a plan destined to be fraught with difficulty, their enthusiasm for the project was boundless, and David was pleased to see how the work had given Angus a new lease of life.

For thirty years educationalists had done their utmost to eliminate Gaelic from the schools. Children, fluent in the tongue which they had learned in their cradles, were punished soundly for speaking it in the playground, and in those families where the grandparents could speak no English, the little ones suffered agonies of confusion in moving between their homes and the schoolroom. It was Angus's dream that one day every Scottish child would have access to the wealth of Gaelic literature.

Yes, it pleased David to know that Annabel and Margaret were able to see so much of each other. Since their move to Connel, Margaret had called upon her mother every week. Even when Michael required the car, she was able to hop on the train and travel the eight miles from Oban in comfort.

David had been rather distressed on the first occasion that his daughter had arrived on her own, driving Michael's Model T Ford. Motoring seemed to him to be a rather dangerous exercise for a woman, especially on the Highland roads with their many hazards. His protests had received short shrift, however. The women had all sided against him, of course. They usually did, these days. Both Annabel and Millicent had laughed at him for being an old fuddy duddy. Well, perhaps they were right . . .

He stepped out on to the terrace.

From here he could see a locomotive bound for Ballahulish, threading its way between that complex construction of ironwork that is the Connel Bridge. Against the low afternoon sun, its silhouette of delicate tracery was most pleasing. It was not at all the eyesore it was claimed to be by local reactionaries.

How resistant people are to change, David thought, smiling to himself as his glance fell on his splendid Argyll Tourer, standing on the drive beside the house. The car had been the suggestion of his son Hugh, who had himself added a motor vehicle to the assets of the Eisdalsa practice as soon as he had taken it over from David.

'It will take hours off your travelling,' Hugh had insisted, when David complained about the long journeys he was obliged to make into areas where the only choice for travel was between horse-drawn cart or Shanks's Pony.

He smiled to himself, remembering the prediction that he had made when, with youthful enthusiasm, his boys had looked forward to the age of the motor car.

'No internal combustion engine will ever be able to negotiate Kilninver Brae,' David had predicted, with great conviction.

Nowadays Hugh made that particular ascent most days of the week, while David himself was not even daunted by the prospect of a trip to Campbeltown, along the tortuous coast road.

Although it was midsummer, the light breeze blowing in from the sea was quite chilly. David filled his pipe to the brim from a leather pouch, then tamped the tobacco well down before, his back to the wind, he attempted to strike a match.

Satisfied at last with the thin plume of blue smoke arising from the bowl, he stepped down on to a rough pathway and threaded his way between outcropping boulders, rough grass and heather. Here and there a small spinney of stunted willows or a dense stand of gorse broke up the sparse vegetation. David wondered how Annabel could ever hope to make a garden out of this barren ground.

He could hear someone working down by the shore: the steady rhythm of a pick in expert hands, and the occasional scrape of metal spade upon stone. He followed the sounds until he came upon the site of this activity.

David had engaged their housekeeper's husband and his boy to assist Annabel with the heavy work of clearing the ground and creating the framework of her new garden. Suddenly the sounds of activity ceased. On turning a corner he found all three workers contemplating a thicket of gorse and ferns clustered around a natural outcrop of rock. Annabel had her dress protected by a leather apron, and her hair scraped back under a Paisley-patterned scarf. The men, despite the breezy spring day, wore their shirtsleeves rolled up, their bare arms scratched and bleeding from attacking the thorn bushes.

A flat patch of ground, perhaps thirty feet across, had already been cleared and the topsoil dug over. Annabel, a pad and pencil in her hand, was perched upon a convenient boulder. She had obviously been making notes as the men laboured.

'I think it will be unnecessary to remove that stone,' she decided. 'We could make a feature of it . . . grow a vigorous rambler over it perhaps.'

David was amused to note the look of relief on the face of the younger Murchieson.

Donald, his father, looked dubious. To his mind gardening should begin with level ground and no obstacles. If Mrs Beaton wanted her garden to look like a natural piece of countryside, why bother to go to all this trouble in the first place? He liked his plants in orderly rows, and preferred vegetables to flowers. 'If you canna eat it, why grow it?' he would demand of his friends in the taproom of the Dunstaffnage Arms of an evening.

On this occasion, however, he kept his peace. If the doctor was satisfied, who was he to argue? The job paid well and that was all that mattered.

Annabel glanced up at that moment and noticed David for the first time. She slipped off the rock and came towards him.

He caught his breath at the sight of her. She had never looked happier – or lovelier. The original golden colour of her hair had faded somewhat, but obstinate wisps escaping from beneath her scarf still shone brightly in the afternoon sunshine. The lines about her blue eyes deepened as she smiled her welcome, a clear sign that she was more accustomed to laughter than to frowning. Her face, generally pale, glowed with enthusiasm, clusters of freckles on her nose and cheeks adding a touch of youthfulness to her finely drawn features.

David wondered, not for the first time, at the strength of his feelings for his wife after thirty-six years of marriage. Her recent stand in opposition to his decision to move to Dunbarton had only served to heighten his regard for her. The threat of losing her had scared him.

'You've caught the sun,' he observed. 'That will be jolly sore tomorrow!' He touched her cheek lightly with his fingers and she noted how cool his hands were.

'Have you finished your report?' she enquired, sorry that he had had to remain so long indoors on such a lovely day.

'Nearly,' he replied, absently, contemplating the bare ground at his feet. 'What is happening here?' he asked, anxious to show an interest in what she was doing.

It had been one of her accusations, on that dreadful day when they had faced each other across his desk at Tigh na Broch, that he took no interest in any of his family's activities; that he was too absorbed by his own problems and made no attempt to understand hers. She showed him her sketch.

'This is to be the flower garden,' she explained. 'Donald will lay turf for a lawn in the centre. Here there will be herbaceous borders . . .'

Earnestly, Annabel outlined her plans while David, listening intently, put his arm around her shoulders and guided her up the steep path towards the house.

Six hundred miles to the south, behind prison walls, Wee Annie McGillivray allowed herself a moment of self-pity. If only she had not been so firm in her resolve to remain in Britain, she might even now be with her family, enjoying freedom and the challenge of a new life in Australia.

She heard sounds of a disturbance outside in the road, beyond the prison walls.

By standing on the plain wooden stool, and hoisting herself up by the bars, she was able to peer over the sill and look down on to the heads of the small crowd, mainly women and children, gathered there.

It must be Sunday, she thought. That was the day when the working-class women of London could find time to come and support their imprisoned sisters.

Despite the rain, the crowd swayed to the rhythms of a Salvation Army band, playing familiar hymns which all could sing, both inside the jail and out. The words, rewritten for the purpose, reflected the sentiments displayed on the flags and posters.

Banners fluttered in the wind above the sea of umbrellas and sopping wet bonnets.

NEVER GIVE IN, urged one. WOMEN DEMAND EQUAL RIGHTS UNDER THE LAW, declared another which, supported on two long poles, was stretched across the width of the pavement. A poster had been hurriedly plastered to the wall of a warehouse building opposite. It depicted working women and their babies and stated, MOTHERS DEMAND THE RIGHT TO VOTE.

Annie detected the hand of Sylvia Pankhurst in that particular one. It was very professionally produced.

On the same wall, painted in red in sprawling letters three feet high, were the words: THE WOMEN'S SOCIAL AND POLITICAL UNION, and beneath them, FIGHT FOR THE RIGHT TO VOTE!

Whenever the crowd spotted a hand waving from one of the cell windows, a great roar of support went up, putting heart into the inmates of Holloway Prison's political wing.

Suddenly a small group of mounted policemen emerged from out of a cul-de-sac, effectively cutting off the only escape route from the street. It was clear to Annie that they had been in position all along, waiting only for an appropriate moment to strike.

A line of horses advanced along the street, parting the solid mass of people below the prison walls and squeezing them up against the buildings on either side. Retaliation from the crowd was almost impossible. A few demonstrators fought off the approach using the poles which moments before had been supporting their banners. This only served to disturb the horses who let fly with their hooves and Annie saw one young woman struck on the head and left lying bleeding in the roadway.

Until now the dispersal of the demonstration had been relatively orderly, but as the people were forced into the narrower street and passageways nearby, some struggling began. There was a sharp cry as a horse stood on some luckless female's foot, and screams from a group of women who, with their babies clinging to their skirts, were forced up against the wall of the jail by a huge chestnut gelding.

There were scuffles as additional groups of policemen, on foot this time, moved into the rapidly diminishing crowd, arresting anyone they could lay hands on. Umbrellas, which until this moment had been keeping off the heavy downpour, now became weapons, their sharp ferules used to prod both horses and policemen alike.

Indiscriminately, women were thrown to the ground, over-powered by hulking male figures, and led screaming to the waiting black police vans. Many such arrests were made, but the majority of the demonstrators managed to filter out between the rows of policemen, suffering no more than torn clothing and a few bruises.

The street was suddenly quiet, the only sound the bell of an approaching ambulance, summoned to the aid of the stricken woman who lay spread-eagled on the pavement below Annie's cell.

Sickened by the behaviour of the policemen, men with wives and children of their own no doubt, Annie dropped down to the floor of her cell. There had been no provocation to warrant an attack upon these defenceless people. Only when the officers had moved in, had there been any suggestion of a riot.

She had seen similar incidents so many times in the past year: the women trying to keep their demonstrations orderly and peaceful; the men stepping in only to create turmoil.

She recalled her very first experience of a public meeting.

Could it really be ten years since the night she had half dragged, half carried her injured American friend, Alice Packstone, from the riot at St George's Cross to the Western Infirmary? She remembered the shock of finding Dr Hugh Beaton, her old school friend, on duty that night, and smiled as she recalled his kindness in paying for a cab to take the two girls back to their digs.

Her mind turned to memories of her dear friend, Margaret Beaton. Born on the same day in November, 1881, she and the doctor's daughter had been friends throughout their childhood. With her own brother and sister so much older than herself, it had seemed natural for Annie to spend much of her time in the Beaton household. Margaret's brothers, Hugh and Stuart, had been the girls' constant companions. Only when Annie won a scholarship to the Merchants' Ladies College, in Edinburgh, were she and Margaret parted. Since that time they had met only occasionally . . . the last time had been at Margaret's wedding.

The two older Beaton brothers had also gone away to school leaving Margaret at home with her mother, her invalid brother Ian and her writing.

During the school holidays, when they had all been at home together, Hugh, anxious to excel in his medical studies, had attached himself to his father and they had seen little of him. Stuart, on the other hand, preferred the sea and fishing from the island. Many long days had been spent by Margaret, Annie and Stuart in his small sailing dinghy, exploring the multitude of tiny islands scattered in the Sound of Lorn.

Even when Stuart forsook the company of the girls and associated with the local fishermen, Annie had refused to be left out. By offering to do the most tedious jobs, tarring the hull of a rotting dinghy, gutting fish or mending nets, she could spend endless wonderful hours in Stuart's company. Annie's love for Stuart Beaton was worn upon her sleeve for all the world to witness. Only Stuart himself had been too blind to see it.

A rattling of bolts brought Annie back to the present with a jolt. The square peep-hole in the door was slammed open and a harsh-voiced wardress demanded, 'Pint!'

Annie struggled to her feet and placed a pint-sized enamel mug on the hatch flap. A thick gruel of oatmeal and water was ladled into it and thrust back through the hatch. The lumpy mixture had overflowed and clung to the outside of the vessel in a slimy glutinous mess. Annie ate the thick gruel absentmindedly, still distracted by her memories.

Prison food differed little from meals she had experienced as a child, in the years during which her widowed mother had been forced to support her family alone.

Unlike her comrades, many of whom came from comfortable middle-class backgrounds, Annie McGillivray had quickly adjusted to prison fare. The plain diet, the senseless orders, harsh prison clothing and heavy boots she could tolerate. It was only the loneliness, and the empty hours of boredom, she found difficult to bear.

Annie could not help wondering how the fastidious Christobel Pankhurst would have enjoyed her Sunday supper.

Christobel had fled to Paris when threatened with repeated imprisonment, on the pretext that the organisation must have a leader 'on the outside'. Her mother Emmeline, her sister Sylvia, and countless unnamed heroines were left to carry the burden of imprisonment and all it was to imply in the future. There was most certainly no love lost between Annie McGillivray and Christobel Pankhurst who lacked the common touch of her sister Sylvia. It had been to Sylvia's East End branch of the WSPU that Annie had reported when she first came to London. Despite her middle-class upbringing, Sylvia had a very clear understanding of the lives endured by the working-class women of the East End. She had lived among them for many months, sharing their poverty, witnessing the humiliations and indignities heaped upon them both at work and in the home. Her views were understood and approved by the quarryman's daughter from Argyll.

Annie placed her empty mug on the scrubbed wooden table, hoping there would be an opportunity to rinse it out when the time came for ablutions. She settled back on her narrow mattress and allowed her mind to wander back to the time when she had first come to London.

It had been the day after the 'Battle of St George's Cross'.

Alice Packstone, having partially recovered from her wounds, was due to return to the States at the end of the following week. She had insisted, therefore, that Annie proceed with her own journey to London, to join up with Sylvia Pankhurst.

While seated in the railway carriage, awaiting departure, she had been startled to have Hugh Beaton burst in upon her, demanding that she forego her trip to London, and begging her to return to Eisdalsa as his bride. She remembered how appalled she had been at his proposal.

Intense, unimaginative Hugh had never figured in Annie's ambitious plans. Now, had Stuart Beaton made the same offer, she would have accepted him without a second thought. But Hugh – stodgy, predictable, conventional Hugh – was not for Wee Annie McGillivray. What an embarrassment she would have been to him, with her abrupt habit of calling a spade a spade!

She listened for the sound of footsteps in the corridor . . . a signal that the next stage in the monotonous routine of the day was imminent.

What am I doing here? she asked herself for the umpteenth time. Was their cause really worth all this . . . this senseless incarceration? She could be so much more useful out there, where she would be able to focus attention upon their grievances by means of her own particular skills.

Would winning the vote really bring women everything they dreamed of? Once they had gained the recognition they sought, would the women of Britain thank them for their sacrifices? How many of them would exercise their right to vote and, more important, put themselves forward for election to office?

She knew that people like her friend Margaret Beaton, and her mother Annabel, considered the Suffragettes too extreme in their programme of direct action. Her former schoolteacher Elizabeth McIntyre, that great advocate for women's rights, believed that they would gain the franchise through informed debate alone and was totally opposed to violence.

Maybe Annie's friends were right. When she considered those women who *had* made a breakthrough into any of the male provinces, she had to admit that it had always been by stealth rather than by vulgar publicity... look at the female doctors whose numbers could have been counted on the fingers of one hand until the last decade of the previous century. Unlike her sister Kirsty, a doctor who had died tragically of cholera while treating her patients back in the 1880's, most of them were from wealthy middle-class families and had never needed to practise medicine once they were qualified. The gaining of a medical degree had been their only goal – it was just a game to many of them.

That was the whole point: such women could afford to make a show, write their pamphlets, issue their sophisticated protests, and yes, even go to prison. For at the end of the day they could always retire to their comfortable mansions and bask in notoriety for a short time, secure in the bosom of their understanding families.

Working-class women, once committed to prison for however short a time, would wear the stigma of it to the end of their days. They could wave goodbye to any chance of decent employment and the honest cab drivers and stall-holders of Hackney and Bow were unlikely to invite ex-convicts and trouble-makers to become the mothers of their children.

Yes, it was the women of the working classes who most needed to have their plight recognised – those who suffered the indignity of being considered of less account than the most stupid, idle and criminal of men. Forced to work for slave wages, unable to gain recognition for their demands for the most basic improvement, either in the workplace or in the home, without even the right to claim the custody of their own children... these were the women who required a champion.

Annie, my girl, she told herself, you have had all the advantages that are denied to most working-class girls. You owe it to those less fortunate to use what you have learned to best advantage. And that, she decided, will best be done from outside these prison walls!

For a time, Annie dropped off into a restless slumber in which images of the past and fears for the future coloured her dreams.

'Everybody up! Stand by your beds!'

Annie started, instantly awake.

The door of the cell was thrown open with a clang and, on the instruction to march, Annie joined the line of prisoners shuffling towards the ablutions block – a last call before the final ceremony of locking up for the night. At least the daily visits to the washroom were not as dreadful as her first experience of the bathhouse routine.

On admission to the prison every woman was forced to take a bath, a rule with which Annie could find no fault. For some of them it was the first time in their lives that they had been totally immersed in water.

Annie had found that there was no distinction between the grades of criminal with whom she was obliged to bathe. While they had waited in a line to be ushered into the bathroom, six at a time, there had been sufficient opportunity for her to identify thieves, drunkards, prostitutes and even murderesses amongst her companions. When her time had come at last, she had been made to strip naked, her own clothes bundled together and carelessly labelled.

Six enamelled slipper baths stood in a row down the centre of the room.

Annie had been relieved to see that each was being refilled with clean water. Her satisfaction was short-lived, however, for as she approached her appointed tub she could see the layer of scum forming on the surface of the water, left over from the previous occupant.

As if it had not been sufficiently humiliating to be left standing stark naked before the eagle-eyed wardresses and her fellow prisoners, Annie had been mortified when one of the wardresses, believing her to be too gentle with herself, had snatched up a coarse scrubbing brush, covered it liberally in caustic lye soap and commenced to scrub Annie's arms and shoulders until they were red and sore.

How relieved she had been to emerge from the water and rub herself dry on the coarse towelling. The harsh chocolate brown serge of the prison uniform she had been given scratched her skin unmercifully, while her prison boots had quickly raised a crop of painful blisters.

That had been nearly four weeks ago. Annie kept her eyes on the ground, speaking to no one as the slow file of prisoners wound along the corridor, through the ablutions block and back towards the cells. In three days she would be released.

The door was slammed shut behind her. Twelve more dark, solitary, interminable hours before the next distraction.

She picked up her bible, the only reading matter permitted, and flipped through the pages unable to concentrate. If she could only sleep, the time might pass more rapidly. She put down the book and closed her eyes, but could not dispell the images of home which would keep her awake until the early hours.

Annie had no quarrel with the magistrate concerning her sentence for she considered that she fully deserved the treatment she had received at the hands of the court.

She had gone into the public gallery that day, having briefed an inexperienced young solicitor who had agreed to defend two of her comrades arrested in Hyde Park during an open-air rally.

Martin Strong had listened carefully to all Annie's prepared arguments, upholding the defendant's right of free speech, and protesting that it was the male hecklers who had been responsible for the ensuing disturbance.

The prosecution alleged that stones had been thrown, and a policeman, unseated by his mount, was nursing a cracked skull in St Bartholomew's Hospital.

Explaining that his clients had had no weapons of any kind, and could not therefore be accused of having caused the affray, Martin concluded, 'The defendants regret any injury to the police officer, your honour, and would wish to send him their good wishes for a speedy recovery.'

'Yes, yes,' the Magistrate interrupted testily. 'We know that the defendants did not throw the stone themselves, Mr Strong. That is hardly the point at issue. Were these women demonstrating in the park, or not?'

Sensing a trap, Martin Strong was forced to reply, 'Yes, your honour.'

'And, as a result of this . . . demonstration, was there, or was there not, an affray?'

The solicitor gulped his reply.

'There was, your honour.'

Annie had all the while been biting back her comments. Unable to contain her anger a moment longer, she had shouted from the public gallery, 'What is illegal about any citizen of this country standing up in a park and voicing an opinion?'

'Silence,' roared the magistrate, purple with indignation.

'Surely the right of free speech applies to women as well as men?' Annie continued, 'Or is that just a myth? Is freedom of speech just one more prerogative of men which women must be denied?'

The magistrate's response was entirely predictable.

'Constable, arrest that woman,' he demanded.

A burly policeman made a rough grab at her, catching her about the waist. Infuriated at the liberty he was taking, Annie struggled, her arms waving above her head. In the ensuing scuffle the man's helmet was dislodged. All self-control now abandoned, Annie grasped the helmet and cast it into the well of the court.

Onlookers in the public gallery cheered and hooted. The court officials found it difficult to suppress their mirth and even the two women in the dock joined in the laughter.

The magistrate, hammering upon the bench with his gavel, eventually restored the courtroom to order, and Annie was led away to be sentenced next day to one month in Holloway Prison.

On her release from Holloway, having served the full term of her first prison sentence, Annie McGillivray was determined that she would never again be caught up in any militant activity of the Union. Accustomed to winning her point by reasoned argument, she did not subscribe to the destruction of property or injury to persons. She found it ironic that she should have a police record of violence towards an officer of the law.

Her role since coming to London had been to attend public

meetings addressed by the organisation, keeping in the background while making note of comments made from the floor as well as by the speakers. This monitoring of events had proved useful in compiling a defence for those women subsequently arrested for causing an affray. She was also able to refute many of the worst fabrications of over-active journalistic reporting.

As one who had served a term in jail, however, Annie was now considered sufficiently experienced to be able to contribute to public meetings. With many prominent members of the organisation under lock and key, and others languishing abroad, it was only a matter of time before she was called upon.

A meeting was organised in the Central Hall in East London, late in October, 1913, at which a distinguished Member of Parliament had agreed to give an address. Unfortunately, on the evening in question he was delayed at the House by a protracted debate.

The capacity audience was becoming restive and the ladies of the platform party felt obliged to call upon Annie McGillivray to give an impromptu speech.

Somewhat reluctantly, she found herself thrust towards the front of the platform.

'Keep them occupied for as long as you can,' a voice whispered, 'he must come soon.'

When they saw that Annie was about to speak, the audience hushed expectantly, and the girl from a remote Hebridean island found herself addressing a crowd of more than a thousand people. They were London women from every class of society, of many races and different religions, but tonight they were united in their purpose. Annie's words could not have fallen upon more receptive ears.

'Sisters . . .' Her voice faltered as she gazed across a sea of upturned faces. There was a wave of restlessness at the back of the hall as people strained to hear. She raised her voice and the fidgeting ceased.

'My friends,' she continued, 'I come from a Scottish village, unknown to most of you. It is a small community where every person depends for survival upon the help of family and neighbours. Yet even in such rigorous circumstances, not the slightest measure of equality exists between men and women.

'Before the slate quarries closed down, the company which employed the men to work there provided a house, medical care and good schooling for its employees, relying upon the wives to feed and clothe the workers, and to nurse them when they were sick or injured. Yet when a man was killed at his work, or injured so that he would never work again, all such benefits were withdrawn, and the homeless widow was left with only the charity of the parish to support her. Sisters, I put it to you that a woman in such circumstances should be entitled to a pension, in recognition of her own contribution to her husband's working capability.'

There were murmurs of agreement and encouragement from the floor.

'A woman labours for as many hours as her husband, but she has no right to any part of the income which he enjoys. Often she must beg for a portion of the money he earns, in order to provide for herself and her children. How many of you, I wonder, receive a fair proportion of your husband's wages?'

The comments from several parts of the hall were ribald and humorous. A ripple of laughter swept through the audience.

'If a man chooses to spend the larger part of his income on his own self-gratification, there is absolutely nothing that his wife can do about it. If he chooses to spend all his money in the tavern, she has no redress in law!'

Wild agreement came from all parts of the hall.

Annie waited for silence. 'In the marriage bed,' she lowered her voice significantly, but her words rang clearly to the far end of the building, 'the wife is expected to submit, no matter what form of bestiality or brutality her husband chooses to inflict upon her. If she refuses him, through fear of injury or an unwanted pregnancy, he has grounds for divorce. If he beats her into submission, the police turn a blind eye.'

There were a few startled exchanges between the women on the platform. Once in full flight, however, nothing would have stopped Wee Annie McGillivray at that point.

Lowering the pitch of her voice again, to dramatic effect, she continued, 'In our small community, some years ago, a young woman, a simpleton with the mind of a child, was raped.'

One of the platform party, indignant that such an unacceptable subject should be introduced, would have interrupted at this point had not her neighbour prevented her. 'Don't you see,' she persuaded, 'Annie is speaking in a language they understand? Look at their faces!'

'In due course,' she continued without a pause, 'in a sea cave, all alone, this poor creature gave birth to her child. Soon after, through fear and ignorance, she dashed the baby's head upon a rock and killed it.'

There was an audible sigh from the body of the hall.

'Did the police hunt down the rapist?' she demanded. 'No, they did not! In that small community it would not have been a difficult task to identify the father of the child. There were plenty of individuals who might have given evidence against him. No, they locked the girl away in an institution, for the rest of her life, and prided themselves on having spared her the hangman's noose.'

The audience roared its disapproval.

'When we ask our lords and masters for the vote . . . no, when we *demand* that they give us the vote . . . we are seeking only those rights which are already enjoyed by fifty per cent of the population. While any man, be he lord or scavenger, may register his vote, no woman, however knowledgeable, may do so.'

'And quite right too,' came a deep male voice from somewhere near the doors at the back.

There was a howl of disagreement, and the offender shot out through the swing doors, in fear for his life.

Undeterred, Annie went on, 'What we want is the right to free speech. How many of our sisters are languishing in jail for expressing just such views as I have put forward tonight?'

'You're next!' The laconic remark made the audience laugh and there were some drunken catcalls from the shadowy area beneath the overhanging gallery.

'We demand freedom from poverty,' she shouted above the ensuing hubbub.

'We demand our fair share of the wage packet.' Loud cheers greeted this.

'We need to be able to end an unsatisfactory marriage. Why should it be only the rich who may divorce, simply because they can afford it?'

Roars of protest accompanied this last remark, but there were many in the hall who supported Annie's view.

She continued: 'We want freedom from the tyranny of men and from the fear of unwanted pregnancy.' Again it was the middle-class women on the platform who showed disapproval. Annie ignored them.

'We demand freedom from want, freedom to eliminate the dirt and degradation of poverty from our lives, and we ask for an opportunity to be involved in constructing a society which will bring about such changes.'

She was coming to an end now and with her hands held up in supplication, demanded, 'Give us the vote! Put women in a position where their views may be expressed without fear or favour, in the very seat of government itself! Sisters, we must be represented in Parliament!'

From the wings there stepped forward a single male figure. He applauded her roundly. After a moment's hushed astonishment, the entire audience rose to its feet to join in.

The elegant gentleman, in immaculate evening dress, unconventional only by virtue of the large orange rosette worn in his button-hole, seemed to have been recognised immediately by many in the hall.

As he joined Annie in the centre of the stage he was clapping his hands, slowly at first, then as the audience joined in, faster and faster. Soon the auditorium was ringing with cheers and applause. The Liberal member for Woodhamstead East shook Annie by the hand and the audience roared its approval.

It was at that moment that she was struck full in the face by a soft tomato. The juice spread into her eyes and the mess splattered her snowy starched shirt-front. As the MP went to her aid, he too was struck, this time by a rotten egg which landed on his shoulder. The stench was awful!

Turning his back to protect both himself and Annie, a second egg struck him on the back of the head.

Now more tomatoes, oranges and rotting fruit of all kinds sailed through the air, mostly landing harmlessly on the rapidly emptying stage.

The main body of the audience, momentarily shocked into inaction by the savagery of the attack, now turned upon the intruders, using whatever weapons came to hand. Handbags, umbrellas and hat pins were used to good effect, and had it not been for the intervention of the police, there might well have been charges of homicide that night.

The more cautious amongst the onlookers took advantage of the darkened auditorium to slip away through the side exits before the house lights went up, but those upon the platform, seeking to escape by the back stairs, found themselves immediately surrounded by constables.

That the attack had been engineered there was no doubt. A few of the most drunken and verbose of the intruders were taken into custody, more for their own safety than from any intention of charging them. The officers were undoubtedly targeting the leaders of the Suffragettes.

A uniformed sergeant approached Annie, laying his hand firmly upon her shoulder. Her other arm was taken in a vice-like grip by a red-faced young constable.

The MP stepped forward to intervene.

Instantly recognising the statesman, the police sergeant saluted smartly.

'Good evening, sir,' he said. Then, seeing the gentleman attempting to release the constable's grip upon Annie, 'You will excuse me, Mr Rosenstein, sir,' he continued, 'but I would not wish to be forced to charge you with obstructing a police officer in the execution of his duty.'

Reluctantly, Rosenstein released his hold on the officer's arm. 'No, Sergeant of course.' Self-consciously he gave Annie a helpless shrug and stepped back while the sergeant made his arrest.

'Miss McGillivray, I am arresting you for disturbing the peace and for incitement to riot . . .'

'Oh, for God's sake!' protested Rosenstein, but was silenced by the sergeant's withering glance.

Annie made no protest, but she squirmed as the constable tightened his grip.

'And there will be a further charge of resisting arrest,' he continued. 'You are not obliged to speak, but anything you do say will be taken down and may be used in evidence against you.'

He licked his pencil as he completed his notes, gave her a moment to reply and then, very deliberately, tucked the book into his top pocket and turned to another unfortunate captive. Emmanuel Rosenstein stood by helplessly as they dragged Annie away to the waiting Black Maria.

Inside the wagon, battered and bruised, were several of her colleagues. The doors were slammed shut and as the iron-bound wheels of the carriage rumbled across the cobbled roadway, shaking the passengers uncomfortably on their narrow wooden seats, the women began to sing defiantly. Outside, many of those who had attended the meeting now gathered to shout their encouragement to the prisoners. As members of the Constabulary looked on helplessly, uncertain how to proceed without further orders, the crowd thronging the street took up the song of those within.

Chapter 8

For her second term of imprisonment, Annie had been classed as a category two prisoner, which meant that she was allowed some books and writing materials, and was permitted a limited amount of social discourse with other prisoners. A further six weeks of the mindless inactivity which she had endured on the previous occasion would certainly have sent her crazy.

Once every day the women were allowed out into the prison yard for thirty minutes' exercise and recreation. It was upon such brief periods of social intercourse that the leadership of the WSPU relied, in order to pass messages to those of their members under sentence. One prisoner might have a visit from lawyer or friend; another would bring with her, upon sentence, instructions from on high to be conveyed to her fellow inmates while strolling in the prison yard. So efficient was the organisation that every suffragette could be contacted in one way or another. On just such an occasion Annie received the instruction, 'Hunger strikes are to begin, immediately.'

If a cause is worth fighting for, it is worth dying for, was the maxim. This peculiarly self-destructive form of protest had proved to be a most effective method of gaining publicity. There was nothing the press and the public at large liked better than a few martyrs, whatever their cause.

Immediately the word was out, all the political prisoners refused food, allowing themselves only minimal amounts of water each day.

By the third day, Annie found that she was too weak to go to the exercise yard. When the wardress came to release her from her cell, she remained stretched upon her narrow cot, unable to respond.

'You had better go outside,' declared the woman, not unkindly, 'or the doctors will be round with the trolley to see that you take nourishment.'

Annie turned her face to the wall. She knew only too well what the wardress meant; was prepared for it, in fact. Had she not seen the effects of forcible feeding upon a number of her friends?

She did not know how long it was before they came for her. In her weakened state she drifted in and out of sleep and lost all notion of time passing.

There it was at last, the anticipated sound of a metal trolley rattling on its journey along the corridor. Suddenly the noise ceased. The trolley had stopped before reaching her cell. They were going to deal with another prisoner first.

Her senses sharpened by anxiety, Annie strained to hear sounds from the adjoining cell. There was a muffled argument followed by a clatter of instruments and metal bowls scattered across a concrete floor. Her neighbour was putting up a hard fight.

Annie was suddenly transfixed with fear as a wild, high-pitched scream of terror rent the air, echoing from wall to tiled wall, the length of the building. There followed a silence so deep that it was almost more terrifying than the noise.

In the calm which followed, Annie at last allowed herself to relax. In her anxiety, she had been holding her breath almost to the point of asphyxiation.

Breathe deeply, she told herself. Don't let them see you are afraid. Relax. Tension will only make things worse!

The trolley was coming closer. It stopped outside her own cell. A key scraped in the lock and the door was flung back, ringing as it struck the wall. Annie tried not to flinch.

There were two doctors wearing long white coats. Annie had never seen them before. The matron from the prison infirmary she did recognise.

A senior prison officer manhandled the trolley into the cell while a second officer followed with a sturdy wooden armchair which he placed in the centre of the narrow space left by the cot.

Wordlessly the matron unbuttoned Annie's prison gown,

tugging it down roughly from her shoulders and exposing her bare breasts.

Wielding an icy stethoscope, one doctor examined her heart and lungs. Apparently satisfied that she was fit to endure the coming ordeal, he nodded to his colleague. The matron stood by, her face expressionless, as the two prison officers half carried Annie to the chair and attempted to strap her in.

Her struggles, at first feeble, became fiercer as indignation overcame her weakness. Annie felt her adrenaline rising and fought off the men vigorously. Experienced as they were, the jailers were ready for her. Each grabbed a forearm, forcing it down on to the solid arm of the chair, and quickly snapped manacles over her wrists.

She kicked out with her feet then, upsetting various buckets and bowls which were being carefully arranged beside the chair by the matron.

In a matter of seconds they had secured her feet also. Annie was now helpless, able only to prepare herself mentally for them to do their worst.

Suddenly her head was forced roughly back, and she found herself gazing at the cracks on the ceiling of her cell.

She tried to concentrate on these as she held her jaws clamped fast together. She was determined to resist the vicious metal gag held by one of the doctors.

In her ear she heard the whispered words of the matron.

'Allow him to fix the gag, dear. This one needs no excuse to use the nasal tube.'

Annie had heard about the nasal tube method. One woman who refused the gag had had a feeding tube thrust up her nose. Unfortunately, in the struggle which followed, the tube had missed the oesophagus, passed down the prisoner's windpipe and penetrated the lung. Liquid food had flooded her pleural cavity, and she had died painfully of pleurisy some weeks later.

Annie relaxed her jaws. In an instant the doctor had his hand inside her mouth and was tightening the cruel metal instrument over her gums. Dissatisfied with the result of his efforts, he grabbed a second gag and forced it into the other cheek.

Annie's resistance now was reduced to rolling her head from side to side, to make it difficult to tighten the clamp. The movement incensed the doctor, who continued screwing on the instrument until her gums were bleeding. Blood gushed from her mouth, spattering the front of her gown and soiling the matron's starched apron.

While the woman wiped the blood from Annie's face with a piece of cotton, she caught sight of the rubber tube in the hands of the second doctor.

Her eyes, wide with terror, rolled back beneath their lids until she was forced to shut them tight. She felt the tube thrust roughly over her tongue and gagged as it met and entered the opening to the food canal. As she choked and swallowed involuntarily the tube was sucked in. Deftly, the doctor slipped it down, down, while she felt its sharp edges rasping at her delicate membranes.

When she dared to open her eyes it was to see the first doctor holding a large funnel connected to the open end of the tube, and the matron pouring something out of a large enamel jug. In seconds she was aware of a warm sensation as the liquid food slid down into her stomach. When enough of the nourishing broth had been passed down, and the doctors had removed all the apparatus, Annie felt a moment of extreme relief.

Then the retching began. Her whole body strained with the effort to reject the food which had filled her empty stomach so abruptly. A means of preventing her suicide it might be, but no finer torture than this could have been invented.

Again the matron, trying to be helpful, murmured to her, 'Try to keep it down, dear. They will only do it all over again if you bring back too much.'

But she did bring back too much. With a catastrophic spasm, her stomach finally rejected the greater part of the fluid which had gone in. They caught most of it in a bucket, measured the quantity and decided that insufficient food had been retained.

Totally helpless now, Annie could do nothing to resist their second attempt to feed her. The whole ghastly process was repeated down to the last detail, save only that without her resistance the men were able to insert the tube using only one gag, in the side of her mouth which had been the least lacerated.

Perhaps because her system had become inured to this intrusive method of feeding, or maybe because in her semiconscious condition Annie was unable to make any voluntary effort at rejection, she retained more food than she vomited. The doctors, satisfied that she would live to see another day, packed up their apparatus and departed.

Exhausted, mutilated, aching and sore, Annie gave way at last to tears.

She wept for her mother, as she had not done since she was a child; her mother who was thousands of miles away, quite unaware of her plight and unable to help her even if she had known.

She wept for her dead sister, Kirsty, whom she had worshipped, and for the father she had never known. She longed for the green islands of Eisdalsa and Seileach, for the sweet, cloying scent of the yellow gorse, and the tangy salt air of home.

To the imagined sounds of great Atlantic rollers crashing along the shore, at last she slept.

Annie's torment was repeated on the following day, when she again refused normal food. The process of forcible feeding was continued until she lost count of time altogether. At last, when she was weakened to the point of exhaustion and very close to death, they removed her to the infirmary. Here, without her permission, she was fed intravenously for two days. When eventually they brought her a thin broth to eat herself, she did not refuse it. All the fight had gone out of her.

Prison rules allowed those confined to the infirmary one visitor. Annie, assuming that this would be a member of the organisation, was surprised to discover, upon waking, that her visitor was a man.

It took her a few moments to recognise the Member for Woodhamstead East.

'Mr Rosenstein?' she croaked, her throat still very sore from the feeding tubes.

'Ah, good.' He beamed at her and leant forward to take her hand. 'I was beginning to think I would be obliged to leave without having spoken to you. I have been sitting here watching you sleep for the pasty twenty minutes.'

'It is most kind of you to take the trouble,' she whispered, barely audibly.

Gently he placed two fingers across her lips.

'Do not try to talk. I can see that the effort is very painful to you.'

She made a movement of protest, but he stilled her with a slight pressure on her wasted arm which rested limply upon the counterpane.

'Just listen to what I have to say to you, and if you agree, nod your head. Understand?' She nodded.

'I carry a message from my mother who, having read the transcript of your speech in *The Times*, has followed reports of your imprisonment with concern and admiration. She has charged me with the responsibility of insisting that, upon your release, you will accompany me to our home in Hampshire, where she can supervise your recovery.'

'But she knows nothing about me . . .' Annie attempted a reply.

'There you go again,' he interrupted her. 'We will not discuss it further now,' he continued, smiling sympathetically. 'On the day of your release I shall come to fetch you. If you have alternative plans by then, I am sure that Mother will understand, but you will make her very happy if you do accept the invitation.'

Too feeble to protest further, Annie smiled wanly and Manny Rosenstein took his cue to depart.

When he reached the door of the ward, he turned again. 'I know that you are quite determined to carry on the fight,' he observed, 'but let the doctors make you well enough to travel. You can do more useful work outside than in!'

She lay still, eyes deeply sunken in their bruised sockets, the whites red with ruptured blood vessels from the strain of the forced feeding. What a poor little thing she was, he thought. But even as he pitied her feebleness, he recalled the fiery speaker he had witnessed addressing the meeting at the Central Hall.

'You wait,' he called, 'we'll soon have you back in harness.'

Annie watched him go, trying to fix in her mind the image of this man who had appeared so unexpectedly.

He was dark, of course, like so many members of his race. His thick wavy hair was cut short and neatly combed. A touch of grey at the temples gave him an air of maturity and distinction, while beneath dark, bushy eyebrows his brown eyes sparkled with merriment. Laughter was never far from the surface. A well-trimmed and waxed moustache accentuated his large and sensuous mouth, which curved upwards good-naturedly at the corners.

Slightly built and agile as a cat, his movements belied his age which she guessed must be nearer forty than thirty.

Puzzled by this sudden interest in her well-being, coming as it did from a complete stranger, she drifted once more into sleep.

Manny Rosenstein meanwhile strode along the stark, scrupulously clean and cheerless corridor to where the matron waited impatiently, tapping her tightly laced and highly polished boot on the tiled floor. She had been obliged to change her stiffly starched apron and frilled bonnet for the third time that day, and was unashamedly wishing all the Suffragettes in her charge either turned loose on that undeserving rabble out there, or dead of starvation if that was what they wanted!

'When will she be fit to travel?' enquired the MP. His soft voice and charming smile had won him the adoration of half the female hearts in the constituency of East Woodhamstead, and with them the votes of their husbands.

Beneath a formidable exterior, hardened by the exigencies of her profession, the matron melted. Who would not be moved by his obvious concern for Annie McGillivray?

'The sooner she is gone from here the better, the poor young woman. She has a lot of courage that one . . . she's not like the rest, you know. She is not one of your ladies of quality who joined, looking for some diversion from their cosy, boring lives. Young madams still looking for "Nanny" or a lady's maid to answer to their every whim. It's hard on that sort, of course, but a little harshness does them no harm. This one is different . . . well, she's already had her share of troubles.'

Once launched upon this speech, the matron's voice softened as she described Annie.

'One of us, she is . . . understands the ordinary woman. She comes from among real God-fearing, working-class folks. If she thinks this cause is worth fighting for . . .' She halted in mid-sentence, suddenly realising that she had completely reversed her opinion of a few moments before.

Manny Rosenstein regarded the matron with renewed interest. If Annie elicited this kind of response from women of the lower classes, she would, as he had already suspected, be a most valuable tool in the political battle which he and his colleagues were planning.

'Take good care of her, Matron,' he said, and removed from his wallet a crisp white five-pound note.

'She is to have the best food you can buy with that. I am going right away to the Magistrates' Court to apply for her release into my charge. It may take a day or two, but I shall be back to claim her very soon.'

The matron, used to taking orders, made no protest. She accepted the note which she tucked into her apron pocket, and gave him a neat curtsy.

'Never fear, sir,' she assured him. 'Miss McGillivray will be ready and waiting for you.'

The journey seemed endless to Annie in her weakened state. It had proved impossible to find one comfortable position in which to rest her head, despite the luxurious upholstery of the first-class railway carriage. Every jolt jarred through her whole body. Nevertheless she managed at last to drift into a fitful doze.

She came to with a jerk, to find herself looking out upon an unfamiliar landscape of low rounded hills, green meadows and tidy red-roofed villages.

In the opposite seat, her escort looked up from the papers he was studying, and smiled.

'I must have dropped off,' she murmured, her voice still husky. 'Where are we?'

'We shall be coming into Andover very shortly,' he told her.

She nodded and feigned sleep, to avoid disturbing him further. It had taken two days for Manny to get her prison sentence curtailed. The magistrate had finally agreed to grant her release, on licence, on Mr Rosenstein's personal assurance that he would be responsible for her good behaviour. She must forego all demonstrations and political meetings of any kind, for an indefinite period.

In her present condition, Annie could make no protest at the terms imposed upon her freedom. She herself had given no guarantees, however, and if and when the time came for further action, she would have no compunction about defying the law. Mr Rosenstein would just have to face the consequences of his rash promises.

The train began to slow down and Manny Rosenstein slipped the documents he had been studying into his red box. Despite her weakness and discomfort, Annie had not failed to be impressed by the sight of the ministerial attaché case. For the first time she was made patently aware of the company she was keeping.

Very soon now they would be meeting Manny Rosenstein's mother, and Annie was apprehensive at being entertained by the owner of the largest clothing manufacturing and retailing business in the country. She had read somewhere that the Rosenstein Empire had had its origins in a small tailoring business set up by Joseph Rosenstein, a Polish Jewish immigrant fleeing from oppression in his own country. At the time of his death, his wife Rebecca had been expected to sell up and retire to the country with her two sons, Emmanuel and Daniel. Instead she had taken up the reins of management herself, and by a combination of acumen, perseverance and inspiration, had turned Rosensteins into a multifaceted business consisting of mills and factories in several parts of the country and a retail outlet in the high street of every major town.

Annie was under no illusion as to her appearance, for although the matron, as good as her word, had seen to it that her diet included eggs, fresh milk and nourishing beef tea, her skin still wore its deathly pallor and her eyes remained bloodshot.

She examined her dress, smoothing the dark blue-serge down over her knees, and tightening the belt at her waist lest her skirt should sag when she stood up to leave the train. At least her white linen blouse was freshly laundered, although no amount of patient rubbing had done anything to remove the stains from the eggs and squashed tomatoes thrown during the demonstration.

Her Russian boots in soft black leather, which buttoned from ankle to knee, had been burnished until they gleamed. Annie suspected that she had the matron herself to thank for these attentions to her dress. The poor woman had been quite beside herself with emotion when Annie had left the prison on Manny Rosenstein's arm.

Not everyone in Holloway had been as considerate. In fact, Annie suspected that had the Governor known of her activities on Annie's behalf, the matron's position on the staff might well have been in jeopardy.

Before taking her leave, Annie had been obliged to attend the Governor in his office.

'Well, madam,' he had addressed her in sarcastic tones. 'Perhaps we have taught you a lesson or two in good manners? I hope so.'

He was a tall, thin man with a high forehead and scarcely any hair. The gold-framed spectacles which perched close to the end of his sharp, aquiline nose gave him an appearance which had reminded her of the stern schoolmaster, Mr Ogilvy, who had terrified Annie and her schoolmates in the early days of their childhood.

'Rest assured,' he had warned her, 'that should you return behind these walls, the regime will be no less stringent, and the consequences of your actions no less painful. I take no pleasure in the use of force, especially upon females, but the law is the law. I trust that you will reflect upon your experiences here when you begin to recover your health and strength. Let us hope that they will deter you from further transgressions.'

Annie had remained silent, too weak to retaliate in the spirit which had brought her to this place, but no less resolute in her determination to continue the fight.

Although the cab had been drawn up close to the prison entrance so that she should experience no obstruction on leaving, this had not deterred the newspaper reporters who had gathered to witness her departure. Even in all the excitement, it had occurred to her to wonder how they knew that she was to be released at that time.

Manny rose to his feet as the train drew up at Andover Station. He guided her gently through the crowd of passengers milling about on the platform and soon they were outside in the station yard. Apparently from nowhere, a splendid Rolls-Royce car drew up beside them, and a neatly uniformed chauffeur sprang out to open the door for them.

'Good afternoon, Mainwaring,' Manny greeted him.

'It's a pleasure to see you, sir,' the man replied.

Handing Annie into the car, Rosenstein explained, 'This is Miss McGillivray, who is to be my mother's guest for a while.'

Mainwaring gave Annie a rapid glance of appraisal before responding politely with, 'Good afternoon, miss.'

She could only smile feebly, and nod her acknowledgement when he solicitously tucked a soft woollen rug around her knees.

The journey had been too much for her. As the car drew away from the kerb she felt tears of weariness gather behind her closed eyelids and tumble uncontrollably down her cheeks.

Perturbed by her sudden collapse, Manny leant across and mopped up her tears with his handkerchief. As though comforting a lost child, he put his arm around her shoulders, drawing her towards him. She sobbed soundlessly into his collar for some minutes, then, too weary even to weep, lay back against the soft leather upholstery with her eyes closed. He continued to hold her hand until the car had swept into a tree-lined drive and drawn up before an imposing stone staircase.

'I think I'm going to need your assistance, Mainwaring,' Manny observed quietly when the chauffeur opened the door. Together the two men half carried Annie up the flight of steps to where Rebecca Rosenstein waited to greet her guest.

Chapter 9

Margaret Brown surveyed her handiwork with some satisfaction. The little cottage gleamed from her efforts with beeswax and brass polish and the cast-iron range wore that soft bloom which can only be achieved by regular rubbing with blacklead.

Now that her parents had finally vacated the cottage, she had been able to arrange her grandmother's furniture as she remembered it. The cosy room appeared as though Morag Beaton had only just stepped outside and would be back at any minute.

There was the sound of chattering, a titter of childish laughter and a crunching of small feet on the path outside.

Before Margaret could move to open it, the door was flung wide, letting in the afternoon sunshine.

Margaret's niece, Morag, was the first to enter. She stood on the threshold for a few moments, taking in the changes. Then, as though satisfied with what she had observed, she stepped into the room, flung her thin little arms around Margaret's neck and kissed her on the cheek.

'It looks lovely, Auntie,' she exclaimed. 'Different, but lovely.'

Pleased at so positive a response to her labours, Margaret was about to show the little girl some of the pretty china she had unearthed when Morag's brother, Ian, burst into the room.

'Hallo, Auntie,' he called excitedly, then, conscious of the weight of his seven years – he had had a birthday only a week or two before – confined his greeting to a polite handshake.

Solemnly, Margaret took the rather dirty little paw.

'Well, Ian,' she asked, 'what do you think of my cottage now?'

During the period in which Annabel and David had occupied Margarét's wee house on Eisdalsa Island, the children had been frequent visitors. The house had always been somewhat cluttered, however, because Annabel had brought with her from Tigh na Broch many of her favourite pieces of furniture. Margaret had stored the original contents of her grandmother's house in the attic rooms or the shed outside.

Her parents' large double bed had nearly filled the tiny bedroom on the ground floor, and the loft rooms had been stacked with books, crockery and ornaments of every kind.

To the Beaton children visiting their grandparents, it had been the warmth of the welcome they received which had mattered, not the cramped conditions of the house. Besides, they had rarely spent long indoors, because a visit to the island had meant an adventure with their grandfather. With David they had explored the old quarry workings, played hide and seek in the caves along the shore and scrambled up the screes of waste slate to peer down into the clear blue waters of the sea-filled quarries, where fish, trapped by the falling tide, slid languidly between the rocky outcrops far below the surface.

Ian now made a beeline for the stairs, really no more than a wooden ladder, and disappeared into the loft.

Morag walked around the room from object to object. She allowed her hand to rest lightly on a mahogany balloon-back chair. She fingered a delicately embroidered antimacassar hanging over the back of a velvet-upholstered armchair, then lifted a porcelain figure from the little side-table to examine it more closely, before replacing it very carefully.

All the while Margaret watched her, saying nothing.

'Auntie,' the child said at last, 'do you ever feel that you have been in a place before, that you are looking for things that you know you will find, and yet you are quite certain that this is definitely your first visit?'

'Sometimes,' said Margaret, gently. 'Most people do. It is called déjà vu.'

'I have been here before,' Morag translated. Margaret was impressed with the nine-year-old's facility with the French language.

'Of course, I've been in this house before,' her niece went on, 'but I have never seen it like this, arranged as Great-grandmama

The two women exchanged glances.

'My daughter seems to be taking charge already,' observed Millicent, smiling. 'I must say, it looks a lot better now that Mother's stuff is all gone!'

'It is as near as I can remember, just how my Granny used to have it,' said Margaret.

'I wish I had known Morag,' Millicent sighed. 'Hugh always talks so fondly of his grandmother.'

'She was a remarkable person for her generation,' Margaret recalled. 'She believed that a woman could be the equal of a man in anything. She and Father used to have arguments about it all the time. Papa hated the idea of girls taking up the professions,' she continued, rather wistfully. 'Even when Grandmother left me the money for a university education, he would not let me go.'

She wondered why, after all this time, she should be unburdening herself to Millicent in this way. It was not as though they had ever been that close. Yet somehow, here in this room, now that it looked like her grandmother's home again, all her girlhood hopes and dreams had come flooding back.

'I didn't know,' Millicent murmured, 'about the reason for the legacy, I mean. Hugh has never shown any kind of resentment that Morag left everything to you, but I did wonder why she excluded the boys from her will.'

'I suppose,' Margaret replied, perhaps facing up to the truth for the first time, 'it was a gesture of defiance. She was taking a poke at the impenetrable barrier which men have placed between women and the path to the professions. Unfortunately,' she paused reflectively, 'Papa won in the end.'

'Not really,' said Millicent, thoughtfully. 'After all, despite the lack of a university education, you have become an authoress. That has been an important foray into the men's world, has it not? George Eliot and the Brontë sisters could only get their work published by using a man's name! You were not obliged to deceive anybody.'

Margaret had never looked upon her achievement in quite that way herself, nor had she previously regarded her sister-in-law as a modern woman.

It had always bothered Margaret that Morag had made her the sole beneficiary in her will, instead of dividing her small fortune more equitably between her grandchildren. Hugh and Stuart had never made any reference to the bequest, either at the time or subsequently. Only Margaret seemed to be concerned at the unfairness of the situation, and sought now to redress the balance by making the house available to her brothers if they wanted to stay here.

'Now that I have the cottage back to rights,' she told Millicent, 'I hope the whole family will make use of it and enjoy it. You and your friends are welcome to come over and stay on the island whenever you wish. The Whylies have already promised to visit in the autumn, and Stuart is bringing a friend with him on his next leave.'

'I met Elizabeth Whylie briefly, only once,' said Millicent, 'the first time that I visited Tigh na Broch. She seems to have been an important personality in the district. One often hears her name mentioned in the village, even now.'

'This house was built for her, you know,' Margaret explained, 'by her first husband, Captain McIntyre. Grandmother bought it from her when she took over the job as head-teacher of the village school, and moved into the schoolhouse on Seileach.'

'She seems to have been an exceptional teacher,' observed Millicent.

'She was quite a radical lady in those days, a great advocate of higher education for women,' Margaret recalled with a smile. 'Both Kirsty and Annie McGillivray won scholarships to the Merchants' Ladies College in Edinburgh as a result of her encouragement, and Mary McDougal went to the teachers' training college in Glasgow. Mrs McIntyre intervened with the Marquis of Stirling to gain bursaries for them.'

'Hugh has often mentioned Annie McGillivray,' replied Millicent, 'but I have never heard of another sister. What does she do?'

'Kirsty McGillivray trained to become a physician but unfortunately died of cholera before she was fully qualified.' Margaret vividly recalled the energetic young woman who had won the hearts of the people of Eisdalsa with her selfless devotion to the sick and dying. 'It was during the epidemic here in, '85,' she explained. 'Kirsty was nearly nineteen and had been studying medicine for two years. When she heard about the cholera epidemic she came home to help. Father was against it . . . he thought his patients would not want a woman physician . . . but he was so hard pressed that in the end he had to accept her offer of assistance. He was quite wrong about the people . . . they loved her.

'The trouble was nearly over . . . there had been no new cases for a week when she came down with the fever. She died a few days later.'

'How terribly sad,' said Millicent, 'I never knew. Poor Anne has had such a hard life . . . to lose both her husband and her daughter. I do hope that she is happier now.'

Millicent had known Anne McGillivray only as Mrs McDougal, during the short period between Anne's marriage to John and her departure for Australia. Annabel spoke frequently of her friend, but this other daughter had never been mentioned.

'Kirsty McGillivray was our idol when Wee Annie and I were growing up.' Margaret was now absorbed in her reminiscences. 'She was the embodiment of all our own ambitions. Annie wanted to be a lawyer and perhaps become a Member of Parliament, while I would have been content to be allowed to study literature . . . I just wanted to go to university.'

'Wasn't that a strange ambition for a girl like you?'

Millicent's idea of a 'blue stocking' was a frumpish, rather plain person of limited funds who, lacking all hope of finding a husband, was obliged to study in order to acquire the means of making a living.

'After all,' she insisted, 'you already had everything that any girl could want . . . a good home with loving parents, a comfortable life, good looks and every prospect of a good marriage . . . Wee Annie McGillivray on the other hand, was a fatherless waif from a working-class background. She had to educate herself if she was to make anything of her life.'

'I only ever wanted to be a writer,' Margaret persisted, as if

Millicent had not spoken, 'I was convinced that university was the place to go to widen my experience. Grandmother once told me that for inspiration I had only to look around me.'

As clearly as though Morag was seated in the room with them, Margaret heard the words which she now repeated: 'In a small village like this, you will find humanity in all its guises . . . every facet of man's behaviour is to be seen on either side of your own front door. You have no need to go further afield.'

'And was she right?' Millicent asked.

'To a certain extent, I suppose she was,' Margaret agreed, 'but it has never compensated for being denied the education which I so badly wanted.'

Fearing that she had unwittingly opened an old wound, Millicent sought for a change of topic. 'Annabel tells me that Annie McGillivray is in London working with the Suffragettes?'

'Yes,' Margaret confirmed. 'By her efforts she puts us all to shame. Were I not married, I might have joined her!'

Both these young women followed the activities of the Women's Social and Political Union with great interest and both supported the principles of that organisation. They could not, however, agree upon the more militant activities of the Suffragette Movement.

Margaret considered that the breaking of windows, physical attacks upon Members of Parliament, and rioting in the streets, were all justified, if such methods served to draw attention to the cause of women's suffrage. She had considerable sympathy with those who were imprisoned and went on hunger strike in order to make their case.

Millicent, on the other hand, abhorred all forms of violence, and expressed a distaste for the masculine styles of dress worn by the more prominent suffragists. In her opinion, a woman had a far more powerful means of getting her own way than by imitating men. A lawyer's daughter, Millicent had learned very early the power of diplomacy, and was not averse to the use of feminine wiles to achieve her objective.

'You mark my words,' she observed on this occasion. 'When the men are called away to the war, all that stuff about our physical frailty, and the female's inability to learn without taxing her poor little brain, will quickly be forgotten.'

Margaret would have liked to continue the discussion, but at that moment Morag appeared with their meal, and there was a need to see the children seated at the table. Just as she was about to call the boys, Millicent remembered that there was a pressing matter she wished to discuss with her sister-in-law.

'Mother has been working so hard this summer,' she said, 'I wondered if we could organise her birthday party for her at Tigh na Broch this year, and save her all the preparation?'

Annabel had for many years used the occasion of her birthday to organise an annual family reunion. Despite the long distances the young Beatons had had to travel when they were studying away from home in the city, no one had ever declined the invitation. In recent years only Stuart, whose movements were always unpredictable, had been absent.

'I think that's a fine idea,' Margaret agreed, 'but if the weather is good enough it might be fun to have a family picnic here on the island. Papa loves a romp with the children.' She paused for a moment and then added, mischievously, 'Why don't I invite Annie McGillivray to join us, and we can have a Suffragettes' meeting!'

'I want to go to a party,' cried a little voice, muffled by the thickness of the cupboard wall. Ian forced back the sliding door.

'Aunt Margaret says I may sleep in here, Mummy. May I sleep here after Grannie's party? May I, Mummy . . . please?' He came tumbling out of the box bed, turning to replace the panelling. He had forgotten baby David who, left behind in the darkness, screamed in terror. A few moments of panic and pacifying went by before Ian dared broach the subject of the party again.

'I want to meet a Suffragette,' he blurted out, as soon as the baby had stopped wailing. 'What's a Suffragette, Mummy?'

From the tiny kitchen it was his sister, Morag, who replied: 'A woman who is going to put you men in your place!' she called, and Margaret was startled by an echo from the past. Despite the higher pitched, girlish tones of her young niece, she detected something of the more mature voice and mannerisms to come. It might have been her grandmother speaking.

Chapter 10

❦

Annabel had been busy all week, preparing the ground for her autumn planting. Wisely she had consulted Katherine McLean and her husband, Archie, about the most suitable shrubs to grow on the high banks which fell away abruptly to the shore on the northern side of the garden. As a result Katherine had promised a supply of rare rhododendrons, developed at Johnstones, their estate on Seileach.

The lawn, turfed rather late in the season, had nevertheless rooted well during a prolonged period of rainy weather in June and July. Annabel's herbaceous beds had also flourished with the ample watering, and luscious foliage abounded even if the flowers had been spoilt by the continuous deluge.

'Next year,' Annabel assured herself, in the way so many gardeners do, 'the garden will be a kaleidoscope of colour.'

She descended the wooden staircase which, upon David's insistence, had been stoutly constructed to give access to both the summer-house, halfway up the cliff, and the garden below.

'I suppose the next thing,' David observed, as Annabel dropped into the chair beside his own, on the little terrace in front of the wooden building, 'will be one of these new hand-pushed lawn-mowing machines.'

The location of Annabel's lawn did not lend itself to mowing in the usual manner, by a pony-drawn contraption. She was constantly thrusting pages of gardening magazines under David's nose, showing all the latest gadgets for trouble-free cultivation, including the kind of grass cutter which was said to be so lightweight that even a lady could use it. Pretending to ignore her attempts to interest him in the subject, David had nevertheless taken note. He smiled to himself, imagining her expression when he revealed his birthday gift, bought for once well in advance of the day, and concealed at the back of the garage.

'Here is a letter from Stuart, at last,' she said, withdrawing an envelope from the pocket of her gardening apron. 'He is to take four weeks' leave, beginning on Sunday. I do hope he will be here before the twenty-third.'

'Why,' David enquired, archly, 'what is so special about the twenty-third of September?'

She looked up quickly, then seeing the slight twitch at the corners of his mouth and the twinkle in his eye, knew that he was teasing her. He never forgot her birthday.

Ignoring his question, she glanced again at the letter which she had scanned only briefly before coming to find David.

'He has been promoted to Surgeon Commander and is to take special training at Haslar Hospital before returning to the ship,' she related breathlessly.

David nodded contentedly at this news. He had been disappointed when Stuart had chosen to pursue his career in the Royal Navy, but at least he was making good progress.

'Decide what you want to do, then make the best shot at it that you can,' had been his advice to his sons. Well, Stuart had certainly done that.

He had hoped that Stuart would succeed in the career in surgery which David had at one time mapped out for himself. His own hopes had been dashed by the untimely death of his father, Dr Hugh Beaton, which had resulted in his taking over the Eisdalsa practice, in order to support his mother.

The way things were shaping up, Stuart might even now find himself engaged in surgery of the most desperate kind. David had dealt with some very unpleasant wounds while serving with the Eisdalsa Company of the Argyll and Bute Volunteers, and they were gained in battle training only. What injuries his son might encounter in a war at sea, he hardly dared to imagine.

David was justly proud of the progress made by both his sons. He was delighted to see how well his elder son, Hugh, had settled into the Eisdalsa practice. He had taken over at a time when the quarries were closing down, and many families were moving away from the parish. By dint of hard work, and a willingness to extend the boundaries of his sphere of operation, and because of his skill as a general practitioner, Hugh had nevertheless restored the practice to its former strength. He had lost business from the quarries, and in particular from the quarrymen's health insurance scheme, but he had gained patients from the steadily growing population of visitors, tourists, holiday makers and a small contingent of artists, writers and naturalists who found the area to their liking and came to settle.

It was at moments like this that David's thoughts wandered to his other son, Ian, who had been an invalid from infancy, and whose life had been so tragically cut short when he was only just seventeen. Had he lived, David had no doubt that Ian would have been the finest doctor of them all.

The Doctor waited impatiently for his wife to reach the end of the letter. When she came to the last paragraphs she read them aloud, with a hint of frustration,

I have a chum on board, a second lieutenant, Daniel Rosenstein. As I suggested in my last letter, I invited him to accompany me to Argyll, but unfortunately he had previously agreed to spend a few days with his mother in Hampshire. She is at present nursing one of these Suffragette women, recently released from prison, and Dan is determined to meet her while he has the opportunity.

This means that we will not be home by the 23rd as I had hoped and consequently I shall miss your birthday party. I must buy a really special present to compensate, and you will have plenty of visitors, what with Hugh's brood as well as Margaret and Michael, so I don't suppose I shall be missed too much!

I look forward to having you to myself for a few days when we do arrive . . .

David could see that Annabel was hurt. He took the letter which she was holding out to him.

'It will only mean waiting a few more days, my dear,' he soothed her. 'Does it really matter so much?'

Shaking her head and swallowing the threatening tears, Annabel responded too brightly, 'Hugh and Millicent are planning a family picnic on the island for my birthday, provided the weather remains good. Margaret suggests that you and I sleep in the cottage overnight, to save the long journey home in the dark. There was even a suggestion from Morag that she and Ian might stay with us. I think we shall have to agree or the children will be very disappointed.'

'What? Oh, yes . . . of course,' David answered absently. He had been reading Stuart's account of the refit of the *Hampshire*, and had paid only scant attention to what his wife was saying.

'Whether Michael will join us depends on the good people of Oban, I suppose.'

'On a Saturday night?' David observed dryly. 'He will be lucky to get away before midnight!'

Since his appointment as senior consultant at the Oban Hospital, Michael Brown had catered for the medical needs of a growing population in the town of Oban, which claimed to be the gateway to the Hebrides. His life seemed to be a constant battle to obtain sufficient resources to cope with the variety of problems arising in such a widespread and varied community. The hospital was too small, and the number of beds available inadequate for the size of the population which it served. The nursing staff were too few, while the medical staff consisted of himself, a young and inexperienced registrar, and what help he could elicit from the small group of general practitioners in the district.

Both David and Hugh had turned out from time to time, and even David's brother Angus had been winkled out from his comfortable little practice on the Island of Mull, to cover in an emergency.

'Margaret thinks that Heather will be home in time for the party,' Annabel continued. 'I gather that she has some project requiring research amongst Angus's books and is going to spend a few days with him on Mull.'

David glanced up from the page he was reading. 'Oh, good,' he observed. 'It seems a long time since she was last here.'

Annabel and David had taken the Brown children to their hearts and treated them as their grandchildren although they would have liked to see Margaret with babies of her own. Whether the absence of children was deliberate or an act of God, neither had ever dared to enquire. Michael was a good enough doctor to know where to get specialist advice if he needed it. Annabel had never liked to suggest that their daughter might be taking steps to avoid pregnancy, but she had her suspicions, and while she herself could see no harm in it, if that was what they wanted, she knew that David would have very different views on the subject. She kept her conjectures to herself.

Well, anyway, she consoled herself, it will be nice to have everyone there . . . who can be.

Annabel's party provided an opportunity for the three doctors to get together after all. A spell of fine weather having reduced the number of patients at Oban to manageable proportions, Michael was able to snatch a day's holiday.

When the women declared their intention of taking the children to the shore to lay out the celebration meal, the men begged a few minutes in which to talk over those topics which were uppermost in their minds: the threat of war and its possible consequences to them all. They had lit up their pipes and cigars, and having exhausted the main talking points, were relaxing contentedly in a haze of blue tobacco smoke.

'What do you think about all this suffragist activity, Pa?' Hugh winked at his brother-in-law, knowing that the subject would raise David's temperature by a degree or two.

There had been widespread newspaper coverage of the hunger-striking suffragists all over the country. The lengths to which women were prepared to go to obtain recognition for their cause had surprised many people hitherto indifferent to their demands.

'Such idiocy could only be perpetrated by a bunch of ignorant females,' David observed, laconically. 'They harm only themselves, and if they suffer permanent damage as a result of starvation, they have only themselves to blame!'

'I have never had any experience of real starvation,' Michael admitted. 'There was plenty of poverty in Edinburgh, of course, and many cases of malnutrition, but actual starvation . . .' He left the sentence uncompleted.

David Beaton and his father had served the needs of the Eisdalsa community for more than sixty years, in good times and in lean ones. He had seen hungry people, lacking all but the basic necessities, but never a fatality due to actual starvation.

'Even the poorest cotter on the estate,' David mused, 'had access to a fishing line, and with wild berries and roots to supplement what meagre portion of meal the parish allocated to them, they survived. When things became easier, they put on weight quickly and regained their strength although, of course, they were always more susceptible to any infection going the rounds.'

'If a person refuses all food,' Hugh considered, 'there must come a time when the brain cells are so seriously affected that they cease to carry out their normal function.'

'And what would be the first area of the brain to be affected, do you suppose?' David queried, peering over the top of his spectacles in a manner familiar to both Hugh and Michael from their student days. They answered now as they might have done then.

'The autonomic system,' suggested Hugh.

'Which would lead to ineffectual peristaltic movement of the alimentary tract . . .' Michael added.

'And,' concluded David, 'that would mean a very slow recovery to normal peristalsis . . . if any.'

'My God,' exclaimed Hugh. 'I wonder if these women have any idea what damage they are doing to themselves? Can they really believe that obtaining the vote is worth so heavy a price?'

'Oh, I think they are well aware of the risks they take,' said Michael, thoughtfully. 'I only hope that in a hundred years from now, when women have the freedom and the enfranchisement that is craved so urgently, their granddaughters and great-granddaughters will remember these brave women, and appreciate the sacrifices they made.'

David gave a snort of disapproval. No doubt Michael's ear was

constantly bent on the subject. He had obviously been indoctri-
nated by his wife, since Margaret made no secret of her support
for the Sufragettes.

Hugh remained silent. It was constantly in his mind that Wee
Annie McGillivray could be mixed up in this business. They had
lost contact over the past year or two, but he knew that she had
been working with the Pankhursts in the East End of London. He
scoured the pages of the *Clydesman* daily, for any mention of her
activities, but that organ of Scottish respectability had no intention of publicising, and thereby encouraging, the escapades of a
few Scottish women activists.

Ian Beaton, breathless and red in the face from running in the
hot sunshine, burst into the little parlour.

'Grandmama says if you don't come now, she will give your
mutton pies to the seagulls!' he announced, and ran to David's
chair and began to pull him up forcibly.

'Oh, do come along, Grandpa,' he insisted, 'I really think she
means it!'

'I am quite sure that she does,' agreed David, laughing, and
allowed himself to be dragged out into the autumn sunshine.

Stuart Beaton, M.D., B.S., resplendent in his brand new uniform
of Surgeon Lieutenant Commander, R.N., emerged from the
tailor's emporium where he had spent a satisfying morning being
fitted with all the trappings of his newly acquired status.

The gold rings, two and a half on either sleeve with, alongside,
a narrow stripe in red to signify his profession, shone just a little
too brightly. He was as conscious of them as is a bride of that
narrow band of gold on the third finger of her left hand.

A few weeks of salt air and tropical sunshine would, he felt
sure, soon dull the braid to a more modest colour.

Under peacetime conditions a naval surgeon would not normally expect promotion to Lieutenant Commander in under five
years, but when preparations for the *Hampshire*'s extended
mission to the South Atlantic were already well underway, Stuart's
immediate superior had been struck down by a recurrence of
malaria. As a consequence, Lieutenant Commander Travers was

refused permission to sail with the ship. There had been insufficient time for the Admiralty to find a replacement for the surgeon commander, and so, on the captain's recommendation, Stuart had found himself stepping into his chief's shoes at a moment's notice.

Acting Lieutenant Commander Beaton glanced at his watch. He was late. Dodging between the busy traffic, he crossed the road and took a short cut through a narrow passage to emerge on the sea front.

The arrangement had been that he would meet Dan at noon in the Admiral Nelson, and it was already fifteen minutes past the hour. He pushed open the swing door into the main lounge and fought his way through the lunch-time crowd towards the bar.

Second Lieutenant Daniel Rosenstein, fourth officer aboard H.M.S. *Hampshire*, leapt to his feet when Stuart approached.

'What will it be, Commander?' he demanded, smiling broadly.

'A beer if you please, Lieutenant.'

Dan leant across the counter to attract the barman's attention.

'All set to go, are we?' he enquired, as with consummate skill he hoisted two foaming tankards above the heads of those thronging the bar, and led the way to a side-table.

'Mother has sent the Lanchester down to pick us up,' he announced, taking a long pull at his drink. 'Mainwaring is waiting for us outside, even as we speak.'

'Who the hell is Mainwaring?' Stuart demanded, and nearly choked on his beer when Dan replied: 'The chauffeur, of course, who else?'

He finished his pint and thumped the pot down on the polished table. 'Come on,' he urged, 'we don't want to hang about. I'd like to be home in time to have dinner with the old girl.'

The two had met briefly at the training establishment where Stuart had been introduced to the basics of seamanship before taking up his posting aboard H.M.S. *Hampshire*.

Having learnt to tell the bows of a battleship from the stern, the correct manner of taking a salute, and when and when not to wear his cap, Stuart had been sent on a so-called familiarisation course where he had concentrated upon the more common ailments of seafarers. As this consisted in the main of the identification and treatment of venereal disease, Stuart had found the course to be, in his terms, a doddle. He had seen it all before when, during his residency at the Infirmary, he had been obliged to attend at the out-patients' clinic which dealt largely with seamen and prostitutes, just off Glasgow's Broomielaw Quay.

When he at last reported for duty aboard his ship, he was pleased to find at least one familiar face amongst a sea of strangers. He and Daniel Rosenstein had struck up a friendship which had developed into the kind of David and Johnathan relationship so often attained in the close-knit community aboard a naval vessel. They had been very close for more than two years, but in all that time there had been no mention of chauffeur-driven limousines or any other of the accoutrements of the upper classes. Stuart began to feel a little apprehensive about this visit to his friend's home.

The stylish motor car, its spotless grey paintwork and bright nickel-plating on bumpers and headlamps gleaming in the last rays of a dying sun, slid silently to a halt before a wide stone staircase. The noble mansion of Overavon, its white portico of Portland stone supported by tall Palladian-style pillars, was bathed in the warm pink glow of a fine autumn evening.

The butler, a slightly built, immaculately attired gentleman, stepped forward to greet them as they mounted the steps to the main door.

'Mr Daniel, sir,' he exclaimed effusively, 'what a pleasure to have you home again.'

'And what a great pleasure it is to *be* home, Bates,' cried Daniel enthusiastically, wringing the man's hand warmly. The butler beamed.

'This is Surgeon Commander Beaton, Bates,' Daniel added, waving a hand vaguely in Stuart's direction.

Bates acknowledged him politely, and conducted them up a long flight of stairs to a wide gallery which stretched across the whole front of the house, giving a view across the park, to the distant hills of the South Downs.

A rather short, stout lady waited for them at the top of the stairs, leaning heavily upon an ebony cane. Dressed entirely in black, she was more than a little reminiscent of Queen Victoria. She was a little above five feet tall and her hair, which was streaked with grey, was scraped back into a neat bun and covered with a lacy black cap.

As Stuart approached, Rebecca Rosenstein extended a gnarled and withered hand, whose swollen joints and reddened skin told their own story of rheumatoid arthritis.

He held the hand gently for an instant before releasing it. Rebecca smiled at him.

'Welcome to Overavon, Commander Beaton,' she greeted him. Despite her crippling infirmity, her voice lacked nothing in strength and sweetness of tone.

'It is very kind of you to invite me, Mrs Rosenstein,' he replied, smiling.

'Daniel has referred to you so often that I feel I know you already,' she continued politely, and leaning upon the arm of her son led them to a group of chairs set before one of the great stone-mullioned windows.

Daniel excused himself almost immediately, leaving Rebecca to attend to his guest.

'I am sure that you must be ready for some refreshment, Commander,' she said, as Stuart helped her carefully into her chair before seating himself.

Leaning forward, she rang a small silver bell.

'It is by great good fortune that Daniel's leave should fall at this particular time,' she remarked, 'especially since he has brought you with him.'

Noting Stuart's surprised expression, she went on, 'In fact, to put it plainly, Commander Beaton, I have need of your services as a physician.'

Perturbed, he began to protest, 'But surely, madam, your own physician . . .'

She raised a hand to interrupt him.

'Not for myself,' she explained. 'It is for a young person whom I have staying here at the moment. She had undergone a severely testing ordeal which has left her weak and dispirited. Unfortunately, because my own physician has no sympathy with the cause which has been responsible for her condition, and considers her to be suffering self-inflicted pain, they do not get on together. My young lady guest has a somewhat forceful personality. The good Dr Stobbart prefers his female patients to be rather more submissive.'

Stuart detected a twinkle of amusement in those dark eyes and suspected that Rebecca might well have crossed swords with the family physician herself.

'What my visitor needs,' she continued, 'is someone effective enough to command her recuperation, yet sufficiently understanding of her cause to gain her confidence. Perhaps you have guessed already that she is a Suffragette, recently released from Holloway Prison?'

'If the lady has refused the ministrations of Dr Stobbart,' he replied, 'I see no ethical reason why I should not attend your guest, but I cannot guarantee to overcome her stubbornness, if she refuses my advice.'

'If you will just see her, Commander Beaton, I feel sure that you will be able to help her.'

He knew very little about the Women's Suffrage Movement, other than what he had read in the papers. His sister and her friends had been going on for years about equality of the sexes and so on, but he had taken little interest in their discussions. In the entirely male environment in which he now existed, the activities of these women had received only cursory and often derisory consideration.

Seeing that his hostess was at least in sympathy with the cause of these Suffragettes, however, he was too polite to voice his own opinion.

Flushed from her afternoon nap, Annie McGillivray stretched her cramped legs under the silk coverlet, enjoying the luxurious feel of soft material next to her tender skin. She sipped her tea and gazed out over the green lawns towards a magnificent stand of elms, marking the boundary of the Great Park.

Her chaise-longue had been placed in the window of the high-ceilinged chamber. Heavy damask curtains covered the stone mullions, into which had been set a pair of magnificent Georgian windows. It was a far cry from the humble quarryman's cottage in which she had lived with her mother. She was still puzzled as to why she was here.

Enfeebled by her experiences in jail, she had not had the will to argue with Manny Rosenstein about coming to Overavon and had submitted without complaint to the attentions of an elderly family retainer named Emily Clegg, who had at one time been the Rosensteins' nanny.

She appreciated Rebecca's kindness, but resented the overbearing, chauvinistic manner of her physician, and had behaved so badly on his last visit that he had refused to attend her again. While this was precisely what Annie had aimed at, Rebecca was clearly put out, fearing that neither she nor Nanny Clegg was competent to deal with Annie's condition.

The altercation with the doctor had been the only occasion upon which Annie had felt sufficiently incensed to show any of her usual spirit. She was withdrawn, and deeply depressed. A terrible feeling of lethargy had fallen upon her and she seemed incapable of summoning either the will or the strength to respond to the kind attentions of her hostess.

She yearned for she knew not what . . . the mountains and moorlands of Argyll . . . her family and friends . . . her home? Oh, if only she could be there now, within sight of the sea, the sounds of her childhood ringing in her ears.

There was a light tap on the door.

'Are you up to seeing a visitor?' Nanny Clegg enquired, coming in to collect her tea tray. 'Mr Rosenstein's brother, Daniel, is here and has brought a friend with him. Madam thought it might cheer you up a little to meet them.'

Annie made no response to this. Why did they not understand? She did not need visitors, she just wanted to be left alone.

Assuming her silence to convey assent, the elderly nurse turned to the two figures waiting on the landing behind her.

Annie watched beneath lowered eyelids as Dan advanced into

the room, smiling, his hand extended. She saw him hesitate for a brief moment, shocked by her appearance. To disguise his embarrassment, he assumed a manner and a voice much heartier and louder than usual.

'I am Daniel Rosenstein, Manny's brother. I hope they are taking proper care of you?'

Annie raised a limp hand in acknowledgement, but then she caught sight of the second visitor who had stepped forward into the light.

'I fear we are intruding, Dan.' Stuart laid his hand upon his friend's sleeve. 'Perhaps we should return later . . . when the lady is feeling a little stronger.'

The voice was unmistakable. Despite the unfamiliar uniform, she was certain that she recognised that tall slim figure with a shock of wavy auburn hair.

'Stuart?' she murmured, and tried to rise from the couch.

He turned back at the sound of her voice. Rays from the setting sun illuminated her features clearly for the first time.

'Annie?' His voice faltered. 'Annie McGillivray? Oh, Annie, what have they done to you?'

Oblivious to the others in the room, Stuart knelt beside her and gathered her in his arms. He held her tightly as tears of relief poured down her shrunken cheeks, soaking the jacket of his splendid new uniform.

'Oh, Stuart,' she sobbed, 'if you only knew how I have longed to hear a voice from home!'

Emily Clegg, standing with her hand on the doorknob, motioned to Daniel who hovered uncertainly in the shadows. Silently, they departed.

It was a long time before either of them spoke again.

The weeping had clearly exhausted Annie. Stuart eased her back against the pillows and took hold of one bony wrist. Her pulse was racing. He turned up the gas jet. Now he could see her more clearly.

'Mrs Rosenstein tells me you do not get on well with her physician,' he remarked, mildly. 'What have you got against him?'

'Pompous . . . pig!' she managed, shocking him with her

vehemence, but at the same time reminding him of the Annie he remembered so well. There was hope for her yet!

'He is only trying to help you get well,' he rebuked her gently.

'I need no help from a man like that!' she protested, indignantly. 'All he can talk about is how foolish I have been.'

She raised her head momentarily from the pillow, and gazed at him, anxiously.

'You don't think that what we are doing is foolish, do you?'

'No,' he reassured her, although he could not accept that any political battle should demand this degree of self-sacrifice.

She lay back, satisfied.

'Mrs Rosenstein has asked me to take a look at you,' he told her. 'Do you have any objection to my taking care of you?'

'Please, Stuart,' she whispered, 'please help me. I will try to get better . . . for you.'

He squeezed her hand reassuringly whilst agonising over the change in her appearance.

He recalled how Annie had looked the last time he had seen her.

It was on Margaret's wedding day. Annie had appeared as a *new* woman in her dark costume cut in masculine style, with lapels on the jacket, a plain white shirt and even a tie, knotted like a man's. She had worn no hat, he remembered, and smiled when he recalled the tongue-wagging that had caused amongst the village matrons as she walked into church. Her bared head had gleamed like a raven's wing in the coloured light which filtered through the stained-glass window. It was not gleaming now, despite the soft lamplight. She was Margaret's age, a little beyond thirty, but already he detected streaks of grey in her undressed hair.

'What you need,' he announced briskly, 'is some good nourishing food, and plenty of exercise. You can't go on languishing here like some latter-day Elizabeth Barrett Browning, you know!'

She tried to smile.

'Food nauseates me,' she told him, despairingly. 'Swallowing is painful and the fear of vomiting makes me gag.'

'We will take it in easy stages,' he promised, gently, and rose to his feet.

'First, a small glass of whisky,' he decided. 'I never knew a true

Scot who gagged on a dram of the usquebaugh. It's not called the water of life for nothing, you know!'

He looked about him, then, spotting the cord hanging beside the fireplace, went over and pulled it.

'Let's see how good the service is in this hotel.' He laughed lightly and she was forced to smile.

When the servant arrived, Stuart went to the door and gave some rapid instructions in a voice too low for her to overhear. The maid departed, returning quickly with a decanter of whisky and two glasses. One of the footmen entered with Stuart's medical case and placed it on a side table.

'Now then,' he said, employing his best bedside manner, 'a very small dram for you, and a very large one for myself.'

She laughed, and if the effect was a trifle ghoulish in that wasted little face, at least it was a beginning. She had not laughed for a very long time.

Having made a thorough examination of his patient, Stuart began her treatment immediately.

He decided to call off the visit to Scotland. It was clear that Annie's positive response to his strict regime was associated with his own presence upon the scene. Her progress depended as much upon a desire to please him as upon any determination of her own to get well. To leave her now, even in the hands of the kindly Nanny Clegg, would most likely bring about a relapse.

Stuart wrote to his mother, explaining the circumstances, knowing that Annabel would wish him to do whatever he could to help Anne McDougal's daughter.

It was Michael Brown who had come across an article about Annie in a popular London newspaper.

He was walking his wards, talking to Sister as they moved from one patient to the next, when his glance fell upon the name 'McGillivray'.

'May I take a look at your paper, Hamish?' he asked the old man in the end bed.

Gnarled fingers released the crumpled sheets as the grey head appeared from behind the sports columns on the back page.

'Aye, Doctor,' he responded, his ageing voice high-pitched, like the cry of a seagull. 'It iss only the football that I am looking at, just, and that iss a load of English rubbish, so it iss!'

'Soon as we get you out of there, we'll be signing you on for Celtic,' Michael laughed.

'Och, and what would a good Protestant Highlander be doing playing for a bunch of Catholics, I would like to know?'

'They'd probably lose, with you playing,' suggested Michael, grinning at the Sister across the bed.

The old man contemplated this for a moment. 'Oh, aye, so they would.' He nodded, satisfied with that idea and released the newspaper, lying back against his pillows with a beatific smile on his lips. Michael retrieved the paper and turned quickly to the front page where he read again the headline which had caught his eye.

The photograph purporting to be of Margaret's friend, Annie McGillivray, was unrecognisable. He put this down to poor quality newsprint, and turned to the article on the inside pages.

It was all there. Annie's early life, distorted by over-enthusiastic journalism, her speech, the circumstances of her arrest. The words 'hunger strike' stung him.

He went back over the two previous paragraphs and re-read them. He folded the paper without comment and tucked it under his arm.

'All right if I keep this, Hamish?' he enquired. The old man's soft snoring was all the permission he required.

'Mother!' Margaret hurried down the path towards the spot where she could see Annabel digging in uncultivated ground beside the loch. It really was too bad of her to be working outdoors in such a cold wind!

Annabel straightened up at her call, and put down her garden fork. She waved, and tucked a stray piece of hair back under the scarf which was tied around her head, in the way a tinker's woman would wear it.

'Whatever are you going?' demanded Margaret. 'Surely you can wait for a better day? It is far too cold in this wind!'

'Not really, dear,' Annabel replied, placidly. 'If these bulbs do not go in now, there will be no daffodils in the spring. I like to begin planting in August and then put in a few each month until December. That way we shall have flowers from February until April.' She wiped her hands on her gardening apron and held out her cheek to be kissed.

'This is a nice surprise.' She kissed her daughter affectionately. 'Did you come by car?'

Margaret normally drove herself the eight miles from Oban to Connel. 'No,' she replied, 'Michael has had to go to Inverary to a meeting today, and this was far too important to wait until he gets back. I caught the train,' she explained as she led her mother back into the house.

Annabel was alarmed at the serious tone of her daughter's voice. 'What is it? What has happened? Is there something wrong with one of the children?' she enquired anxiously.

Margaret smiled reassuringly. 'No, it's nothing to do with the family, Mother. It's something that Michael discovered yesterday in *The London Times*.

They entered the lounge by the garden door from the terrace. Here it was possible to sit in comfort and view the loch.

When they were settled, Margaret withdrew from her handbag a newspaper clipping which she spread on the table in front of Annabel.

On seeing the photograph of Annie McGillivray outside the jail, she gave a little shriek of recognition, then taking a closer look at the ghastly portrait, cried, 'Why, what has happened? What have they done to her?'

Margaret remained silent as her mother absorbed the contents of the article. At last she looked up, pale and anxious.

'What if her mother gets to hear of this, and she so far away?'

'That was my first thought too,' said Margaret. 'We must try to contact Anne McDougal before she reads this somewhere for herself.'

'What could we tell her?' Annabel queried. 'Unless we see Annie for ourselves first.'

'I have been planning to go down to London to visit my publisher,' Margaret observed. 'If I knew where to find her, I would visit Annie. It should not be too difficult to trace her. The newspaper editor will probably be able to help.'

The problem was solved far more simply.

Mrs Murchieson, Annabel's housekeeper, appeared at that moment with a heavily laden tea-tray. When she had set out the cups and arranged a place of freshly baked scones on the table, she straightened up and took from her pocket a large white envelope made of expensive paper, and carrying a most impressive coat of arms.

'The afternoon post, ma'am,' she announced grandly, and handed the envelope to Annabel.

Recognising Stuart's handwriting, she tore open the letter and read rapidly.

'What an extraordinary coincidence!' she exclaimed. 'You remember Stuart delayed his visit because he had been invited to the home of a shipmate? Who should he find there, being nursed back to health, but Wee Annie McGillivray herself!'

Annabel read on to the end of the letter. Her disappointment at Stuart's decision not to come home at all was plainly written in her face. She handed the letter to Margaret while she herself rose and went over to the window. She studied the view avidly for a few moments, trying to compose herself.

'Stuart must be very concerned about Annie's condition to forego his leave in this way?' Margaret suggested.

Annabel sat down again and poured herself another cup of tea. Throughout her life medical business had always come before her own personal needs. Now she found herself fighting back tears of frustration and disappointment. In her heart she knew that Stuart was right to stay with Annie. Someone had to take care of her in her mother's absence.

Margaret, sensing her distress, leant forward and patted her comfortingly on the knee.

'Never mind, Mama,' she said, 'Stuart will come and see us just as soon as his ship docks in the Clyde. At least we now know where Annie is. Perhaps, when you reply, you will ask if I may visit her?'

* * *

Fourteen days was all too short a time in which to judge the effect of Stuart's ministrations. His patient began to take her meals with the rest of the household, but merely played with her food, consuming very little.

Daily, he increased the amount of exercise she took. At first it had been a few steps around her bedroom. After a day or two he had helped her down the stairs to take dinner, and sit with her hostess for a while afterwards.

During these encounters the two women seemed to strike up a rapport. In seeking to understand what it was that drove women like Annie to such lengths to gain recognition for their cause, Rebecca asked many searching questions, and when the answers did not satisfy her, she said so. Some rousing debate ensued, in which the two young men participated. In defending her cause, Annie would become flushed with impatience or indignation. To Stuart this was a sure sign of recovery. Like Annie herself, he had been more disturbed by her mental attitude than by her physical condition, which he was certain would be put right in the course of time.

'I can understand that the women of the working classes feel repressed by their husbands,' Mrs Rosenstein mused. 'Many men drink and gamble away the family's income without a thought for their responsibilities. I cannot for the life of me see, however, how winning the vote is going to make the slightest difference to that situation.'

Annie looked at her quizzically. Did Mrs Rosenstein truly not understand the significance of enfranchisement, or was she just egging her on?

'The vote,' she began to explain in the simplest terms that she could muster, 'is a kind of symbol of hope, a recognition that women are the equal of men in every level of society. By exercising the right to vote, a woman will not prevent her husband from beating her, but she will be entitled to protest about it, and she will have a platform for that protest! In time she may even be placed in a position to change the law in order to prevent him.' She was warming to her subject now.

'In the workshops where clothing is manufactured for the

Rosenstein shops, how many women hold posts of responsibility?' she demanded of Rebecca, knowing full well what the answer would be. Without waiting for a reply she continued, 'Your women, without doubt, work hours as long and as arduous as their male counterparts, but do they receive equivalent wages? Of course they do not! That is surely the reason why the bulk of your workforce are women. The mills in the north, and the biscuit factories in Reading and Birmingham, employ women because they are a source of cheap labour.

'Women workers are not demanding better conditions than men,' she went on, 'all they want is equal consideration, an equal opportunity to voice their concerns, and equal wages for equivalent work. Is that too much to ask?'

Annie felt herself flagging. Realising suddenly that she had been less than gracious to her hostess with her accusations, she coloured deeply and apologised.

'Forgive me, Mrs Rosenstein,' she begged, 'that was inexcusable.'

'Nonsense, my dear,' Rebecca demurred. 'They are your principles and you must stick to them through thick and thin! I was once an employee of Rosenstein's myself, before I married the boss!' She laughed good-naturedly, her plump bosom wobbling with her exuberance. 'I know what it is to be patronised by a male colleague, believe me. I understand how a woman feels when she sees a man getting away with slovenly work, while depending upon his female inferiors to cover up for him. I have seen men taking liberties with female staff, knowing that they dared not complain for fear of losing their positions.

'I appreciate what you are saying about equality of status and opportunity for advancement,' she continued, 'but I cannot believe that simply by winning the vote, women will attain any of these objectives. Certainly it will do nothing to change the inbred attitudes of men towards women in this country.'

'Very soon there is going to come a time,' Annie replied, quietly, 'when women will be required in the factories as surely as today they are needed in the home. Then we shall see a change of attitude on the part of the men.'

Chapter 11

The Lanchester drew to a halt outside Overavon House and Mainwaring hastened to open the rear door to assist Margaret Brown to alight.

To her surprise, her brother Stuart came bounding down the steps to greet her. She had understood that he had already returned to his ship and would not be there when she arrived.

As they embraced, she stared apprehensively over his shoulder towards the magnificent portico of the great house.

Smiling at her startled expression, he murmured, 'It is a little overwhelming, isn't it? Don't worry, Mrs Rosenstein is one of the nicest women you could hope to meet. You'll love it here!' He continued, 'I just couldn't miss this opportunity to see you . . . I managed to slip away from the ship for a few hours.'

Stuart slipped an arm through hers, and together they climbed the stairs.

Margaret had been led to expect a large house, but never in her wildest dreams had she envisaged anything like Overavon. It was as grand as Holyrood Palace itself!

She took in at a glance the huge oil paintings which lined the walls, the magnificent oak staircase and richly piled carpet into which her feet sank at every step. Nervously, she followed Stuart into the drawing room to meet their hostess.

'Mrs Rosenstein,' Stuart introduced them, 'this is my sister Margaret Brown.'

'Margaret,' repeated the older woman, 'may I call you that? Mrs Brown seems so terribly formal.' She placed her withered hand in Margaret's, and smiled.

Margaret turned now to Stuart, an anxious frown on her face.

'Tell me about Annie,' she requested. 'Is she as poorly as the picture I saw indicates?'

'She is still very ill,' he replied, 'little more than a living skeleton. She has undergone a most traumatic experience. When any individual refuses food to the point of starvation,' he explained, 'the body will eventually reach a stage where it ceases to crave for food. It is then very difficult to persuade it to receive nourishment again in the normal way.'

Margaret shuddered at the thought. 'Poor Annie, it must be very distressing for her,' she whispered, horrified.

Stuart nodded his agreement, and then went on, 'The forced feeding did such a lot of damage. There is so much internal bruising and so many abrasions that to swallow anything at all is agonising.'

Margaret gazed at him in shocked surprise.

'What must be done to help her?' she demanded.

'All we can do is to try to get her to take a little food several times a day,' Mrs Rosenstein intervened. 'The nurse and I have been taking it in turns to try to encourage her . . . unfortunately, even the softest morsels cause so much discomfort that she soon gives up trying.'

Margaret turned to Stuart as though for confirmation.

'Unless she takes proper nourishment, the healing process will inevitably be very slow.'

'Will she ever recover completely?' Margaret asked, fearing to hear his answer.

'I am sure she will.' Stuart wished he was as convinced of this as he tried to appear. 'It will require constant surveillance on the part of those nursing her, and a great deal of perseverance from everyone concerned.'

Mrs Rosenstein patted Margaret's hand, sympathetically.

'I am sure that Annie will recover more quickly now that you have come,' she assured her.

'How long do you think it will be before she is fit to travel?' Margaret felt obliged to remain with Annie now that her problem had been made clear. Michael had given his full support to his wife's visit to Overavon, but she knew how much he disliked her being long away from home. It was something she tried to avoid, even though her work often demanded a considerable amount of travelling.

Stuart's reply was unexpectedly optimistic. 'With you to help her,' he said, 'I would hope for more rapid progress. She should be able to travel home in a week, or at the most two, provided the journey is made as comfortable as possible.'

Margaret still felt uneasy. She looked from one to the other in alarm. Stuart appeared to be holding something back.

'What is it?' she demanded. 'What is worrying you?'

He hesitated, unwilling to admit to his fears, but knowing that he must tell her the worst possibility.

'The psychological damage caused by her experiences has made great changes in her personality,' he explained. 'You will find our patient very different from the Wee Annie we all knew.'

Margaret gasped. 'What do you mean?' she demanded. 'Are you suggesting that starvation has affected her mind?'

'There may well have been physical damage to the structure of the brain and nervous system, which could lead to permanent changes in her mental responses,' he replied miserably. 'She is so traumatised at present that it is hard to tell if she is withdrawn because she chooses to be, or because she cannot help herself.'

Alarmed by her brother's assessment, Margaret was now even more anxious to see Annie for herself. 'Where is she?' she demanded. 'I must go to her straight away.'

'She is waiting for you in her room,' said Mrs Rosenstein.

As they mounted the stairs together, Stuart warned, 'Be prepared for Annie's very changed appearance. We have been trying to bolster her self-image, and we have managed to prevent her from looking in a mirror since she left the prison infirmary. Try not to show any sign of your distress when you see her.' He tapped on Annie's door and drew back to allow his sister to go in alone.

'Annie?' Margaret advanced cautiously into the room.

The invalid occupied her usual position on the couch beside the window overlooking the drive and the park beyond. She sat in shadow, her back to the window and her face almost obscured in the dim light.

At the first sight of her friend, Margaret struggled for control. She found it difficult to believe that such a change could be wrought in so short a period.

Despite Stuart's careful ministrations and Miss Clegg's motherly attentions, Annie still looked wizened and emaciated.

Oh, God! Margaret clapped a hand to her mouth to prevent herself from crying out. She looks so old!

'Margaret,' Annie's voice had not lost its huskiness, although speaking now caused her less pain, 'how good of you to have made the journey to visit me!'

Margaret threw her arms about her friend.

'Oh, Annie, it is so good to see you,' she cried. 'Mama sends her love and Father has sent Stuart a whole lot of suggestions about your treatment. You know how he is . . . never will accept that the younger generation know anything . . .'

She rattled on, somehow managing to disguise her concern with a smokescreen of chatter. She described David and Annabel's new home, talked of Hugh's children who were all getting so big and cheeky, told her how Heather had attained a first in Medieval History at Oxford and about James's new appointment at the Glasgow Royal Infirmary.

At last, when Annie showed signs of tiring, Margaret clasped the invalid's hands once again.

'When you are fit to travel,' she insisted, 'you must come home to Argyll. Mother and I will see to it that you get all the care and attention you require. Think of all the medical attendants who will be available,' she continued, lightly. 'Hugh wants you to go and stay at Tigh na Broch, but I thought you might prefer to live in my cottage on the island for a spell. It is so tranquil there. The quarries are all filled with water – like huge lakes – very clear and blue on a fine day. Oh, do say that you will come?'

'I suppose so.' Annie closed her eyes, content to let her friend do the thinking for her.

'First of all,' Margaret decided, 'we must make you well enough for the journey. Mrs Rosenstein has kindly invited me to stay with you until you are fit enough to travel back to Scotland.'

Annie nodded bleakly. She knew that Margaret deserved a more enthusiastic response, but she was too weary . . . Soon her eyelids drooped, and her mouth fell open just enough for her visitor to detect a gentle snoring. Straightening the rumpled bed covers, Margaret kissed her friend lightly upon the brow and crept silently from the room.

Stuart had waited impatiently by the landing window while his sister was with Annie. Although he tried to concentrate on the scenes of activity taking place in the fields beyond the parkland, his mind kept wandering back to his patient. He turned sharply when he heard the sound of a door closing gently behind him.

'Well?' he asked, eagerly.

'She is sleeping,' Margaret replied as she came and put her arms around him, seeking comfort.

They stood silently, hugging one another, until at last she drew away, wiping the tears from her cheeks.

'Poor Annie,' she sighed. 'She seems so very low.'

'When she is well rested, there are moments when her mind is as sharp as always,' he tried to reassure her. 'We must hope that she will soon recover completely.' He slipped his arm about his sister's shoulders and together they descended to the hall below.

The steamer's bows cut sharply through the glassy-still waters as she glided northwards between the islands and the mainland of Argyll.

Although the day was calm and a bright sun shone in an almost cloudless blue sky, there was an autumnal chill in the air. Annie, gazing out at the passing scene, shivered involuntarily, and Margaret gave her an anxious glance.

'Are you cold?' she enquired, solicitously.

Annie shook her head. 'Just a little tired,' she replied. She rested her head against the upholstered seating and closed her eyes.

They had taken the overnight sleeper from Euston in order to minimise the effects of the long journey upon the invalid. Mrs Rosenstein had insisted upon their travelling first-class, which had meant that they had been left undisturbed when the train pulled in to Glasgow in the early morning. Nevertheless, it was now several hours since they had joined a merry crowd of

Glaswegians taking a late holiday 'doon the watta' aboard the Clyde River boat.

Having disembarked at Ardrishaig on Loch Fyne, their short trip along the Crinan canal had, in contrast, been quiet and uneventful, the number of travellers for the West Coast ports being much reduced at this late stage in the season.

Once aboard the coastal paddle steamer, the two women had been able to find a comfortable seat in the passenger lounge where they could rest undisturbed for the remainder of the journey.

Annie had specifically requested that they take the sea route home. Now Margaret wondered if it had been wise to resurrect memories of times past in this fashion. As Annie spoke of other similar journeys with her mother, brother and sister, her eyes filled with tears.

'While I was living in London,' she mused, 'I did not miss them too terribly. It was no different from their being here still, on Eisdalsa. Now, coming back to an island devoid of family and the friends I grew up with, I am not sure that I shall be able to cope.'

Margaret too had wondered how Annie would manage on her own.

'You will not be allowed to feel lonely,' she assured her in a cheerful manner. 'Hugh's children are bubbling with excitement about your visit. You will like Millicent, I know, and there are one or two friendly old faces still to be found on the island. As for medical care, apart from Hugh there are two other Beaton doctors aiming to keep an eye on you, not to mention my Michael.'

'Two?' Annie knew that David would be calling on her. Her mother's friend, Annabel Beaton, had written to inform her that Dr David would be checking on her condition before reporting to the family in Australia. The old Annie might have protested that this was unwarranted interference in her personal affairs, but the truth was that not only was she too weak to protest, but in her heart she wanted her mother to know of her plight. It was unlikely to bring Anne McDougal scurrying home again, but at least the burden of her ill health would be shared with the one person who loved her unconditionally.

'Uncle Angus has taken a surprising interest in the Movement these past few years,' Margaret went on. 'I have no doubt that he will wish to discuss the politics of women's suffrage with you.'

Noting her friend's look of alarm, Margaret laughed. 'Oh, don't worry, he's on your side!'

A change of tempo in the paddle wheels indicated that the ship had negotiated the narrows between the islands of Lunga and Fladda and was now entering the wider waters of the Sound of Eisdalsa.

'Let's go out on the deck,' suggested Annie. 'I am anxious for my first sight of Eisdalsa.'

There was a welcoming committee waiting for them on the quay.

Heather Brown had been determined to see Annie comfortably settled on the island before returning to Oxford. Understanding her stepmother's dilemma, torn as Margaret had been between her responsibilities towards her husband and a desire to take care of Annie until she was well enough to travel, Heather had offered to return to Oban and keep house for her father. Since she had also promised that she would undertake some research in Angus Beaton's unique library of Gaelic manuscripts, she had returned to Argyll with the approval of her college tutor.

On the island of Mull, the twenty-five miles of road between Craignure, where the ferry from Oban docked, and Bunessan, where Angus lived, were tortuous, and Heather had been obliged to make the journey several times a week. Her activities would have been very much restricted had not Angus Beaton offered her the use of his new 15/30 Albion.

Mull is as mountainous, boggy and treacherous as any place in the Highlands, and David had been horrified to think of Heather bounding across the island in all weathers. Michael Brown, however, did not share David's concerns about women driving motor cars. He had taught both his wife and his daughter to drive, and had every confidence in their ability to handle a vehicle in the worst conditions. Once Angus had satisfied himself that the girl could handle the Albion on the difficult terrain, he too was happy to let her go her own way.

None of them could have guessed at the importance of this experience to Heather. The skills and knowledge which she gained in those few weeks were to be of inestimable value to her in the years ahead.

On the day of Margaret's and Annie's return to Eisdalsa, Heather had arrived early at Tigh na Broch, this time driving her father's car.

Millicent looked up as wheels crunched on the gravel outside the morning-room window.

'Surely Hugh cannot be back so early?' she muttered to herself, and went to the door to see what was amiss.

'Hallo, Aunt Millicent!' cried Heather as she leapt from the vehicle and tore a long chiffon scarf from her head. 'I have come to welcome Mama, and give her a lift back to Oban when she is ready.'

'That was thoughtful of you, dear.' Millicent greeted her with a sisterly kiss.

Although Heather was really of the next generation, she and Millicent found that they had a great deal in common, both being incomers to the Beaton family. From the first, they had struck up an easy relationship, which had quickly blossomed into a firm friendship.

'I don't know how you manage it,' declared Millicent, enviously, as she watched Heather satisfy herself that the hand-brake of Michael's car was securely fixed, and placed a rock beneath the back wheel to ensure that the vehicle did not roll backwards down the sloping driveway. 'I am quite sure that Hugh would never let me near his car, even were I able to drive it!'

'I will teach you, if you like?' offered Heather, pulling off the leather gauntlets which were standard wear for motorists. 'Then, if Hugh won't let you drive his, you can always demand a car of your own. After all, in these remote parts, a woman needs a means of getting about.'

Morag and her brother came tearing round the corner of the house. They had been playing on the hillside above when the sound of the vehicle interrupted their game. Thinking their father was home unexpectedly early, they had come rushing to greet him.

On seeing that it was, in fact, only Cousin Heather who had arrived, Ian, who was far more interested in his uncle's car, gave a cursory nod of recognition in her direction, and jumped into the driver's seat. He honked the horn, twice, and sat with his hands on the wheel, pretending he was really driving.

'Do take care, Ian,' his mother remonstrated, with a helpless look at Heather.

'Oh, it's quite all right, Mother,' the boy called out. 'Uncle Michael always lets me!'

Morag, always pleased to see her grand, grown-up cousin, gave Heather a mighty hug in welcome.

As Heather followed Millicent into the house, with Morag clinging to her free hand, she smiled. 'I'm sure he will not harm the vehicle,' she said. 'I am only concerned that he might damage himself.'

Millicent turned back to the open door.

'Ian, come along in,' she called. 'It is nearly time for the steamer. You must wash your face and comb your hair if you are going to meet Aunt Margaret.'

Seeing the lad hesitate, Heather added, 'If you hurry and tidy yourself, I will give you and Morag a ride in the car.'

This was sufficient to make him jump down from his perch and follow them obediently into the house.

At the top of the gangway Annie paused, drinking in the sights and smells of her youth. The village seemed strangely quiet and for a moment she wondered what it was that she was missing. Of course, it was the constant churning of the water pumps in the quarries, now long silent. Margaret touched her arm. The deck officer was clearly eager to disembark his passengers and be on his way.

'Hang on tight to the rail as you go down,' Margaret urged. 'I'll cope with the baggage.'

Heather and Morag were already halfway to meet them and quickly relieved Margaret of her load. Ian stood at the foot of the gangway chatting to the seamen.

On the dock the Beatons gathered around their visitor, making her welcome.

'The cottage is all ready for you,' announced Morag, excitedly. 'Granny and I worked on it all day yesterday to make sure it was aired and dusted.'

'That was very kind of you,' said Annie. 'I am sure it will be splendid.'

'Here, let me take that,' Ian demanded importantly, laying hold of a carpet bag which was almost as large as himself.

'You take these,' suggested Margaret, handing the boy two smaller bags and lifting the larger one herself. 'Run and ask the ferryman to wait for a moment. Miss McGillivray cannot rush, you know.'

Ian scampered down the flight of wooden steps which led to a landing stage below the steamer pier, calling out as he did so.

'Hold on, Baldie. There's quite a party of us to cross over.'

The elderly ferryman looked a trifle cross at the prospect of some heavy rowing until, glancing up at the descending passengers, he recognised an old friend.

'Why, if it iss not Mrs McGillivray's wee girlie,' he cried. 'A pleasure it iss to see you, Miss Annie, so it iss.'

Had she been less concerned about keeping her balance, Annie would have hugged the old man. She was so happy to find at least one figure from her past life on Eisdalsa. Archibald Campbell had been the ferryman, taking passengers to and fro across the Sound, as far back as Annie could remember.

'You are looking well, Baldie,' she greeted him. 'How is Mairi?'

'Och, she is not the woman she was, Miss Annie. It fair broke her heart when our Wullie took his brood awa' to America to look for work, I can tell you. They're all gone now, you know, all the young ones. Only us old 'ns left. You will be finding the island a wee bit dull, I'm thinking.'

'I am hoping for a little peace and quiet,' she assured him, 'but I shall look forward to having a crack with you and Mairi, just as soon as I get settled in.'

With the party all seated in the broad-beamed dory, Baldie signalled to Morag and Ian to sit side by side on the middle thwart.

'Come along now,' he urged them, 'you can each take an oar to help us across.'

The ferryman himself took the second pair of oars and pulled strongly for the island. The children's contribution was less powerful, but they were proud to be of assistance, and in the calm waters the small boat cut cleanly through the waves, making the five-hundred-yard crossing in record time.

'Aunt Annie, are girls ever able to become doctors?'

It was Saturday afternoon, and much to Morag's delight she had been allowed to cross over, alone, to the island with some messages for Annie McGillivray.

'Sometimes.' Annie looked up from her writing, and seeing that her visitor was intent upon staying, laid down her pen and resigned herself to the interruption.

'Why don't you fill the kettle and we will have some tea?' she suggested, opening the front of the range to stoke up the fire. 'There should be some muffins in that order from the bakery.'

Morag, always eager to be of help, busied herself with the tea tray, while Annie searched for the muffins amongst the groceries which Morag had brought her from the village shop on Seileach. Soon they were comfortably settled beside the fire, munching contentedly.

The Eisdalsa air had certainly sharpened Annie's appetite. She had been on the island a little over a fortnight and already Hugh was able to report a marked improvement in her condition.

'You were going to tell me about women doctors?' Morag prompted.

'There have been some,' Annie told her. 'They are, or were, mostly from wealthy families who could support them during their struggle for recognition.' She spoke briefly of such figures as Elizabeth Garrett Anderson and Sophia Jex Blake, who had pioneered training for women doctors.

'Why did they have to struggle,' asked the girl, puzzled. 'Everyone in my family has a path mapped out for them from birth – school, Watson's College in Edinburgh and University Medical School – all the boys that is. I've often wondered why none of the girls wanted to do the same.'

'Even if they had wanted to, it is doubtful if they would have been encouraged to become doctors,' Annie replied. 'When I was young it was considered inappropriate for a woman to study medicine. My sister Kirsty began her medical training in 1884, knowing that even if she were to pass all the examinations, she would not be given a degree from the university. Women were not able to matriculate in those days, although they could practise under license from the Society of Apothecaries.'

'Is she a doctor now?' Morag enquired, enthusiastically.

'No, she died when she was eighteen.' Annie looked wistfully into the fire, remembering the grown-up sister whom she had worshipped. 'She came home from college to help the doctors during the cholera epidemic that year, and caught the disease herself.'

'How horrible!' Morag's romantic ideas about doctoring had not included the possibility of danger to herself.

'Your grandfather never really approved of her working with the sick.' Annie recalled the scene at Kirsty's deathbed. 'Despite the fact that, when she died, he had to concede that she would have made a very fine doctor. Dr David always maintained that women were not strong enough, physically or mentally, for the job of a physician, and Kirsty's death was enough to confirm his opinion. I cannot think that he will ever change his mind on that point.'

'He's wrong. I know he is!' declared Morag with all the certainty of a ten-year-old. 'I am going to be a doctor, and neither Grandfather nor anyone else is going to stop me!'

'Bravo!' cried Annie. 'Just you stick to your guns. We'll make a suffragist of you yet.'

'I'm not sure that Mother would approve of that,' mused the girl. 'She says that Suffragettes defy the law and sometimes go to prison.' Realising that she had broken her promise to her mother not to mention Annie's recent experiences, she clamped her hand to her mouth in dismay and reddened with embarrassment.

'At times,' Annie said, smoothly, 'it is the only way to make oneself heard. Many women feel so strongly about their claim for equality under the law, that they are willing to die for it.'

'They are very brave,' Morag observed, looking hard at her and thinking, *You are very brave*.

'So, what do you propose to do about becoming a doctor?' Annie enquired more cheerfully.

'I suppose that I shall have to talk to Father about it,' decided the girl. 'With him on my side, I might be able to persuade Mother, and even Grandfather, that it's a good idea. To be honest with you, I dread to think what they will say when they hear what I propose to do, but nevertheless I must raise the subject soon if I want to go to the right school.'

'That sounds to me like a pretty courageous action,' Annie declared, smiling. 'One worthy of a true suffragist!'

A high-pitched scream from the kitchen brought Millicent Beaton hurrying downstairs.

Daisy, the general servant of the Beaton household, was standing in the middle of the stone-flagged kitchen floor, staring in horror at an enormous green caterpillar. Equally distressed by its unfamiliar surroundings, the unfortunate creature was making a determined retreat towards the open door into the yard.

'When I catch that young monster, I'll skelp him until there is not an inch of skin left on his buttocks,' declared the stout body. She lowered the frying pan which she had grasped in her panic, intending to kill the invader. No sense in squashing it all over the flagstones. That would mean a serious cleaning operation.

As Daisy watched the caterpillar's retreat, Annabel picked up a paper and persuaded the creature to climb aboard, so that she might transfer it more swiftly into the garden.

'I just reached for a match,' Daisy explained when her mistress returned. 'How was I to know that the boy had chosen an empty box for his wormie? I tell you, Mrs Beaton, ma'am, it is not safe to open anything these days, for fear of discovering one of Master Ian's creatures inside.'

'You have to examine the containers for signs of air-holes,' Annabel laughed. 'Ian is very careful to see that his animals have sufficient food and air! It is very naughty of him to leave his captives in the kitchen, however. The garden shed is the place for such treasures. I will tell him not to do it again.'

While Millicent found Ian's obsession with creatures, living or dead, distasteful, Hugh was highly amused by his son's proclivities and encouraged him to the extent of providing proper scalpels and scissors for the dissections which he carried out. Hugh had even produced an ancient microscope for the boy, one which had been discarded by his father many years before.

The other member of the household who took an interest in Ian's activities was Morag.

While Ian was encouraged in his investigations, Morag was left in no doubt that such interests were for boys alone. It was unladylike for a girl to chase butterflies with a net and mount them on pins. To scramble about on the cliffs in search of birds' eggs was undignified and near-impossible in the flounced petticoats and frilly pinafores worn by the young ladies of Eisdalsa.

Morag's opportunities to study zoology came only when her brother was otherwise occupied. She would creep into his room, examine his current project and attempt to trace blood vessels and nerve pathways herself, or she would mount tissues on the little glass slides and study them under the microscope. When she showed interest in the carcasses being prepared for roasting in the kitchen, she was fobbed off in her questioning by Daisy, or set to carry out some alternative task by her mother. Millicent suspected her daughter of harbouring an interest in biology but did nothing to encourage it and the subject was never raised with her husband.

Morag's request to her father came, therefore, as a bolt from the blue.

'Grandpa used to take you out on his rounds when you were ten, didn't he?' she demanded.

Hugh Beaton and his daughter were enjoying a rare moment of intimacy; he was sorting through his patients' records and Morag was dusting and rearranging bottles of pills and potions on the dispensary shelves. This was a task which she enjoyed more than any other, as it was an opportunity to familiarise herself with the difficult names on the labels and to ask occasionally what this or that medicine was for.

While her brother was eager enough to study the substances and their use, Ian considered himself above polishing and dusting and was happy to leave such dismal chores to his sister.

'Yes, I must have been about your age when I began visiting patients,' agreed Hugh, absently.

'May I come out with you sometimes?' she burst out, with sudden recklessness.

Hugh, startled by the urgency in her request, did not know how to answer. He had no wish to discourage some worthy notion of concern for the welfare of his poorer patients.

'I think that you would find it all very dull after a while, Kitten,' he surmised. 'There must be many more interesting pursuits for a little girl with time on her hands.'

'If you want a job,' observed Millicent, interrupting their discussion by carrying in clean towels for the surgery, 'you can come and help me to sort out the linen closet.'

'Morag was asking if she might accompany me on my rounds,' Hugh told his wife, noting the anxious look on his daughter's face with some amusement.

'What on earth do you want to go visiting a lot of sick people for?' Millicent enquired. 'Why, you might catch something and give it to your brothers. The idea doesn't bear thinking about.' She dismissed the proposal, and Morag's face fell.

'Oh, I don't know,' Hugh considered. He was sensitive to his daughter's distress and was inclined to rally to her support.

'There is no reason why the child should not accompany me when I go to see some of the older folk,' he continued. 'There are plenty whose ailments are confined to the aged, and would be no danger to her. So many of the grandparents in these parts have their own little ones far across the seas, and yearn for the company of children.'

When Ian heard that Morag was to accompany their father on his rounds on the following Saturday morning, he protested loudly.

'I'm the one who is going to be a doctor,' he declared. 'I should visit the patients with Father if anyone does!'

Morag was dismayed by this suggestion. If her brother came too, he would hog all her father's attention, asking his endless questions and making her take a back seat.

'Sorry, old man,' Hugh replied, to his daughter's great relief. 'In another year or two, perhaps. You are rather too young to start right away.'

'Why?' demanded the seven-year-old, unused to having his requests denied thus.

'Because,' replied his father, 'ten seems to be the age to begin sick-visiting!'

So began a period of absorbing interest for Morag.

It was not long before Hugh became aware that his daughter was genuinely anxious to learn about his patient's ailments and their treatment. On the long drives from one house to the next, they would exchange opinions about the progress of this or that person, and Hugh was surprised to discover that Morag's observations were often more insightful than his own. He was reminded of his own early ventures into the world of medicine and the chagrin he had experienced when his younger brother, Stuart, apparently so careless of his studies, would time and again beat him to the correct solution to a problem posed by their father. Was it possible that his daughter shared her uncle's intuitive approach to medicine?

'Well now, how are ye today, Andrew?' Hugh enquired, pausing in the doorway to McAllister's cottage in order to accustom his eyes to the dim light.

'Och, nae sae bad, Doctor.' McAllister half rose from his chair, but Hugh motioned him to stay where he was.

'And how is the cough?'

The old man was about to declare the cough 'nae sae bad' also but began rasping and choking on the words.

''Tis that ol' pipe that's the cause of it!' complained the tiny woman to whom McAllister had been married for fifty years and more.

'I've tell't him, Doctor,' she protested. 'If I've tell't him once, I've tell't him a thousand times, that ol' pipe will be the death of him!'

'Mrs McAllister,' Hugh greeted the woman, at the same time motioning Morag to enter the cottage.

'See here,' he announced, 'I have brought my young assistant with me today, to meet my patients. Now then, Morag, come over here and tell me what you think of Mr McAllister.'

Morag swelled with pride at being introduced in this fashion. She entered the room, marched over to Andrew McAllister's chair and solemnly took the patient's hand.

'How do you do, sir?' she enquired solicitously. She retained his hand long enough to take a hold on his wrist. She turned the hand palm upwards and glanced swiftly over it before letting it fall.

'Well, bless me,' replied the old man, 'I feel a sight better for seeing you, missie.'

The effort of speaking made the old man cough all the more. Without a word, Morag reached for the sputum bowl which was kept always at his side.

'Here,' she said, handing it to him without a qualm.

The old man used the bowl and she replaced it.

'I hope you feel more comfortable now?' she enquired politely.

'Quite the little nurse, isn't she?' observed Mrs McAllister, going to the dresser for the box of biscuits which she kept ready to offer to any young visitors.

Hugh, hiding his astonishment at the proficient manner in which his daughter had carried out the simple but unpleasant task, smiled at the old woman.

'Beatons are born to it, ma'am,' he replied proudly, and took out the bottle of cough medicine which he had prepared for Andrew.

When they had taken their leave of the old couple, Hugh and Morag skirted the end of the harbour, going towards Margaret's cottage.

'Well, miss, what did you make of our patient's condition?' he demanded.

'His chest was very wheezy, Father. I think Mrs McAllister is right about the smoking – it does him no good,' she replied.

'You are both right,' he agreed. 'But an old man in that condition has few pleasures to look forward to. Were he to stop smoking now, he might extend his life by a few months, but what miserable months they would be! Far better to opt for a shorter life but one with a measure of enjoyment attached to it.

'Thou shalt not kill,
But should not strive
officiously, to keep alive.'

He quoted the old axiom which his father had taught to him.

'If old Andrew gains comfort from a pipe or two of tobacco and a dram of whisky now and again, who am I to deny him? He knows as well as you and I that neither is good for him.'

'His skin is very thin,' observed Morag. 'I have never seen veins so clearly as on Mr McAllister's hand.'

'We have several layers of skin,' Hugh explained, 'including one which is largely fatty tissue. As people grow older the fat layer disappears and the skin looks paper thin. Then you can see quite clearly the path taken by the veins.'

'I should like to know about the skin, and what is wrong with Mr McAllister's lungs, and why Aunt Annie is so thin . . . and everything!' declared the little girl.

'I will look out some books for you to read,' decided Hugh. Then, as they approached Annie's door, 'As far as Miss McGillivray is concerned, she is thin because of her experiences in prison. All she needs to restore her to full health is to eat well and take plenty of exercise.'

A thought struck him.

'How would you like Annie to be considered your very own case?' he asked her. 'It would mean using all your powers of persuasion to make her eat properly, and I would have to rely on you to see she gets plenty of fresh air and exercise.'

Morag was beside herself with delight.

'Oh, may I, Daddy? May I have my very own patient?'

'I shall expect properly written reports on her progress, mind you,' said her father, amused and not a little impressed by her enthusiasm.

'I shall keep a special journal which I shall write up after every visit,' Morag decided. Then, hesitating for an instant, she asked, 'Do you think that Annie will mind having me for her nurse?'

'I am sure that she will be delighted,' replied her father.

'Can we start straight away, today?' demanded Morag.

'Why not?' Hugh smiled at her. 'I am not so busy this morning that I cannot spare an hour to walk to the top of the ridge, if you can persuade Annie to come along too.'

They entered the house to find her busy with her book.

'Good morning, Auntie Annie.' Morag darted towards her and gave her an affectionate kiss on the cheek.

'Daddy and I have come to take you out for a walk,' she declared, pausing only momentarily to take a breath. 'Ian says that he saw some late-flowering orchids in the upper meadow last week. Oh, do put down your pen and come with us!'

Annie would have protested that she was far too busy, but she caught Hugh's pleading look. He was willing her to make the correct response. She glanced again at Morag's eager little face and knew that she could not refuse the child.

'Oh, if I must,' she submitted, 'I will just fetch my coat.' As she disappeared into the bedroom, Hugh smiled at his daughter and grasped her hand. 'Well done,' he murmured.

They struggled up the steep slope to the summit of the ridge of granite rock which stuck out across the island like a gigantic crest. At the top they paused for breath, while Morag pointed out those of the many islets in the bay which she could name. On such a bright, clear day it was possible to see all the way to the Isle of Colonsay itself.

As the child rattled off a string of Gaelic names, Annie began to join in.

When it came to the last, a mere pinnacle of rock surrounded by huge choppy waves, it was Hugh who shouted the name into the wind.

'Sgeir Bhuidhe!' he cried, and the other two cheered.

For a time they all three stood silently contemplating the vast arena of the Sound of Lorn.

Hugh recalled other such days long ago. Days when he had dreamed of a future in which Wee Annie McGillivray had figured significantly. They had all gone their separate ways, of course, and Hugh could not grumble at his own fate.

David Beaton had wished to quit the family practice at the very point in Hugh's career when he had decided to leave the city hospital for a more peaceful, rural occupation. He was seeking a place where his children might grow up in the sweet clean air of the Highlands, and not the choking atmosphere of Glasgow or Edinburgh.

It had been the most natural thing in the world for Millicent and himself to move into Tigh na Broch, as his parents moved out. The villagers had been delighted to see yet another generation of Beatons occupying the old house, and immediately took the new doctor to their hearts.

Annie too remembered earlier times. Days when she had scrambled over the rocks like a monkey in pursuit of Stuart Beaton and his cronies. In the hope that he would cast her an encouraging smile or exchange a word with her, she would have followed him to the moon. In those days she had seemed not to notice that it was always Hugh who waited for her when the going got tough. He had been the one to haul her up when a boulder was too large, or to catch her as she jumped.

Her mind flew now to those days at Overavon when she would emerge from a deep pit of misery and pain to find Stuart standing there, looking so anxious. Her skin tingled even now at the memory of his hand upon her wrist, of his stethoscope exploring her chest, his cool touch upon her abdomen. All so professional, all so caring . . . a doctor's concern for his patient. The old feelings had come over her then. If only he would notice her in that other way . . . look upon her with the same longing which she had for him. She shuddered at the thought of what she must have looked like on their first encounter at Overavon. It was a wonder he had recognised her at all.

Stuart had been caring and considerate but in all respects their relationship had been the distant one of doctor and patient – nothing had changed since the days when, as children, they had frolicked together up here on the ridge.

Morag's heart was so full that she thought she must burst with happiness.

At last her father had taken note of her aching desire to learn more about his work. He had allowed her to visit a real patient, and had given her a 'case' to herself. If Aunt Annie was to be her responsibility from now on, she must find out about the correct foods to give a person for a balanced diet. She had heard Grandpa use the term when justifying smoking his pipe.

'I have a well-balanced diet, my dear,' he would explain to Grandmama, 'that is what is essential to good health. A pipe of tobacco now and again never hurt anyone.'

She squatted now upon her own special rock, hugged her knees, and thought happily about the future. Surely there must be a girls' equivalent to George Watson's Academy for Boys!

'Why do the boys in this family all go to George Watson's College, Father?' she asked Hugh, on one of their subsequent drives together.

'In your grandfather's day,' he explained, 'it was because the Marquis of Stirling was a benefactor of the school and could nominate as pupils children from his estates. Now it has become the tradition for Beaton boys to go there.'

'What about the girls?' she demanded, knowing the answer.

'There have been so few in each generation, and as doctor's daughters they were never sent away to school. There was no need.'

'But suppose a girl wanted a profession? To be a teacher say, or a nurse like Grandmama?'

'No Beaton lady has ever needed to work for her living,' Hugh responded with some pride.

'If I wanted to be a doctor . . .' there it was out at last '. . . I would have to go away to school first, wouldn't I?' Morag demanded.

'You would certainly need more science and mathematics than you can get at the village school,' her father replied, a little more circumspect now that he realised the direction this discussion was taking. 'You would need to learn Latin and Greek,' he added, hoping to put her off.

'I have already learned quite a lot of Latin grammar,' the girl assured him. 'I quite enjoy it!'

'Look here,' he said, remembering a conversation he had had with Elizabeth Whylie a few weeks previously, when she and

William had stayed on the island for a holiday. 'How would you like to go to Mrs Whylie's school in Dumfries? I know that for a girls' school they do an inordinate amount of science. Mr Whylie himself teaches physics and mathematics. We could see how you got on there before making any decisions about your becoming a doctor.'

The child was ecstatic.

'Oh, Daddy, could I really go away to school? I would work so very hard. I know you would be proud of me, and I do so want to be a doctor like Mrs Garrett Anderson.

Oh, ho, thought Hugh, so that's it. Annie McGillivray has been filling her head with stories.

To Morag he replied, 'Let us take it one step at a time. I think I can persuade your mother to let you go to Elizabeth's school, but any suggestion that you might be preparing for a career in medicine we will keep strictly to ourselves for the present. Let's see how you get on with your studies first.'

He comforted himself with the thought that she might tire of the idea of becoming a doctor when confronted with the vast amount of information that she would be required to learn. He should have known his daughter better than that!

Chapter 12

Ann McDougal put down the empty pail, pushed back a lock of hair from her damp forehead and watched, absently, while the chooks pecked at the meal and scraps she had spread before them. One would think it was the first food they had eaten for a week!

It had been a busy few months since the day of the house-raising. She laughed to herself at the fright she had had on seeing that little family of Aborigines, squatting just outside the firelight while the newcomers feasted with their neighbours at the end of the day. How stupid she had been to fear those quiet, friendly people who wanted nothing but to satisfy their curiosity, and perhaps sample a little of the white man's good living!

On hearing a distant clink of harness, Anne shaded her eyes and gazed into the distance where her husband was turning the plough at the end of a furrow.

John McDougal had shed a few of his sixty-seven years during the six months since they had arrived at Kerrera Station. The climate seemed to agree with him. Those old rheumatic pains, which were the legacy of a lifetime in the damp, chill winds of Western Argyll, seemed to have deserted him completely. He was bronzed by the Australian sun, and the musculature of his shoulders and upper arms was now that of a much younger man. Any misgivings which Anne might have felt about persuading him to come here had been set aside.

A cloud of dust away over to the east told her that Jack and Vicky were on their way back to the homestead. She hurried indoors to prepare the midday meal.

After their initial encounter with the Aborigines on the night of the house-raising, Jack McDougal and his father had found their way to the tribal encampment. With sign language, and a little pidgin English, a bargain had been struck with the headman and three of the men agreed to accompany the Scotsmen back to Kerrera Station. They were put to work erecting fences to contain the stock.

The crafts associated with farmwork are best taught by example. Day after day Jack would demonstrate a particular task which the Aborigines were delighted to imitate. There were difficulties, of course, in a system of training in which the 'how' was taught without the 'why', but gradually the Aborigines came to understand the ways of the newcomers and a relationship of mutual respect developed. As John expanded his activities to encompass the entire extent of his holding, more of the tribe were employed. Kerrera Station began to look more like a farm, and less like an untamed stretch of wilderness.

In return for their labours, the Aborigines received food, blankets, and the European cooking pots and tools which were much favoured by native Australians. John was careful to observe the rule that they be paid in kind and not in money, but in particular he ensured that they had no access to alcohol.

Many of the problems which had seemed so daunting to Jack and his father on first encountering the outback were solved for them by the Aboriginal workers.

It was these men who led them to the best stands of blue and white gum from which to obtain suitable timber for fencing. While the McDougals struggled to work the fibrous timbers with their good steel axes and saws, brought with them from Scotland, the black men, using the most primitive of tools, seemed able to cut and fashion the wood with consummate ease.

The Aborigines found water located at the more remote parts of the spread, and under Jack's direction dug the shafts for the artesian wells which were, eventually, to make Kerrera one of the most successful farms in the district.

Once she had organised the homestead to her satisfaction, Anne engaged one of the Aboriginal women and her daughter, to help with work in the house and dairy.

These two, never having set foot inside a white man's house before, were amazed at everything they were shown. Common implements – spoons, forks, china dishes and ornaments – had them completely baffled. The few treasured pieces of furniture which Anne had brought across the seas from home were a source of constant interest. It was nothing for Anne to come across one of them carefully opening and closing the drawer of her mahogany tallboy, just for the pleasure of feeling the wood gliding in and out so effortlessly.

The uses to which the various objects should be put also caused confusion. Anne frequently had to rescue some precious piece of china from destruction over the hot stove, and on one famous occasion was devastated to find the girl mixing dough for the week's supply of bred in a chamber-pot.

It had taken very little time for the newcomers to realise just how little regard was given to the Aboriginal population of their adopted land. It had horrified Anne to hear her neighbours discuss them as if they were animals, to be used and abused as their masters thought fit. There were those amongst the white Australians who would see the native population completely wiped out, as they had indeed been eliminated from Tasmania. For the most part they were content to allow these misused and abused people to destroy themselves, by indulging in the worst excesses of European culture: gambling, fighting, fornication, and the excessive consumption of alcohol. In order to achieve these goals, they turned to crime and, as a consequence, suffered all the related penalties, sometimes with fatal results.

Perhaps even worse were the diseases brought to Australia by the white men. A common cold which Europeans might shrug off in a few days, could lay a black man low and would probably turn to pleurisy, while tuberculosis and venereal disease killed without mercy. Amongst the children, measles was the greatest scourge. Two of these lively little youngsters died of the disease during the McDougals' first year at Kerrera.

Anne stepped on to the veranda and beat the metal triangle to warn the men that it was time to come in to their midday meal.

Shading her eyes she watched the approaching cloud of dust. Her stepson would soon be joining them at the table.

As Jack McDougal cantered towards the house, mounted on the tall roan horse which he had recently acquired at a fair in Southern Cross, he cast a professional eye over the nucleus of his flock. He was more than satisfied with the progress of the animals he had bought from Mick O'Flannery.

Only last evening, he had at last felt ready to write his first letter to Jean Parsons. After several attempts to make a suitable beginning he had settled for '*My dear Jean*', and proceeded to give a careful account of events since their arrival at Kerrera. Suspecting that she would be more interested in the house than the farm, he gave a detailed description of every room, hastening to add:

> *I shall begin to build a separate house for myself as soon as the wet is over and we have harvested the first season's crops. Anne and my father are very accommodating, but I do feel that I need a place of my own.*

His style was stilted. Unaccustomed to writing any letters other than those connected with the business, he found it difficult to express his personal feelings. When it came to his flock, however, he found that his pen just flew across the paper, his hand having difficulty in keeping up with his thoughts:

> *I made a careful selection from the lambs. All the ewes will be kept for breeding and also for their wool, of course. Of the rams, I separated out the best three as tups, and retained the remainder for meat. We kill the animals as and when Anne requires them for the homestead. Mutton forms the major part of our diet, I'm afraid, but that is nothing new to we Highland Scots. More importantly the meat is used to pay the Aboriginal workers for their labours.*
> *I have discovered that it is common practice out here to cross the more common blackface sheep with the merino ram from South America. The result is an animal capable*

of withstanding the drought while producing excellent wool. An added bonus is that the meat from such a combination is of acceptable quality. Although it will be a while before we know whether wool or mutton is going to bring us the highest return. I shall need to introduce a good merino ram to the flock as soon as I can afford it.

I wait eagerly for this season to pass, determined to make the journey to Adelaide just as soon as circumstances allow, for I want so desperately to see my Jeannie again.

He wondered if perhaps he had dwelt at too much length on matters relating to the farm, but satisfied himself with the thought that Jean was a farm girl herself and would forgive his single-mindedness.

I hope that you are well and happy, my dearest. I shall wait anxiously for your reply.

My loving thoughts are with you always . . .

He addressed the envelope to the 'Women's Immigration and Overseas Appointments Society' – it was the only address Jean had been able to give him – and left it in the post bag, to be taken to the post office in Southern Cross the next time Billy drove in for supplies.

As always, it was Vicky who reached the homestead first.

Coming to a sudden halt, she stirred up the dust around Anne's feet and flopped down, tongue lolling, while Anne filled a pail of water from the trough.

Always perfectly mannered, the collie nuzzled her mistress's hand before bending her head to drink.

Anne ran her hand along the bitch's flanks.

'If I didn't know there is no other dog for fifteen miles around,' she murmured, 'I would swear that you are in the family way.'

The collie pricked her ears, and rolled over to expose her belly where her swelling glands and prominent teats told their own story.

'Hallo, Ma,' Jack greeted her as he rode up, 'I see you've noticed that our Vicky is torrach!'

'But where could she have found herself a mate?' demanded his stepmother.

'A wild dog . . . dingoes they call them,' he explained. 'I saw her playing with him a few weeks ago. Now, whenever we go out to the far paddock, he follows us and watches Vicky working the sheep. He just sits there, up on the hillock, in the shade of a clump of wattles, and watches.'

'Will she be all right, bearing pups from a wild creature?' Anne demanded anxiously. 'What sort of offspring will she produce from such a union?'

'They're called kelpies,' Jack told her. 'It's been quite common practice out there for a long time to cross-breed with dingoes.'

'Do you mean to say you actively encouraged Vicky?' Anne asked, astonished that Jack should have been so reckless with his beautiful collie bitch.

'I think you are in for a surprise,' he laughed. 'A good kelpie should have the intelligence of the best collie, and the native instincts of his dingo brothers.'

As though to reassure Jack that she was not about to let him down, Vicky crept up to her master's side and licked his fingers affectionately.

Billy Blue Gum was returning from the town with supplies for Kerrera Station. He blessed the day that John McDougal had offered him work and rescued him from a life of drudgery and torment at Dooley's stables.

There were aspects of his old life which he still missed very much – the occasional visit to the race track, and the drinking and gambling that followed, for instance. Most of all he missed working with Dooley's beautiful race horses, for although Kerrera now boasted a large number of stock horses, there were none to compare with the Irishman's well-bred sprinters.

'I'll just have to make the most of you fellers,' he murmured as he touched the left-hand gelding lightly to make him keep in step with his partner. Billy crooned softly to the horses, a form of mouth music, strangely rhythmical, which the two animals seemed to enjoy, for they responded by picking up their feet and trotting along with an easy gait.

John McDougal was a decent boss. He sometimes harangued Billy for being lazy on the job and for oversleeping after a night at the go-down, but harsh words didn't bruise your arms or break your nose the way Dooley's swift left hand had done for similar misdoings. The old man was worried about his failing health. Billy knew, because all the time he was drawing his Aboriginal foreman to one side and saying: 'Now then, Billy, you're going to have to learn to do this yourself. I might not always be around to show you, you know.' They were always talking about this war 'back home'. Billy didn't see what it had to do with Mr Jack or any other of the Pommie farmers hereabouts. If they had had such a good life in the 'old country', what had brought them here to take over his homeland? Never one to look a gift horse in the mouth, however, Billy did as he was told, doing his best to carry out all the tasks John McDougal gave him and trying to remember his instructions, confident that the elderly Scot was a man of his word.

And then there was Mrs Anne . . . such a kind lady. Billy thought the world of her. If anything were to happen to the master, Billy would have to be around to see that she was all right.

As he neared the homestead, the stockman whipped up the team, approaching the house with an air of urgency which had been completely lacking for all but the last mile.

'Letters for you, missus,' he called, as Anne appeared on the veranda to greet him.

Climbing down from the driving seat, he handed the reins to one of the little group of Aborigine children who always hung around the homestead. The boy held the horses still, while the rest of the children unloaded the supplies and carried them with much chattering and laughter into the house.

When they had all wandered off once more, Anne turned over the correspondence that Billy had brought her. Most of the envelopes contained seed catalogues or farming journals, but amongst them there were two letters of a more personal nature, one for herself and the other for Jack . . . posted in Adelaide. Who did he know in Adelaide? She wondered. She seemed to recall that Hamish's friend Tom Pain had gone there but this looked like a business letter, the envelope had been typed.

Setting aside Jack's correspondence, she studied her own letter.

The writing on the envelope was unmistakably that of Annabel Beaton. Letters from home were precious, their contents to be pored over again and again, until every nuance was devoured, every item of information absorbed. There was to be no time for such indulgence now, however, for at that moment she heard sounds of the men coming home for their evening meal. Annabel's letter would have to wait until she was alone. She tucked it into her apron pocket and hurried towards the kitchen.

'What's become of the little collie bitch, Jack?' asked Cal McKinley as he wiped a piece of bread around his empty plate, reluctant to let even a morsel of gravy escape. 'Haven't seen her around this week.'

'Nursing a litter of pups down in the barn,' Jack replied proudly. 'Five of them there were. One's a wee bit dwannie . . . sickly,' he added hastily. On occasions he forgot that not everyone appreciated his rich Scottish vocabulary. 'The rest are fine, healthy kelpie pups.'

'So that's why that ole dingo dog's been hanging around the top paddock?' declared Billy. 'Is he the mate?'

'Reckon so,' agreed Jack.

'Gee, I'd give anything to own a pup of your Vicky's. I'm darned if she ain't the cleverest little bitch I ever seen working the sheep,' sighed a jackeroo who had arrived earlier in the week looking for work. There was little money to take on extra hands, but Jack had agreed to give the itinerant farmworker bed and board in exchange for a few day's fencing and ditching.

'Kelpie like that'd bring in five pounds of anybody's money at one of the shows, Mr Jack,' declared Billy. ''Specially if he was part-trained before you sold him.'

'Really?' Jack was genuinely surprised at Billy's estimate. Five pounds was a lot of money. He would never have thought he could get anything like twenty pounds for the pups. Why, that would be enough to take him all the way to Adelaide and back on the train, and maybe buy a good merino tup as well.

As the meal came to an end, the men were reluctant to rise from the table. Night after night they would sit on, discussing the day's work, debating the latest sports reports and the growing tensions in Europe which suggested that at any day a full-scale war might break out.

John McDougal viewed the mixed group of men gathered about his table that evening with great satisfaction. There were still many white Australians who regarded the Aborigines as little higher than the animals, and would no more consider sitting down to a meal with black men than they would drink beer with a bunch of gorillas. Anne McDougal and her husband were considered unusual in having so soon found common ground with their black neighbours. They recognised the Aborigines as being the real owners of the land which had been leased to them by the Australian Government, and insisted that the black farm workers should share their meals, and live alongside the white men in the bunkhouse. If a European jackaroo chose to object to black-skinned workmen sharing his ablutions or bedding down beside him, he could move on, for no amount of complaining from the white men would induce John McDougal to separate them. Despite all the tales told about their slothfulness, John had found his black workers to be honest, hard-working and respectful. He had no complaints, and what was good enough for him should be good enough for all!

So it was that at Kerrera Station black and white men sat together at table. Their clothes were identical: coarse cotton shirts and hard-wearing canvas trousers. All had the clean shiny look of men fresh from the yard pump. Their speech carried the intonations of a wide variety of European countries, as well as the distinctive tones of the native Australian, but the language they used was English. There was no problem of communication for they all had a common purpose: to wrest from the unforgiving, inhospitable environment a living for themselves and their families.

An hour or so later, in the privacy of her bedroom, Anne again took out the letter she had received that afternoon. Eagerly she examined the Oban postmark. It had been sent only six weeks ago and must have come by one of those fast new mail ships, to have arrived so soon.

Hungry for news, she scanned the pages rapidly the first time, leaving aside for the moment Annabel's description of her new house and garden. She came to a section relating to the suffragist movement. Mention of Wee Annie rested her attention:

> *... whatever you may hear to the contrary, I can assure you that, despite all her tribulations, Annie is well on the road to recovery. After staying with friends of Stuart's in Hampshire, she returned to Eisdalsa with Margaret, and is at present residing on Eisdalsa Island with Hugh and my little granddaughter, Morag, in attendance. She could not be better cared for were she the King himself! It was very fortunate that Stuart was on leave at the time of her release, and able to help her through the worst stages of her recovery ...*

Anne went back a page and studied Annabel's account more carefully. She was appalled to learn of Annie's arrest and imprisonment. Hoping to spare her friend the worst details of her daughter's ordeal, Annabel had made only a brief reference to the hunger strike and entirely omitted details of the girl's treatment while she was in prison.

Unaware of the worst aspects of Annie's imprisonment, Anne consoled herself with the thought: Whatever my Wee Annie has been through, she is now in safe hands.

She recalled all those other occasions when the Beatons had come to the rescue of the McGillivrays. Whenever tragedy had struck at her family, one or other of the Beaton doctors had been there to give comfort and support.

She read the remainder of Annabel's letter, but found it difficult to concentrate upon topics other than her daughter's health. She put the letter aside to read again when she felt calmer.

As the Australian summer had approached, Jack found it more and more difficult to sleep in the stuffy atmosphere of the little room they had built for him at the side of the main house. He took his bedroll out on to the veranda at the back and by the light of an oil lamp read his first letter from Jean. She explained why she had typed the envelope:

> *My employer is very suspicious about any letters I write of a personal nature. She does, however, expect me to type her business letters for her, so it is less likely that she will notice this one going out to the post if the envelope looks like the rest . . .*

Whatever kind of a situation is that? Jack wondered. Where a grown woman is not allowed to write to her friends!

> *I would never have found my way from the boat into the centre of Adelaide had it not been for the kindly assistance of Tom Pain . . . you remember, Hamish's friend on board the* Geraldtown? *He gave me a lift in his cab and set me down outside the offices of the Women's Migration and Overseas Appointments Society.*
>
> *My employer, Mrs Savery, has two little nieces, orphans, to whom she acts as guardian. They are rather difficult children but I think they have met their match in me. I understand that I have now held the position of governess for a longer period than any of my predecessors.*
>
> *Poppy is the more biddable child. She is only six and never really knew her own parents – they died of fever while running a Methodist Mission on Papua, New Guinea. Estelle is eleven and at a difficult age. She is old enough to remember her parents, and resents anyone who tries to usurp their position in her life. She is crafty though. She sucks up to her aunt in an abominable way, flattering*

*her and ostentatiously running all her many errands,
while behind Mrs Savery's back she has nothing good to
say of her at all. So unpleasant is she at times, that I am
inclined to think she is more like my mistress's own
daughter than her niece.*

*The house is large but rather ramshackle. We live well
out of town, on the Fleurieu Peninsular, at a place called
Kuitpo Creek. I think the estate was bought by Mrs Savery's
grandfather who seems to have been something of a
mixture between a businessman and a pirate. At any rate,
he made a great deal of money, which he lost later gambling on the Stock Market.*

*Although the work is not hard, and I live comfortably
enough, my employer makes my life intolerable. Were I able
to pay her back my fare, I would leave tomorrow. As it is, I
shall just have to stick it out until my year's contract is up.*

*I look forward so much to seeing you when you come to
the stock fair in Adelaide. How I would love to accompany
you back to Kerrera straightaway! I fear, however, that I
shall not be able to leave this position until the end of April.
I hope you will not get impatient and find yourself another
'farm girl' to take my place!*

*My one friend in this bleak landscape is Tom Pain. If it
were not for his occasional visits to the house, I think I
should despair utterly.*

*He has set up a small garage at the end of town with a
petrol pump, a repair workshop and a second-hand
limousine which is for hire. It was quite by chance that Mrs
Savery's car was driven in there one day for petrol. Since
then she regards Tom as her own personal mechanic. He
comes out to the house whenever the car refuses to start, or
if Mrs Savery chooses to hire his impressive Rolls-Royce
rather than use her own much smaller vehicle.*

*When I tell Tom of the awful things that Mrs S. and the
children get up to, he makes such a joke of it all that I
cannot help laughing too . . .*

Jean's letter ended with the endearments which he was longing to read. Jack was a little disturbed at her constant references to Tom Pain, though. He was a nice enough fellow, of course. Flora, in particular, had taken to him, as he recalled . . . but he did seem to be filling a place in Jean's life which should, by rights be Jack's and no one else's. The sooner he got the pups sold, and himself on the train to Adelaide, the better.

By late-August, a piece of land had been cleared some half a mile from the homestead, close by a convenient water-hole and a shady stand of wattle and gum trees. Here Jack intended to build a house for himself.

Anne and John were somewhat surprised by their son's anxiety to have a home of his own. After all, it was not as though he had any marriage prospects. He was already over forty and there was a scarcity of women in this sparsely populated district. His parents could not have failed to notice his attachment to Jean Parsons while on board the ship, of course, but nothing had been said about her since they had landed in Australia, and Anne had assumed that it had been no more than a shipboard romance.

She appreciated her stepson's concern that she and John should have the place to themselves, though. After all, they had lived cramped together ever since her marriage and it would be nice to have John to herself during their declining years.

All afternoon Jack had been digging the foundations of the main building. The soil was sandy, but after nine months' continuous drought it was rock hard. With pick and shovel he cut out his first trench, eighteen inches wide and two feet deep. At this rate of working it would be a week before he was ready to start mixing the concrete.

He stopped for a moment to wipe the sweat out of his eyes.

Great black cumulus clouds had been building up all through the afternoon. The air was noticeably more humid than it had been earlier in the day. Maybe the old Aborigines were right about the good wet they said was coming!

With this amount of overcast, it would soon be dark. He lifted the pick and tackled the next part of the trench.

It was a matter of pride for Jack that he should build this house by himself. Until he was forced to seek help to raise the walls and roof, he intended to do everything, working on it whenever he could spare the time. Already he had refused help from his father and from some of the men. It was good of them to offer to put in time after the normal day's work was finished, but Jack was quite determined to build his house alone. If he had no money to offer his bride, he had at least his health and strength. He would prove to her that he was capable of creating a home for them with his own bare hands.

It was already getting dark. There was no dusk out there in the bush. One moment it was bright daylight and the next it was black as pitch until the moon came up. He downed tools and made his way to the homestead as Anne struck the bell, calling the men to supper.

In the early hours of the morning the first raindrops fell like pebbles on the corrugated iron roof.

The occupants of Kerrera Station were roused from sleep by the continuous drumming, and ran out into the deluge in their nightwear. For a long time they enjoyed the sheer pleasure of being drenched in the cool rain. They inspected the roof and its drainage system, noting with satisfaction that the water-butts were filling nicely. Jack climbed the ladder to peer into the great storage tank which they had constructed during the first week, and which had remained tantalisingly empty ever since. The water had already risen to the first foot mark.

Refreshed and ready for sleep, the McDougals returned to their beds to drowse away what remained of the night-time hours.

In the morning Anne woke to the sound of the kookaburra's cackling cry and the flapping of wings as a swarm of parakeets rose from the gums by the water-hole and beat a flight-path over the roof of the house.

She was immediately aware of a freshness in the atmosphere and a remarkable fragrance.

Unable to contain her curiosity a moment longer, she leapt from her bed and dragging a loose wrapper around her, went out on to the veranda.

During the night, the parched ground of the paddocks had absorbed the moisture like a sponge. Already seeds which had lain dormant for a year or more were beginning to sprout, creating a green bloom over the surface of the sandy soil.

Away to the south-east, where the ground dipped to form a shallow basin two or three miles in diameter, she caught a glimpse of something reflecting from the surface of the soil. She blinked, shaded her eyes for a better view and then let out a whoop of joy.

'Merlin's Lake,' she cried, laughing until the tears rolled down her cheeks. 'It's Merlin's Lake!' Without thinking about the distance she began to run towards the great shining sheet of water.

Jack, emerging from sleep with an aching head and an unpleasant taste in his mouth, was slow to grasp what was happening. He met his father in the hallway.

Having been wakened by his wife's cries, and fearing some terrible disaster, John was trying, somewhat unsuccessfully, to pull on his clothes while running, desperate to go to Anne's aid.

The two men arrived on the veranda together. They scanned the horizon for a sign of what it was that had disturbed Anne and saw her running figure, and beyond the glittering surface of the lake.

With greater circumspection than had been displayed by his wife, John McDougal led one of the horses out of the stable and harnessed her to the little trap which they used for getting about the farm. Jack saddled his roan, and within minutes the men were following in Anne's footsteps.

She ran and ran, but no matter how far she travelled, the waters still seemed a long way ahead.

After covering more than two miles on foot, Anne crested a small hillock which marked the boundary of the crater in whose base the water had gathered. She sat down on a boulder to regain her breath.

By the lake's edge, swarms of birds had already gathered. A mob of kangaroos, the big reds of the western outback, had assembled on the far bank, while nearer to hand a crowd of smaller wallabies cavorted in and out of the water.

So entranced was she at this scene of unusual activity that Anne was unaware of her husband's approach until the trap had drawn up beside her.

'You must be tired after that run,' he said, laughingly. 'Hop up and I'll take you the rest of the way.'

She noticed that Jack too was smiling at her. Glancing down, she realised for the first time that not only was she still wearing her nightgown, but she had not even stopped to put on her shoes. In her excitement she had been oblivious of the stony ground, and unaware of the numerous nicks and gashes on the soles of her bare feet.

'You must think me crazy,' she said, blushing. 'It was just that I had become convinced that Mick's story of Merlin's Lake was a "Pommie teaser", so I was overjoyed to see that it really does exist!'

John gave her a hand to climb aboard and the little party covered the half mile or so to the water's edge. So intent were the wild creatures in their enjoyment of God's bounty, that they hardly lifted their heads as the McDougals approached.

Jack knelt on the ground and took a handful of the water which he held to his lips to taste. It was brackish but not undrinkable as the animals had already shown. Clearly, however, as the sun evaporated much of the moisture, the remaining solution would become more concentrated until eventually only a salt-marsh would remain.

To the Scotsmen, used as they were to a constant supply of fresh water from the mountain springs feeding into bottomless lochs, the notion of salt-marshes was foreign. For this reason they had ridden across this very basin many times in months past, quite unaware that it was the bed of a lake, not recognising the strange succulents as plants associated with salt water.

'When the gold-mining started,' Jack pondered, 'they tell me that the only source of water was salt-lakes such as this. They had to organise a desalination system which was so expensive that it was only the gold-mining industry which could afford to pay for it.'

'Life must have been terribly hard for the women in those days,' mused Anne and then, realising what she had said, she began to laugh hysterically. Here she was, sympathising with her sisters who had pioneered life in the outback, when only a month or two previously she had been convinced that no one could possibly have endured such hardship as that to which she and her family had been subjected.

'One thing is certain,' said John, 'there must be a good permanent source of water down below. While the lake remains, we should mark out a few likely sites for sinking bore holes. I'm surprised that the Abos did not suggest that we tried a well out here.'

They turned for home, not noticing the little group of figures gather on the rim of the basin, in the far distance. As the white men drove off, leaving the magical stretch of water to the animals, the black men began a slow chant and a strange, mystical dance, summoning upon themselves the blessings of their ancestors.

As though in answer to their incantations, in a day or so the first seedlings burst their buds and the desert began to bloom. For many nights it rained, and as day followed sunny day the normally barren soil became a carpet of gloriously coloured flowers.

At last the rain clouds of an Australian spring passed, the plants formed their seeds, shrivelled and died, and all that remained of Merlin's Lake was a crust of white salt crystals and a border of greyish-green plants of goosefoot, prickly saltwort and seablight, similar to those to be found anywhere on the salt-marshes of Britain and Europe.

Kuitpo Creek,
10 January, 1914

My Dearest Jack,
How soon can you come to fetch me?

I have had the most terrible row with my employer. She intercepted your last letter, the one which you addressed to Kuitpo Creek, and has accused me of carrying on a clandestine liaison. She assumes that I have used her solely as a means of establishing myself for long enough to find a husband! I have tried to explain that I had no intention of leaving her service until my contract was up, but she is adamant that I must go at the end of the month.

She had already demanded a replacement from the WIOAS, so as from February I shall be unemployed, with no place to go!

Although I long to see the last of this place, I am sorry that things have ended in this way, if only because I had hoped to come to you with my first year's earnings of £100. I am not sure exactly what will happen about the money because Mrs Savery is refusing to discuss the matter of payment. She is quite determined that if I do not complete the contract, I am entitled to nothing. Can this be correct?

I long to see you again, my dearest.

Write soon and tell me that you are on your way!

Please direct any further letters to the office of the Women's Immigration and Overseas Appointments Society.

Your, Jean

Jack had taken his letter to the barn, about the only place where he could find a little privacy. At his feet Vicky lay quietly, herself enjoying a moment of respite from her boisterous family. He laid down the letter and fondled the animal's silken ears. His thoughts were in turmoil.

He had to go to Adelaide at once, yet how could he? The farm was doing well, but every halfpenny accumulated was immediately ploughed back into the business. He had no money for a railway ticket for himself, let alone Jean.

The pups were getting noisy again. The litter, now nearly three months old, had grown healthy and strong. In their play they demonstrated all the herding instincts of their mother. They were going to be excellent sheep dogs, every one.

Jack picked up the dog which had been the runt of the litter. He was the image of Vicky in every respect save for a patch of golden fur on either cheek and at his rump. So closely did he resemble his dam that Jack had called him Albert after the Prince Consort, as Vicky had been called after the late Queen.

The name had quickly been shortened to Al.

Although the last pup delivered, and hence the smallest at birth, Al had gained weight remarkably quickly. Too weak to fight for his own nipple to latch on to at feeding time, he had been obliged to rely upon Jack or Anne to see that he had his fill. A strong bond of affection had grown up between the three of them, and Vicky, appreciating the extra care that was being lavished upon her tiny offspring, seemed to favour him herself. Jack fondled his favourite of the brood thoughtfully. Vicky was getting on in years. He should be thinking of training another dog to take her place.

He contemplated the noisy bunch as they scrambled about in the hay. If Mackintosh was right, the sale of four of the pups should bring him in twenty pounds which would be more than enough to take him to Adelaide to collect his bride.

He nuzzled the soft fur of the pup wriggling in his hands. 'But not you, little laddie,' he whispered. 'You are staying with your ma.'

Part 2

1914–1916

Chapter 13

Annie read Margaret's letter with some amusement:

You will recall our discussion with Mama and Millicent concerning the Scottish involvement in the Suffrage Movement? To prove her point, that there was some activity on this score, Millicent organised a lecture in the Drill Hall last week, which was addressed by two ladies from the Scottish Federation of Women's Suffrage Societies. Well, as a result of a most interesting and enlightening discussion, we have all joined! I hasten to add that the reason which persuaded Mama more than any other was that the Scottish Sisterhood is totally opposed to militant action and seeks to obtain the vote through lobbying persons of influence in the Government and elsewhere.

Heather was spending a few days with Michael and myself at the time, and she was rather more impressed with a notion purporting to have come from a Dr Elsie Inglis of Edinburgh. In the event of a war, Dr Inglis is proposing to set up a Field Hospital entirely manned by females, surgeons, nurses, administrators and ambulance drivers, which she will offer to the War Office as a unit. I don't need to tell you how Heather leapt at the idea of being able to drive heavy motor vehicles in a good cause! I sometimes wonder whether an MA (Oxon) is absolutely necessary for a woman who wants so badly to be a lorry driver!

Annie's second letter bore an Australian postage stamp and was in her mother's unmistakable handwriting.

There had been a number of letters since news had reached Kerrera Station of Annie's imprisonment and subsequent illness. At no time did Anne McDougal remonstrate with her daughter about her militant activities. Apart from a brief reference to Annie's health, and a message of thanks to the Beatons for their part in her recovery, she had confined herself to news of events at Kerrera and secondhand accounts of the progress Dougal and Mary were making to Keningo.

Jack sold four of Vicky's pups last month for a surprising sum – about five or six pounds apiece, I believe. Quite out of the blue, he announced that he was going to Adelaide to buy a Merino ram ... not a word about any other intention he might have! Imagine our surprise, therefore, at receiving a telegram saying that he would be staying over in Adelaide to get married, and would we collect his prize ram from Southern Cross? There was no mention of whom he was marrying and we had some agonising moments, I can tell you, worrying about the kind of girl he might find in the big city who was willing to marry at a moment's notice, and come out into the bush without first seeing what it was like! I can't tell you how relieved we were when he came driving up to the house in Mick O'Flannery's wagon, with Jean Parsons beside him. We had shared a cabin with Jean on the ship, and were very good friends, but they never gave a hint they were planning to marry. When I laughingly told Jack how his father and I had worried about the kind of girl he was bringing home with him, he looked quite amazed that we had not known it would be Jean. It had never occurred to him that we were not aware of his plans.

You will be pleased to know that Vicky's remaining pup, whom we have called Al (short for Albert), is turning out to be an excellent sheepdog just as Jack had hoped. Vicky teaches him all he needs to know ... It is lovely to see them together, working the flock. Vicky is getting quite old, and in this climate is unlikely to live much beyond twelve years.

Jack will be heartbroken when she dies, but at least he now has Al to replace her.

Jean Parsons was working in Adelaide as a governess. Although not as well qualified for the job as your 'Aunt' Elizabeth, we thought she might be the person to start a school for the local children, but she and Jack are more concerned for the moment to build their own wee house, and Jean is proving a great help to me in the dairy. She was brought up on a farm in Kent, and makes an excellent farmer's wife.

We have eight Aborigines under the age of thirteen on the station here, and the McNaughtons, our nearest neighbours, have a family of twelve children from nought to fifteen, most of whom can barely read or write. John is very keen to get some kind of a school started soon. We could have done with Mary's help. It is a pity she and Dougal are so far away.

You would not believe how changed John is by the life out here. He seems so much younger and more vigorous, and is making long-term plans for the development of Kerrera into a township.

The school is only one of his projects. Almost as important to him is the establishment of a proper medical service, including a bush hospital. Wouldn't it be marvellous if we could persuade one of your Beaton doctors to take on the job? In the meantime I have to cope with emergencies as best I can using what little nursing skill I acquired on Eisdalsa, and a medical kit which David Beaton gave me before we left. Cuts and bruises I can cope with . . . I have even made a possible attempt at suturing a few really bad cuts. I have been midwife at two successful birthings so far, but when it comes to such conditions as infantile paralysis (there is a great deal of it, particularly among the Aborigines) and other fevers, like malaria for example, I am lost. I have written to David and talked to the doctor at Southern Cross but both assure me that there is very little to be done for such cases . . .

Annie put her letter down on a table already strewn with papers, most of them relating to Rebecca Rosenstein's business affairs.

When she'd received Rebecca's invitation, she had at first wondered if it was wise to return to Overavon, where the house was bound to be a constant reminder of the miserable aftermath of her imprisonment. However, Mrs Rosenstein's offer had been too good to ignore. If it had been a simple matter of a job for herself, acting as legal adviser and personal assistant to the lady, Annie might well have refused, but Rebecca had coupled her proposal with the suggestion that Annie might also use the resources of the Rosensteins' retail empire to assist the women's movement. Annie felt that she owed it to her sisters in the WSPU to accept such generosity.

At the sound of an approaching vehicle, she hurried to the tall library window which overlooked the long drive from the main road and was in time to see the Rosensteins' limousine glide to a halt before the main entrance.

Before Mainwaring had a chance to open the doors, his passengers had alighted and were charging up the stone steps like a couple of schoolboys.

Both Dan Rosenstein and Stuart Beaton looked bronzed from the past few months at sea. Annie's heart missed a beat when Stuart, removing his cap as they approached the door, lifted his glance towards her and for a brief moment their eyes met. She saw him smile and raised her hand in acknowledgement.

Manny Rosenstein, unaware of his brother's arrival, entered the library with a sheaf of documents under his arm, thrust the pile on the table where Annie had been sitting and threw himself into a winged armchair which was placed to one side of the great marble fireplace.

'Now then, Annie,' he declared, 'there are some important matters which I must discuss with you.'

She turned round, startled by his voice.

'Your brother Dan has arrived with Dr Beaton,' she told him. 'I was just watching the servants unloading the car. One might think they were home for good, from the amount of luggage they have brought with them!'

'Before we go to greet them,' Manny interrupted her, brusquely, 'there is something I have to ask you. Can you bear with me for just a moment?' He looked more strained than she had ever seen him.

'If it is about this problem of the shops being vandalised, I believe that I have the answer,' she reassured him.

'No, it's nothing to do with that,' he replied, his voice softening. He came and sat down beside her, taking her hand in such a manner that she was compelled to turn and look at him.

'We have come to rely so much upon your wise counsel these past few weeks,' he said. A little shame-faced, he continued, 'I must confess that in the beginning, when Mother suggested your coming here to work, I wondered if it was a good idea. She was very anxious to ensure that you could not put yourself in a position which would lead to further imprisonment. She hoped that by working quietly in the background, you could do so much more to help the cause . . . she is genuinely interested in improving conditions for working women, you know. Also, she regards your presence here as her way of showing support for the Women's Movement.'

A look of bewilderment swept across Annie's face. She knew all of this . . . what was he really trying to say?

'What I had not realised, although I should have guessed from your wonderful speech that night when we first met, was that you have far more to offer than merely providing my mother with business advice. A few women like you in government, and we would be less likely to get ourselves into the sort of mess we are in today.'

Carried away by the force of his argument, Manny was gripping her hand so tightly that she cried out in pain. Mortified, he relaxed his hold instantly, apologising as he did so.

'Forgive me, dear Annie, if I seem overwrought. I have been wanting to speak to you on this subject for so long, and today I am determined to address you. I have been rehearsing my words all the way from London.'

Annie could think of nothing but the fact that Stuart Beaton was in the house, and must be wondering why she had not hurried to greet him. She was taken off guard by Manny's next question.

'You are happy here at Overavon, are you not?'

'But of course I am happy,' she replied. 'No one could be more welcoming and kind than your mother, and I find my work on behalf of the company both absorbing and satisfying.'

'Would you be prepared to make this your home permanently?' His gaze was so intent that she was forced to look away.

'I . . . I don't understand,' she murmured. For such an eminent politician he seemed inordinately tongue-tied.

'I am asking you to marry me and become the mistress of Overavon,' he said at last. 'You could help me with my political work, and maybe when the time is right, we will be able to find you a parliamentary seat for yourself. Think of that . . . Annie Rosenstein, the first female Member of Parliament!'

Annie was stunned. No such idea would ever have occurred to her. Marriage to anyone other than Stuart Beaton was unthinkable . . . and it didn't seem possible that he would ever ask her. When at last she replied, she sounded far more in charge of her emotions than she felt. Her whole body seemed to be responding involuntarily to this unexpected proposal; her face was flushed, her heart pounded and her palms were sweating.

'I am very conscious of the honour that you do me in making such a proposal,' she began, fumbling for the right words, 'but I must confess, Mr Rosenstein, that you have taken me completely by surprise.'

'Don't give me your answer right away,' he protested, hating her formal use of his name, and fearing that if she did give an answer immediately it would be the wrong one. 'Take all the time you need, but please understand that I love you deeply, and have done so since that first encounter at the Central Hall.'

'I will think about it,' promised Annie.

He lifted her hand once again and this time pressed it to his lips.

A light tap upon the library door forestalled any further

conversation. A footman entered, announcing starchily that Mrs Rosenstein requested the pleasure of their company at afternoon tea in the Long Gallery.

Annie excused herself, feeling the need for a few moments alone to recover from the shock of his proposal, so Emmanuel Rosenstein went alone to greet his brother and his friend.

When Emmanuel joined his mother however, he was relieved to find that Dan and Stuart had already gone to their rooms to unpack.

'Well?' she demanded the moment he sat down. 'Have you asked her yet?'

'I beg your pardon?' Manny flushed with embarrassment.

'Oh, come now, Manny, don't tell me you have put it off again!'

'If you must know,' he replied irritably, 'yes, I have just asked Miss McGillivray for her hand in marriage.'

'And?' Rebecca demanded.

'She has asked to be given time to consider the proposal.'

'Of course she has,' retorted his mother. 'No young woman of any breeding is going to give an immediate reply, unless it is *no!*'

Conversation at dinner was dominated by the recent experiences of the two officers in the South Atlantic. Manny, always anxious to get his military information at first hand, questioned his brother at length during the soup and the entrée. By the time that strawberries and cream had given place to the cheese board, the subject of *Hampshire*'s recall to home waters after only six months of her three-year posting had been thoroughly analysed. It was a clear indication of the seriousness of the situation in Europe.

Dan related how, when their ship had arrived in the Solent on 1 August, she went almost unnoticed amidst the vessels assembled for the annual Review of the Fleet.

'It was quite amazing,' he recalled. 'There were we, slipping quietly into our berth in Portsmouth Dock, with our crew engaged in the most rapid preparations for an imminent departure, while all around us the sirens were sounding on battleships dressed overall for a public holiday! As we loaded the magazine with shells, it was to dance music blaring forth from a dozen deck parties. The people were lined up along the promenade . . . the deckchairs must have been three deep . . . and as they munched their sandwiches, we winched aboard six additional machine-guns.'

'I don't believe too many of those people watching were fooled, you know,' said Stuart, thoughtfully. 'There is no doubt that the real intention was to impress our enemies with the strength of our naval forces.'

'It certainly impressed me,' laughed Daniel, excitedly. 'It was a stirring sight to see, all those ships . . . every one ready at a moment's notice to break out her battle flags.'

Daniel, who had monopolised the discussion for most of the meal, now turned to Manny. 'What's going on, Big Brother?' he demanded as soon as the servants had cleared all but the port, and left the scene. 'We passed three old fifteen thousand-ton merchantmen as we sailed down the Solent. I'll swear they were swinging 4.7-inch guns aboard one of them. Are we that short of proper naval vessels?'

'You know better than to ask me anything like that,' warned Emmanuel

'That's just his way of saying he doesn't know,' laughed Annie. The excellent meal and a glass or two of fine Burgundy had helped her to regain her composure, following Emmanuel's bombshell of the afternoon. She took up the discussion with her customary ease. 'From what I hear, one Department of State has absolutely no notion what any of the others are thinking about. Perhaps we should be glad that the War Office is actually doing *something* for a change!'

Stuart, who had been very quiet all evening, was surprised at Annie's forthrightness. He knew it was stupid of him to expect her to be as dependent upon himself as she had been when they were last in this house together, but he could not help regretting, just a little, her new found self-assurance. He was pleased that she was well again, of course, but he had so much enjoyed their previous intimacy.

Her promised correspondence from Eisdalsa had consisted of short and rather stilted notes at first, but recently she had filled pages with amusing details about happenings on the islands and the activities of his family. He had begun to look forward to receiving her letters, scanning the postbag anxiously whenever one of the Navy's supply vessels managed to catch up with the *Hampshire*.

He had been surprised and delighted to learn from Mainwaring that Annie had returned to Overavon, anticipating their meeting with mounting excitement all the way from the station. When she failed to appear to greet him, he had been hugely disappointed and wondered if she for some reason objected to his visit. While he had been welcomed royally by Mrs Rosenstein and her household, and even Emmanuel had appeared pleased to see him, Annie had scarcely exchanged a word with him all evening.

'What are you finding to amuse yourself with these days, Annie?' he asked now, determined to get her to acknowledge his presence at the table. 'The WSPU seems to have become dormant of late.'

Was he genuinely interested, Annie wondered, or simply looking for a way of baiting her? Having been obliged to miss Stuart's arrival while Manny held her attention in the library, she had felt uncomfortable about making the first approach.

'Mrs Rosenstein was kind enough to offer me a position as her legal adviser,' Annie explained, thankful that he had at last given her the opening she had been waiting for. 'I returned to Overavon two weeks ago.'

'And a most excellent job she is making of it,' Rebecca emphasised.

Unable to put ministerial matters out of his mind for any length of time, Manny suddenly broke in. 'That reminds me of something I intended to ask you earlier, Annie,' he said. 'When women are recruited into munitions factories, as they most assuredly will be, there are going to be numerous problems of welfare and social importance which do not normally concern employers of male labour. Do you think you could draft a list of points to be raised in this connection? One likes to be prepared.'

Annie had had occasion to visit a number of the Rosensteins' clothing factories since she had taken up the task of legal adviser to the company. She had produced several reports exposing inadequate facilities, unsafe practices, and instances of appalling abuse in some of the workshops. Rebecca Rosenstein, while sympathetic to Annie's pleas for better working conditions for the mainly female employees, was at heart a hard-headed business-woman. She had been unwilling to spend money to improve matters. Sensing that she was about to be criticised on this score, she attacked her son, quite sharply.

'How often do I have to tell you, Manny,' she protested at her son's request, 'Annie is not your private secretary, she is my legal adviser!'

'I think I understand what the minister requires, Mrs Rosenstein,' Annie interrupted, quietly. 'I can acquire much of the information he wants from the reports which I have already compiled. It will be a small task to list the essential requirements for women employed in factory work.' She turned to Manny. 'There is of course a difference between work in a clothing factory and employment in an establishment making armaments . . . perhaps even explosives. I will need access to information relating to the types of chemicals to be handled.'

Manny looked a trifle nonplussed. He had hardly expected such a detailed response to his request.

'I had in mind washing facilities, protective clothing . . . that sort of thing,' he muttered. 'However, should there be any requirement for you to know what materials are to be handled, I will see to it that you receive the relevant information.'

He rose to leave. He kissed his mother lightly on the forehead, and shook hands with Stuart and Daniel.

'Enjoy your leave,' he told them. 'It may be a while before you get another!' His words were heavy with meaning. No one was under any illusions now. War was inevitable . . . it could come any day.

Emmanuel approached Annie, who looked up at him and smiled. 'I shall be looking forward to hearing from you,' he said, blandly.

'Goodbye, Manny,' she replied, and offered her hand to be kissed for the second time that day.

Stuart Beaton, witnessing their leavetaking, felt oddly discomfited by what he saw.

Once Manny was out of the way, Stuart was pleased to find Annie treating him in much the same friendly way as she had done in the past, before her illness had placed a barrier of professional etiquette between them. During the day she was absorbed in her duties, but in the evenings the three young people were free to walk, drive out into the country, and visit some of the charming little villages which nestled among the chalk downlands.

On the first Monday in August, Daniel decided to go riding on the downs overlooking the Thames Valley. Stuart, whose experience of horses was restricted to riding his father's carriage ponies bareback around the farm at Tigh na Broch, retired to the library to lose himself amongst the Rosensteins' collection of first editions of nineteenth-century writers.

At the enormous library table, Annie busied herself with writing the report which Manny had requested. Stuart was perched on a tall set of library steps, in one of the dark recesses at the back of the room. Glancing up from time to time, he was comforted by her presence. It seemed so natural for them to be here together, each warmed by the other's proximity. This was much the same as when they had all been children together at Tigh na Broch. As the only girl in the Beaton household, his sister Margaret had been encouraged to invite her schoolfriends to their home, and in particular Wee Annie McGillivray. He recalled long wet summer afternoons when they had all gathered in his brother Ian's bedroom, playing games to entertain the invalid, reading books and listening to Margaret's endless tales of magic and adventure.

He glanced across the room. Annie's face was suddenly illuminated by a shaft of sunlight which had filtered through the great Gothic window. Even after all this time she was still painfully thin, but her beautifully sculptured features, emphasised at this moment by the deep shadows surrounding her eyes and mouth, had a nobility about them. She would never regain the bloom of youth, but she had become a stunningly attractive woman.

She looked up, saw him gazing at her, and smiled. Instantly there was a radiance about her which had been absent seconds before. His heart leapt.

Like Daniel, Stuart was only too aware of the imminence of the disaster which was about to alter all their lives. He also craved something tangible to hold on to, something to give a meaning to the future, whatever it might bring. Could Annie be the anchor he was looking for?

Suddenly he slapped together the covers of the book he was examining. The noise startled Annie and she looked up, inquiringly.

'It's a beautiful day,' he said, 'far too good to be stuck indoors. Why don't we ask for a picnic lunch and drive up into the hills? They tell me there is a white horse somewhere near here, carved in the turf.'

'At Uffington,' she enlightened him. 'I went there earlier this year. It is certainly worth seeing. Its origins must be as ancient as Stonehenge, so they say.' He felt once again an unreasonable twinge of jealousy. Who had she gone with, he wondered. Emmanuel? almost certainly. He thrust the unsettling thought from him.

'You may borrow my little Morris motor, if you like?' she continued. 'But I'm afraid you will have to go alone. I must finish this report for Manny before tomorrow.'

'Oh, come on,' he insisted, 'it will do you good . . . you spend far too much time in this stuffy old room. Let's say it's doctor's orders!'

The offer was irresistible. It was a beautiful day and Stuart's leave would not last for ever. Anyway, had she not been longing for him to make just such a suggestion, all week?

'Oh, very well,' she conceded, trying to sound casual about it. She laid down her pen and reached for the bell.

Annie had accustomed herself very quickly to this new lifestyle, Stuart reflected. How could an impecunious naval surgeon hope to compete with the owner of Overavon?

Quickly he thrust the thought from his mind. After all, he had only seen the fellow kiss her hand . . . something he probably did to every woman he met!

* * *

They left the Bath road at Hungerford and drove north towards Wantage. It was only when Annie turned off the main road on to a steeply sloping, unmade track, that the little tourer began to protest.

The car, a small saloon recently introduced by Morris Motors of Oxford, had been provided by Rebecca, to allow Annie to travel conveniently between the various company establishments.

Stuart had made no suggestion that he should drive, and Annie had appreciated that. Most men, when offered a lift in her car, seemed to assume immediately that they would take the wheel, even without a by-your-leave. Stuart seemed perfectly content to be a passenger, and indicated in no uncertain terms his admiration for her driving ability. When the car came to a sudden halt, its narrow tyres caught in a sun-baked rut formed from winter mud, Annie managed to slam on the hand-brake before the vehicle started to slide backwards down the hill.

Since the engine had stalled, it was necessary to secure the vehicle properly before they could attempt to get her going again. Stuart leapt out and found a sizeable flinty rock, which he thrust under the rear wheel. They both remained silent for a few moments, trying to get their breath back.

'The slope flattens out a short way ahead,' he observed, having walked a few yards beyond the bonnet so that he might peer around the corner of the lane. 'I'll give her a swing on the handle to get her started. If you can just manage to get her into first gear, and let the clutch in very gently, you might make it to the plateau without my weight. I'd do it myself, but I think it will require a shove from behind to get you moving.'

She did as he instructed, concentrating hard upon getting the clutch and accelerator to synchronise as she had been taught. Once she felt the tyres grip, however, she was so anxious not to lose the advantage that she opened the accelerator with a jerk. The car shot forward under the joint impetus of Stuart's muscle and her own engine.

Taken completely by surprise at this sudden movement, Surgeon Commander Stuart Beaton, R.N., fell flat on his face in the roadway. There he lay, stunned, while Annie pulled around the corner and brought the Morris to rest on a level, grassy patch of ground to one side of the lane. There she sat, hands resting lightly on the wheel, while she allowed the breeze to restore her overheated face to normal. It was a few minutes before she realised that Stuart was not coming to join her. Switching off the engine once more, she jumped down on to the road and ran back to where she had left him.

He lay just where he had fallen, arms spread above his head, having held on to the car until the last possible moment.

Thinking he must be unconscious at the very least, Annie ran to him with a terrified cry, dropped on to her knees in the dust, and tried to turn his head so that she could see his face. She wiped the dirt from around his mouth and placed her cheek close to his lips to see if she could detect his breathing.

'Oh, my darling,' she cried in her distress, 'please wake up . . . please don't die!'

'It's a good job I don't have a cracked vertebra,' he murmured, opening one eye, which glinted wickedly. 'That movement would have finished me off nicely!'

'I thought you were dead!' she declared, sitting back on her heels. 'You were just pretending!' she added in a tone of disgust.

'Are you disappointed?' he asked, and sat up gingerly to finger a large white bump which was developing rapidly on his forehead.

'It would probably be best to wash that with some of the champagne we have in the picnic basket,' she suggested, starchily, annoyed with herself for her emotional outburst.

He looked up at her, half ashamed at having teased her. 'I really was stunned for a few moments,' he protested. Then, seeing again that worried look, hastened to reassure her. 'If you will give me a hand, I think I can manage to stand up now.'

Leaning on her willing shoulder, maybe just a little too heavily, he managed to reach the car, sat down on the grass verge and leant back against the rear wheel with his eyes closed.

She studied him anxiously for a few moments. The swelling was really quite alarming. She reached for the wine, which was packed in the bottom of the picnic hamper to keep it cool, and with a proficiency which might have surprised her mother and her friends on Eisdalsa, she uncorked the bottle with a minimum of spillage, catching the overflow on a napkin and using this to dab at his forehead. Dissatisfied with the result, she wet the cloth again, more thoroughly this time, and applied it to the swelling.

'Hey, don't use too much,' protested the invalid, grabbing a glass. 'It will do more good inside than out!'

Convinced at last that he was going to live Annie sat down beside Stuart on the grass and held out her glass to be filled. The chilled wine washed the dust from their throats and the cares from their minds. Annie found that the champagne gave her a warm sensation in her stomach and a tingle in her spine. Most of all she could feel herself relaxing. After a few moments she began to giggle.

'You weren't really hurt badly at all, were you?' she demanded, playfully pummelling him. Her balled fist caught a bruised spot on his rib cage and he winced. Instantly she was all contrition.

'Oh, Stuart, I'm so sorry. Did I hurt you?'

She put down her glass and knelt over him, anxious to know what harm she had done.

He caught her in his arms and held her to him.

'No, Annie,' he murmured, 'you could never hurt me.' He lifted her chin so that he could study her face, and was startled to see tears glistening in her eyes. Gently, he wiped them away with his kisses. His lips brushed hers, and she responded, opening up to expose a tip of pink tongue between pearl-white teeth. He kissed her lingeringly, his fingers wandering over her breasts, firm beneath the thin stuff of her blouse. Finally, unable to breathe, she forced him away. They stared at each other for what seemed like an eternity.

'Oh, Annie,' he murmured, 'what a fool I've been. All those years when we were growing up . . . I deliberately ignored you. The other fellows used to make jokes about you being my girlfriend. You know the sort of thing.'

She placed her fingers over his lips to silence him. He caught her hand and held it.

'I suppose because you were there so much of the time,' he continued, 'I looked on you as another sister.' He grinned, sheepishly. 'You don't seem anything like a sister to me now!'

She smiled, hesitating to speak lest the spell be broken.

He kissed her again, a long hard kiss, his tongue seeking and finding hers. When both were gasping for breath, he released her and ran his fingers over her cheek and across her brow, stroking the locks of hair which had come adrift.

'I have wasted so much time . . .' Stuart would have continued with his self-recriminations had she not got to her feet, offering her hand to help him up also.

Annie repacked the picnic basket. Neither of them seemed interested in eating anything.

'If we are to see this White Horse,' she decided, 'we had better be getting along.'

Stuart looked a trifle crestfallen. Just at this moment he had other things in mind than viewing ancient monuments.

She took his hesitation for an indication that he was still suffering from his fall. 'Maybe you would rather we went straight home? Are you still feeling unwell?' she asked solicitously.

'No, I'm fine,' he assured her. He cranked the car, and climbed back into the passenger seat.

It was dusk by the time the little Morris headed back down White Horse Hill to regain the road for Ashbury. Here they turned back towards Lambourne where, because they had eaten nothing all day, Annie pulled into the forecourt of a country inn.

In the landlord's tiny 'snug' they finished their meal of rare steak and fresh vegetables, and sat on over the remains of a bottle of Burgundy. Before long, the public bar began to fill up with people, and for the first time that day, Stuart and Annie remembered that this was a Bank Holiday.

'It's been a wonderful day,' Annie sighed, reaching across the table for his hand.

'I found the horse something of a disappointment,' he replied, eyes twinkling.

'Oh, I don't know. I thought he was rather nice . . . symbolic rather than nautralistic,' Annie responded.

'I must say, it didn't look much like a horse to me,' protested Stuart.

'It was quite clear from the road,' she replied seriously, and then, seeing his grin, slapped him playfully. 'You're teasing,' she cried. He caught her hand before she could strike him again and, turning it palm up, kissed it.

'It's a Palaeolithic horse,' she explained seriously. 'It must have been how the cave men saw them.'

'One wonders how Palaeolithic Man saw Palaeolithic Woman,' he mused. 'Equally disjointedly, no doubt!' He paused for a moment, then, still smiling, concluded: 'I think I prefer a nice complete twentieth-century woman, especially if she looks like you!'

The noise from the bar next door was increasing. People seemed to be agitated about something. Voices were raised, not in anger exactly but rather excitement . . . or panic perhaps?'

The hatch flew up and the landlord poked his head through.

'Sorry, sir, I hope you weren't waiting to be served?' he apologised. 'There's such a crowd in the public, you'd think they were celebrating the Relief of Mafeking rather than the declaration of war!'

'What's that you say?' demanded Stuart.

'Old Bill Penny, the village bobby, came down from the station house just half an hour ago with the news. We've declared war on Germany, along with France and Belgium.'

Stuart felt for his wallet. 'I must settle up, Landlord,' he declared. To Annie he said, 'I'm sorry, my dear, but we will have to get back to Overavon right away. There will probably be a telegram recalling us to the ship.'

It was quite dark by the time they set off. Stuart drove by the light of the acetylene headlights which Annie had never had occasion to use before. The one advantage of travelling by night was that the roads were relatively empty, until they joined the London to Bath highway. Here they were caught up with a convoy of army wagons moving off Salisbury Plain, presumably en route for the Channel ports.

It was with considerable relief that they were at last able to turn off the main road just before Newbury, and make their way over the escarpment, south towards Overavon.

Above the house, Stuart pulled in to the side of the road and switched off the engine. He turned towards her, seeking the outline of her face in the darkness.

'There may be no time to speak again, after we go in,' he said, hands resting on the steering wheel. 'God knows when we will see each other again, and there is something that I have to know before I leave.'

'What is it?' she asked.

'What is your relationship with Manny Rosenstein?' He barked the question, half afraid to hear the answer.

The darkness hid her astonishment.

'I don't understand,' she said, her voice trembling. 'What do you mean?'

'Is there anything between you?'

'Manny was very good to me after my imprisonment . . . partly, I suspect, because of the political advantage which he gained from our association.' She hesitated then added, 'No, that is unpardonable. He does not deserve such an uncharitable thought.'

'He seems to think he has some prior claim upon you,' observed Stuart, harking back to his arrival at Overavon when Manny had monopolised all of Annie's time.

'He uses me as a sounding board,' she explained. 'Seems to think that I have the ears of the women's movement. It's quite amusing, really, because I have had no personal contact with the Pankhursts since my release from Holloway.'

'So what exactly is your position in the household?' demanded Stuart.

'I am employed by Mrs Rosenstein, and answerable only to her. Sometimes I oblige Manny with a little legal advice also, but my responsibility is to the Rosenstein business . . . that's all.'

'I had been led to believe that there was more between you,' he told her, relief causing him to hammer out the words.

'Who could have given you such an idea?' she cried. Had he some inkling of her conversation with Manny on the day that he and Dan had arrived at Overavon? She had given very little consideration to Manny's proposal, putting aside her decision while Stuart's close proximity confused the issue. After today, however, there was no question what her reply to Emmanuel must be.

'Nothing has been said outright,' he told her, 'but both Mrs Rosenstein and Dan have hinted that you might be the next mistress of Overavon.' He paused, glad that the darkness hid his face.

'Manny *has* asked me to marry him,' she confessed. Even in the dim light, she could sense the anxiety in his eyes.

'What did you say to him?'

'I told him that I would give his proposal my earnest consideration,' she said, looking straight into the blur which was his face.

'You could do a lot worse.' Stuart's words were painfully strained.

'What would a little country bumpkin like myself be doing as a mistress of a great place like this?' She waved one arm in the direction of the house, whose windows were ablaze with light.

There was a long silence.

'Annie, you will marry me, won't you?' pleaded Stuart, so softly that she was uncertain whether the words were his or merely her own thoughts.

Could this really be happening to her . . . after all these years? She leant towards him, allowing her fingers to trace the contours of his face.

'Oh, Stuart,' she whispered, 'of course I will.'

They kissed, gently.

'And so as to scotch all these silly rumours,' she continued suddenly, 'we'll go down and announce it, right away.'

He caught her in his arms then, covering her face and neck with his kisses. After a time, he jumped down from the car, swung the handle to start the engine, and climbed back in beside Annie. He rested one arm along the back of her seat so that she could snuggle into his shoulder, and steered with his free hand. Slowly, they drove down the hill towards the entrance to Overavon Park.

* * *

David Beaton pushed open the swing door and crossed the tiled entrance hall with barely a glance at the female receptionist behind the glass panel. Silently she ticked another name off her list. They were nearly all there . . . only Dr Angus Beaton to come. She had watched the Mull ferry steam into the harbour ten minutes ago. He would soon be arriving.

The Superintendent's office, which, other than the wards, was the only room in the hospital large enough to accommodate more than a couple of people, was already crammed.

David took his place at the back of the room and absent-mindedly filled his pipe. From behind the desk, Michael Brown cleared his throat unnecessarily loudly, and David glanced up to see his son-in-law shaking his head. He placed the unlit pipe in his mouth, indicating that he was not actually smoking it. Michael smiled, then turned to answer a question put by one of the other doctors.

Angus Beaton, limping slightly after the long climb up from the harbour, slumped down on the seat beside his brother and took out a large pocket handkerchief.

'My goodness,' he declared, mopping his brow, 'had I thought about it, I would have taken a cab up the hill. There was a good strong breeze aboard the boat, and it seemed an ideal day for a walk. It was only when I started up the road that I realised just how hot it really was.'

David observed his brother intently. At sixty-eight he was still a fine figure of a man. Carrying no spare weight at all, Angus was remarkably active for one of his age. Nevertheless, David thought, he's too old for this lark. We'll have to find him something to do which doesn't require too much travelling about!

Michael rapped the table in order to gain their attention.

'Gentlemen, I have called you together to see how we can co-ordinate our activities in the light of yesterday's devastating announcement. As you will appreciate, other than the occasional casualty at sea, we are unlikely to be directly involved in the coming conflict. There will, however, be problems arising from the departure of some of our younger colleagues for the front.

'Drs MacKinley and Fergusson are reservists, and are awaiting a call to join their regiments. Their departure will leave two parishes completely without medical cover, and the hospital will be deprived of Dr MacKinley's surgical specialism.'

There was a general murmuring as the local practitioners began to discuss among themselves the problems arising from this announcement.

'I have received this communication from the Admiralty,' Michael continued, once the noise had died down. He took up a heavily embossed piece of notepaper and read: 'There being no naval hospital within reasonable reach of the Western Islands, it has been decided to make use of the civilian facilities provided at Fort William and Oban for dealing with any casualties arising from enemy attack at sea in those areas. All naval personnel receiving initial treatment in civilian hospitals will be transferred to naval establishments as soon as possible. It is not considered that casualty figures will be high enough to warrant the provision of extra staffing for the hospitals concerned. Additional supplies of dressings and drugs will be despatched forthwith.'

There was a buzz of excitement amongst the doctors. The younger ones, already committed to military service, observed the proceedings with an air of condescension. They could just imagine these old buffers lavishing all their attentions on the odd seaman with a gashed hand or an appendicitis. They themselves were going to the front . . . to the real fighting . . . and they couldn't wait to get into uniform.

Hugh Beaton raised his hand to speak.

'Mr Chairman,' he began, 'many of us have widespread parishes to cover, which means that a deal of time has to be taken up in travelling. It seems to me that the problem of limited staffing might be relieved somewhat by establishing collection points for patients . . . village surgeries, as it were, to avoid doctors and nurses having to travel great distances from house to house. My own local midwife has already suggested that she use her spare bedroom as a lying-in hospital for the district, eliminating the inevitable night-calls out into the wilds.' There were general murmurs of approval. 'It will, of course, take a certain amount of capital to get such arrangements established. Is there any indication of an additional source of funds to be called upon during the hostilities?'

'Other than the supply of materials, as indicated by the Admiralty letter, no,' was Michael's answer. 'That is not to say,' he added hastily, 'that we may not approach the authorities with some concrete proposals. If you are all in favour of Dr Beaton's suggestion, I will put it to the County Council immediately.'

The discussion meandered on at a leisurely pace for the reminder of the afternoon. Angus found himself nodding off in the hot August sunshine, which was now penetrating the single window with relentless accuracy.

The weary assembly was suddenly alerted by the arrival, bells clanging, of the new motorised ambulance, of which the town was justly proud. There was a scuffling in the corridor outside, and the rapid clack-clacking of nurses' heels on the polished linoleum warned them all that this was more than a routine emergency. Michael hurried to the door with David close behind him.

Sister had already assembled four trolleys and it was on to these that the mangled bodies were being loaded with extreme care.

'What happened?' Michael demanded, moving rapidly from one cot to the next, trying to ascertain which were the most urgent cases.

The ambulance driver, having unloaded his passengers, had come into the vestibule to give his report.

'It was a fishing boat,' he told them. They say she hit a mine outside Tobermory Bay. The Oban lifeboat brought them in . . . these four were thrown clear by the explosion. There was no sign of the other two crew members.'

David, examining the tourniquet on a partially severed leg, signalled to the orderly to wheel the man away to the theatre. 'This looks like an amputation,' he told Michael. 'I'll take it, while you attend to those burns.' He indicated two of the men whose faces were nothing more than an unrecognisable pulp of charred skin and blood.

Michael nodded his agreement, and catching sight of his young registrar, Dr MacKinley, called him over. The young man was looking pretty sick; his estimation of what life was going to be like in the front-line had taken a decided down-turn in the last few minutes.

'See what you can do for the fracture case, Neil,' Michael ordered. 'If you need any help, I'm sure that Dr Angus will lend a hand.' Leaving the younger man to make his own arrangements for his patient, Michael followed his burned casualties to the ward.

Sister had already assembled a team of nurses, two of whom were no more than eighteen years of age.

'Has either of you ever seen a severely burned patient?' she demanded, sharply.

'No, Sister,' said Mairi Ramsay, her eyes wide with fear.

'Well, just remember, no matter how unpleasant you find his looks, your patient is hurting much more than you are!' Then, a little more gently, she added: 'Just get on and do exactly what I say. You will soon find that you get used to the sight.'

Mairi quickly discovered that what Sister had said was true. As she swabbed away the destroyed tissues with extreme care, she began to see only the wound, and not the man beneath. What she would never forget, however, until the day that she died, was the sweet cloying scent which was a mixture of fuel oil and roasted flesh.

Annabel lifted her cup to her lips, sipped the refreshing beverage, and then abruptly set down cup and saucer on Margaret's polished table.

'That's the third vessel to drop anchor in the bay since noon,' she observed as the grey-painted sloop came up to its mooring and began to swing with the tide.

'My goodness,' laughed Margaret, 'with all these sailors in town, the good burghers of Oban will be having to lock up their daughters! I wonder if Heather is aware of what she is missing?'

Annabel watched a jollyboat lowered, crowded with matelots. 'Poor boys,' she murmured, 'they will not find much to entertain them.'

'That's a point,' said Margaret, thoughtfully. 'Other than the bars, there really is nowhere in the town for so many young men to go to in their free time.'

'Stuart says that the living conditions aboard any vessel smaller than a destroyer are pretty terrible,' observed Annabel. 'When they sling their hammocks there is not an inch of space between the men. Washing facilities are very cramped, and they have the greatest difficulty keeping themselves and their uniforms clean.'

'If there is going to be a permanent naval force operating in these waters,' said Margaret, 'then the problem will last for as long as the hostilities continue.'

Annabel could see that her daughter was busy hatching some plan. 'Well,' she demanded, 'what have you in mind?'

'What is needed is some kind of club house. A place where the men can have a meal and a cup of tea . . . not all of them drink alcohol,' she protested, when Annabel raised her eyebrows. 'There should be a reading room, a quiet place where they can write their letters home . . . baths and showers for those from the smaller ships who don't have those facilities . . . and somewhere where they can get their laundry attended to.'

'It would take a great deal of money to set up.' Annabel felt that, noble as the idea seemed, the voice of reason must prevail.

'We could raise it by public subscription,' Margaret suggested. 'You remember how we used to hold soirées and ceilidhs at Eisdalsa to raise money for the Technical Institute and for Father's little isolation hospital? Well, what is to stop us from doing the same thing here? The fund-raising itself will provide entertainment for the sailors as well. No one ever said that one had to be miserable all the time, just because the country is at war!'

'Then there is the question of suitable premises.' Annabel felt she was being the Devil's advocate, but in fact her doubts served only to strengthen her daughter's resolve.

'I have already thought about that,' Margaret assured her. 'There are two disused churches in the town – and St Barnabas's has a superb hall beside it. We could talk to the Church Commissioners, see if they will let us use the buildings.'

After a long period of fragmentation, following the Disruption of 1843, a number of smaller nonconformist congregations had in recent years joined together to become the United Reformed Church of Scotland, leaving empty several older church buildings such as St Barnabas's. There was an added bonus. The building in question was close to the north pier, and very convenient for the men coming ashore from vessels moored in the bay.

'I believe that Minister McCulloch at Eisdalsa might be able to put us in touch with the right people,' Annabel contributed, warming to Margaret's idea. 'If we can gather some volunteers from amongst our friends, we could start a canteen and then work up to the other refinements you mentioned.'

The two women sat long into the evening making lists. There were lists of people who might volunteer their services, and people who would almost certainly contribute to the funds. They made lists of furniture and equipment required to set up the canteen and suggestions of whom to approach to supply these items. When David eventually arrived to drive Annabel home to Connel, the Sailors' Rest and Recreation Centre for Oban had been planned, if not already established.

Chapter 14

This was not the first visit that Eddie Makepeace had made to Keningo. He had come once or twice during McKenzie's managership. Then he had been unimpressed by what he had found. In fact, when Doug McGillivray had turned up in Perth nearly eighteen months ago, full of enthusiasm and eager to get started, Eddie had been tempted to send him straight back home . . . particularly since he had a wife and kids with him.

We all have to live, he had excused himself at the time, and if I don't appoint a manager for the mine, I can kiss my job goodbye.

He had allowed McGillivray to go off into the bush without knowing what the conditions there would be like. A year-end report showing that, despite all, the Keningo mine had managed to equal the previous year's output, did nothing to lessen Makepeace's apprehension at facing the new manager for the first time since his installation.

The supply truck from Kalgoorlie had pulled up inside the gates just as the hooter was sounding for the end of the day's work. Men began to emerge from all corners of the enclosure.

They were a strange mixture of white men and Aborigines, but they had one thing in common: although they showed every appearance of having done a hard day's work at the rock-face, all seemed cheerful. Makepeace was struck by the comparison with his previous visits when there had been an atmosphere of resentment and distrust amongst the workforce.

'Howareyer, mate?' the foreman, Dai Jones, greeted the truck driver. Then, looking beyond the driver and recognising the figure of Edward Makepeace, he straightened up deferentially.

'G'day, Mr Makepeace,' he said, hurriedly. 'You'll be wantin' to see Mr McGillivray, I reckon. I think you'll find him over in the winding shed.'

'Thank you, Jones,' Makepeace replied, swinging himself down from the cab and grasping the Welshman's outstretched hand.

He turned to dismiss the driver with a curt nod and a word of warning. 'I shall be ready to drive back to Kal' at noon tomorrow and not a moment later. See you moderate your celebrations accordingly.'

The driver, who was only too familiar with Doug McGillivray's ban on mid-week drinking, doffed his cap elaborately and replied sarcastically, 'Chance would be a fine thing, I'm thinking yer worship!'

Whistling a familiar Irish ditty, he started the engine and backed his vehicle out through the gates of the compound. Moving in fits and starts across the uneven surface, he turned his lorry towards the village street and Walt Wilson's store. Despite the rules, he reckoned he might find a bottle of something cool waiting for him there!

Eddie found Doug McGillivray supervising repairs to the winding gear. It was clear that the manager was no idle bystander in the work. His hands and forearms were smothered in thick black grease.

'G'day, Mr McGillivray,' Makepeace shouted above the noise of the machinery. Doug turned to see a dark figure silhouetted against the sky. For a moment he did not recognise the stranger. He stood up and, wiping his fingers, tossed the rag of cotton waste to his Aboriginal assistant before shaking the outstretched hand.

'Just a routine visit,' the agent explained, seeing the expression of curiosity on Dougal's face. He steered the Scotsman away from the winding shed and as they walked together towards the office, they exchanged the usual pleasantries. It was only when he had satisfied himself that there was no one to overhear their conversation that Makepeace told Doug the purpose of his visit.

'You sent some samples for assay a month or so ago,' he began, settling himself comfortably at McGillivray's desk.

'Yes, I did,' Doug agreed. 'The initial analysis seemed too good to be true, so I sent samples to Head Office. Do you have the results with you?'

'Oh yes, I have the results . . . that's why I'm here.'

A trifle dramatically, he withdrew from an inside pocket a thick white package and thrust it across the desk. He watched Doug tear open the envelope and begin to study the summary sheet before continuing, 'With things shaping up so badly in Europe, gold reserves are going to be of major importance. I have been sent to emphasise that what you do here at Keningo in the next few months will directly affect Australia's ability to take part in this war when the time comes. The owners are under pressure to increase output of gold from all their mines but this new seam at Keningo promises to be of such importance that they wish to give its exploitation absolute priority. Now then,' he leaned forward, grabbing the arms of the old Windsor chair, 'what steps have you taken to get it under production?'

'As yet, none,' Doug replied, 'other than to take those samples and reseal the gallery. Most of our output since January has come from the seam that Jones uncovered before my arrival, last April. That exposure has just about been worked out. I had planned to make a start on the new seam as soon as the assay was confirmed.'

Makepeace stood up and went to the window. Silently he studied the yard for a few minutes. The headframe straddling the open mine shaft towered above the rest of the plant. On his previous visit this enormous steel structure had been red with rust and in need of extensive maintenance. Today it was freshly painted and seemed to be in good repair. There was an air of order and efficiency about the whole place. New sheets of corrugated iron, coated in red iron oxide paint, now roofed the crushing and washing sheds, both of which had been in a derelict condition on his last visit. What had been untidy heaps of ore haphazardly dumped to await treatment, were now confined to an orderly row of bunkers at one side of the compound, while the sludge – the liquid material resulting from the treatment of crushed ore – waited in tail pools for transportation to the processing plant where the gold would finally be separated out.

Festoons of electric cable, strung from tall poles and crossing the yard in all directions, took Makepeace by surprise.

'Electricity?' he queried. This was a quite unexpected innovation.

'Not as expensive as it might seem,' Doug assured him, hastily. He had reported his intention to electrify the mine but had gone ahead without receiving confirmation from Perth. 'My son Hamish did the work at very little cost to the company.' Noting Makepeace's dubious expression, he hastened to add, 'The boy completed his apprenticeship as an electrician before we left Scotland. I can assure you that the improved lighting below ground has reduced the number of accidents both to men and equipment, as well as speeding up the work.'

As Makepeace resumed his seat, Doug continued, 'There could be an interesting additional benefit. I have been looking into electrolytic methods of extracting precious metals. I believe that with a small additional outlay we could set up a system to get the maximum amount of gold and in addition silver and some of the rare metals which might be valuable for munitions manufacture . . .'

Makepeace remembered the conversation they had had in Perth a year ago and had to concede that the Scottish engineer had more than fulfilled his promise on that day. If he was new to gold-mining then, he had certainly mastered every aspect of the work since.

'I think I must explain,' he admitted, 'that I came here today wondering if you were the right man to take on this fresh phase of production. My bosses were concerned to know whether you were capable of exploiting the new find to the full. You will understand that their interest is not merely patriotic? The investors are baying at their heels for increased profits.'

'Gold-mining shareholders are no different from those in the slate industry,' Doug assured him, laughing.

'Anyway,' Makepeace continued, 'now that I have seen what is happening here, I cannot think of any man in the company's employ who could have done a better job with Keningo. I am convinced that, given greater investment, you can make this the most productive mine in West Australia!'

Doug went to a cabinet and extracted a set of documents and a roll of drawings. 'I've already compiled a report on the new extraction system that I want to install,' he said, stretching the first of the plans across the top of the desk. 'See . . . there is room for another building here, alongside the generator housing. That will avoid too long a run of high-tension cable. Of course, the generator we have at present is a very small affair, sufficient to provide lighting and little else. For the electrolytic process we are going to require a much larger machine altogether . . .'

Makepeace was a little daunted by Doug's enthusiasm. While the manager was anxious to outline his plans immediately, Eddie, who had been travelling since early morning, was tired and hungry.

'It's getting late,' he said, interrupting his colleague's excited explanations, 'and I have still to find somewhere I can get a room for the night.'

'I am sure that Mrs McGillivray will insist that you take supper with us,' Doug assured him, 'and I suspect that she will also expect you to stay overnight.'

'That's extremely hospitable of you, old man,' said Makepeace rising to his feet, eager to take up Doug's offer at once. 'Perhaps we can go over your plans after we have eaten?'

As Doug had suspected, Mary was adamant that their visitor should not only dine with them but also spend the night under her roof.

'I had anticipated lodging with Mrs Bowler,' the agent explained. 'She has always been most obliging in the past.'

'Nonsense, Mr Makepeace,' Mary insisted, 'I will not hear of your paying for accommodation when our house is at your disposal. Pray be seated. Hamish, offer Mr Makepeace a drink,' she instructed, and to her daughter, 'Flora, go and make up your bed with clean linen. You can sleep in here for the night.'

'Oh, really, Mrs McGillivray, I would not want to put any of your family out . . .' protested Eddie Makepeace.

'If you only knew what a joy it is to have a visitor,' she replied. 'We are so cut off out here, Mr Makepeace, that we are quite starved of news and interesting company.'

So eager were the young people to hear what was going on in the city that it was late in the evening before Doug and Eddie were left alone to discuss matters concerning the mine. They pored over Doug's plans until well into the early hours, so that when Eddie Makepeace at last retired to his bed, he slept so soundly that even the morning siren calling the men to work did not disturb him.

When he at last appeared for breakfast it was to find that Flora had been left to wait upon him since her mother had urgent business elsewhere. As he prepared to tackle the mountain of bacon, eggs and fried bread which the girl placed before him, he enquired how the Australian outback compared with her former home.

'Oh, it's all right, I suppose,' she replied rather disconsolately. 'It's just that nothing much happens around here, most of the time.'

She spared him her usual tirade about the lack of companionship, and having nothing to do all day but clean up the continuous influx of dust and dirt from the parched countryside.

'Surely a young lady like you should be away at school in the city?' Eddie suggested. 'Doesn't Mr Jones send his girls to some posh place in Adelaide?'

'Well, yes . . .' She hesitated to tell him that Mary had been so horrified at the standard of reading and writing achieved by the Jones girls after three years at their Australian boarding school that she had refused point blank to allow Flora to go with them. 'But I'm a bit too old for conventional schooling,' she explained. 'My mother is a qualified teacher, you see, and she has continued my education since we arrived at Keningo. I am even allowed to help her in the school she has set up for the miners' children.'

'You want to be a teacher too, I suppose?' He shovelled in a mouthful of food. He enjoyed hearing her speak. Despite all these months in the outback, Flora had not lost her Highland brogue.

'Oh, no!' she contradicted him. 'It is not a job that I enjoy. I had an aunt, Kirsty, who was a doctor . . . for a time I thought I might like to be the same, but I am not clever enough for that so I thought I might train to be a hospital nurse.'

'The way things are shaping up, there is going to be a need for plenty of nurses, I reckon,' Eddie observed. 'Why don't you write to the big hospital in Adelaide? It's called the Royal . . . an old school chum of mine is a surgeon there.' Encouraged by her obvious interest, he continued generously. 'If you like I could write to him on your behalf. Find out what it takes to get a training.'

The enthusiastic response which his suggestion elicited changed Flora's demeanour so completely that Eddie was quite startled by her sudden vivacity. Her eyes flashed and her cheeks coloured. By gosh, he thought, this girlie will stir a few hearts in a year or two, and no mistake!

'Oh, Mr Makepeace,' she cried, excitedly, 'would you really do that for me? I want so much to do something useful with my life but I have no idea how to go about it.'

'It will be no trouble to contact Percy Farmer,' he assured her. 'It's time I did so anyway. We haven't set eyes on one another for more than five years.'

'There is just one thing,' she pleaded. 'Will you please say nothing to my mother about this?'

Makepeace was about to protest that he could not do anything without her parents' knowledge when she reassured him: 'It's not that I intend to run away without telling her or anything like that . . . but Ma is a worrier, and I would rather have some concrete proposal to put to her before I even suggest that I might be leaving.'

Eddie wondered how the McGillivrays would view this level of interference from himself on so short an acquaintance; it was not as if he were an old family friend. The previous evening he had been guilty of influencing Hamish also.

'Have you considered what you might do if there is a war in Europe, young man?' Eddie had enquired when the men sat on after the table had been cleared, talking of the subject uppermost in every mind.

'I had thought about returning to Scotland and joining our local regiment – the Argyll and Sutherland Highlanders,' Hamish told him.

'I believe that here they intend recruiting technicians like yourself into a separate unit, the Royal Australian Engineers,' said Makepeace. 'It would be an opportunity to make use of your training as an electrician . . . preferable to being a front-line infantryman, anyway.'

All Hamish's notions of what battle was like came from reading the *Boys' Own Paper* as a lad. He was inclined to dismiss Makepeace's suggestion out of hand. He thought he knew what soldiering was all about, and was determined to be in the thick of the fighting. He could see, however, that his father might support his resolve to join up if he thought his son was going to be doing something safe, behind the lines . . . perhaps he *should* enlist in the Australian Expeditionary Force? Once he was away in Perth, signing-on, his parents would not be able to stop him from joining the real soldiers.

At noon, Doug and his foreman, Dai Jones, waited with Eddie Makepeace at the compound gates. The carrier was loading the last of the packages and produce for delivery to Kalgoorlie.

'If the boys at Canberra are so keen on increasing gold production,' Eddie was saying, 'they will have to provide a suitable workforce.'

'I'd be very grateful for a couple of experienced miners,' Doug told him. 'There have been quite a few men passing through lately who were from the Balkan countries. Their English is poor but they know a lot about mining.'

'I'll see what I can do,' Eddie replied, tapping the valise which now contained all Doug's suggestions for the new process. 'And I'll see that this stuff is placed in the appropriate hands immediately.'

As he swung himself up into the cab of the carrier's lorry, he called back, 'I'll be in touch as soon as possible . . . thank Mrs McGillivray for her hospitality. Cheerio!'

The lorry lurched forward, leaving behind a great cloud of dust. By the time it had cleared, the ramshackle vehicle was already almost out of sight.

While Mary had been dismayed on first viewing the bush

settlement of Keningo, she quickly discovered that she was more at home in this mining community than she had ever been during the long weeks aboard ship and the short time they had spent in Perth. To her there was nothing unusual in the idea that people made the most of what was available and did not allow themselves to pine for the unattainable. There was great satisfaction to be had from overcoming the difficulties of life in the outback, and even more in working to enrich the lives of others.

Mary had immediately identified the need for a system of education in the settlement, both for the white and the Aboriginal children. Her observation of the Jones girls had suggested to her that the standards of private boarding schools were not high, while day schooling for working-class children simply did not exist in such remote areas as Keningo.

Within weeks of their arrival, she had travelled either on foot or in the jaunty little trap which Doug had found for her on one of his infrequent visits to Kalgoorlie, to each of the outlying homesteads. In addition she had called upon most of the families located in the settlement itself. Her purpose had been to make herself known and to sound out the residents on the subject of setting up a school.

Madge Bowler had not exaggerated the strong feelings of resentment engendered in some of her neighbours when Mary had suggested that white children should sit side by side in school with the Aborigines. Others, however, were only too pleased to find someone willing and able to provide an education for their little ones, and made no objection to her pupils being of both races.

Her little school had opened the previous July, in a disused shed belonging to the mining company. At first there had been a majority of black children for their parents were most anxious to avail themselves of this opportunity, despite the necessity of having their offspring mix with the whites. Very soon, however, dissenters both black and white overcame their prejudices when they saw what benefits their neighbours' children derived from their days in Mrs McGillivray's school.

Flora, very much at a loose end now that her mother had

decided not to send her away to school in Adelaide, had agreed to assist. Reluctant at first to become involved in her mother's project, she eventually allowed herself to be persuaded into decorating the miserable hut which was all that the mining company could provide as a schoolroom. In no time at all, a giant-sized alphabet, with everyday objects illustrating each individual letter, ran around the room at eye-level, and colourful displays of the children's own work brightened up the ugly walls of corrugated iron.

School started very early in the day, and was dismissed before the heat of the noonday sun turned the shed into an oven.

When school had started, Flora had found that she had a particular gift for working with the smaller children, and that teaching them in her mother's way, through the experience of handling natural objects and exploring the environment in which they lived, was actually fun. Her days now filled with her activities in the schoolroom, Flora settled down to wait for word from Eddie Makepeace.

A few days after the agent's visit, Mary received a reply to a letter she had written to the State Legislature, requesting that her new school should become registered, and eligible for State funding.

Mrs D. J. McGillivray   *The Department of Education*
Keningo Settlement   *State of Western Australia*
Kalgoorlie District   *Perth WA*
Western Australia

3 June, 1914

Madam,
I am instructed by the Education Board of the State Legislature to inform you that your request for registration of a school at the settlement known as Keningo has been deferred pending the report of the State's Inspector of Schools.
In this connection Mr Aloysius Montgomery, M.A.

*(Melbourne), will call upon you at an unspecified date
within the next twenty-eight days. Please ensure that suitable accommodation is provided for his overnight stay . . .*

Mary laid down the letter and glanced around her makeshift
schoolroom.

It compared most unfavourably with the magnificent building
where she had last been employed, which had been constructed
to house the school for slate quarriers' children on the Island of
Lunga. The walls here were sheets of iron with a single small
window and a few unused bolt holes through which to view the
outside world. Despite Flora's valiant attempts to cheer it up, the
building was little more than a miserable hovel. She looked
despairingly up at the roof of rusty corrugated iron which over-
lapped the walls, leaving a gap of several inches at the eaves.
Through this opening, noisy parakeets shuffled to and fro, while
on the exposed wooden beams supporting the roof, two huge
goannas acted as animated fly-papers. How could the government
inspector be persuaded to pass such a building as suitable for a
school?

They had done their best to make the place inhabitable. The
benches and stools were rough-hewn, the work of willing parents
co-opted to help get the school underway. Outside, in the far
corners of the yard, two sets of earth closets served as latrines.

Mary, suspecting that school materials might be scarce in
Keningo, had had the foresight to bring with her from Eisdalsa a
large amount of equipment no longer required when the island's
school closed. Slates, copy books and reading primers for every
age group had been provided by the quarry manager, William
Whylie, before his retirement. Whatever else this government
inspector found to criticise, it would surely not be her library.

The noise from the yard had reached a crescendo. Whatever
could Flora be thinking of to let things get so out of hand? Mary
wondered and went out to see for herself.

To one side of the school yard a number of sawn pieces of tree
trunk had been set up for the children to climb upon. At the
moment these served as a grandstand, commandeered by the

boys. Little girls stood in giggling groups around the central figure of a small Aboriginal boy who, with a fork-ended stick, held prisoner the largest and most fearsome-looking black snake that Mary had ever seen. The child held the serpent so firmly that all its sinuous writhings could not set it free. Until the moment when Mary had appeared, the children had been egging on the Aboriginal boy to torment the captive, cheering at each agonised movement of the unfortunate creature.

Taking their cue from the horror on their teacher's chalk-white face, however, their screams of laughter died on their lips and suddenly the whole yard was so silent that Mary could hear her own heart beating.

'Marty Mallacoota,' she addressed the boy, firmly but quietly, 'are you able to hold that creature there while I clear the yard?'

'Yes, missus,' the child replied, mystified at his classmates' sudden silence. 'I can hold this old red-belly all day if you wants, missus,' he assured her proudly.

'Very well.' Mary addressed the remainder of the children. 'You will file into school in the usual manner. Lucy Milman,' she picked out the oldest and most reliable of her pupils, 'see that everyone gets on with some useful work until I come.' The girl acknowledged her order, and led the class into the schoolroom.

'Now then, Marty.' Mary turned back to the Aboriginal child and his captive. 'What do you propose to do with the snake?'

'If I was at home, I'd kill him and eat him, missus. My mama, she makes good snake dinners.' The boy moved the forked stick slightly, encouraging the animal to believe it was about to be freed, but as it began again to wriggle and lash out with its tail, he prodded with the stick even more fiercely, keeping it pinned firmly to the ground.

'How would you kill it?' Mary was now so intrigued by the boy's expert handling of the creature that much of her initial horror had dissipated.

'Cut off its head, missus,' he declared, and holding the stick now in one hand only, he searched in his pocket for a clasp knife which he knew he should not have been carrying in school. Looking a trifle shame-faced at this flagrant disregard for the rules, he handed Mary the knife while he concentrated on securing the reptile.

Without comment, she handed it back with its blade open. She saw the knife flash in the sunlight, but so swift was its descent that she was unaware of the child's action until the snake's head lay severed on the ground while the body continued its involuntary movements for several seconds. As she watched, Marty kicked away the head with its lethal fangs, and slit the animal along the length of its red belly, allowing the viscera to fall free. Then he rolled up the body and tied it deftly with a length of tough raffia-like grass.

Relieved, his teacher let out her breath.

'You had better take that straight home to your mother, Marty,' she said, and was gratified to see him dig a hole in the sandy soil in which both head and intestines were swiftly buried.

'And, Marty.' The child looked back as he opened the yard gate. 'You must never again play with snakes on the school premises.'

'Yes, missus . . . sorry, missus,' he replied, and skipped off gleefully, knowing how pleased his mother would be with his offering.

Mary stood for a moment on the porch, before going back into the schoolroom. As she took in a few deep breaths and felt her hot face begin to cool, she saw Flora approaching from the direction of the village.

'Where have you been?' she demanded of her daughter. 'You were supposed to be keeping an eye on the children's play.'

'I'm sorry, Mother,' Flora replied, 'but I caught sight of the carrier's truck, and since there was a passenger I thought I should go and investigate, just in case it was your inspector fellow.'

'And was it?' Mary demanded, feeling herself grow hot again.

'Yes,' replied Flora, 'but I took him into the house, showed him the room we had ready for him and how to operate the shower, and left him recovering from his journey. When I produced a bottle of cool beer he looked as if he might settle in for the afternoon!'

'Thank goodness you went,' Mary sighed, relieved. The story of the great black snake could wait.

* * *

After a comfortable night and a good breakfast, Aloysius Montgomery, M.A. (Melbourne) was quite prepared to be lenient in his criticism of Keningo School, its children, premises and schoolmistress. He and Mary visited the school building early, before the children were due to arrive.

The condition of the hut was no worse and no better than any he had seen in these outback communities. When the people themselves lived in hovels, how could one expect their school buildings to be of any higher standard?

The presence of the huge monitor lizards was something of a shock, but rather those, basking on the rafters, than have the air filled with the flies and mosquitoes which generally plagued these country places.

The yard made a good play area. Well-fenced, it ensured the children's safety while at play, and deterred would-be truants from running off before school was over for the day. The earth closets were pretty primitive, but relatively clean.

He was going through the curriculum which Mary had devised for the various age-groups, and admiring the small library which she had been able to amass, when Flora, who had been deputed to organise their assembly in the yard, led the children into class.

They stood politely until Mary bade them good morning and then they sat.

Aloysius Montgomery remained standing, his mouth hanging open in surprise, brown eyes staring blankly at the assembled children through the thick pebbled glasses which told their own story of severe myopia. He thrust spread fingers through his bush of black hair, greying only slightly at the temples, and stared, speechless, at Mary McGillivray.

At last he managed to splutter one word.

'Natives?'

Mary looked startled. She had come to accept antagonism from a few ignorant and bigoted people, but this reaction from one purporting to be educated and intelligent shocked her profoundly.

'Aboriginal men work side by side in the mines with white Australians and white Europeans,' she told him. 'Black and white women shop in the same company store, and share the same water pump in the village street. Why should the children be segregated?'

'But they are ineducable,' he insisted. 'How can you teach heathens, with no more intelligence than a bunch of monkeys, to read and write? What is more important, how can you expect white children to learn in the presence of such ignorance? Why, they do not even know the difference between right and wrong!'

Mary thought of the episode with the snake the day before. Whatever his motives, Marty Mallacoota had saved other children from what might have been a lethal attack by a vicious animal, one of the deadliest of Australian reptiles. Not only had he demonstrated how to catch and kill the snake, but he had cleaned it, carefully disposed of the offal and provided his family with a meal. Only a fool would describe Marty Mallacoota as ineducable!

'They are all little children, Mr Montgomery,' she replied, coldly, trying hard to keep her temper. 'There may be a difference in the colour of their skins, but I see nothing in their behaviour in school, or in their ability to learn, which one could attribute solely to this. Some pupils are very bright, others find learning difficult . . . and in this latter category I would place as many white children as Aborigines. Some of the children's problems may well be attributable to their home circumstances, and certainly in this respect the Aborigines are at a disadvantage when dealing with a curriculum imposed by white educationalists. From his own sphere of experience, however, the native child has as much to contribute to the whole body of knowledge in the school as has the white child.'

Stunned by the sight of white Australian children sitting side by side with blacks, Montgomery had scarcely heard a word she said. He proceeded to gather up his papers, forms which he had been completing during the course of his discussions. He tore these into pieces and threw them into the waste-paper basket.

While Mary looked on, quite bemused by these activities, he reached for his hat, picked up his bag and made for the door. There he turned.

'A word of advice, Mrs McGillivray. The Australian Government provides schools for white Australian children. It also provides for the education of Aboriginal children in the recognised reserves. It does not support the notion of mixed race schools, and I hope to God that I shall never see the day when it does. Do not think that you can come here with your newfangled notions of integration and change overnight arrangements which had held good in this great land of ours for a hundred years!' He stalked out into the glare of the noonday sun.

Flora, seeing how distressed her mother was by this unwarranted outburst, quietly instructed the youngest children to take up their slates and practise writing their letters. Following their daughter's lead, Mary too busied herself with her pupils. She tried not to think about the outcome of this strange encounter with the Schools Inspector. Would they close her school down? she wondered. Could they . . . if she made no demands upon the State's purse? She had only applied for registration in order to gain some financial assistance.

It was pointless to speculate. No doubt she would have her opportunity to put her case to a higher authority before any really drastic measures were taken against the school. In the meantime she would carry on as if the inspector's visit had never taken place.

The men were all in the canteen when the news came through.

It was a rare thing to see Walt Wilson on horseback. He galloped into the yard and pulled up his mount inexpertly, sliding to the ground rather than dismounting in the accepted fashion.

'Where's the boss?' he demanded, throwing the reins over a convenient hitching post.

'Over in the office,' Dai Jones called out, emerging from inside the building. 'What's up?'

'It's on . . . that's what's up!' Walt replied, making his way towards the office building on the far side of the yard.

The men looked at one another, mystified.

'Waddayer mean . . . what's on?' they called after him.

'The bloody war . . . that's what!' Walt called over his shoulder and disappeared inside the hut.

They had all gathered in the yard by the time Doug emerged, followed closely by the storekeeper.

'Well, you've all heard the news,' he addressed them. 'It seems that the British Government, the French and the Belgians, have declared war on Germany.' Everyone yelled excitedly. They might have been watching a goal scored at the Saturday football match.

'I have no doubt there will be some of you busting to get into this fight . . .' Out of the corner of his eye, Doug caught sight of Hamish standing at the rear, and paused for a moment recalling their recent conversation with Eddie Makepeace. 'But before you make up your minds, I want you to know that the Australian Government values your work here so highly that there are promises of Government investment in the plant, and a chance to bring the extraction process right up to date. So, if you feel it is your bounden duty to go off and join the army for King and Country, well, that's up to you. But if you decide to stay here and get on with the job, you will be working just as surely for the war effort, and no one will think any the less of you.'

There was a general buzz of conversation for a few moments, then some of the older men set off for home, anxious to talk over this momentous news with their wives and families. The young men huddled in groups, discussing what they felt the future might hold for them. Most of them, like Hamish, had already considered what they would do should there be a war.

Over by the crushing plant, a small group of Aboriginal workmen had huddled together, uncertain of their position in this new situation. They had for a long time been aware of a peculiar restlessness amongst the white men. Now it was clear to them that their European masters had brought upon themselves this tragedy which was unfolding in that land across the sea that most of them called home.

Seeing the Aborigines gathered there, Doug wandered over to join them and addressed his remarks to their headman, Alfie Mallacoota, father of Mary's little snake charmer.

'This is not your fight, Alfie,' he said, 'but it could affect things around here nonetheless. If the white boys go away to join the army, it will mean that you fellows will have to take on more of the work.'

'We here to help, boss,' Alfie replied, cheerfully, and his mates all nodded enthusiastically, their white teeth gleaming. Doug clapped a friendly hand on their leader's shoulder. 'Thanks, Alfie,' he said, gratefully. 'We'll talk more about this once we see just how many of the men we have left.'

Mary would be waiting for him; he must get home to her before Hamish dropped his own private bombshell.

Very quickly an Australian Expeditionary Force was mustered and sent to occupy the Pacific territories colonised by Germany. After this, no further demands were made upon the Australian Government by the Allies in Europe for many months.

Makepeace, as good as his word, had rapidly mustered support for Doug's new electrolytic process and before the Australian summer had reached its height, wagon loads of materials and equipment had been shipped into Keningo from all quarters of the continent. Hamish was persuaded to remain at the mine while the installation of the new equipment was put in hand. When he read of the first wave of Australian troops, languishing in the sunny climes of the southern Pacific Ocean, he was not sorry to have held back. He was, after all, engaged in work of vital importance to the war effort.

By the time that the year 1914 came to a close, the electrolytic processing plant was operating satisfactorily. Three Serbian mining engineers who, having once escaped the tyranny of foreign invaders in their own country, had no intention of returning for the fight, had been recruited in Perth and sent to work under Doug McGillivray. Their lack of English had been a barrier at first, but within days Mary had organised evening classes for them in the schoolroom. With the help of a mixture of French and German, languages in which Mary was proficient and of which the men had some understanding, they were soon able to communicate sufficiently to carry out their work. Apart from a number of minor accidents, attributed to the handling of unfamiliar materials and equipment, production figures showed every sign of breaking all records.

In January 1915 Hamish received his call to join the colours in

Perth. On the afternoon of 18 January, Walt Wilson, excited by the rare opportunity to deliver an officially worded telegram addressed to one of the few younger men of the settlement, came running up the street, waving a yellow envelope. Mary was working in her garden, carefully tending the one or two rose bushes she had persuaded to grow beside the path to the main door. She looked up at Walt's shout and felt her hands begin to tremble. She laid her secateurs carefully on the veranda rail before she dropped them, and walked down to the gate, wiping her hands on her flowered apron.

Wordlessly she took the envelope from Walt, and turned away, unsmiling.

'This letter came for Miss Flora by the carrier, 'Walt called after her, anxiously. She turned back to accept the second communication. Even her distress at receiving the telegram could not stifle her curiosity about Flora's letter. Who could be writing to her daughter from Adelaide?

She thanked the storekeeper and went into the house. It would be an hour or more before Hamish came in from the mine and Flora had gone with the trap to collect butter from Jones's farm. With a sense of foreboding, Mary filled a kettle and set it to boil. When she had brewed her tea she carried the tray out on to the veranda and set it down on the rustic table which Hamish had made for her. She ran her hand over the polished red jarrah wood, remembering the pride with which her son had presented the table to her on Christmas Day. It had been his first attempt at joinery, and she was very proud of it. He had promised to make her a deckchair for her birthday to go with it. There wouldn't be time now. She stifled a sob and stirred her tea vigorously.

From along the street she heard the sound of a vehicle approaching and looked up to see a rather splendid open tourer draw to a halt outside her gate. From out of a cloud of dust emerged a figure whose appearance was at first unfamiliar to her. Once he had removed hat and goggles and wiped a spotted handkerchief over his dust-caked face, however, she recognised Hamish's friend, Tom Pain. He had visited them only once since their arrival at Keningo. Mary recalled her concerns on that other occasion, fearing that Hamish would be anxious to rush away with his friend. How gratified she had been when her son had declined Tom's invitation to join his motor garage enterprise, explaining that he was committed to helping his father at the mine.

Today was different. She was certain that Tom was here on other, more pressing business.

'Mrs McGillivray,' he called, flinging the gate wide and hurrying towards her, 'how are you, ma'am?'

'Why, Tom,' she mustered a smile, 'what a pleasant surprise. Do come and sit here in the shade.' She fussed around him, pulling up a second chair. 'I am sure you could do with some tea . . . I will fetch another cup.'

Without waiting for an answer she disappeared inside the house, leaving her guest to settle himself. He looked about him approvingly. What a difference they had made to the place since he had called here last. The paint was fresh, and sheets of new iron indicated where Doug had made repairs to the roof. He recalled their complaints about the soaking they'd received at the first fall of rain after their arrival! He took a deep breath, enjoying the fragrance of Mary's roses. He hated to be the one to disturb her idyll.

'Is Hamish about?' he enquired when his hostess returned. 'I am sorry to appear rude, but my business with him is urgent. I must be on my way again within the hour if I'm to make Southern Cross tonight.'

'Southern Cross?' Mary repeated, bewildered. 'But that's more than a hundred miles away.'

'Yes,' he agreed. 'Without incident, it will take four or five hours by road. That's why I really cannot hang about.'

Their conversation was cut short by the arrival of Flora, who waved to her mother as she reined in the pony and steered the neat little trap into the yard at the side of the house. Because she was unaware of their visitor's arrival, it was several minutes before she appeared, hot and perspiring freely. She had taken her time stabling the horse and watering him.

When she saw Tom, she gave an exclamation of both delight

and anguish . . . what must he think of her, looking so dirty? Then she noticed that he too was streaked with dust and more than a trifle warm, and they both broke into peals of laughter as they hugged one another affectionately.

'Why, Tom,' Flora cried, 'Hamish never said you were coming.'

'He is not expecting me,' was the reply, 'and I'm afraid that you may not be so welcoming when you know what I have come about.'

He tailed off, lamely, noting Mary's despairing glance.

'You have come to take him with you to Perth,' she responded in a toneless voice.

'How did you know?' Tom asked, mystified.

'A telegram came for him not half an hour before you arrived,' she explained, then turning to her daughter, commanded, 'Flora, run down to the compound and fetch your father and Hamish. Tell them to come at once.'

For an instant the girl looked helplessly from one to the other, but finding no explanation forthcoming, flew off down the village street, her feet hardly touching the ground.

'You must eat before you leave. I'll go and prepare something,' Mary told her guest. 'If you would like to take a shower, you know where it is.' She disappeared once more into the house, anxious to shed her tears in the privacy of her own kitchen.

Only a few minutes passed before Hamish and Flora came hurrying in from the mine with Doug close upon their heels. As Tom and Hamish exchanged greetings, Mary handed her son the yellow envelope. He hesitated for a moment, regarded his mother's red-rimmed eyes a trifle impatiently and tore it open.

'I'm to report to the recruiting office in Perth by the twenty-third,' he said, looking to his friend for confirmation.

'Mine said the same,' said Tom. 'But I received it two days ago.'

'Does that mean that Jack will be called at the same time?' Hamish asked.

'I expect so,' replied his friend. 'I put through a cable to Kerrera Station before I left, telling him to meet us at the

Pioneer's Hotel at Southern Cross. We might just as well all enlist at the same time. There is more chance that we will stay together if we do.'

Mary put her hand to her mouth to stifle her cry of distress. 'Oh, no, they'll never take Jack,' she insisted, 'not now that Jean is going to have a baby!'

'I can't see a wife and bairn keeping Jack from doing his duty,' said Hamish, rather pompously. While he had doubts about the sentiment expressed by his son, Doug had to agree that Jack McDougal was not the man to be left behind in a fight such as this. Seeing the two young bloods girding themselves for war, Doug was tempted to join them himself. Had it not been for the discussion he had had with Makepeace on the importance of the work he was doing at the mine, he felt sure that he would have been.

In a flurry of embraces and garbled messages – 'If you should see John and Anne, tell them I shall be writing soon' from Mary, and from Flora: 'Give my love to Jean . . . tell her I am actually knitting something for the baby!' – the tourer drew away. The backfire from its exhaust could still be heard even after the car had disappeared from sight.

It was quite late in the evening when Mary remembered Flora's letter. The three of them were unusually quiet as they sat around the kitchen table, trying to ignore the chair vacated by Hamish. Mary, distraught after the day's happenings, had neglected to remove her pinafore before sitting down to eat. Her hand now strayed to the pocket in search of a handkerchief and came in contact with the envelope.

'Oh, my goodness!' she declared, withdrawing it. 'I quite forgot. This came for Flora this afternoon.' She re-examined the address before handing the letter to her daughter. 'Whoever do you know in Adelaide?' she demanded.

Flora's heart missed a beat. Could it be from the hospital? Had Mr Makepeace remembered after all? It had been a long time since his visit . . . she had begun to suspect that he had forgotten all about his promise to her to speak to his friend.

> *The Royal Hospital*
> *Adelaide*
> *South Australia*
> *10 January, 1915*

Dear Miss McGillivray,
Recruitment of Nurses – Emergency Programme
I understand that you have expressed a desire to enrol at this hospital in order to train in nursing duties.

Normally we would expect a candidate to write a formal application before being invited for interview, but in view of the recommendation received from our Chief of Surgery, Mr Farmer, I am willing to invite you to attend for interview on the first day of February at ten o'clock. If suitable for training, you will be enrolled immediately to begin a period of six weeks' initial instruction before being allowed to work on the wards. You must expect to be away from home for at least two months before any leave can be granted. Your parents should understand that there is every possibility of an overseas appointment, once your probationary period in this hospital has ended.

Please notify this office of your anticipated date and time of arrival.

Yours sincerely,
Amelia Elliot (Matron)

Flora was speechless with excitement. She read the contents of the letter again, studying every detail in case she had missed anything. At last, she handed it to her mother.

As Mary read, she felt the bottom dropping out of her world. She had been prepared for Hamish's departure at a moment's notice, but this was quite unexpected.

'I don't understand,' she said, bleakly. 'Who is this Mr Farmer? I have never heard of him.' She handed the letter on to Doug who read it through without comment before laying the paper down, very deliberately. Both parents waited for their daughter's explanation.

'I . . . I didn't expect it to happen this way.' Flora hesitated. 'Mr

Makepeace said he would make some enquiries and let me know how I could go about applying for training. It seems that things have moved along faster than he anticipated.'

She gave her father a beseeching look . . . surely he would understand that this was not what she had intended?

Doug was no help to her. Too stunned to make any comment, he filled his pipe with the deliberate motions reserved for those times when he was thinking deeply.

'Honestly, Ma,' Flora pleaded with her mother, 'I expected to get information and perhaps a form to fill in . . . I did intend to discuss it with you before things got this far, really I did. Mr Makepeace said that he knew this Mr Farmer from their student days and that he would find out for me how to go about making an application. I promise you, that was all . . .' Her voice trailed off as she watched the expression on her mother's face.

'So you're going to leave me too, are you, you naughty girl?' The quiet comment was more withering than any argument with raised voices. 'I suppose it was only to be expected of you,' Mary concluded, wearied to death by the day's happenings.

'Oh, Mother, Dad, don't you see . . . don't you understand that I have to do what I can? If I can't go to fight with guns and bayonets – and believe me, if it was allowed, that's what I would do – I can at least make myself useful with splints and bandages.'

'They must be desperately short of nurses if they are willing to take you on the say-so of someone whose only knowledge of you is through a third party,' Doug observed, thoughtfully. 'Perhaps she is right, Mary, perhaps she ought to go?'

But Mary ran sobbing from the room.

'You have only a few days to prepare your mother for this, Flora,' Doug said to his daughter. 'Be gentle and understanding with her. You and Hamish are all she has left to care for in this world.'

'That's nonsense, Pa,' Flora insisted, kneeling by his chair and placing her head in his lap as she had done as a child. 'Mother has you, whom she cherishes most of all . . . and there's Grandmother at Kerrera Station and Grandfather McDougal at Eisdalsa. She has plenty of people to worry about!' They shared a secret smile. So often in the past they had laughed together over Mary's habitual worrying.

Dougal stroked the girl's hair, so much like her Aunt Annie's, raven black and shining in the lamplight. She was like Wee Annie in so many ways. He could just see Flora shouting from a soapbox, or chained to the railings at St George's Cross.

'Do you mind my going very much, Pa?' she asked softly.

'I shall miss you,' he replied. And Flora was satisfied with that. It meant that he had accepted that she would be going. 'Remember what I said about your mother,' he repeated. 'Treat her kindly. She'll come around to it in the end.'

Chapter 15

❧

Solway Academy
25 November, 1914

Dear Miss McGillivray,
I said I would let you know all about my first impressions
of school, just as soon as I could. We are allowed to write
one letter a week, on a Sunday, and of course I had to fulfil
promises to Mother and Grandpa and everyone.

There was some uncertainty at first whether I would be
allowed to come away, what with the war and everything,
but in the end Father was persuaded that life should go on
as normally as possible, so here I am.

The school is very big compared with our little village
school. There are a hundred girls in all, fifty of whom are
boarders like myself.

We sleep in dormitories of ten pupils. Ours is a bit bare,
but the beds are comfortable enough, although the girls say
it can be very cold in the winter.

We are doing all the usual subjects but, in addition, Mr
Whylie takes us for physics and astronomy, when he is not
busy at the munitions factory in Annan, and Mrs Whylie
has engaged the local pharmacist to teach another girl and
myself chemistry. Christina Bell, that's the other girl also
doing chemistry, wants to be a doctor like me, so we have
become best friends!

Our Latin teacher is a frightful old dragon called Miss
Bashford. She wears knitted woollen suits which sag from
too much washing and stretching, and long strings of
amber beads. She wears her hair in a tight bun and seems

to use a whole packet of hairpins to secure it. Even so, it's all wispy by the end of the day! Anyway, Latin is awful. If it was not absolutely necessary to do it to become a doctor, I would ask to be allowed to give it up.

Our French teacher is a Belgian refugee, a dumpy little woman called Madame Hersche. Mrs Whylie took her in, together with her daughter who is twelve. Every householder in the district was asked to give a home to a refugee and dear Mrs Whylie was of course one of the first to offer. The daughter, Tilda, attends school with us, and her mother teaches the first years French. I am not surprised that they wanted to leave Belgium. Tilda says that German soldiers bayonet babies and eat them, and they rape young girls like us. What does rape mean? Madame is very nervous, rather sweet really, but if we get too talkative and do not pay attention, she weeps. Do you think this is because of her experiences?

Grandma wrote that you have met Uncle Stuart since he came back from the South Atlantic. Did he see any penguins and whales, and most important of all, were there any albatrosses, like in Coleridge's poem? I can't wait to see him for myself.

Mother says that Aunt Margaret is organising a rest room and canteen for sailors in Oban, and that when I am home on holiday I may help. Christina Bell is green with envy. Her brother is in the army but she prefers naval uniform!

I hope that you are taking good care of yourself, eating properly and taking lots of exercise. There you see, I am still practising my bedside manner with my very first patient! Incidentally, Mother still does not know that I am planning to be a doctor. Father says I have to lead up to the idea gently, so please don't mention it should you write to her.

I sometimes get a little homesick and the best cure for that is a letter, so please write as soon as you have a minute to spare.

With much love, from your devoted friend,
Morag Beaton

P.S. Mrs Whylie has seen the address on this letter and has enclosed a note of her own.

Solway Academy
25 November, 1914

Dear Annie,

Annabel has told me of your engagement to Stuart ... at last! I always felt that you two should marry one day. I hope that you will be very happy.

Don't forget that William and I will expect an invitation to the wedding – provided of course that you decide to wait until Stuart has sufficient leave to do the job properly!

When I saw the address on Morag's envelope I was stricken with conscience that I had not written to you for so long. She does not know it, but I have taken a peak at her letter ... the little monkey! How very perceptive children can be, and how forthright. None more so than you yourself at Morag's age, I remember!

William was so determined to be involved with the war effort that he offered his services to the local munitions factory. At first they were very sceptical but I think he must have told a fib about his age. Anyway, they were impressed with his knowledge of explosives and so on from his work in the slate quarries, so they offered him the post of Welfare and Safety Officer ... and a good thing too. You would not believe the appalling conditions under which those young women are expected to work. Why, they even have the nickname, 'the canaries', because they go quite yellow with the toluene in the explosives.

I must not hold up Morag's letter, lest she miss the afternoon post.

Again, I wish you much happiness upon your engagement.

William sends his kindest regards.

Yours truly,
Elizabeth Whylie

Annie folded both letters, smiling to herself at Morag's graphic description of Miss Bashford and her shapeless woollens. It was good to hear from Elizabeth, who had been the schoolmistress at the Eisdalsa school when she and Margaret Beaton were girls. Her references to William and his work at the munitions factory interested Annie greatly. She tucked the pages under her blotter and continued with her work.

Stuart and Annie had not, after all, made the announcement of their engagement when they returned to Overavon on the evening of 4 August. They had found Mainwaring with the Rolls parked before the main entrance, doors wide open and the engine running. Stuart's bags stood beside Dan's on the step, and the butler was overseeing their loading into the boot.

Stuart had brought the little Morris to a halt immediately behind the other vehicle, in time to see Dan come bounding down the steps.

'Thank goodness,' he had exclaimed. 'I was wondering if we would have to send out a search party! All hell has broken loose . . . we are to report back as soon as possible. The *Hampshire* sails at dawn.'

There had been hurried, strangely impersonal goodbyes. By the time the silver-coloured limousine had disappeared into the darkness of the night, Annie began to wonder if the happenings of the day had not all been a dream.

There seemed no point now in making any announcement about her engagement to Stuart. She resolved to keep her news to herself until she had a chance to explain her new circumstances to Emmanuel.

When Annie alighted from the Rosenstein Rolls outside the door of Number 10 Downing Street on the afternoon of 18 September, her appearance created considerable interest among the rabble of newspaper reporters waiting hopefully for any snippet of news, but there was nothing to connect this elegant young woman, arriving in aristocratic style, with the scarecrow figure of a Suffragette who had emerged from Holloway jail twelve months before. Thankfully she went unrecognised, and before any reporters could interrogate her, was hurriedly ushered through the main door and into the imposing reception hall beyond.

'Ah, Miss McGillivray, please do come this way.'

The Pickwickian figure in morning coat and striped trousers who had greeted her, led her to a chair, busied himself with her coat and gloves, and having offered her a cup of coffee, which she declined, bade her wait.

'The Minister will not keep you long, madam,' he explained. 'Things are very much at sixes and sevens, you understand.' He pulled out a gold watch from his vest pocket and consulted it, muttering incoherently as he bustled off to shepherd in the next appointment. Annie was reminded of the White Rabbit in *Alice in Wonderland*, and could not help smiling.

At that moment a door flew open to reveal Emmanuel Rosenstein, splendid in a dove-grey suit with a tiny rose in his buttonhole, which was precisely the correct shade of magenta. His immaculate grey silk cravat was secured by a diamond pin of almost indecent size. What a fine figure he cut, Annie thought. Any girl might be pleased to have such an eligible bachelor courting her. Over Manny's shoulder she noticed the portrait of some long-dead naval officer and was reminded of Stuart. She must find an opportunity to give Manny her answer today.

'Ah, my dear,' he greeted her in proprietorial manner, 'Mainwaring managed to get you here in good time. I am so pleased to see you.' He leant forward to kiss her on the mouth but she changed position at the last moment and his lips brushed her cheek, clumsily.

'Perhaps you can give me some explanation as to why I have been summoned in this imperious manner?' she demanded. His telegram had contained a terse instruction to attend a meeting . . . no explanation given, not even worded as a request. It had been an order!

'That you will learn soon enough,' he replied. 'Your memo on the requirements of women employed in munitions factories was received very favourably. Some very important people wish to question you about it.'

The White Rabbit had reappeared.

'They will see you now Minister . . . Madam.' He held open the inner door to allow entry and closed it soundlessly behind them.

Annie was led into a somewhat gloomy chamber where several elderly gentlemen were seated around a large oval table. Some of them shuffled peremptorily to their feet at her entry, while others appeared welded to their chairs. In the general bustle of her arrival she took stock of the company.

David Lloyd George she identified by his shaggy mane and bushy eyebrows, which were such a gift to the newspaper cartoonists.

Really, she thought, his looks are quite extraordinary and his stature not the least imposing . . . I cannot imagine why women should throw themselves at his feet as one is led to believe!

Winston Churchill's face was also well known to her. As a war correspondent during the South African campaign, his photograph had appeared frequently in the daily newspapers. The First Lord of the Admiralty was a somewhat florid gentleman with receding hair and a tendency to hanging jowls. Despite the fact that he could not be more than forty years of age, Winston Churchill had a decided pot belly which was the result, she suspected, of persistent over-indulgence in rich food and wines.

He it was who opened the questioning, staring at her with such a penetrating gaze that she herself was forced to look away. He began by examining her at length on the notes she had prepared for Emmanuel, without once referring to the document himself, suggesting that he had thoroughly absorbed its contents before their meeting. At first she felt flattered that he had taken such an interest in her little offering but on reflection, she realised that this was merely an example of the remarkable abilities of this man, who contrasted so vividly with the other gentlemen present.

Those in uniform were either gruff and blustering, or cold and aloof, but none of them impressed her as being able to come to a decision on any matter. The other gentlemen, mainly civil servants she supposed, tried hard to ignore the fact that she was a woman when forced to address their questions to her.

She was left reeling from the manner in which the Chancellor of the Exchequer, David Lloyd George, introduced the subject of the recruitment of women to munitions work. Forgotten were all those harsh, dismissive words against the Suffragist Movement, the arguments against women taking any kind of administrative role in society. Woman's place was no longer in the home, it seemed, woman's place was now behind the factory bench, in order that the menfolk could be released to fight in the trenches.

'Miss McGillivray, we are about to launch a recruitment drive to encourage young women into war work of many kinds,' she was told. 'What, in your opinion, are the main factors which should be brought to their attention, to encourage them to enter the factories?'

'I believe that the mere fact that their brothers, husbands and lovers are away, fighting in France, will be sufficient encouragement in the first place,' she replied, 'but once the first flush of patriotism wears off, I suspect they will begin to examine their situation with a more critical eye.'

The heads around the table nodded, sagely. They all appreciated the fact that women recruited from the middle and upper classes would expect a cleaner environment than their male colleagues were willing to accept. The matter of washing facilities, adequate lavatories, and even rest rooms for women taken unwell while at work, had already been considered.

'We have taken your proposals for the welfare of women to heart, Miss McGillivray,' a nameless individual in civilian dress commented, ticking off items on a list before him. 'Every one of the new factories will have special facilities for ladies included in the plans for construction. Established premises will be put to rights as and when circumstances allow.'

Annie turned upon the speaker, quite forgetting the company in which she found herself. 'To hear you talk,' she said, 'one would never imagine that women already work in factories up and down the country and have been doing so, in the most degrading of conditions, since the beginning of the Industrial Revolution!'

Manny Rosenstein, fearing that his protégée was about to launch into one of her more militant speeches, tried to divert her.

'The Prime Minister is seeking to find the right enticements to persuade ladies of breeding and good education to work in the factories . . .' he began. 'They will naturally be expecting rather better conditions than those traditionally provided for female workers.'

Immediately she turned upon him.

'Oh, I see,' she replied, coldly. 'Those women who have always been forced to accept the most basic of circumstances can expect no change in their condition then, is that it? These new arrangements will apply only to your ladies of breeding. Pray how do you propose to separate the two?'

Most of the individuals around the table appeared not to understand the question. Churchill leant forward, clearly impressed by her outburst and eager to hear more.

'Do you think that you could enlarge upon your comment, madam?' he asked without a hint of sarcasm.

'With the experienced foremen and supervisors away at the war, who is to train this new female workforce? she demanded. 'The only women with the knowledge and skills to show your "lady" recruits what to do, will be those who have until now been systematically denied recognition of their abilities in the workplace. If you have any notion of placing ladies of quality in positions of authority in the factories, merely because of their status in society, you will find that those who are asked to work under their command will simply refuse to do so!'

Churchill interrupted with a roar of approval. 'Bravo, madam,' he cried. 'We·are not talking here about the Army, gentlemen, where young, unblooded subalterns are carried through the battle by their more experienced NCOs.'

Around the table the military personnel looked shocked, but Lloyd George was seen to smile. Winston had little respect for the Army's ways of doing things.

Annie continued as though there had been no interruption.

'Those women who organise the work will have to be given equal status with their male counterparts.' She paused deliberately, gazing at each of them in turn, aware that she now had their full attention.

Churchill sat back, beaming. It seemed she had clinched some previous argument for him. Not prepared to allow him this self-satisfaction, however, she continued.

'Almost more important than the questions of welfare and organisation is the question of remuneration. Where women are given tasks formerly carried out by men, they must receive the wages of a man. If women are elevated to the status of supervisors, they must be given the authority and the salary appropriate to the task.'

A long silence followed her comments. Suddenly realising the enormity of her statement, Annie coloured a deep red and sank back in her chair, determined not to embarrass Manny any further.

Lloyd George spoke for the first time. Ignoring her outburst he said, 'We had in mind certain slogans which we wish to test out on you, my dear.'

Annie cringed at his condescending familiarity.

There followed a list of innocuous statements persuading women to fight side by side with their menfolk; words like 'loved ones' and 'homeland' figured significantly. To all these Annie merely nodded disinterestedly. When addressed directly for an answer, she took one last swing in defence of her position.

'Slogans and emotive pictures may gain recruits initially,' she responded, 'but they will expect more than fine words!'

They all stood up when she left the room. Only Churchill looked at her directly, and he was smiling. After a few minutes, while she was left cooling her heels in the corridor, Manny joined her. Surprisingly, he did not upbraid her for her outburst.

'They were impressed,' he said. 'One of them even commented that it was a pity there weren't a few like you in the Cabinet!'

'In which case it is a pity they are all so adamantly opposed to women's franchise,' she retorted, having recognised around that table some of the staunchest opponents of the Suffrage Movement.

Rain had begun to fall in blinding sheets as they approached Reading. Mainwaring was forced to reduce speed. The street lamps, turned into brilliant stars by the raindrops, blinded them. Annie's sympathies were with the chauffeur. It must be very difficult to drive in such circumstances . . . but at least the Rolls had a windscreen wiper. In her own little car it was necessary to open the screen when it rained, in order to see where one was going.

Once through the town the lights disappeared and they could relax again in the comfortable shelter of the magnificent limousine.

Manny could contain his impatience no longer. He turned to Annie, grasping both her hands in his, eyes blazing in the dimly lit interior.

'Am I to have my answer now?' he demanded.

Annie, who had been rehearsing this speech for days, found it difficult to look him in the eye as she began: 'I am deeply conscious of the honour which you have done me in asking me to be your wife . . .' Emmanuel moved a little closer, expectantly '. . . but I fear that I cannot accept your proposal.'

She could see that her refusal came as a great shock to him. Could it be that he had persuaded himself that her reticence was merely some feminine trick to stimulate his amorous feelings towards her? It was quite obvious that he had never considered the possibility of rejection.

His face drained of all colour.

'May I ask why?' he demanded, still reeling under the shock of her refusal.

'I am engaged to marry Stuart Beaton.'

'Ah, so that's it.' He leant back against the upholstery and was silent for a moment. 'When you were ill and he so solicitous, I did wonder. Was that when . . . ?' His voice was calm but his hand was shaking as he continued, 'Since you have known one another for so long, I assumed that it was merely a platonic friendship.' He swallowed painfully before asking, 'For how long have you been engaged?' He was trying to sound matter-of-fact, but his expression and his voice betrayed the extent of his hurt.

'Since the fourth of August,' she answered.

'The day that war was declared,' he murmured.

There was a sudden spark of hope in his eyes. She realised with dismay that he concluded her engagement to Stuart had been an impulsive gesture at a time of panic and uncertainty. Perhaps he hoped that their attachment might just as easily be broken?

Hastily she took steps to dispel any such notion.

'I have always held a special place in my heart for Stuart ever since we were children. His recognition of the strength of feeling that he has for me came, I think, as a great shock to him. Perhaps it was the urgency of the situation . . . the feeling that because of the war it was time to put our lives into some semblance of order . . . who knows? Suddenly we were both made aware of a deeply felt love for one another.'

Manny's face fell.

Annie felt real affection for this kindly man who had taken care of her when she was at a low ebb, but she feared that any display of concern for him at this moment might give him unreasonable grounds for hope. She resisted the desire to show him any sympathy.

'When do you plan to marry?' he asked, as calmly as he could.

'As soon as Stuart can arrange leave,' she answered. 'We hope to be married in Scotland.'

For some time Manny remained silent, gazing out into the darkness and seeing only his own reflection in the glass. At last he turned towards her again and in a strained voice said, 'There was one item of news that I was saving as a surprise. There seems little point in holding back now.'

Annie looked up expectantly.

'Do tell me, please?'

'After you left the meeting . . .' he began, hesitantly.

'Yes, what did they say?' she demanded, eagerly.

'There was talk of appointing you Director of Women's Welfare in the Department of Munitions Manufacture,' he told her. 'Since you are soon to be a married woman, I assume that you will not wish to be considered?'

'Why not?' she protested. 'My husband will be away for much of the time, and your colleagues were discussing the employment of women in general. I don't recall there being any ban upon married women offering their services. What better example could there be than to have a married woman, whose husband is in the fighting forces, in a senior position in industry?'

Despite himself, Manny could not help but smile. She had been touched on the raw by his suggestion that her married status might impair her ability to work. He wondered how her future husband would view the prospect of a working wife.

'Then you would still consider such a proposal, should the post be offered to you?' he asked.

'Of course,' she replied without a moment's hesitation.

The night train to Glasgow slowed as it approached Beatock summit, huffing and puffing like an elderly stallion. At last, with a tremendous sigh of escaping steam, it came to a halt in the dimly lit station. Somewhere towards the front of the train a few doors opened and slammed and then a heavy silence fell upon the occupants of the carriage. The young sailor in the far corner suddenly grunted, snored loudly as his head fell back against the antimacassar and then became silent once more as, with his head resting on the shoulder of the little woman in widow's weeds at his side, he slept again. Heather smiled at the woman who dared not move lest she wake the sailor. It's all right, her smile in return seemed to say, the poor laddie needs his rest!

Heather settled back in her corner and dozed, allowing her thoughts to wander over the events of the previous week.

Frustrated beyond imagining by the lack of any response to her application to be accepted as an ambulance driver, Heather had returned to Oxford for the Michaelmas term. It might be that the university itself would be considering forming a unit similar to the Scottish Women's Hospitals, the title used by the Scottish Federation of Women's Suffrage Societies.

Dr Inglis, she had been informed, had offered the services of her unit to the War Office, but the suggestion of a field hospital staffed by women surgeons had been flatly dismissed. 'My dear lady, go home and sit still!' was the reply Elsie had received from one official. Miss Inglis had immediately made her offer to the French and the Belgians. Those women anxious to get to the front line now waited eagerly for some response from either or both of these Governments.

Despite the war, the shops in the centre of Oxford were

displaying their usual festive fripperies and there was an air of joviality and anticipation on this cold December afternoon. It would soon be time for the Christmas break.

With her head down against the chill easterly wind, Heather nearly collided with the muffled figure ahead of her. She pulled her bicycle to an abrupt halt just in time, and made an ungainly descent to the ground. Bloomers or plus fours might be more acceptable apparel for cycling, but ladies wearing trousers were not admitted to the Bodleian Library, even in 1914.

'Heather . . . Heather Brown, by all that's wonderful! Well, this is a piece of good fortune!'

Heather had met Daniel Rosenstein only once. It was during the time that Annie McGillivray was recuperating at Overavon. Having travelled over from Oxford to see her stepmother, she had been delighted to encounter her Uncle Stuart, who with his friend Dan Rosenstein had managed to wangle a forty-eight hour pass. Annie McGillivray being too poorly to sustain more than a brief conversation with her visitors, and Stuart and Margaret having a great deal to discuss concerning their patient's welfare, Heather had been somewhat neglected. Taking pity on her, Dan had volunteered to take her on a tour of the stables and gardens. She had not set eyes on him since. In fact, had he not spoken, she might never have recognised him.

'Why, Mr Rosenstein,' she exclaimed. 'This is a surprise. I thought that you and Stuart must be on the high seas by now?'

'I've been attending a course at the Morris Motor works,' he explained, and laughed at her look of astonishment.

'No, we don't intend to *drive* the old *Hampshire* to Berlin . . . it was a course on aero engines.' Heather still wondered why the gunnery officer of a battleship needed to know anything about aeroplane engines but realised that she should not be asking such questions.

He took her bicycle and pushed it for her as they walked side by side along the narrow pavement.

'I can't tell you how pleased I am to see a friendly face,' he went on. 'Here was I, wondering how best to spend my last hours of freedom, and you come along and nearly run me down.'

She would have protested at the exaggeration, but he continued without pause. 'You must have dinner with me this evening. Come on now, you cannot deny me that pleasure . . . it may be the last meal that I ever take in civilised society!'

'Oh, Daniel,' she exclaimed, 'how can you be so flippant?' She felt a cold chill down her spine when she thought about it. Every day there came news of merchant shipping sunk by German U-boats. It was inevitable that the *Hampshire* should herself be exposed to similar attack.

'I understand that your ship is in Glasgow for a refit?' Heather observed. 'Only this morning I received a formal invitation to Annie and Stuart's wedding at Eisdalsa.'

'I shall be leaving for Scotland early tomorrow,' Dan explained. 'After a short spell of duty on board, Stuart and I will be taking a few days' leave to attend the wedding. I'm to be his "second".'

'I have never considered marriage to be a duel,' she laughed. 'Don't you mean best man?'

Dan shrugged. 'Whatever you say!' He grinned.

'Have you ever been to Eisdalsa?' Heather asked.

'No,' he replied, 'but the way Stuart talks about it all the time, I feel that I know every blade of grass already!'

They had reached the library by this time. Heather repossessed her bicycle.

'I have some work to catch up on,' she explained. 'Where shall we meet for dinner?'

'I could come and call for you?' he suggested.

'Not a good idea,' she replied. 'I shall have to sneak out without the Proctor seeing me. They're a bit strict with female students, you know!'

'But you're not an undergraduate,' he protested.

'Nevertheless.' Heather shrugged resignedly. 'It would be best if we arranged to meet somewhere.'

They had agreed upon a little restaurant just off the High Street where they were less likely to be spotted by any of Heather's friends.

At their first meeting, Daniel had been only mildly attracted to the blue stocking from the Highlands, but seeing Stuart and Margaret so taken up with Annie's problems, he had felt obliged to entertain the girl himself. During their walk around the estate, he remembered, she had been rather silent, more concerned about her sick friend perhaps than she was ready to admit. The only time she had shown even a flicker of excitement or interest was on seeing some medieval wall paintings which had been uncovered quite recently, during restoration work on the thirteenth-century church in the village.

Tonight, however, he found himself increasingly attracted to her. She was most vivacious – determined to be amusing, and interested in every topic of conversation. Dan suspected that she viewed the occasion as an opportunity to do her 'bit' for the war effort by entertaining a poor sailor, away from home and soon to go off to fight.

He regarded her closely as she attacked her lamb chops with enthusiasm. She was a handsome woman, tall, with that hint of auburn in her hair which marked her out as a Highlander. Her eyes were blue as the skies above the Hebrides, and her skin had the soft bloom of one who was raised on mountain water and salt sea air. He could picture her with her hair blowing loosely in the breeze, standing upon some rocky cliff facing out to sea . . . He began to fantasise. Could it be that some day she would be waiting there for him?

He felt oddly disturbed by the feelings which she aroused in him. Why, he hardly knew the girl. Quickly he brushed aside the thoughts which were troubling him and concentrated upon the dessert trolley which, despite wartime restrictions, seemed generously loaded.

There was a sharp chill in the December night when they emerged from the brightly lit restaurant. Heather drew her heavy woollen coat closely about her shoulders. As her eyes adjusted to the gloom she looked upwards, admiring the indigo blue of the star-spangled heavens.

'It's so beautiful,' she sighed, 'it seems a pity not to make the most of such a glorious evening.'

'How about a walk along by the river?' Dan suggested, and was surprised how overjoyed he felt when she agreed.

The lights of the ancient city were dimmed, a precaution, against the threat of Zeppelin raids, but there was a moon three-quarters full, and the stars seemed large and close enough for them to be able to reach up and pluck them from the sky.

Dan pushed open an old iron gate and they slipped through into Christchurch Meadow. Heather had stood at this very spot on the towpath earlier in the year, watching the 'eights' battling their way towards the finish. Now the waters lay oily-still in the moonlight and only a clump of brown and withered reeds floating on the river's surface indicated the direction of its flow. Disturbed by their footsteps, a coot scuttled out suddenly from below the bank and half ran, half flew to the opposite shore. Startled, Heather grabbed Daniel's arm.

'Are you cold?' he asked, and without waiting for her reply, he placed an arm around her shoulders, drawing her close. They walked on companionably.

Beyond the meadow the towpath widened out into a tarmacadamed forecourt linking a dark boat house with the river bank. Piled upon this, upside-down for the winter, punts which during the long summer days had populated the river, lay abandoned until spring. One lone craft, lashed securely to stakes at both bow and stern, rode upon the water. It must have been on the river only that afternoon, for the cushions were still on board.

On impulse, Dan handed Heather, mildly protesting, down into the tiny craft. He cast off both ropes and leapt aboard himself, grabbing up a paddle to fend the boat off from the bank.

Heather lay against the pillows and watched as, with surprising expertise, Dan poled his craft into midstream and allowed it to float along with a minimum of effort on his part.

'This is a bit different from steering a battleship,' she remarked, pulling gently at the rudder line resting over her shoulder and watching his expert handling of the pole.

'Yes,' he replied lightly, 'she responds much faster!'

'I can see you've done this before,' she told him.

'At Marlborough, actually,' he replied. 'I was at school there, until I went to Dartmouth Naval College when I was sixteen.'

'Don't they have punts at Dartmouth?' she asked, continuing, with a wicked smile, 'What a pity. I have always thought a punt the ideal vessel for courting. What does a sailor do to entertain the ladies at Dartmouth?'

'One takes them for a cream tea at Mrs Oakes's Parlour on the waterfront,' he replied, laughing. 'The food was so poor in college we were always starving!'

After a time he pulled out of the stream and made for an overhanging willow. Under the canopy formed by its bows, he secured the punt and moved to occupy the cushions beside Heather.

For a while they lay looking up at the sky through the overhanging branches, and talked. After a while they fell silent. Heather, her mind far away in the Hebrides, remembered other nights as clear and bright. She was suddenly aware that Dan was gazing at her with an intensity which startled her. In the Oxford University of 1914, the women's colleges were convent-like in their regulations. Although she had been away from home for three years, Heather had never before found herself in so compromising a position. She moved slightly, and sensing her disquiet Dan caught hold of her hand. His grip was firm and warm. Strangely the gesture made her feel more secure, and she relaxed sufficiently for him to take the other hand as well. Leaning towards her, he kissed her tenderly and was rewarded by soft inviting lips parting to allow his tongue inside. With a little moan of pleasure he released her hands only to grasp her more firmly by the shoulders. They kissed again.

Struggling with the heavy woollen coats which each of them wore, Dan began, gently and systematically, to unbutton her dress so that he might slip his hand inside her bodice. She shuddered in anticipation as he probed beneath her tightly laced chemise and loosened the strings. Soon his fingers caressed her soft warm breasts and played gently with her hardened nipples. She gave an ecstatic little gasp as he lowered his lips to hers once more, and they kissed passionately.

Heather did not know how long they lay there in the boat. It was the sound of Old Tom striking once which finally alerted them to the lateness of the hour.

'Good lord!' Dan struggled into an upright position and turned to help as Heather hurriedly adjusted her dress. 'I shall have to get back to my digs. I have to catch the train for London which leaves at seven-thirty if I am to make the connection for Glasgow by ten o'clock.'

Their passage back upstream to the boatyard took all of Dan's attention, and it was not until they had secured the punt and were hurrying along the towpath towards Magdalene Bridge that either of them made any mention of the future.

'Shall I see you at the wedding?' Dan asked, holding the gate for her to slip through.

'Of course,' she replied.

'No doubt it will be a pretty quiet affair,' he suggested. 'Eisdalsa is a very small place, isn't it?'

Heather laughed. 'What it lacks in size it makes up for in entertainment,' she told him. 'I think you might be in for a very great surprise!'

They approached her college by way of a narrow passage which ran alongside the gardens, and stopped at a spot where the ancient brick wall had deteriorated substantially over the years, leaving useful footholds.

'You don't propose to go over there?' Dan viewed the sheer brickwork in alarm.

'There's nothing to it,' Heather said, expressing greater confidence than she felt. Nothing would have made her confess to this being her first attempt in three years to scale the wall. Her fellow students had assured her that it was an easy climb. 'Just give me a bunk up and I'll be over in a jiffy.'

She gave him one last, fleeting kiss. 'See you in Scotland,' she whispered, and waited for him to lift her up to the first foothold.

Annie had returned to Overavon, convinced that she would hear no more of the Government appointment at which Manny had hinted. She felt sure that he had only proposed her for the post because he thought that as his wife it would be a convenient way for her to contribute to the war effort. How ironic that he should now consider the work unsuitable for a married woman!

Letters from Stuart were few, but when they arrived they were many pages long. He wrote daily, mailing his communiqué when an opportunity presented itself. He was not allowed to say what he was doing, of course, but he spoke of day-to-day happenings aboard the ship, describing in picturesque and often amusing terms his shipmates and their peculiarities. There was a hint that a refit would be bringing the *Hampshire* into dry dock very soon and he hoped that this would be the opportunity they needed to arrange the wedding.

'*It looks as though Highland dress might be appropriate since we shall not be too far from home.*' Annie caught her breath. How wonderful! The refit was almost certainly going to be on the Clyde. '*But my fellow officers are insisting on dress uniform, swords and all . . .*'

Delighted at the prospect of marrying with her friends around her, Annie hurriedly made plans for her return to Scotland.

Stuart's telegram announcing his arrival at Greenock, and giving the date of his leave, arrived on the same day that she received a letter from the Ministry of Supply inviting her to take up the post of Director of Women's Welfare and Inspector of Factories (Munitions and Armaments Manufacture). Her appointment was to commence on 12 January, 1915.

In normal circumstances she would have chalked this up as a great victory for women's emancipation, and shared her rejoicing with her friends in the Movement. As it was, she was obliged to spend the next few days making last-minute arrangements for her wedding.

On the day of her departure, Rebecca summoned Annie to her withdrawing room.

Since Annie had refused Emmanuel's proposal of marriage things had been rather awkward between Rebecca and herself. Once she was no longer the prospective daughter-in-law, Annie's position in the household had become that of an employee rather than a member of the family.

Now, in a strained atmosphere, they exchanged trivialities for a few minutes over a cup of tea.

Rebecca Rosenstein had aged during the past months. Annie, absorbed in her work, and having deliberately distanced herself from the social activities of the household, had failed to notice the steady deterioration which had taken place in her employer. The arthritis which had plagued her for several years seemed to have defeated Rebecca at last. She appeared more frail, her skin had taken on the pallor and texture of that of an old woman, and Annie noticed that as she lifted her teacup, she had difficulty in keeping a steady hand.

Suddenly Annie was filled with compassion for her.

'It seems a pity that your wedding should have to be such a rushed affair.' Rebecca spoke in the tightly clipped manner which she had adopted since the day Annie had announced that she was to marry Stuart Beaton.

'We are lucky that Stuart will have fourteen days' leave,' she replied. 'It means we can be married in the church of Eisdalsa.'

She looked up at Rebecca as she spoke, and was surprised to see tears trickling down the older woman's face.

'I have been very unkind to you these past weeks,' admitted Rebecca, dabbing at her eyes with a lace handkerchief. 'It was so difficult for me to accept that you do not love my *son*. I had built up such hopes for the future, you see . . . a future in which you were to play a major role.' She choked on the words. Annie went to her and put her arms around her.

'It is not that I do not like him,' she said, gently. 'I have a great affection for both your sons, and shall be eternally grateful to Manny, and to you, for giving me shelter and helping me to recover from . . . well . . . you know. But I have known Stuart Beaton since we played together as children,' she continued. 'In those days he was my idol. When he came here with Dan and took care of me, my feelings for him had not changed but there was absolutely nothing to indicate that he felt anything at all for me, other than the concern of a physician for his patient.'

Rebecca stroked a wayward lock of hair out of Annie's eyes, and with gentle fingers erased an anxious frown from the younger woman's brow.

'What changed things?' she asked, wanting to keep Annie

talking, wanting to repair the damage which her attitude over these past weeks had done to their relationship.

'I don't know,' Annie replied. 'Maybe it was the war. Suddenly it seemed important to have roots . . . someone to think about, some hope for the future. Who can say? That day, when we drove over to see the White Horse, Stuart discovered that he was in love too. I think for him it was like a bolt of lightning . . . the realisation that his need for me was as great as mine for him.' Her voice trailed off, and there was a far-away look in her eyes.

Rebecca, now the more composed of the two, squeezed Annie's hand and smiled. 'I hope you will be very happy, my dear.'

Relieved that at last she had made her peace with her benefactor, Annie pulled herself to her feet and went to the window. Mainwaring should be driving the car round at any time now.

Rebecca settled herself into a less painful position. 'Manny tells me that you have been assigned to the southern region of the country for the first few months,' she observed. 'I hope that you will use Overavon as a stopping-off point when on your travels. You will come and visit me, won't you?'

'Nothing shall keep me away,' Annie replied, smiling.

'Help me up,' Rebecca demanded, suddenly, 'I have something for you.' Stiffly, she shuffled to her walnut escritoire, and struggled with the lid. Annie hastened to help her. From one of a row of small drawers Rebecca withdrew a flat box covered in red leather which she handed to Annie to open.

'I want you to have this,' she said. 'My husband gave it to me when we became engaged. Wear it on your wedding day, as a token of our friendship. I wish that I could be present in person, but this will have to suffice.'

On a bed of black velvet lay an exquisite necklace; undoubtedly the diamonds were real and of the very best quality. Annie gasped in surprise.

'I can't accept this,' she declared, 'you must keep it for your real daughter-in-law. This is a family heirloom.'

'It is mine to do with as I choose,' Rebecca insisted. 'Please take it with my blessing.'

Annie, quite speechless, closed the box and threw her arms around the frail woman. The strength of her hug made Rebecca wince with pain, but nevertheless she smiled as Annie murmured, 'Thank you . . . for this and for everything you have done for me.'

'Get along with you,' Rebecca insisted, anxious to be alone now that matters had been put to rights between them. 'I heard the car drive up just a few moments ago. You must not miss your train.'

Annie kissed her again on either cheek and grasped her handbag, tucking the necklace carefully inside.

'I'll see you again, very soon,' she asserted.

'Goodbye, my dear, and good luck.' Rebecca turned to the window and Annie fled through the hall and ran down the steps to the waiting Rolls.

She was surprised to find a small crowd gathered around the car. As she reached the bottom of the stairway, the butler, Bates, stepped forward with a parcel in his hands, wrapped in coloured paper with ribbons and bows in silver.

'A small wedding gift from the staff, Miss McGillivray. We hope that you and the Commander will be very happy.'

Speechless, Annie took the package from him. She was near to tears. Here was she, expecting to leave as if under a cloud, and they were all being so nice to her. Even the stiff-lipped house-keeper kissed her on the cheek and old Nanny Clegg, who had cared for her during her illness, hugged her so tightly that her hat was set askew. A young gardener's lad whom she hardly knew gave her a posy of gardenias from the greenhouse and when she looked around for the head gardener to see if he approved, she found his grizzled old face wreathed in smiles.

'Thank you,' she managed through her tears, 'thank you all so much. I shall be seeing you again very soon, I hope.'

Mainwaring, aware that time was passing and there was a train to catch, ushered her into the car. The sound of their cheerful farewells was still ringing in her ears as they reached the end of the drive and turned into the main road.

Chapter 16

From Pulpit Hill Annie could view the entire panorama of Oban Bay, from the island of Kerrera on her left hand, to the distant hills of Movern and the Nevis Range on her right. There was a light dusting of snow on the nearby hills of Mull, while the surrounding mountains stood out sharply against the horizon, white-capped and gleaming in the bright sunlight.

In her hand Annie held the long red box containing Rebecca Rosenstein's gift. She opened the lid and took out the diamonds, holding them up to the window to admire the fine stones. Moving across to the cheval mirror which stood in one corner of the room, she fastened the necklace about her throat and decided immediately that the jewellery could not be worn with the ruffled blouse and the suit she had chosen for the wedding. She began to struggle with the clasp.

There had been no time for complicated dressmaking, but Annie would have chosen to be married in a tailored woollen costume anyway. She never felt comfortable in elaborate dress.

There was a light tap on the door before Margaret entered.

'I thought you might like a cup of tea,' she said, and paused when she saw Annie was already dressed. 'Oh, I didn't realise you were up.'

Seeing Annie struggling with the necklace, she put down the teacup and went to her aid.

'What a perfectly lovely thing,' she declared, admiringly.

'It was given to me to wear at the wedding,' Annie explained, 'but it looks quite wrong against this blouse.'

Margaret had to agree that Annie was right. 'It really cries out for a low-cut bodice,' she decided.

'It seems a shame,' sighed Annie. 'I can't think there will ever be an occasion to wear it, other than tomorrow.'

'Oh, I'm sure that's not true,' Margaret laughed. 'Just you wait until Stuart is a famous surgeon . . . you will forever be receiving invitations to splendid events.' Thoughtfully she measured Annie with her eyes. 'I have an idea,' she said at last, then hesitated, unsure how she would respond to her suggestion. 'But you may not want to consider it.'

Suddenly making up her mind she hurried out of the room, calling back over her shoulder, 'drink your tea . . . I won't be a minute.'

William and Elizabeth Whylie had arrived on the evening train, alighting at Connel station to find both David and Annabel Beaton waiting to greet them. Morag, jumping down ahead of her escorts, ran along the platform and threw her arms around her grandfather.

'Hallo there, Kitten,' he greeted her, grabbing hold of his hat which she had dislodged in her enthusiasm. 'How's my favourite granddaughter?'

'Oh, you are a silly, Grandpa!' the child replied. 'You only have one.'

'That makes it all the easier to decide.' He pushed her gently to one side while he kissed Elizabeth lightly on the cheek and shook hands with William.

Formalities over, they wasted no time in bundling the visitors into the car for the short journey to Creag an Tuirc.

'I thought a light supper would be preferable to anything too heavy,' Annabel said as she helped Elizabeth to unpack. 'I know what it is like after a long journey.'

'Is Morag staying here tonight?' Elizabeth asked, lifting out her wedding outfit and taking care to shake out the creases.

'No,' Annabel answered, 'David will drive her to Eisdalsa as soon as we have eaten. Her mother wants to dress her tomorrow.'

'She is so excited,' explained Elizabeth. 'She tells me she has never been to a wedding before and has little idea what to expect. I have tried to explain her duties, so I dare say she will perform to everyone's satisfaction. The questions she asked . . . it makes one wonder how less gifted girls could ever have managed to be bridesmaids!'

'Yes, she does rather like to know every detail,' laughed Annabel. 'What about her school work . . . is she keeping up with her classmates?'

'She is way ahead of most of them,' Elizabeth assured her. 'I can see her being ready for Medical School by the time she is seventeen.'

'Medical School?' Annabel repeated, startled.

'Oh, dear, have I let the cat out of the bag?' Elizabeth looked quite concerned. 'I thought you all knew that she intended to become a doctor?'

'Well, I must admit to being a little suspicious when she demanded to accompany her father on his rounds at the age of ten,' Annabel replied. 'Hugh's story was that his elderly patients were starved of young company and that her visits did them good. Somehow I think your explanation is the more convincing.' A slow grin spread across her face. 'I wonder what David will say when he hears about it?'

'Remembering his attitude towards working women in general, I did wonder how Morag had persuaded him.' Elizabeth grinned.

'Morag obviously believes that it is not yet time to reveal her intentions,' observed Annabel, thoughtfully. 'Perhaps it would be as well if we do not mention it to the others.'

'Is Stuart not staying here before the great day?' Elizabeth asked, surprised not to have seen him already.

'No, the men thought it would be more convenient if they stayed at Tigh na Broch. Stuart and his best man, that is. I believe that their fellow officers have taken rooms at the Army and Navy Club in Oban.'

One of the larger of the seafront hotels had been transformed into a club early in the war, providing for officers similar facilities to those offered to other ranks by the Services Canteen.

'You must be disappointed not to have him here with you on his last night of freedom,' Elizabeth commented, wondering if she and William had been the cause of Stuart's having to lodge elsewhere.

'From what I heard,' Annabel observed, dryly, 'there are plans afoot for a certain amount of celebration tonight, to which we ladies are not invited, so maybe it is as well that they are spending the night at Eisdalsa! We are sure to see something of Stuart and Annie while they are here. They are spending their honeymoon on the island, in Margaret's cottage.'

Sounds of male laughter from below reminded the two women that they must join the men for supper if Morag was to be delivered to her mother at a reasonable hour.

The church had begun to fill up a full half hour before the ceremony was scheduled to begin. The Reverend John McCulloch poked his head around the vestry door to find out how things were going, and was gratified to see Stuart Beaton and his friend hovering in the vestibule. He approached them, hand outstretched.

'Stuart, my boy, it has been a long time.' He shook the bridegroom's hand warmly.

'Mr McCulloch, sir, you are looking very well, if I may say so.' Stuart noted the frail hands and the deeply shadowed eyes. The old chap must be getting on for eighty. It was hardly surprising if he was showing signs of wear. Thrusting these thoughts aside, Stuart continued to smile broadly.

'May I present my brother officer, Daniel Rosenstein.'

McCulloch greeted Daniel. 'What a pleasure to see so many of Stuart's fellow mariners here today,' he said, casting an approving eye over the row of officers from the *Hampshire*, all clad like the groom and best man in their full dress uniform.

McCulloch continued, somewhat apologetically, 'It is usual to go over the service with the bride and groom before the ceremony, but in these days there is too little time for the niceties. I hope you have witnessed enough weddings, Stuart, to know the order in which we do things?'

As a child Stuart had possessed a treble voice of a quality to gladden not only his mother's heart, but those of all the ladies of the parish. He had served in the Kilbrendan Church choir for several years and attended many a wedding service. Convinced that he knew every word of the wedding vows by heart, he replied, reassuringly, 'I am certain we shall manage admirably.'

Dan regarded his friend with some amusement. He had always been led to believe that on his wedding day the groom was supposed to be a nervous wreck. Was not that the reason for his requiring a friend to stand up with him at the altar? Yet here was Stuart, reassuring the *priest* that everything would go well . . .

Stuart caught sight of his mother, fussing over the seating arrangements for the Whylies, and hurried down the aisle to greet her. It had been so long since his last leave, she wanted to gather him in her arms and hug the life out of him. Instead they embraced with great care – neither wishing to disturb Annabel's elaborate hat.

'Come, dearest,' he said gently, 'let me introduce you to my friend Daniel.'

He led her to where Dan waited beside the front pew.

'Mr Rosenstein,' Annabel said, holding out her gloved hand, 'I am very pleased to meet you at last. We were so much looking forward to your visit last year.'

'Mrs Beaton, ma'am.' Dan stepped forward and placed the proffered hand to his lips. In these modern days, Scottish matrons were no longer accustomed to such demonstrations of gallantry. Annabel blushed prettily and Stuart felt sure that Daniel had won his mother's heart.

'Perhaps, had we come that September,' observed Dan, amused 'we might not be here today!'

Annabel looked puzzled for a minute, then smiled. 'Of course . . . it was on your visit to Overavon that Stuart met Annie again. How silly of me not to remember.'

Sounds of activity in the porch indicated that the bride had arrived. Within a few minutes Margaret Brown hurried down the aisle and joined Michael and Heather, while Millicent slipped in beside Hugh. With her handkerchief, Millicent dabbed at something sticky on her youngest son's mouth, and straightened Ian's tie. She looked across at Hugh and smiled. Everything was going to plan . . . so far.

Seated in front, Annabel was obliged to turn around in order to survey her little family. She was so glad that the men had decided to wear full Highland dress – it added so much colour to the scene. Hugh's boys, too, looked quite angelic in their miniature kilts complete with sporran. Contentedly she turned back to admire her younger son, his smart uniform decorated for the occasion with white bows on his cap and in his lapel. She had been shocked to see how thin and gaunt he had become. It was unlikely that they would ever know just what tribulations these poor boys had to endure while away at sea.

The last wedding she had attended here had been of such a different character. She recalled her dear friend Anne McGillivray standing at the alter rail beside the grey-haired, rather stooped figure of John McDougal, and her thoughts strayed to Wee Annie's mother . . . so far away on her daughter's wedding day. Well, they had done their best to make up for the absence of Annie's family. David had been most moved when the couple had asked him to give the bride away. She must be sure to take note of every detail of what happened in order to write Anne an eyewitness account.

Glancing across the aisle to where Elizabeth and William Whylie sat, she caught a glimpse of William in profile and realised how old and tired he looked. He had accepted a very responsible job at a time in his life when he should be resting and taking life easy. David too was busier now than he had been when he ran the Eisdalsa practice, having accumulated more duties as each of the younger medical men in the district had been called up.

She bent her head and began searching for the first of the hymns on the board. The book almost fell open at the number. 'Love divine . . .' But of course.

Really it was a remarkable turn out, she told herself, considering the short time allowed for the preparations. There was a fair smattering of uniforms. Many of the men wore the Black Watch tartan of the Argyll and Sutherland Highlanders, the local regiment. And what a lot of sailors there were! The McPhersons, the boat-builders of Eisdalsa island, were well represented among those in naval uniform she noticed, and behind Hugh and Millicent sat Stuart's friends from the *Hampshire*. She hoped they had enjoyed themselves last evening.

She had taken immediately to Daniel Rosenstein. She must remember to ask after his mother. Mrs Rosenstein had been kind to Annie and had made both Stuart and Margaret very welcome in her home.

There was no doubting that Stuart was a happy man today. Annabel was so pleased that he had decided to marry. When the war was over, perhaps he would be content to take up a practice somewhere nearby and enjoy a more settled, family life. She could imagine the beautiful, clever children he was going to have. Wee Annie was such an admirable wife for him. It would be a pleasure to welcome her into the family.

Katherine McLean, official organist now that Mr Bloar was fighting in France, was playing something by Bach. Annabel glanced around again. Yes, there was Archie McClean, her husband, seated right at the back, unobtrusive as always. It had been so thoughtful of Katherine to offer her beautiful home, Johnstones, for Stuart's wedding reception. Everyone had rallied round to find enough food and drink, of course, but to have one's entire household disrupted for someone else's wedding – well, it just showed how lucky they were to have such friends.

Katherine struck up the 'Wedding March', and all heads turned to watch the bride walk down the aisle on the arm of Dr David Beaton.

Annabel had expected that Wee Annie McGillivray would choose to wear something very plain, a well-tailored suit perhaps. She was astonished to see the bride in a gown of glistening white silk and a veil of fine lace. It was only as the procession swept close by her that she recognised Margaret's own wedding dress. How well it looked with that beautiful necklace . . . could they be real diamonds? she wondered. Annie's dark hair, highlighted by strands of silver, waved gracefully beneath a neat headband of fresh flowers, picked only that morning from Katherine McLean's greenhouse. The bouquet was a simple spray of white gardenias and asparagus fern. As she turned to hand the flowers to Morag, Annie caught Annabel's eye and smiled. Her look seemed to say: I know we can trust you not to give away our little secret.

Morag Beaton, the single bridesmaid, waited calmly behind the bridal pair, the skirt of her dark blue velvet gown brushing

Annabel's knee. She smiled happily at her grandmother and Annabel felt the first tears welling . . . and she had vowed that she would not cry! The child carried a delightful little posy of many colours. In future, the heavy scent of freesias would always remind Annabel of this moment.

Annie shivered a little as Margaret removed the warm cape which she had held around her during the journey from Oban. Up to this moment it had all been such a rush that she had hardly had time to feel nervous.

It was a long time since she had stood in this church. The damp musty smell of old stonework evoked memories of Sundays long ago; of endless sermons when she had struggled to keep awake; of precious moments when at Christmas, by candlelight they had sung the ancient carols; of a day in summer when she had stood between her brother and her mother and watched them lift Kirsty's coffin – a wreath had slipped off she remembered, and Dougal had stepped forward to catch it.

Dr David had done her proud. He looked so distinguished in his kilt. She rested her gloved hand on his arm, and smiled up at him.

'Ready?' he asked.

She nodded, just a trifle nervously, and as the first notes of the organ heralded their entrance, was aware of her new shoes slipping slightly on the cold marble tiles. She grasped David's arm more tightly, and he instinctively pulled her closer. David had always been like a father to her. She had known no other. As they walked down the aisle, heads turned. There was Stuart's mother – she wondered whether Annabel would recognise the wedding gown? It had been such a hurried decision that they had scarcely had time to press out the creases, but when she had seen herself in the mirror, Annie knew she had been right to accept Margaret's offer. This was what a girl should look like on her wedding day. Her hand wandered up to touch the diamond necklace. Rebecca would be pleased that she had worn it.

Here was Mr McCulloch standing before them, his black stock relieved by preaching bands of lace, worn especially for the occasion.

She hardly dared look at Stuart, but felt his nearness as her bare upper arm rubbed lightly against his uniform jacket and her gloved fingers encountered his. David had switched to her other side in readiness to give her hand to the groom. Suddenly she felt overwhelmed by the atmosphere of warmth and tenderness emanating from this great gathering of their friends. If only her mother had been there too, everything would have been perfect.

Stuart had borne all the usual ribaldry associated with the marriage of a young man, with good humour. It had been a merry party of officers from the *Hampshire*, together with one or two of the groom's medical colleagues from university, who had boarded the train from Glasgow the previous day. They had taken over a carriage to themselves, and if they made rather more noise than was normally acceptable upon the Highland line, well, what of it? The guard, whose son was serving in a minesweeper somewhere in the North Sea, was not disposed to make a fuss, and ignored the occasional complaint from less indulgent passengers.

Up to the moment when he had found himself standing waiting for Annie to join him in the church, the preparations had all seemed quite superficial and without much meaning to Stuart. As the minister had said, he had witnessed such ceremonies so many times in the past that they held no mystery for him.

At the first notes of the organ, the congregation rose to its feet and Stuart turned his head slightly, to catch a glimpse of Annie as she came down the aisle.

The vision of loveliness advancing towards him on his father's arm quite took his breath away. Could this really be his Annie? She of the dark suits, the knotted ties and sensible brogues; the tough Suffragette who stood on platforms to be pelted with rotten eggs. Was this the little ghost-like figure whom he had rediscovered at Overavon?

She stood beside him now, gloved fingers touching his briefly in greeting. As she turned to hand her bouquet to Morag, Stuart cast a bewildered glance at his father, who nodded reassuringly and actually winked.

Stuart's knees had turned to jelly, he felt sure he must collapse at any moment. He glanced nervously at Daniel to find his friend surreptitiously tapping his jacket pocket to make sure he could feel the ring.

Mr McCulloch was speaking. The words were familiar but Stuart was in a panic. When did he have to say something? Would he have to remember the words for himself? He was sure he had forgotten them.

'I require and charge you both . . .' He tried to concentrate on the words, but his eyes kept straying towards the silk-clad figure at his side. The necklace was magnificent. He wondered where it had come from?

'Stuart William Angus, wilt thou have this woman . . .' She had so much colour in her cheeks today, it must be the sea air. Those few weeks on Eisdalsa had done her the world of good. He hoped she would consent to remain living on the island until the war was over. He would feel more at ease if he knew that was where she would be, safely out of harm's way.

'. . . as long as ye both shall live?'

Suddenly he was aware that everyone was looking at him, expecting him to answer.

'I will,' he spluttered, turning red with embarrassment. He had fluffed his lines! Annie, by contrast, answered without hesitation, which made him feel even worse.

It was over. They had made their vows and Stuart had only stumbled slightly over the Annie Elizabeth – no one had told him her second name was Elizabeth. At last the veil was thrown back, and he could take a proper look at his bride.

He felt daunted by the enormity of the commitment he had just undertaken. Annie's happiness and well-being were now his responsibility. He glanced down at her delicate hand, resting confidently in his own, the simple gold band that had tied them together gleaming brightly in its newness. She smiled up at him, radiant with happiness, and he knew that whatever trials he must face in the months and years to come, that look would be with him always.

With the sounds of the organ still ringing in their ears, Stuart and Annie emerged into the cold December afternoon to be greeted by a piper and a guard of honour formed by the officers of the *Hampshire*, who with their swords raised formed an archway of glistening steel.

There was a brief pause while a photographer recorded the scene and then the bridal pair was ushered into the waiting limousine – Callum McKenzie's taxi, splendidly decorated in white ribbons.

Annie leant forward and gave a regal wave to the guests who had positioned themselves along the driveway as far as the church gates. She sat back at last when the car turned into the lane and the friendly salutations were lost on the wind.

Suddenly conscious of Stuart's eyes upon her, she turned to him.

'Hallo, Mrs Beaton,' he said, slipping his arm around her shoulders.

'Hallo, Mr Beaton,' she replied, happily, and sank into his embrace. Pulling away the veiling without any regard at all for her coiffeur, he buried his face in her hair and kissed the nape of her neck.

Glancing up, Stuart caught sight of Callum McKenzie's interested face in the driving mirror. With a deft motion he lowered the blind across the glass partition, obscuring the driver's view.

Morag had asked several people why it was called a 'wedding breakfast' when they were eating at four o'clock in the afternoon? So far she had not found a satisfactory answer, perhaps because most of her informants had been of the uniformed variety and clearly delighted in teasing Annie's little bridesmaid.

She had been thrilled to find herself seated between Stuart and his best man, and just wished that Christina Bell were here to see her, surrounded by all these splendid figures in naval uniform. Mrs Whylie had told her that throughout the day the best man was not only responsible for directing the proceedings on behalf of the groom, but was also the official escort to the chief bridesmaid. While Daniel Rosenstein had carried out his duties faultlessly during and after the church ceremony, she found his attentions wandering now that her Cousin Heather was seated on his other hand. Really, it was too bad of him!

They had told her there would be speeches when the meal was finished. She was not looking forward to that. Grandpa, for one, was difficult to stop once he got started.

Mama had made the syllabub, Morag could always tell. It was her mother's favourite recipe and guaranteed never to go wrong. She scraped her spoon carefully around the glass dish to be sure that not a scrap was left then frowned as she glanced across at Annie's plate which lay untouched before her.

Stuart caught her eye and grinned. He leant towards Annie and whispered something in her ear. Morag's empty dish was spirited away from under her nose and suddenly there was Annie's in its place.

'Shouldn't she be eating it herself?' Morag protested. 'She ought to have something . . . she only picked at her salad.'

Stuart had heard all about Morag's solicitous management of Annie's recovery the previous year.

'I think she is a little too excited to eat just at present,' he told the child, seriously. 'I'll see she has something later.'

Satisfied, Morag plunged her spoon into the delicious creamy mound, savouring the envious looks of her two brothers who were seated some feet away, under the watchful eyes of their parents.

Morag was dismayed to hear the tell-tale squeaks and groans which heralded the playing of the pipes. From a tiny child she had always protested at the sound which appeared to send her grandpa and father into raptures of delight. Now the piper was in full flow. He swept into the great dining room, kilt swinging and sporran dancing to the rhythm of the march. There was a gasp of delight from all sides.

Despite the restrictions imposed upon them by food shortages, the wedding cake had tree tiers and was iced in white sugar – a work of delicate filigree and dainty floral patterns. It stood on the table before the bride and groom, Stuart's polished ceremonial sword beside it, winking in the light from half a dozen chandeliers.

Twice around the room marched the piper, to the tune of 'I got a Kiss o' the King's Hand', finally coming to a halt right behind Stuart's chair.

He rose to his feet amidst calls and cheers, took up the sword and brandished it. There was some wild cheering. He invited Annie to help him cut the cake. They all clapped and sang 'For They Are Jolly Good Fellows!' until at last the bride and groom sat down and the speeches began.

Morag was agreeably surprised to find that her grandfather's speech was funny. To begin with, because he was speaking from knowledge of both bride and groom since the day each was born, he could recall the kinds of incident designed to make both of them blush and everyone else dissolve into fits of laughter: how Annie had been known as 'the shadow', because she had a reputation for keeping up with the boys in all their games, and was always in trouble for getting dirty and tearing her clothes, and how Stuart could be guaranteed to be playing truant from school as soon as the mackerel were spotted out in the bay!

Morag had never heard some of the stories before . . . it made the grown-ups a little more human, somehow. She began to wonder what sort of capers her own dear papa had got up to?

Now it was time for Stuart to say his piece. There was a hush. Happy faces looked up expectantly, anticipating further excuses for laughter, and Stuart did not disappoint them.

'My father is right about Wee Annie, of course,' he said. 'I wasn't particularly aware of her most of the time, she was Margaret's friend that was all, but my classmates were always going on about her being my girlfriend – which of course, at the age of eight, was a turn-off for any self-respecting wee boy. Anyway she gave up chasing me for a much worthier cause, one which will hopefully reach a successful resolution one day soon. In years to come, when women are not only doctors and lawyers, engineers and car drivers . . .' there was general laughter at this '. . . but also take their seats in Parliament. Think of it, Pa. One day we may have our first woman Prime Minister.' At this there was a sharp intake of breath from Dr David. 'I only hope that when that time comes, people will remember the women who made it possible.' He turned to his bride. 'No man deserves such a precious jewel as this, I least of all!' He raised his glass. 'To Wee Annie McGillivray . . . my wife!' And then he sat down to the cheers and congratulations of his friends.

The speeches came to an end, and as though by common consent dishes were cleared, the huge dining table dismantled and chairs pushed back to make a space for dancing. Donnie Campbell took up his fiddle and out came Gordon McClure's accordion.

Daniel, reminded of Heather's prediction, was forced to agree that a Highland wedding was indeed a very different affair from the rather more formal events which he had attended down south. This was much noisier . . . and far more fun.

To begin with, the guest list had not been restricted to family and close friends. It seemed as though the whole population of Argyll was here, although in truth it was only the parishioners of Kilbrendan. Gillies and fishermen rubbed shoulders with doctors and lawyers. Their host was even now whirling the baker's wife through the measures of the Strathspey while Heather had been spirited away on the arm of Baldie Campbell, the ferryman! If Daniel wanted to see anything of her tonight it was clear that he was going to have to join in.

Suddenly the music came to an end and there she was, beside him, laughing and fanning herself.

'Come along,' she demanded, 'they are going to play a waltz, just to get you sassenachs on to the floor. You'll see . . . by the end of the evening you'll be dancing the reels with the rest of us!'

Stuart led his wife out to open the waltz, and was followed almost immediately by David and Annabel and William and Elizabeth Whylie. Daniel turned to Heather and she crept into his arms, enjoying once again the nearness of him. Her hair brushed his face and he caught the fragrance of violets from the corsage she was wearing. The gentle rhythm of the music increased in pace and the dance soon turned into another frenzy of movement and excitement. Heather and Dan were drawn into the reel which followed in which willing hands steered him through the complicated movements. Stumbling, hesitating, tripping over his own and everyone else's feet, he managed to stay upright until the last notes of the music died.

'I must have some air,' he decided, guiding his partner towards the conservatory door.

Morag, who had had to content herself with partners of her own age all evening, watched them go. Disappointed that the best man had not fulfilled his duties to her satisfaction, she went in search of her grandfather. Surely *he* would be prepared to partner her in a reel?

Daniel and Heather found a secluded seat behind some potted palms. Dan took out a handkerchief and mopped his brow. 'I can appreciate why the Scots consider the kilt a more appropriate garment for these occasions,' he declared. 'It would certainly be cooler for your kind of dancing!'

'No Scotsman ever did anything to make himself cooler,' Heather said, laughing at him. 'It's the cold winds that make us jump about so much!'

'Well, I don't know where you find the stamina for it.' He was still breathing heavily. 'Even the old folks seem to be tireless.'

They sat in comfortable silence for a few minutes.

'What a magnificent view,' Dan commented finally, taking in the entire panorama which lay before them.

The glen ran almost due westwards towards the sea, its valley bottom filled by a narrow loch which snaked between overlapping spurs of the surrounding hills. Beside the loch the level pastures were under intensive cultivation, but higher up the slopes dark trees and bushes clothed the hillsides until, beyond the treeline, they gave way to a scrub of heather and bracken.

'Sometimes in summer, when there is some special event taking place, they hang lanterns in the trees right through the glen,' she told him. 'It's just like fairyland.'

Heather looked dreamily into the far distance. 'Archie McClean created these gardens from the bare hillside,' she explained. 'He used to be a slate quarrier at Eisdalsa, but in the late seventies he went away to Africa and amassed a fortune in the diamond fields.

When he came back, he bought up the entire valley and built this house.'

'His wife – Katherine, is it? – is such a delightful woman,' Dan observed. 'Was it not she who played the organ in church today?'

'She paints the most wonderful flower portraits too. You may have seen some of them about the house?' Heather, who did not know one end of a pencil from the other, had always been filled with admiration for anyone who could draw.

'This glass house is a marvellous idea,' Dan said. 'It makes one feel a part of the garden without having to step outside.'

The conservatory was Archie McLean's only concession to the wild weather conditions on this part of the coast. Here he grew the more tender species which could be enjoyed while winter gales swept down the valley withering leaves and destroying next year's buds on all but the hardiest of plants.

Out in the park it had been necessary to plant native trees as wind breaks. These had now grown to useful proportions. Each season more of the rhododendrons and azaleas from the foothills of the Himalayas and the remote parts of China had come into full bloom, delighting the hearts of all who saw them.

It had never been Archie's intention to keep his new possessions to himself. Despite his great wealth, he had never distanced himself from the villagers and crofters of Seileach. He felt that he owed it to this remote community to put something back into the land which had given him birth. From the very beginning, the people of the parish had been invited to come and go as they pleased about the grounds. Most were familiar with them, and many had attended entertainments in the house. Johnstones had become the focus of the district in the years following the decline of the Eisdalsa quarries.

'Archie planned the gardens,' Heather explained, 'but it is Annie's cousin by marriage, Iain McDougal, who is the gardener. His mother, Martha, is Katherine's housekeeper.'

'Was that the rather florid-faced bull of a young man your father introduced me to earlier on?' Dan asked. 'I was surprised not to see him in uniform.'

'He tried to join up.' Heather jumped to Iain's defence.

'There was something wrong with his heart.'

What a loyal creature she is, Dan thought. Oh, to be defended by such a tiger!

'In any case,' she continued, 'with Archie providing enough vegetables to supply the whole parish and sufficient feed to keep a large herd of beef cattle, Iain is probably doing a more useful job here.'

'The house is most impressive,' Dan commented. 'Is it very old?'

'Goodness, no!' Heather laughed. 'It's late-Victorian, but it does have some delightful rooms. Katherine tells me that she and Archie are planning to convert it into a convalescent home for wounded servicemen – there are quite a lot of seamen brought ashore in Oban and treated at my father's hospital.'

'It would make a wonderful place for convalescence,' Dan agreed, glancing back to where the dancing was again in full swing.

'Lucky the young men who manage to end up here,' he observed. 'Will you be lending a hand, now that you've finished with Oxford?'

'Oh, no!' she exclaimed, realising suddenly how little they really knew of each other. 'Didn't I tell you? I am waiting for an invitation to join Elsie Inglis's organisation, the Scottish Women's Hospitals. I am going to be an ambulance driver!'

'You mean, driving the injured from one place to another for treatment and so on?' he asked, surprised that she should choose such a mundane job.

'I would sincerely hope not!' exclaimed Heather, indignantly. 'I expect to be sent to France. We shall be collecting the wounded from behind the lines and taking them to our own hospitals.

Daniel was horrified. 'But that would be far too dangerous!' he cried.

'No more dangerous than manning a battleship,' she replied staunchly.

Realising that nothing he said was likely to make her change her mind, Daniel remained silent for a few moments. After a while he turned to her again, this time taking her hand in his and lifting her fingers to his lips. 'Don't think too harshly of me for worrying about you,' he apologised. 'You are right, of course, none of us can expect to remain cocooned in safety in today's circumstances. You have every right to do what you think is best.'

He paused, trying to find the words. Was he being too precipitate? But how could he wait? He must return to the ship tomorrow and there was no knowing when they would meet again.

'Perhaps you will think me impertinent to place too much store by our encounter last week . . .' he began.

She made no attempt to withdraw her hand from his grasp.

'But it would mean a great deal to me to feel that somewhere in the world there is someone with whom I might share my innermost thoughts . . . my hopes for the future . . . someone for whom it would be worth struggling to go on living, even when dying seems the easier option.'

She drew back, tears filling her eyes.

'Dearest Heather, do you think that sometime in the future when this . . . this wretched war is behind us . . . could you ever imagine yourself agreeing to marry me?'

She was stunned, thrilled and dismayed, all at the same time. Their meeting in Oxford had been a tremendous emotional upheaval for her. The single-minded desire to gain an academic qualification had concentrated her mind on her studies to the exclusion of all else hitherto. Until that night, she had never experienced romantic feelings for anyone. Since their meeting she had thought of little else!

'Until now, I have never thought of marrying,' she told him. 'Husbands, houses, children, were the things that other girls dreamed about . . . not Heather Brown, historian and teacher. Not me!'

'Perhaps no one has ever told you before that he loved you?' Daniel responded. 'Because that is what I am trying to tell you now. I love you, my darling Heather, and I want to spend the rest of my life with you.'

He sat back, releasing her hands and studying her face, seeking some sign that she felt as strongly as he did. When he drew her close and kissed her tenderly she made no move to resist him.

'I love you too, Dan.' Her reply was almost inaudible.

'You do?' he cried. 'You really love me?' She nodded and kissed him in return. 'But,' she continued, as though she had not been interrupted, 'we both have important work to do, and any long-term commitment might be a hindrance. May we not remain friends for the time being . . . very special friends? I promise I will write and we can meet whenever possible but as for marriage . . . well, perhaps that should wait until after the war.'

She was right, of course. He could see that now. It would be foolish for them to marry. What if she were to have a baby and he was killed? How could she manage to work and bring up a child at the same time? He did not know her very well, but he was sure she would not choose to live on family charity. What an admirable woman she was – practical, sensible, clever and wise – and she had not turned him down completely.

'The ship will be refitting for another ten days at least,' he explained eagerly. 'Will you come down to Gourock and stay until we are ready to sail? I have friends who would be pleased to find accommodation for you.'

'I would like that very much,' she replied, wondering how she was to explain to the family that she would be absent for both Christmas and the New Year celebrations.

'I couldn't get away until Tuesday,' she explained. 'I have promised Mother and Katherine that I will help with restoring Johnstones to some semblance of normality.'

'Then I shall meet you off the noon train in Glasgow,' he declared.

For some time he gazed at her, drinking in every minute detail of her face.

She shifted uneasily.

'I just want to remember you,' he explained. Then, gathering her in his arms, he kissed her once again.

It was well into the early hours of the morning when the wedding party began to break up.

Borrowing Michael's car, Heather and Dan drove the bride and groom to Eisdalsa village in search of a boat for the island. Mr

Campbell, the ferryman, had left the party long ago. There would be no waking him at this hour even had they wished to do so. Stuart decided to borrow one of the little rowing boats tied up beneath the steamer pier. No one would begrudge him the loan on this very special occasion.

What a pair they made: Annie, her white wedding gown trailing beneath a thick woollen cape while her long veil danced behind her in the strong breeze, and Stuart, his cap flat-aback and the gold braid on his winter-warm overcoat gleaming in the moonlight, rowing for all he was worth against the ebbing tide.

Annie turned once to wave to the couple on the shore.

'Those two seem to be getting on very well,' she remarked, as Stuart pulled resolutely for the harbour entrance.

'Humph . . .' He had little breath left for conversation.

'What a tangle of relationships it would be were they to marry,' declared Annie, jokingly. 'Your best friend would become your nephew!'

Imagining Daniel addressing her husband as 'Uncle Stuart', she stifled her giggles, not wishing to disturb the elderly residents whose cottages lay beside the harbour wall.

Stuart, having tied up the boat, hastily scribbled a note and slipped it under the ferry-house door. Mr Campbell would oblige him by towing the borrowed vessel back across at first light.

Arm in arm they took the path around the head of the harbour. There were lights still on in the McPhersons' cottage. Some of the ship-builder's sons must still be at the party. In a little while, no doubt, Katherine McLean would begin cooking breakfast for the most indefatigable of her guests!

Above the door of Margaret's cottage, a lantern, well-shaded to avoid its shining out to sea, lit their way along the path to the door. Some kindly person had thought about them coming home in the dark. Stuart pushed open the door and the ruddy glow of a fire, dying in the range, welcomed them inside. He turned to his bride and lifted her in his arms. She was light as a feather.

Ducking under the low wooden lintel, he carried her inside and pulled the door to behind him.

Chapter 17

Alice Martin folded her sheet. It had been doubled over and stitched down the side to make a bag. They might be forced to share beds with the alternate shift of workers but each girl had her own set of linen. She smoothed the harsh fabric with her hands before placing it with her bolster case in a locker beside the narrow iron bedstead. The mattress was now bare. Two grey army blankets and a pillow in striped ticking were neatly stacked at one end.

'It's time someone invented a shade of rouge to go with this yellow skin,' mused her friend, Sally Smith. She rubbed furiously at the patch of blush-red powder which she had applied liberally to one cheekbone. Sally leant forward, trying to get a clearer image in the ancient mirror which had lost much of its silvering. She wondered if the irritating spot which had kept her awake for most of the night was anything more than an ordinary pimple. It had been there on her right cheek for a long time. She couldn't remember when she had first noticed it. She gazed at the mark intently for a few minutes. It seemed to be getting larger and surely it was darker than the last time she had examined it? Hastily she obscured it with a liberal coating of face powder.

'Did you know that down in the village they are calling us the canaries?' she asked. 'Good, isn't it? We give our all for King and Country, and in return we get a skin like a Chinaman!'

Alice looked thoughtful. 'Do you think it's all right . . . us going yellow like this? Has anyone said anything about it to Mr Whylie?'

'What harm can it do?' scoffed Sally. 'Here, come on, it's nearly time for the shift change.'

She pulled her neat little dairymaid's cap down over her

carefully wound curlers, took a last glance in the mirror, and made for the door of the dormitory hut.

'What about your bed?' Alice called after her.

Sally had been so concerned with her face that she had quite forgotten the routine. She turned back, stripped the linen from her bed and bundled it carelessly into her locker. Alice, taking pity on her friend as she did most mornings, folded the blankets neatly and laid them at the foot of the mattress.

It had been made clear to them from the beginning that there would not be any additional beds provided in the hostel. The workforce had doubled since the factory buildings were completed early in March, but because the women worked in two shifts, it was possible for the night shift to use beds vacated by those working during the day. Despite strong protests as to the inadvisability of so many people living in such close proximity, William Whylie had been forced to accept the situation. All he could do was introduce a number of hygiene regulations and try to see that these were implemented.

The two girls hurried along the corridor towards the canteen. As they passed the bath house they could hear the women who had just come off duty, splashing and singing, glad to be released after a long night in the factory.

In many respects, health and welfare facilities in factories up and down the land had improved as a result of the recruitment of women to replace the men who had gone away to fight. The War Cabinet had fulfilled its promises to make conditions more acceptable for this new breed of workers.

The hostel accommodation, although very basic, was clean, warm and relatively comfortable. The works canteen provided three good meals a day, obviating the necessity for the women to shop for their food, a pastime which could involve queuing for hours every day. There was still a huge gulf between the sexes when it came to working practices, however. Several women had shown themselves to be more than equal to their male counterparts at the factory bench, but when the managers tried to promote such women to posts of responsibility, the men had threatened strike action.

'Going to the dance on Saturday?' Alice asked as they paused before a notice board crowded with messages.

'There's nobody to dance with but spotty schoolboys and men old enough to be my father,' Sally moaned. It wouldn't be so bad if Ralph Dickson, their foreman, was to grace the proceedings, but the only man likely to be present was 'Uncle Bill' Whylie, and he, as like as not, would be bringing his wife.

'I heard that an invitation had been sent to the barracks in Carlisle,' Alice announced, pleased to be the bearer of good tidings.

Sally's demeanour changed instantly.

'Who told you that?' she demanded.

'One of the girls was in Uncle Bill's office and heard him on the telephone.'

'Oh, well.' Sally straightened her overall, smoothing it down over her shapely thighs and squaring her bonnet to cover the curlers as she noticed Ralph Dickson approaching from the direction of the workshop. 'In that case, I might look in for a little while.'

When they came abreast of the foreman the two girls chirruped in unison: 'Good morning, Mr Dickson!'

Ralph nodded brusquely. It didn't do to become too familiar with the staff. Can't afford to have any of them taking liberties, he told himself. It was a pity really that he had encouraged the Smith girl to come and work here. She might have made an entertaining companion had she stayed at the Anvil where he had first met her, serving behind the bar. He should never have persuaded her that she would be better off working at the factory.

Ralph was not pleased to be summoned to the manager's office so early in the shift. Did the boss not realise that he was needed on the floor until the girls were in place, and the morning's jobs had been allocated? This morning he had been obliged to leave this responsibility in the hands of one of the smarter girls. Goodness only knew what the Union boys would say if they got to hear of it!

He met William Whylie outside the office and grinned, comforted by the thought that the Inspector for Women's Welfare

(Department of Munitions Manufacture), would be more concerned with Bill's operation than his own.

In response to William's knock, the voice of Major McFarlane, the factory manager, bade them enter.

'Ah, gentlemen,' he greeted them with unaccustomed formality. 'Let me introduce Inspector Beaton from the Ministry of Defence.'

It would be difficult to assess which of the two men was the more startled as Annie rose from her chair and turned to face them. Ralph Dickson, shaken to the core by the sight of a woman in the role of a government officer, or William Whylie who had last set eyes on Wee Annie, walking down the aisle of Kilbrendan kirk on the arm of Lieutenant Commander Stuart Beaton.

Annie was the first to break the astonished silence.

'William!' she cried. 'What a wonderful surprise. They did not tell me it would be you.'

She took both his hands in a gesture which showed warmth without embarrassing him in front of his colleagues. She wanted to hug him as she used to when she was a little girl.

'It appears that you need no introduction to our Safety Officer, Mr Whylie.' McFarlane was clearly put out at having his thunder stolen. 'And this is Mr Dickson, in charge of the day shift in the factory.'

Ralph stepped forward and shook hands. 'Ma'am,' was all he could manage.

'Perhaps you will tell us what it is that you want to see, Mrs Beaton?' McFarlane hastened to take charge of the situation. 'And we will do our best to accommodate you.'

'It is my responsibility to see that all the statutory requirements regarding the safety and welfare of munitions workers are being met, Mr McFarlane,' she answered. 'I imagine that much of that information lies in the hands of Mr Whylie?'

'He certainly drew up our plan of action with regard to safety, and is responsible for its implementation,' McFarlane agreed. 'Perhaps you would like to take Mrs Beaton to your own office, Whylie, while I rustle up a cup of coffee?'

McFarlane was obviously only too willing to get the lady

inspector off his own back. William was a sufficiently accomplished diplomatist to ensure she saw what she was meant to see . . . and nothing else.

As William ushered her towards the door, Annie turned to Dickson. 'I also wish to observe the workers while they are on the production line, and to speak to a representative group, perhaps during their meal break?'

Ralph's mind immediately flew to the factory, identifying the items he knew needed attention and hoping he could rectify some of the worst defects before she appeared.

'I shall be pleased to show you round,' he told her, 'as soon as Mr Whylie has finished with you.' His appealing glance towards William was loaded with meaning: Hold her off as long as possible. It did not go unnoticed either by Whylie or their visitor.

'See you in a short while, then.' Annie smiled benignly. He was only the last in a long line of foremen she had encountered with plenty to hide from an inspector.

The girls usually sang as they worked. The long lines of shell cases passed up the shed on one moving belt and down the other way on a second. At each station part of the operation of filling the shells was accomplished. Those handling the raw explosive mixture were expected to wear gloves to avoid any direct contact with the body. Phosphorous was a deadly poison, while the toluene in the mixture was responsible for the sickly yellow colour of the munition workers' skin. Even gloves did little to prevent this contamination. The TNT components penetrated surface blood vessels and the toluene was transported in the blood to be stored in the fatty tissues beneath the skin. Since women possess a more extensive fatty layer than men, it seemed that they must inevitably develop a much more obvious colouring than their male counterparts. To Dickson, who had spent a lifetime working with explosives, the phenomenon was a subject of curiosity only. William, however, took a more serious view of the matter. David Beaton had already, at his request, instigated an enquiry.

Sally Smith and Alice Martin worked side by side on the bench. As hour by hour the open shell cases passed before them, measured quantities of the explosives were poured in from an automatic hopper. It was the job of the operatives to tamp down the contents to ensure that there were no air spaces in the mixture.

Sally was the fastest worker on the team. Her long fingers and strong wrists gave her an edge over the other girls. As the production figures mounted, her enthusiasm increased. There were handsome bonuses to be won by those workers attaining the highest output figures. The special gloves with which they were provided were effective in keeping the chemicals at bay but they made the girls clumsy in handling the equipment. Whenever she felt she was unobserved, Sally would remove hers and work with her bare hands. Today, as the girls sang at their work, she knew she was safe from any reprimand. Ralph Dickson had been called away.

The eruption on her cheek was giving her more irritation than ever this morning. Subconsciously she paused every few minutes to scratch at the spot. After a while, Alice, who had been lost in her own private thoughts since they had begun working, looked up at her friend and gasped with surprise.

'You're bleeding!' she exclaimed.

Sally put her fingers to her cheek. When she drew them away, she was amazed to see blood mixed in with the chemicals which covered her hands.

'Och, I've been having a wee pick at it,' she explained, laughingly, and would have gone on with her work had not her friend demurred.

'Go along to the sick bay,' Alice commanded, unable to disguise the worry in her voice. 'Get it covered up. Here . . . use this.' She handed over a clean white handkerchief which Sally held to her cheek, hoping the bleeding would stop. When her companion continued to hesitate, Alice urged her again to go to the infirmary. Sally could not see, as could her friend, the ring of inflamed tissue surrounding the bleeding spot.

There was as yet no sign of the blood clotting and as, despite the handkerchief, drips had begun to fall on Sally's collar, she at last conceded that something would have to be done. She put down her tools and made her way out, coming face to face with Ralph Dickson on his way in.

'What's this?' he demanded, surprised to see Sally of all people leaving her bench.

'Scratched a spot,' she explained hurriedly, removing the handkerchief. Blood still flowed freely from the wound.

'Cut along to see the nurse,' he told her sharply, then noticing the condition of her hands, he became alarmed. 'Don't tell me you've been working without gloves again!' he remonstrated. 'Today of all days! Mark this, all of you.' He raised his voice so that those working nearest the door could overhear. 'Anyone who gets sick after ignoring safety rules can forget about any claims for compensation.' Then to Sally he said, 'Before you see the nurse, wash your hands. Do it now!'

It would be just his luck to have the Beaton woman come across Smith with her hands covered in chemicals!

Two nights before, he had boasted to a colleague in charge of the night shift that Sally Smith was his best worker, and that it was a pity the rest of the girls did not reach her standard. He had failed to explain that part of her success was due to the fact that she consistently ignored the rules about wearing gloves.

Had Annie realised that the safety policy of this factory was in the hands of William Whylie, she would probably have left it off her list of establishments to be inspected. As she would expect, his arrangements were more than adequate and his records impeccable.

'It seems strange,' she observed, putting down the last of the files he had extracted for her to read, 'to be investigating *your* work.'

'Not the first time that a McGillivray has given me advice,' he assured her, remembering how he had leant upon the strengths of her father, James McGillivray, in his early days at Eisdalsa, and later, after Jamie's death, how his wife Anne had supported him as company clerk until her son Dougal had returned from university and taken his place in the quarries.

'I have seen everything I want to here,' Annie told him, not wishing to take up any more of his time. 'Are there any points that you wish to raise?'

'There is the problem of the canaries. I am sure that you have heard the expression?' She could see that the matter disturbed him greatly, and did her best to reassure him.

'As you say, the phenomenon is not new to me,' she agreed. 'I have seen women from most parts of the country who have yellow skin as a result of working with some explosives. All that I can say is that, to date, no particular disease has resulted from this. When a woman ceases work in the factory, the colour fades within weeks and she reverts to normal.'

Clearly relieved, William rose to conduct her on a tour of the welfare facilities before handing her over to Ralph Dickson.

He was justly proud of the little infirmary which he had insisted should be of the highest possible standard.

Apart from the usual cuts and abrasions received by all factory workers, the nurse found herself dealing with problems associated with the female cycle, the occasional unintended pregnancy, and problems of a personal nature related to separation from home and family. Several women had suffered the loss of brothers, lovers, even husbands, at the front. Bereavement was, in a sense, an illness, one with which Christina Fellows had become only too familiar in recent weeks.

Sally Smith's little problem had cost her considerable time this morning. The wound, small as it was, would not stop bleeding. She had begun to wonder if cauterisation was necessary and had just decided to call in the local medical practitioner when William appeared with his visitor.

He was about to explain the purpose of their visit when he realised that the nurse was unusually agitated. He made his introductions brief, allowing the woman a few moments to compose herself before asking, 'Is something the matter?'

Christina looked anxiously in the direction of the factory inspector, and William found it necessary to reassure her.

'Mrs Beaton is here to see what our day-to-day duties involve,' he explained. 'I am sure she will be as interested as I in any unusual case which may have been presented to you.'

'One of the girls, Sally Smith, has come to me having scratched an eruption on her face which will not stop bleeding. I have never seen a malignant mole, but I have every reason to believe that this may be one.'

William appeared mystified, but Annie had heard something like this before, recently, and under similar circumstances.

'I suggest you call in Dr Wallace immediately,' William told the nurse. 'If the young woman needs treatment, see that the doctor understands that the cost will be borne by the company.'

They moved out into the corridor, William realising that he must forego the pleasure of showing off his splendid infirmary.

'That might be a little unwise,' Annie murmured.

'What?' William looked perplexed.

'To admit that the company is responsible for the girl's condition, without being absolutely sure that such is the case.'

She hated to say it, her sympathies being entirely with Sally Smith, but she would not like to see William putting himself into an untenable position.

'Speaking with my legal hat on,' Annie smiled a trifle bleakly, 'it is never wise to admit liability until the evidence is irrefutable.'

'I have only suggested that the company should be responsible for medical fees,' William responded. 'I do not see that that implies responsibility for Miss Smith's condition.'

'On your head be it,' she replied, shrugging off the feeling of disquiet which the incident had caused her.

At the door to the factory block, William paused to allow Ralph Dickson to come and take their visitor off his hands. Before the foreman arrived, he asked, 'Where are you staying the night? I feel sure that Elizabeth will be able to find you a bed if you have not already made arrangements. She would never forgive me for allowing you to leave without taking a meal with us at the very least.'

'I would love to see Elizabeth,' Annie agreed. 'I have made tentative arrangements to return to Carlisle before going on to Lanark in the morning, but a message can easily be sent to the hotel. I would be delighted to spend the evening with you both.'

Arranging to pick her up from McFarlane's office at the end of her visit, William hurried away to meet Dr Wallace.

Ralph Dickson led Annie into the long low building which housed the production line. As they wandered up and down, pausing occasionally to discuss some detail of the operation with one of the workers, Annie observed with some satisfaction that everyone was wearing the prescribed protective clothing, that floors were clear of any obstacles which could result in someone tripping accidentally, and that all fire exits were clear. Instructions in case of fire or other emergency were clearly displayed – an area in which many other establishments failed abysmally. Annie did, however, note the fact that Dickson had had a considerable time to correct any faults. Whether he should be praised for being able to rectify them at a moment's notice, or reprimanded for not insisting on a consistently high standard, it was difficult to say. What was clear, however, was that he knew how things *should* be.

'I am satisfied that measures are in place to ensure the safety of labour on this site,' Annie reported to Major McFarlane at the end of the day. 'It does appear, however, from talking to your people, that there is rather too great an emphasis upon good production figures at any cost. A bonus system which encourages carelessness in terms of safe practices is not acceptable. I feel certain that the men fighting in France would not wish their sweethearts and wives to put their lives in jeopardy for the sake of a few extra shells.'

McFarlane nodded, recognising the sense of what she said. Any suggestion that the work was hazardous would cut down on recruitment, and he could ill afford to suffer any reduction in his workforce.

'It may be that my foremen are a little too enthusiastic. There is strong competition between the different shifts to achieve the highest output figures.' He spoke casually, as though this was a game between schoolboys. Annie had sensed that the pressures upon the workers were very great. No one suggested that they had been told to ignore regulations, but it would seem that certain operations could not be carried out in the time allowed without cutting corners.

'I am not very satisfied with the arrangements for those using the hostel. As a temporary measure I assume that shared beds are a necessity, but I hope that there are plans to ensure that all personnel have a bed to themselves, and in single cubicles to give a little privacy? These women are making considerable sacrifices in order to work here. They are entitled to what comfort we can give them.'

'I will speak to Mr Whylie about it . . . see what can be done,' the manager assured her.

'I hope so,' Annie concluded, 'because I shall be back in two months to ensure the matter has been attended to. Good afternoon.'

Before McFarlane could find a suitable excuse as to why the work could not be set in hand in the time she suggested, Annie had gone, closing the door deliberately behind her.

Elizabeth had been surprised and delighted to see Annie walking up the school drive in company with William. It had taken moments only to arrange for a small dinner party which, at Annie's request, was to include her niece by marriage, Morag Beaton.

Morag was sent for and told to escort their visitor around the building, while Elizabeth concluded her work for the day.

'This,' Morag announced proudly, 'is our scientific laboratory.' She opened the door of a room which was small by the standards of the other classrooms which Annie had been shown. Looking anxiously at the classroom clock, she said, apologetically, 'Will you please excuse me for a few moments, Aunt Annie? My friend Tilda Hersche will be coming out of class very shortly. She is a refugee from Belgium, and I am sure that you will enjoy meeting her. If you don't mind, I will go and tell her that she and her mother are invited to join us for coffee after dinner.'

'By all means,' agreed Annie, 'I shall be honoured to meet your friend.' Left to her own devices, she studied her surroundings with interest. A bench with sinks and Bunsen burners stood along one wall, beneath a wide window which looked out upon the whole panorama of the Firth of Solway.

The opposite wall was lined with glass-fronted cupboards which housed an array of bottles and glassware containing chemicals. A worktable occupied the centre of the room around which were placed sufficient chairs to seat half a dozen pupils, while at the end farthest from the door was a bookcase.

Annie wandered around the table, coming to a halt before the rows of textbooks. She scanned the titles of the books which ranged from *Human Anatomy* and *The Dissection of the Frog*, to *Qualitative Inorganic Chemistry*, *General Science For All*, and *The Mystery of the Heavens*. She took down one leather-bound volume entitled simply *Navigation*, and turned the leaves. The book was scattered liberally with annotations in a familiar hand. Annie caught her breath, startled at the moment of recognition. She turned back to the flyleaf whereon was written, 'Stuart William Angus Beaton, Tigh na Broch, Eisdalsa'.

Hearing someone enter the room behind her, Annie turned to see William looking at her.

'When they heard that we were short of good scientific books,' he explained, 'the Beatons turned out many of the boys' schoolbooks. They are a little out of date perhaps, but the universe does not change all that rapidly!'

'I think that was a splendid idea,' Annie enthused. 'This establishment must be unique in its provision of science in the curriculum – as a girls' school, I mean.'

'A small number of parents express a wish for their daughters to be prepared for entry to science courses at the university,' William explained. 'As you see, the number of places available in each class is limited, but all those who wish to may participate in the lessons.'

As he spoke, Annie had been glancing along the rows of chemicals in the tall glass cabinet. Her glance fell upon a bottle marked 'Phosphorus'.

'That's the same as the material being used in the munitions at the factory, isn't it?' she asked. 'Surely it's rather dangerous to have a bottle of the substance within reach of children?'

'Not really,' he assured her. 'Phosphorus stored under water, as it is in that bottle, is harmless enough. Given a chance to dry out and combine with oxygen in the air, however, it bursts into flame. Munitions containing phosphorus are usually incendiary devices. Here, let me show you.'

William took down the bottle, unscrewed it, and showed her the contents. Sticks of a yellowish-white substance, about the size of her index finger, stood upright in the bottle, entirely covered by water. He placed an asbestos mat at the far end of the table from where Annie stood, and carefully removed one of the sticks. Holding it in the jaws of a pair of long-handled tongs, he cut off a tiny section of the material and replaced the remainder in the bottle.

A large bell jar was placed over the crumb of phosphorus on the mat.

'It will take a few moments to dry out,' William explained. 'Now, watch.'

The material changed colour and began to smoke, giving off dense fumes whose acrid scent Annie could detect, despite the fact that they were apparently trapped inside the glass. Suddenly there was a whooshing noise as air was drawn in under the bell jar for an instant. A flash of blue-white light all but blinded them both, and the bell jar was forced tight up against the asbestos mat with a loud clunk.

As suddenly as it appeared, the flash of light faded away, leaving only a dense white fog inside the jar.

'Touch the glass with the tip of your finger,' William suggested. 'Careful now, it will be rather warm.'

Annie did as he suggested, placing the tip of her little finger on the bell jar. She was amazed at the heat generated by so small a fragment of the substance.

'In using up all the oxygen inside the jar,' William explained, 'the phosphorus creates a vacuum within. Once the oxygen has been exhausted the chemical stops burning as you saw. If, however, the material of the jar had been less tough, there would have been an implosion and the fragments of burning phosphorus, suddenly released, would once more ignite, sending a shower of burning fragments in all directions.'

'A bomb, in fact . . .' Annie's voice trailed off as she envisaged soldiers in the trenches, suddenly showered by such burning fragments, their clothes and hair alight. She shuddered. Then another thought struck her.

'I had had phosphorus pointed out to me as a dangerous substance,' she observed, 'but I have to admit that only your graphic demonstration has alerted me to its full destructive potential. How do the women filling the shells avoid horrific burns themselves?'

'They are issued with gloves, especially manufactured for the purpose,' he told her. 'One of my greatest problems is making the women sufficiently aware of the dangers. The tiniest fragment of phosphorus landing on the skin will cause a burn, and no matter how small, this can become a septic sore in no time at all.'

'Something like your girl today with her bleeding pimple?'

William, suddenly alerted to the possibility, swore silently to himself. Of course . . . that could be it. Sally Smith's condition might well be the result of phosphorus particles on the skin.

Dinner was a happy affair. Annie was not at all surprised to discover that her young niece was encouraged to join in the conversation as an adult. She added a lively freshness to their discussion and Annie was pleased to find that the atmosphere of the school, so different from that of her home, had in no way diminished Morag's determination to become a doctor.

After the meal, Madame Hersche and her daughter, the Belgian refugees, joined them for coffee. It was not long before Tilda began to explain in minute detail what she had heard of the unsavoury habits of the German troops who had overrun her country.

'In one village,' she told them, 'the Germans lined up all the men between sixteen and sixty against the wall of the church and shot them.' Her English had improved beyond all recognition, only a rather charming, lisping accent now betraying her European origins.

Her mother would have silenced her, but Elizabeth encouraged the child. If what she had seen and heard worried her, it was better for her to talk about it.

'They shot the wounded soldiers in our local hospital,' Tilda went on, and realising she had a captive audience, took pleasure in her favourite revelation. 'I am told that they stick newborn babies on to their bayonets, and toast them over the fire!'

At this last, Madame Hersche interrupted. 'Tilda, these are just stories. You must not say what you do not know for certain to be the truth!'

'War is terrible enough,' observed William quietly. 'There is no need to exaggerate the bestiality of man towards his fellows, my dear. The soldiers you describe were bakers and clerks, farmers and fishermen, a few months ago. Just putting on a uniform does not turn them into monsters.'

'It is very hard to understand,' observed Morag. 'Mr Whylie goes off every day to a factory where they make weapons to maim and kill Germans. My father and my uncles spend their time repairing the damage done to our own sailors by German torpedoes. No one has ever explained convincingly what the fighting is all about.'

'Only the politicians know the whole truth of the matter,' Elizabeth told her, 'but some time ago Britain signed an agreement with some of our European neighbours to help them in the event of invasion by a hostile force. When the Germans overran Belgium we were obliged to go to her aid. Apart from the importance of fulfilling our promises, should the western countries of Europe fall into the hands of the Germans, the British Isles also would be under threat of invasion.'

Annie admired Elizabeth's ability to give such an unemotional explanation. It was difficult to deal with such matters without encouraging the hatred which Tilda already displayed against their enemies.

'Each of us, in our own way, must do our best to make these difficult times as easy as possible for those who are doing the fighting,' Elizabeth continued. 'It is no use sending soldiers and sailors to war without ammunition and the weapons to fire it, so William and Annie both make a contribution there. We try to limit the damage to both sides by providing doctors and nurses to tend the sick and wounded. You girls help in your own way, by digging the vegetable garden so that less food must be brought in from abroad by sailors who have to run the gauntlet of the German blockade. You even help by undertaking the household chores so that the servants can be released to work in the factories or join the army.' Realising that she had held the floor for much longer than she had intended, she concluded, apologetically. 'In fact, you are all doing something useful towards the war effort except me!'

'Nonsense,' Annie interrupted her. 'Your role is the most important of all. You are the one who must teach these young women history, so that they understand how wars are started, how they can be prevented, and what part they themselves must play in governments of the future, in order to ensure that nothing like this ever happens again. If the men will not learn their lessons from the past, the women of tomorrow will have to teach them.'

With the children having been sent to bed, and Madame Hersche having excused herself on the pretext of needing to do some marking for the morning's lessons, Annie sat talking with her friends late into the night. Inevitably their conversation reverted to the munitions factory.

Annie had been impressed by William's demonstration of a phosphorus bomb.

'Some of the wounds received by soldiers must be similar to those skin problems of your factory workers. That girl with the facial eruption, for example . . . should she not be treated in a military hospital?'

'I have discussed that particular problem with our local man, Dr Wallace,' William told her. 'He is an elderly fellow, staying on in practice since his son has joined the RAMC. He makes no bones about declaring himself too inexperienced in such matters to deal with injuries related to chemical burns. I have decided to send Sally Smith to Argyll to see Michael Brown. His is not a military hospital, but he has plenty of nasty gunshot wounds to deal with from ships putting in to Oban. It may be that he, or David, will be able to help her.'

'It seems a long way to send her,' said Elizabeth. 'Is there really nowhere nearer where she might receive attention?'

'David tells me that most of the younger specialists have gone to France,' William insisted. 'If she has to see an older man, at least let us send her to someone we can trust to do his best for her.'

Elizabeth was forced to smile. Nothing on earth would ever dissuade William from his belief that David Beaton's was the best medical opinion to be found in Scotland.

Chapter 18

After the first half dozen new miners had appeared, Makepeace's promised additions to Doug's workforce dried up. With so many of his white miners gone to join the army, and only his stalwart Aborigines presenting themselves for employment each day, Doug found himself called upon more and more to work at the rockface alongside his men. He had even been obliged to invite old man McKenzie, the former manager, to handle the office work which piled up during his absences underground.

Output from the mine had remained steady during the last six months, but the new electrolytic installation had dealt swiftly with the backlog of ore awaiting processing, and those working below ground were now hard put to it to keep the men in the extraction sheds busy. New seams had been opened up, often using rather less shoring material than Doug would have wanted for absolute safety, and corners were sometimes cut when it came to observing his own strict rules about blasting procedures. One thing was certain, however: he would have no problem fulfilling his contract with the company this year and the promised bonuses were surely already in the bag.

Believing that the only way to get Makepeace to come up with more manpower, and hoping to obtain a more satisfactory supply of timber for shoring, Doug decided to travel to Perth to iron out his problems with the owners.

Mary saw his trip as an opportunity for her to make the long-anticipated visit to Kerrera and wrote to warn Anne of her intended visit.

Unfortunately Dougal cannot be long away from the mine,

but he has at least promised to come out to Kerrera to collect me on his way home so that he can see you all, and spend one night on the farm before we have to return to Keningo.

Flora seems to be doing well. Her probationary period will be coming to an end very soon, and she is talking of going back to Scotland to do her military nursing. At least, she mentions having applied to the Scottish Women's Hospitals, an organisation I confess I have not heard of. I presume that they offer recuperation for wounded men brought home from the front?

You will know as much as I about the boys. We have had one letter from Hamish from Cairo – I am so pleased that Jack and Tom Pain are with him although it must be strange for the two older men to have him as their officer! There are rumours around here that the Australians might be going to open a front in the Near East. Greece or Turkey have been mentioned, although what these countries have to do with the war in France and the Low Countries I cannot understand. Anyway, anything will be better than the trenches. We saw some newsreel pictures of the fighting at the Bioscope last week. Although the young men all looked cheerful enough, there seemed to be an awful lot of mud . . .

Anne McDougal was speechless with delight. She had not seen her son and his wife since the day the train drew out of the station at Southern Cross. She had been kept informed about progress at the mine, of course, for Mary was a good letter writer, but Anne yearned for a sight of her own family. Keningo might be no more than a hundred miles from Kerrera Station but for the last two years it could have been on the moon.

Anne tucked Mary's letter in her apron pocket and ran out into the yard.

John was supervising the repair of the windmill which pumped water to the homestead from a deep artesian well discovered by Billy Blue Gum, more than a year before. It had seemed to be a simple task to dismantle the gearing on the wind vane, give it a good greasing and replace the worn cogs. Billy was generally adept at mechanical operations of this kind, but today his mind was not on the job.

'How much longer?' John demanded, shading his eyes against the glare of the sun as he watched Billy working, twenty feet up. He was anxious to get the pump operating as soon as possible. The cows would be released from the milking parlour shortly. The discovery of substantial water supplies so close to the homestead had allowed him to increase his herd of dairy cows, giving Jean and Anne an opportunity to employ their skills at cheesemaking. Kerrera cheese was now well known throughout the territory. Its sale in the town of Southern Cross had added significantly to their income.

As though deliberately to provoke him, Billy dropped a spanner which rang a tune as it slipped from metal spar to metal spar from top to bottom of the structure.

John picked up the offending tool and began the laborious climb towards the top. Meeting the Aborigine about halfway up, he handed it over.

'Thanks, boss.' Billy tucked the spanner in his belt and began his ascent towards the top.

'Just a minute.' John caught hold of the man's ankle to prevent him from climbing. 'What is wrong, Billy?'

'It's nothing, boss,' he asserted, rather unconvincingly. 'Just that my boy is sick and I worry about him.' It had been a while after Billy came to Kerrera as a foreman before the McDougals discovered that he had a wife and family. From time to time he would disappear, returning without explanation after a few days to resume his duties. When at last he was persuaded to give the reason for his disappearances, Anne had insisted that his family be brought to live at Kerrera. John had allowed him a piece of ground on which to build them a shack.

The pride of the Aborigine's heart was his eldest son, Taffee. No wonder his mind was not on the job if the lad was ill.

'I'm sorry to hear that,' said John. 'Is there something that Mrs McDougal can do to help?'

Mary Withall

Anne had taken upon herself the role of medic on the spread, and attended to the injuries and occasional sicknesses suffered by the European workers and those of her neighbours who, far from the town, were without a proper doctor in an emergency. The Aborigines tended to practise their own form of medicine, however, and Anne stepped in only when asked.

'Don't think so, Mr John, sir,' Billy replied. 'It the fever . . . takes away the legs . . . not much anyone can do 'bout that.' He sighed deeply, shook his head and resumed his climb. After a few more minutes spent tinkering, Billy Blue Gum raised his hand and shouted down, 'OK, boss. She going sweet as a bird now!'

With the pump working properly it took minutes only to fill the water trough in readiness for the rush of cattle into the yard when they were released from the milking parlour.

Anne came running across to join them, waving a paper.

'Oh, John, such wonderful news! Mary and Dougal are coming for a visit . . .' She stopped when she saw the frown on her husband's face. 'What is it?' she demanded. 'Is something wrong?'

Billy's boy was one of her favourites. John found it difficult to tell her that the child was sick. Amongst the Aboriginal children, infectious illness of any kind often proved fatal.

'Taffee is ill,' he said, bluntly. Then, after a brief hesitation, 'Very ill.'

Anne turned immediately to the father.

'What is the trouble, Billy?' she demanded.

'Him have fever very bad, missus,' the man told her. 'His legs all twisted up. Him crying out in pain all night. His mama take him to the lake this morning.'

'Why the lake?' John queried.

'Merlin's Lake,' Anne murmured. She had heard that the native Australians considered that the intermittent salt-lake was a source of healing.

'I'll take the buckboard and see if I can find them,' she decided, thrusting the letter into John's hand. 'Tell Jean to get on with the evening meal, I may be some time.'

Before he could stop her, Anne hurried off to collect her medical kit, while Billy, goaded into activity by her response to his

310

news, rounded up the team of horses and harnessed them to the farm wagon.

Jean McDougal had slipped so easily into the role of farmer's wife that she sometimes wondered if her time at Kuitpo Creek had not been just a dream.

Life at Kerrera Station could hardly be likened to the Kentish farm where she had spent her childhood, but the daily round of tasks was much the same as she had always known.

John and Anne had made their daughter-in-law so welcome that she could hardly complain when the hours in the paddock and the dairy were long. Nor would she wish to, when they themselves worked equally hard alongside her.

In the first months of her life at Kerrera, every spare minute had been taken up with completing the furnishing of the house which Jack had begun building before their wedding. By Christmas their new home had been completed. It was considerably smaller than John's homestead but it did have a large airy living room, and the two bedrooms could always be extended if there was ever the need. To Jean's delight the small bathroom held a proper cast iron tub as well as the usual shower.

The kitchen was on the back porch, to avoid overheating the interior of the house. At first they had hardly used it because all the farm workers tended to eat together in the main house. But there were occasions when the newly-weds chose to have some time to themselves, and Jean liked to surprise her husband with tempting dishes concocted from the rather plain ingredients available to her. She studied the diet of the Aborigines, and although she was not keen to experiment with snake steaks or fried termite grubs, found many of the plants which the natives used had unusual flavours and textures which helped to make the ubiquitous mutton more palatable.

After their long separation, it had seemed strange to be constantly in Jack's company. They had been shy to begin with. Neither was in the first flush of youth, and each had passed more than thirty years of life in celibacy. Their love making had begun in a tentative, exploratory fashion, neither knowing quite how to behave.

They had married in the Registry Office in Adelaide with Tom Pain standing up as Jack's best man and the Registrar's wife as their second witness. Tom had joined them for a celebration dinner at the Queen's Hotel before hurrying away on some chauffeuring job. She was quite amused at the suspicion with which Jack had regarded her friendship with Tom, but when he saw how kind he had been at a time when she was under great stress, he could not be other than grateful to their mutual friend. By the time that the wedding was over both men were sworn blood brothers – she feared that it was some time during that evening that they had agreed to enlist together. They had also spent their first night at the hotel, a Victorian edifice which had seen better days, as their sparsely furnished room with its narrow bed and sombre dark oak wardrobe, glowering in the corner, indicated.

The newly weds had been so wrapped up in each other that they had paid little attention to their surroundings. Jean smiled to herself now, remembering how they had passed that first night together.

There had been so much news to exchange, so many experiences to discuss, that the bridal pair had sat up most of the night talking. Only as the dawn light had begun to filter through the blinds did Jean find herself curled up in her husband's arms, lying still fully dressed upon the lumpy mattress.

She must have dozed off for a time because she opened her eyes to find Jack gazing down at her, a worried frown on his face.

'What is it love?' she asked, raising her hand to stroke a fallen lock of hair from his brow. 'Why so worried?'

'Are you sure we have done the right thing?' he pleaded. 'You know nothing about life at Kerrera . . . suppose you dinna like living there?'

Your letters have told me so plainly what Kerrera is like – the animals, the buildings, the people. What more is there to know?'

'But it's so far from anywhere,' he insisted, 'and no sae comfortable as yon house of Mrs Savery's.'

'A comfortable house is no substitute for the absence of good people around one. I don't care how much discomfort there is, as long as I have you beside me. I have been so miserable all these months, it was only the thought that you would not let me down that sustained me.'

'The work is hard,' he persisted, 'particularly for a woman. All our neighbours' wives seem coarse and old before their time. It is difficult to imagine that they were once young and beautiful like you. I would not wish you to become like them.'

'I promise to wear a bonnet in the heat of the day, wash only in the softest water and use the best soap I can buy. I shall go to bed each night, my face covered in vanishing cream to allay the wrinkles . . . how will that be?'

'That will do verra well, just so long as you leave a wee place for this.' He leant over and kissed her tenderly on the lips, while his hand searched out the buttons of her muslin gown.

Eager to help him, she wriggled the fabric from her shoulders and slid her arms out of the generous sleeves. His fingers struggled with lacings and hooks for a few seconds until, at last, she lay naked on the bed.

He had moved back then, gazing down at her, absorbed in her beauty. Mechanically he stripped off his own clothes and let them fall where he stood.

Their first coupling had been a fiercely concentrated effort, neither wanting to injure or disappoint the other. They were both tense in their ignorance of how it should be, and when he entered her, she had cried out with the pain. That first shock, however, was quickly dispelled, for as she felt him moving inside her she was overwhelmed by a totally unexpected combination of feelings and emotions. Their movements, in unison, rose to a crescendo which was accompanied by a chorus of bedsprings. The noise was such that, at the instant when both should have climaxed, they collapsed into giggles and the solemn moment had degenerated into a romp.

Jean smiled to herself as she remembered that, and the many other nights they had spent together before that terrible moment when Jack had announced his intention to go off and enlist with Tom and Hamish.

What strange creatures men are, she thought to herself. When she had challenged Jack about his insistence on going to join up with the others, he had told her that he could not allow wee laddies like young Hamish who were still wet behind the ears, to face all the problems they were going to come up against without someone with a bit more experience to keep an eye on them. More likely he reckoned he might be missing something! She laughed aloud and the cow she was milking turned her head to stare. Kicking the stool out of the way she stooped to retrieve the milk. The bucket seemed heavier these days, and she was panting by the time she reached the dairy. She found it necessary to rest for a few moments before lifting the heavy container and pouring the milk over the corrugated metal sheets of the cooler.

She set down the empty pail and her hand rode lightly over the bulge at her waist. Anne had warned her to avoid heavy lifting. She would take her advice from now on.

Making her way over to the water butt, Jean lowered the dipper in and took a long drink of the cool water. At that moment, Vicky came panting into the yard with Al at her heels.

The pup had grown into a fine dog. At first sight he seemed to be in every way a true Border collie. It was only the flash of fawn as he ran which betrayed his parentage. He had his mother's skill with the sheep and his father's strength and natural cunning. Jean was convinced that were he ever lost in the bush, he would survive where a European dog could not. It was his alert expression and the comical way he had of setting his head to one side whenever he waited for an order or wanted her to do something, which had won her heart from the very beginning. While Vicky was undoubtedly Anne's faithful servant in the absence of her beloved Jack, Al would always be Jean's dog.

'Are the men on their way then?' she asked them, watching as the two silky heads came together over the trough. She shaded her eyes to see in the distance that the mob of sheep collected that day for shearing were penned in the far paddock. A moving cloud of dust showed her that the jackeroos were making their way home.

When she had first arrived at Kerrera, Jean had been amazed at the size of Jack's flock after so short a time. Now, with Government aid to increase wool production, the number of animals had trebled. While it gave her no satisfaction at all to have made money out of the misfortunes of war, Jean could not deny that Kerrera Station had been started at a most propitious time.

She got to her feet and returned to the dairy. Usually Taffee was hanging about the yard at this time of day. She had missed him today. She checked that the cooler was doing its job properly, then rinsed out the bucket at the tap and placed it upended on the shelf. Hygiene was an essential part of good cheese-making and they all stuck closely to the rules which Anne had laid down.

Wiping her hands on her apron, she made for the door, only to find her way barred by John McDougal, looking strained and anxious.

'Taffee has been taken ill with fever,' he explained. 'Anne has gone off with the cart to fetch him. I suspect she will want to bring him into the house. Do you think you could prepare a bed for him? Oh, and Anne said that you would attend to the evening meal.'

John hated to put upon his daughter-in-law in her present condition. Anne had specifically warned him that Jean's pregnancy could be complicated were she asked to carry out work which was too physically demanding, and preparing a meal for eight hungry men was no light task.

She gave him a reassuring hug. 'I'll see to it, never fear,' she told him, cheerfully. 'Did Anne say what she thought might be wrong with the boy?'

'From what Billy told us, it seems it could be infantile paralysis,' he replied, gloomily.

'Oh, no!' Jean had lived in Australia long enough to know just how devastating the disease could be. She thought of the tough, lanky little lad who dogged her footsteps as she worked, and who worshipped Anne, his first white friend. How would he cope with callipers on his legs . . . or worse? She hurried off into the house to prepare for the arrival of the invalid.

April marked the beginning of autumn. During the previous months there had been a severe drought, the only moisture to feed the great salt-lake being the heavy dews which fell each morning before sun-up.

As Anne guided the horse down the steep escarpment surrounding the salt-pan, she noticed that a little crowd had gathered, far out towards the centre of the basin.

By the time she had drawn the wagon up at the edge of the cracked and treacherous lake bed, beyond which the horses could not go, she could distinctly hear the sound of chanting. She hobbled the horses and ran across the open ground towards the little knot of people gathered about Billy's wife, Matilda, and her son.

Taffee had grown into a handsome youth since his arrival at Kerrera station. Still thin and wiry as a young sapling, the boy was now nearly as tall as Anne herself. But as she approached the group gathered about him, she could see that the fine strong body had become grotesquely distorted. His back was arched, and his right leg twisted under him. The medicine man, his naked body painted in yellow and red ochre, his face a whitened mask, danced about the boy as he lay upon the ground. At each prod of the priest's staff, the boy screamed out in pain and the women who knelt beside him were obliged to hold him still lest he injure himself in more violent movements.

Anne had seen similar examples of the condition in younger children and knew that this was the earliest stage of the disease. Whereas the white children she had seen had been kept warm in bed and hot fomentations applied to the twisted little limbs to relieve the pain, the treatment here seemed to be to stimulate movement rather than to prevent it.

To one side, some men were digging frantically with their hands into the salt-encrusted surface of the lake. They had reached a depth of a foot or more when one gave a delighted cry and held up a handful of moist clay. Instantly all the others dug with renewed vigour until their efforts were rewarded by the appearance of a few inches of water in the bottom of the pit. After a further half hour of digging, a hole the size of a small slipper bath had been gouged out of the ground, and this had filled with muddy water.

Taffee, meanwhile, continued to writhe with a weak, sporadic jerking of the limbs, crying out intermittently with the pain. Anne observed that the left side of his body acted independently of the right. On the right side, his leg was distorted by muscular contractions and appeared immobile, but his arm still made small involuntary movements. She knew little about the disease, but understood that it was likely to be fatal in those cases where the upper trunk and neck were paralysed. If the rib muscles were affected the patient would be unable to breathe for himself. But perhaps Taffee would recover, even if it meant being a cripple for the rest of his life.

When at last the hastily constructed bath was full, the women lifted the boy gently and lowered him into the pool. The sun was still high in the heavens and Anne felt sure that the water, which must have been close below the surface of the ground, would be warm. Certainly, the additional support afforded by the buoyant solution, rich in salt, appeared to give the boy some relief, for he relaxed, allowing his limbs to float freely.

As the medicine man began a new dance, pointing to the sky with his wand before sweeping it low over the prone body of the victim, the women took up his song, swaying in unison and crooning in a low-pitched, rhythmical chanting.

Anne remained on the edge of the group, knowing better than to interrupt this deeply religious ceremony. She was intrigued to see that, using only the primitive means at their disposal, these people had devised a treatment to relieve the suffering which was not dissimilar from that advocated by David Beaton in his instructions to her.

Earlier in the year, she had witnessed the distress of a neighbour whose daughter had been struck down by the disease. The girl had been left untreated for several days because the doctor was out of town on another call. Anne, needing to equip herself with sufficient knowledge to be able to treat the disease were she to encounter it in the future, had written to David for advice. He had stressed that knowledge of the illness was limited and that other than rest and warmth, followed by support to the affected limbs when the patient became mobile, there was little that could be done.

It had occurred to Anne at the time, that while the sight of a white child in leg braces was not uncommon on the streets of Southern Cross, she had never seen any Aboriginal children wearing them. She had assumed that the disease always proved fatal in the natives and that, as with the European diseases of measles, whooping cough and diphtheria, the Aboriginal children had no resistance to it.

As she stood quietly by, not wishing to disturb the activities of her friends, Anne observed that while Taffee was clearly very ill, he was conscious, and was responding positively to the massaging of his limbs, now being carried out underwater in a systematic manner. To the rhythm of the chanting, one of the women was steadily going over his whole body, kneading and pulling at his muscles, while the boy himself, when bidden, seemed able to make voluntary movements against her palms even with the most affected leg. As she worked, the masseuse gradually straightened the twisted limb, and although this clearly gave Taffee excruciating pain, he bore it stoically. Now, not a whimper was allowed to pass between his gritted teeth.

Then, at a given signal, the action suddenly ceased. There was a brief moment of absolute silence before the priest again intoned his entreaties to the elements. Abruptly, the strange figure turned away and walked off into the bush. The group about the boy watched him go.

After a few moments, as if they themselves were emerging from a trance, they began to bustle about, preparing to carry Taffee home.

Anne stepped up to Matilda, placing an arm about her shoulders.

'Why did you not tell me that Taffee was ill?' she asked, not wishing to sound accusing. 'There might have been something I could have done to relieve his pain.'

'He be OK now, missus,' the woman told her, convincingly.

'At least let me offer him the comfort of the homestead while he recovers,' Anne insisted. 'I can provide him with warm baths without the trouble of carrying him out here every time.'

'There no need for him to come again, Missus Anne,' Matilda replied. 'Now he get better, or he die.'

That seemed to be that.

'At least let me make him comfortable while we wait to see what happens,' pleaded Anne. She felt sure that the treatment she had seen that day was most suitable for the tortured muscles, but she knew enough to realise that only continuous massage was likely to make any difference to the twisted leg.

It was Taffee himself who settled the matter. Still very weak, but relaxed now that the ceremony was over, his eyes widened at the prospect of spending time in a real bed in the master's house.

'Let me go with Missus Anne,' he pleaded, 'I know I can get better along of her.'

'Carry him to the wagon anyway,' suggested Anne. 'We can discuss what is best to do with him as we ride.'

She walked alongside the makeshift stretcher upon which they had carried him from their encampment. When they reached the wagon, Taffee was lifted in and made comfortable on the floor. Anne covered him with a blanket.

'We will take it very slowly, Taffee,' she assured him. 'I will try not to hurt you too much.'

Sure that his mother would not deny him the pleasure of a stay in Mrs Anne's house, the boy nodded silently, closed his eyes, and exhausted by the day's events, slept all the way back to the Kerrera homestead.

Chapter 19

Jean stood up clumsily and stretched her back. She seemed to be top-heavy these days.

Anne had suggested that she leave the milking today, but determined to do her bit up to the last minute, Jean had insisted. Now she could see that it had not been a good idea. The first real contraction gripped her as she made her way laboriously across the yard. She grabbed hold of the water trough and, seeing Taffee watching her from the veranda, called out to him, 'Get Missus Anne, Taffee . . . quick as you can!'

The boy levered himself up from the long chair, grabbed hold of his walking stick and hobbled into the house. Anne's persistence with the hot baths and massage was paying off. He was managing to get about already without the help of callipers, and was determined to throw away his stick one day soon.

Jean lowered herself to the ground, her back propped against the trough, and waited.

It took only minutes for Anne to summon help from the stock-yard where the men were busy turning the manure heap in the hot sun. It was an unpleasant job and one which they were glad to leave, if only for a few minutes.

'Take her into the main house,' ordered Anne.

Jean would have preferred to have the baby in her own house, but she could see how impracticable that would be from Anne's viewpoint. Without Jean to help her she would be hard pressed to keep everything going in and around the homestead for the next few days. It was asking too much to expect her to keep an eye on Jean also, in a house a mile away from her own.

'Tilda!' Anne called, summoning Taffee's mother from the

kitchen. 'Get me some clean sheets from the cupboard, quickly, and make up the bed in the back bedroom.'

Matilda could cope with routine household chores with little prompting, when everything was calm and orderly. The panic into which the household had been thrown in the past few minutes, however, was too much for her.

She went to the linen cupboard, pulling out towels and table cloths and scattering them all about in her wild search for sheets. At last she discovered what she was looking for, but in her efforts to pile the unwanted items back into the cupboard, she allowed the sheets to fall on the stone floor of the scullery. Hastily she picked up the fallen linen and hurried with it to the bedroom.

Anne had made Jean comfortable in the small armchair while they made up the bed. Jean had a wash, using a special scented soap which Anne had put by for just such a moment. She doused herself liberally in eau de cologne to suppress the smell of her own perspiration. It was going to be hot work, having this baby.

The next contraction arrived and she clambered to her feet once more, beginning to pace the room in an effort to relieve the pain.

'Now then,' Anne told her when the sheets had been spread and all made ready for the delivery, 'on to the bed with you.'

'But I'd rather just walk about,' protested Jean.

'What is it you want,' demanded Anne, exasperated, 'to have Jack's baby on the floor? Into bed with you, now!'

With another pain coming fast upon the previous one, Jean conceded that Anne probably knew best after all. She lay down on the bed. This contraction, far stronger than those which had gone before, made her cry out in an alarming manner and poor Matilda, more accustomed to the easy manner in which she and her sisters managed to give birth, ran from the room.

'Get some water boiling on the stove,' Anne called after her. 'And bring me a can of kerosene.'

The pain having subsided, Jean lay back on the pillows breathing more easily. It had all happened so suddenly . . . she breathed deeply and allowed her gaze to wander over the room. Out of the corner of her eye she saw a small army of ants approaching from the kitchen. Whatever it was that had attracted them it seemed to be something about her own person, for they were marching purposefully towards the bed.

'Look!' she cried out in alarm, but Anne was ahead of her. She had anticipated just such an invasion as soon as the sweet cloying odours of the sick room began to pervade the atmosphere.

She took the can of kerosene from Matilda and shooed her back to the kitchen. Splashing the evil-smelling liquid over the floor, she stayed the advancing army. The foremost insects, alarmed by the fluid, turned back against the tide and soon the seething black mass had removed itself almost as fast as it had appeared.

The activity had served to relieve Jean's tension so that she was more relaxed as the next wave of pain began to build. She thrashed about wildly with her hand, seeking something to hold on to. Anne gripped it hard.

'Take deep breaths,' she suggested, 'try to relax . . . there, that's better, isn't it?'

Jean had witnessed many a lamb being born, and calvings too. While it was true that the cows bellowed a bit, she had had no idea just how painful this most natural of all processes could be.

It was hot. Despite the fact that the room Anne had chosen was at the rear of the house and shaded from the noonday sun, the temperature was well into the nineties.

Anne poured water from a pitcher into the washing bowl, added a little carbolic acid solution and wrung out a flannel. She wiped the perspiration from Jean's face and began to loosen her garments, sponging her body all over to cool her.

'Oh, thank you,' Jean murmured, 'I feel like a furnace at full power.'

'I'd give you a little more cologne,' Anne said, 'but it will only bring back the ants. In any case, it's not very hygienic.'

Jean laughed at her; Anne's preoccupation with cleanliness was renowned on the McDougals' homestead.

The contractions began to come more regularly now and at shorter intervals. After all these years, Anne considered herself a fairly well-experienced midwife and felt confident that, barring any unfortunate mishaps, she could cope with the situation.

Nevertheless she had sent one of the lads on horseback to fetch the doctor from Southern Cross. It was only a matter of reassurance for Jean. Anne knew that the baby would be born long before he could get there.

As the afternoon wore on the noise of flies buzzing at the window bothered Jean. Anne wondered if she had been right to exclude the goanna from this room. Perhaps the lizard was preferable to the flies which seemed to get in despite the screens. She would have liked to open a window to catch whatever breeze there was but dared not, lest even more invade the room. She set Matilda to operate the ceiling fan which was worked by the steady pulling of a string. It was an idea imported from India which, if it did not actually create a breeze, was at least sufficient to disturb the heavy atmosphere.

She had examined Jean at intervals, noting the position in which the baby lay and the degree of dilation of the cervix. Everything seemed to go quite normally at first but as time went on and still the final bearing down stage did not begin, she became worried. She felt the abdomen, tracing with her fingers the various parts of the foetus. Under her hand she felt the infant's bottom, pressing upwards, which meant that the baby was face downwards in the birth canal. She could feel the head which seemed to be engaged correctly, but what was this? A protrusion which shouldn't be there. She pushed cautiously at the little lump. Perhaps it was a knee or an elbow? Whatever it was, it was most certainly where it had no business to be.

'There's something not quite right here, Jean,' she said, trying to keep her voice calm. She had no wish to alarm her patient. If she becomes tense now, Anne told herself, goodness knows what harm will be done.

'I'm going to have to feel inside . . . there seems to be some kind of obstruction.'

Jean was almost past caring. She was weak and tired and the agony seemed now to be perpetual. She merely nodded in understanding and resigned herself to Anne's ministrations.

Anne poured more water into the bowl and washed her hands very carefully, scrubbing at her nails until they were red and sore.

She took Vaseline and rubbed it liberally into her fingers before pushing three of them up into the birth canal. Almost at once she felt the downy top of the baby's head. She moved her fingers around the dome of the skull . . . ah, here it was! The tiny shoulder had been hunched up so that it too was trying to force a way out, tight up against the ear. Anne removed her hand, took a large dollop of Vaseline on the tips of her fingers and probed once more. She slipped her fingers round the skull pushing gently against the shoulder until she felt it give way and slip back into position. Now there was nothing to prevent the head from progressing down the canal.

Before she had time to wash off the lubricant, Jean began her final bearing down. Anne hurried to her aid.

'Matilda,' she called, 'take the other leg like this . . . give her something to push against . . . now, Jean, don't hold your breath, pant lightly . . . do an imitation of Vicky . . . that's it . . . here comes another contraction . . . push down now!'

The baby shot out in a gush of blood and fluids and Anne was holding in her hands a greasy little bundle which wriggled fiercely, announcing her arrival with some lusty squawking.

'It's a lovely little girl.' She held up the infant for Jean to see. The younger woman smiled happily and then tears began to form and trickle down her cheeks.

'I wish Jack were here to see her,' was all she said. Even as Anne busied herself with the aftermath of the birth, Jean's eyes began to droop and when the baby, washed and snugly wrapped in her newly crocheted shawl, was laid beside her mother, she was already fast asleep.

John, exhausted by the daily round which had been followed by the excitement of the birth of his first grandchild, had already retired for the night when the doctor arrived. Anne maintained a lonely vigil over her charges.

The baby had woken once and cried. Not wanting to disturb Jean too soon, Anne had given her a few drops of boiled water, which seemed sufficient to satisfy her, because she immediately went back to sleep.

'Trying to come out fighting, must have tired you out too,' Anne observed as she tucked the babe up tight and returned her to her mother.

Anne watched anxiously as Dr Morton examined her patients. He was very gentle with Jean, disturbing her as little as possible. The baby seemed to satisfy him, especially when she opened her eyes and gazed up at him with deep concentration.

'You might almost believe she recognised me,' he laughed. 'I think she'll know me if we meet again!'

'I know babies are always beautiful to their parents,' said Anne, 'but I've seen quite a few, and she is the prettiest yet!'

'Very natural grandmotherly pride,' laughed the doctor. 'Is this your first grandchild?'

Anne laughed. 'Hardly,' she answered. 'My grandson is fighting somewhere in the Near East and my granddaughter, Flora, is a nurse.'

'I find it hard to believe that you have adult grandchildren, Mrs McDougal,' Morton observed. 'You must have been very young when your own babies were born?'

They wandered into the kitchen where Anne had prepared a meal for the doctor.

'You'll stay the night now you are here?' she suggested.

'Thank you, but I must be on the road at first light, Mrs McDougal. Your daughter-in-law is luckier than most, having such an expert midwife to tend her. I know I am leaving her in safe hands.'

When he had finished eating, Annie accompanied the doctor to the stable where his horse was comfortably bedded down for the night.

'Sorry, old girl,' Morton told the beast, 'we have to be on our way.'

He mounted his long-suffering mare, hitched his medical bag over the saddle and leant down to shake Anne's hand.

'You should get some rest while you can, Mrs McDougal,' he suggested.

'That little miss is going to be demanding attention before very long! I'll call back in a day or two, but you know where to get me if I'm needed.'

Not wanting to disturb John, Anne curled up on the couch in the parlour and tried to sleep.

The hot sun, penetrating the linen blinds which John had drawn over the window before he left for the paddocks, eventually woke her in the middle of the morning. She could hear Matilda singing as she slammed pots about in the kitchen. She ought really to go and see what the dear good soul was up to . . . Anne shuddered to remember what a state the place was usually in after one of Matilda's attempts at breakfast.

A thin wailing from the back of the house reminded her of the previous day's events. She dressed rapidly and went to greet her new granddaughter.

Jean lay dreamily upon the pillows. The infant, her cries answered immediately, was sucking contentedly at her mother's breast. An empty cup suggested that Jean had already received some attention.

'Has anyone been looking after you?' Anne asked. 'I'm afraid I overslept.'

'John gave me my breakfast,' Jean replied. 'We both agreed that you needed to sleep in after yesterday.' She laid the baby safely beside her on the pillow and stretched out her arms to Anne. 'Thank you so much for looking after me,' she said, hugging her mother-in-law to her. 'You were wonderful!'

'Oh, I think you did quite well yourself,' laughed Anne. She picked up the baby and cradled her in her arms. 'I had better give this wee mite a bath before I set about doing the milking.'

'John mentioned that he was going to get one of the field hands to see to the milking today,' Jean told her. 'By the way, was I dreaming or did the doctor actually arrive last night, after it was all over?'

'He did.' Anne smiled. 'But you were too exhausted to speak to him.'

'How awfully rude of me,' she said, dismayed. 'What will he think of me? Did he say if the baby was all right?'

'I don't think there can be any doubt about that,' Anne declared, 'but I expect he will tell you himself when he calls back . . . in a day or two, he said.' She bustled about the room tidying up the debris of the night before.

'Whatever John has arranged, there is still plenty to do in the dairy,' she said. She had finished bathing the infant now. She looked anxiously at the baby's navel, which was still bleeding a little, and rubbed in some zinc and castor oil cream. There couldn't be much to worry about there; the doctor had complimented her on the way she had handled things. She had told him about the problem with the baby's shoulder and he had seemed most impressed with the way she had managed it.

She completed the baby's toilet and handed her back to her mother.

'Does this baby have a name?' she asked Jean. 'We are already tired of calling her It or She.'

Jean took the baby in her arms and smiled down into the wrinkly little face. 'As she is a girl, I think Jack would want her to be called Ellen, after his sister,' she said quietly.

Anne was a little startled. Did Jean know the full story of the baby's aunt, she wondered. Ellen McDougal was still alive in the prison where she had been incarcerated for the last twenty years.

'Have you told John that is what you want to call her?' she asked tentatively.

'He seemed delighted,' said Jean. 'He asked that we call her Katrina too, after Jack's mother, so Ellen Katrina she is.'

Anne smiled wanly. So he still thought of them both, even if he didn't mention them. 'I will tell Tilda to listen out for you,' she said. She could see that even the gentle routine of washing and eating had tired Jean. The day was becoming very hot, and her patient was clearly flagging.

'Get as much sleep as you can,' said Anne as she went out, closing the door behind her.

Anne came in from the milking parlour to be greeted by a strange moaning and shouting emanating from Jean's room. Almost immediately the baby began to wail. Anxiously Anne put down the jug of milk she had brought in and went to see what was amiss.

Jean was bathed in sweat. Her sheets were wringing wet and her hair was plastered to her head. She had thrown off the covers and was flailing the air with random motions of arms and legs.

In unison with her mother's lashing and calling out, the infant cried and waved its tiny fists.

Anne noticed the dainty little cradle which now stood beside the bed. So that was what John had been so secretive about all these weeks. Too preoccupied to stop to admire the craftsmanship which her husband had used in his work, she gathered up the infant and laid her in the crib, out of reach of Jean's involuntary movements.

'Oh, Jean,' cried Anne, taking her daughter-in-law's hand. Her pulse was racing and she was so hot. Anne felt the damp forehead. No need for a thermometer to tell her that Jean was in a high fever. 'What is it?' she demanded, as Jean cried out in distress. 'Are you in pain?'

'Hot,' Jean replied wildly. 'So hot . . . burning up . . .' She began rambling, talking one minute to Jack, and another to someone else. Her uncle back in England, perhaps?' 'Rick's afire, Will, have you called the fire Brigade? Wait, I'll fetch a pail . . .' So saying she tried to climb out of bed and Anne was hard pressed to keep her still.

The smell in the room was awful: the odour of putrefying meat. It was like a slaughter house. Anne tore back the sheets. There had been slight haemorrhaging, which accounted for the smell of blood but not so much as to alarm her. No, it was the noxious discharge which concerned her. She had never before seen a case of puerperal fever, but was convinced that this was the problem. She looked at her own hands in horror. They were clean enough – she had after all just come in from the dairy – but who could tell what she had brought in with her in the way of microbes? She remembered everything that Dr David had told her about the microscopic creatures which caused septicaemia. How could she have been so careless as to have infected Jean?

She ran from the room, tearing her clothes off as she went. In the shower she scrubbed herself all over with a hard brush and used a clean towel to dry herself. Wearing a clean set of clothing, she returned to the sickroom where Jean continued to moan incoherently.

'Matilda!' Anne called out, hoping that the Aboriginal woman would appear. She did not. Of course, she would be gone back to her encampment by now. Anne must go herself and fetch water. Carbolic acid, that was the thing ... bathe her in carbolic solution ... not too strong so as to irritate the skin ...

She worked frantically to repair the damage. Satisfied at last that she had cleaned the site of the suppuration as best she could, she concentrated on the fever. Sponging with lukewarm water, she recalled that that was how they had treated the cholera patients and set about it, working tirelessly. She heard the sound of the men coming in from the fields but continued with her task. John stuck his head around the door and was arrested by her sharp cry. 'Don't step inside this room until you have washed and changed your clothes!' She knew she was shutting the door after the horse had bolted, but now that she understood the danger she was determined to do nothing to increase it.

Jean seemed to be resting a little easier. Her ravings had diminished to a soft murmuring and for a while she dozed off.

Anne searched through her medical chest looking for something, anything, which she might give to allay the condition. Tincture of quinine ... they used that for fever, didn't they? It might do some good ... but would it do harm? She thought not, and pouring a little of the concentrated liquid into a medicine glass, diluted it with a little boiled water. She held Jean's head while she forced the bitter medicine down her patient's throat. Jean spluttered, but retained the quinine.

The only other thing that she had was a bottle of Aspirin tablets. Jean had complained of pains in her head. A couple of Aspirins could do no harm, surely? She forced Jean's mouth open and placed the two tablets on her tongue, giving her water to swallow them down.

'What is it?' John asked, anxiously. He had taken her at her word and changed his clothes before returning.

'Fever,' she replied. 'She has septicaemia, and it's all my fault.'

John remembered that when his daughter Ellen had nearly died after giving birth to her illegitimate child, David Beaton had saved her. Surely Anne would cope equally well?

But Anne was devastated. In the early days when her own babies were born, and subsequently when she had helped out at other birthings, she had always been scrupulously clean, observing all the rules Dr David had dinned into her. How could a patient of hers have puerperal fever? In her mind she went over every step she had taken the day before. Everything was clean but of course she had had to use the kerosene to get rid of the ants. Suppose some of them had got through? Then there were the flies. They carried disease, she knew that. She was sure she had washed her hands thoroughly before touching Jean. She had used the Vaseline of course – surely that could not have carried germs?

John could see that nothing he said was going to convince her she was not responsible.

'Oh, John, what if she dies?' his wife cried out in despair. 'How will I face Jack if she dies?'

He took her in his arms, kissing her gently on the brow, knowing that there was nothing more that she could do.

'What can I be thinking of?' she said suddenly. 'The evening meal . . . I have nothing prepared!'

'The men are quite capable of making their own supper tonight,' he assured her. 'I am going now to get something for you, and you must come and eat it when it's ready.' She nodded absently and returned to her patient.

All through the night and for much of the following day, Anne maintained her vigil, constantly sponging Jean's body and every two hours giving the Aspirin tablets. The quinine she was a little more wary of using, still not sure of the accepted dose. As the hours wore on Jean seemed to rest more easily and by the third evening her temperature was down.

So concerned had Anne been for Jean's welfare that she had paid little attention to baby Ellen. Matilda had taken it upon herself to look after the child. She had watched carefully as Anne had instructed her on how to prepare a bottle of cow's milk for the baby and Anne had supervised Matilda's first attempt. Satisfied that the woman knew what she was doing, Anne had returned to her patient and thought no more about it. From then on, whenever Anne saw her, Ellen seemed to be sleeping peacefully.

Jean's milk had never come in properly; her breasts were absolutely flaccid. There was no chance that she would be able to feed the child herself even when she was well again. It was on the fourth afternoon that Anne discovered why Jean's baby was so contented.

She went into the kitchen to make a cup of tea and found that Matilda was entertaining a young friend. The Aboriginal girl was squatting on her haunches, her back supported by the kitchen wall. To one swollen breast clung a tiny dark body, feeding lustily. At the other, Ellen McDougal, having taken her fill, was sucking fitfully, teasing the nipple with her tongue. Taken by surprise, Anne was about to remonstrate with Matilda when she saw the wisdom of what her servant had done. Breast milk was equally good for the bay, no matter what the colour of the woman's skin. How could she even have hesitated? Was not this exactly what women had always done when a mother could not feed her own child?

'Who is your friend, Tilda?' she asked.

'She's my big daughter, Mrs Anne . . . she called Terowie.'

'Thank you for taking care of Mrs Jean's baby, Terowie,' Anne said. And to Matilda, 'While Terowie is feeding both the babies, she must come and live in the house, Tilda. See she gets plenty of milk to drink and good food.'

'Thank you, missus,' said the Aboriginal woman. 'I take care of everything!'

Anne must have dozed off in her chair because she came to with a start. Something had changed. It was the noise, or rather lack of it, which had disturbed her. She had become accustomed to the heavy, laboured breathing of her patient these last few days and now there was no sound at all. Fearfully she approached the bed, hardly daring to look at Jean.

Her daughter-in-law lay still, the sheets and pillow unruffled since Anne had last straightened them. She bent closer to catch any sound of breathing, resting her hands on the bed.

Jean opened her eyes and blinked, a puzzled frown on her face. 'Anne?' she said. She lifted the sheet and took note of her flattened abdomen. 'My baby!' she cried out in a panic . . . 'What has happened to my baby?'

'The baby is well, Jeanie,' Anne assured her. 'It is you who have been very ill.'

'Yes,' Jean said, dreamily, 'I know . . . you looked after me.' Her fingers sought Anne's above the coverlet. 'Thank you, dear Anne,' she said, then turned on her side and without another word fell into a dreamless sleep.

Exhausted after days without proper rest, Anne continued to hold Jean's hand as she allowed her head to sink on to the coverlet. John found her there some hours later. He heard Jean's gentle breathing and realised that all was well. Gently he roused his wife and guided her to bed. Before she closed her eyes again, he said, 'I meant to tell you earlier, Billy met the doctor in town today . . . he told him that Jean was not doing so well and Morton said he would call in tomorrow.'

Annie, who had struggled alone throughout Jean's illness, praying all the time the doctor would return, could barely raise a smile in response.

Jack peered over the gunwale of the barge and ducked down as a shell whistled by, only feet above his head. The brief glimpse had been sufficient to show him that Turkish artillery posts were situated high up on the cliffs to either side of the bay.

'They might have put those out of action before sending in the horses,' he muttered, more to himself than to the men standing nearby.

'I thought this was to be a stealthy landing under cover of darkness?' observed Corporal Simms, taking a tighter grip on the rein. His mount bucked when a star shell suddenly burst above their heads, lighting the whole scene with its intense white glare.

'Whoa there, Birdie!' He patted the horse's neck in the hope of soothing him, but the beast, eyes white with fear, threw up his head in alarm.

Jack McDougal, while retaining a firm grip upon his own horse, turned to face the terrified Birdie. 'Hush, boy,' he murmured, breathing softly into the animal's nostrils. In an instant the horse was quiet. His ears were still laid flat, but the threat that he might launch himself over the side of the vessel had passed.

'Thanks, Sarge.' The corporal relaxed somewhat, and this conveyed itself to his horse who began to nuzzle Jack's grey mare, apparently no longer concerned by the noises of battle.

On the starboard side of the barge, seamen were busily removing the great wooden planks which held the exit ramp in position.

'Any minute now,' Jack warned the men under his command. 'When we hit the beach, lead the horses out in number order . . . no rushing, and no holding back, or you will be putting others in danger.' Even as he spoke, the barge was slewed around so that it came sideways on to the shore. It wallowed in the surf, once again making the horses uneasy.

Jack glanced around at the tense white faces of the young men, hardly more than boys most of them, who had never been under fire.

Jack's maturity – he was the oldest man in the Company – and his rare gift with horses had made him a likely subject for promotion from the outset. Raw recruits, many of them farm boys from the outback, looking for adventure and some relief from the tedium of their lives, required a father figure to look up to, and Jack McDougal had proved to be just the man for the job.

'Remember, lads,' he called out, hoping to calm frayed nerves, 'it's tea and Tommy Cookers for every man who gets his horse to the cliff overhang in one piece!'

'Give me a bottle of real beer and I'm anybody's,' shouted an unidentified voice. There was general laughter. The boys were smiling as the ramp hit the water.

Of the first dozen horses to make the run, two were mown down within yards of the barge. Jack, charging after them, could only cling on to the reins of his mare as she neatly side-stepped a prone companion, landing heavily on her master's foot. Jack swore, but the momentary hesitation allowed man and beast to miss the next shell. It fell harmlessly at the point where they would have been.

In the lull which followed, Jack was able to hobble the last few yards to safety before handing his mare over and throwing himself down on the ground to catch his breath.

As Corporal Tom Pain led the mare away, he spoke soothingly to her. 'Come on, Jeannie lass, I've some fresh water and sweet hay for you over here.'

Jack grinned to himself. He wondered how Jean would take the news that he had called the mare after her. Not every woman would regard it as a compliment. Jean would understand, though. She knew how dearly he loved his animals. She would surely see it as a tribute to her, knowing the pleasure it gave him to use her name constantly.

He got to his feet as the last of the horses arrived from the barge. Another three had been shot down before reaching the cliff, and several of the men were wounded. Corporal Simms was stripping off his pack and webbing.

'Where do ye think you're going?' Jack demanded.

'To carry in those two lads.' He indicated the two soldiers who had been blown up in the first onslaught, with their horses. They lay face down on the sand with the water lapping at their feet.

'No hurry for that, laddie,' Jack told him, kindly. 'They can wait until those Turkish gun positions are overrun. Then we'll bury them.'

'Officer approaching!' One of the sappers, catching sight of a flash of well-polished pips, gave warning.

'Glad to see you, Mr McGillivray, sir!' Jack greeted the young officer. Not wishing to suffer any accusations of nepotism, Hamish and Jack had agreed to keep their relationship to themselves. Only Tom Pain knew that the two were stepbrothers. 'I watched your landing, Sergeant,' Hamish observed. 'Under the circumstances, you did well to get so many men and horses ashore.'

'We were told that we would be landed after the enemy gun position had been overrun,' Jack retorted, angrily.

'The artillery positions up on the cliff were very well-disguised,' Hamish explained. 'No one had spotted them in earlier reconnaissance sorties. We were as surprised as you when they opened fire on the barges.'

Mutely, they surveyed the scene of recent carnage. Other bargeloads had fared worse, it seemed. There must be twenty or more horses lying dead or dying on the shore. Alongside them, bodies of young men lay sprawled – some calling out for help, others still.

'Corporal Simms,' Jack broke the silence. 'Collect a party of six men and go and bring in the wounded. There has nae been any sniper fire for ten minutes.' He looked at Hamish for confirmation.

Hamish took out his service revolver and thrust it into the corporal's hand. 'For the wounded horses, Simms,' he explained in subdued voice.

Corporal Simms saluted and ran off to find medics and a stretcher party.

'At 0600 hours we shall be moving up off the beach.' Hamish turned back to Jack. 'There is a rather narrow pathway up the cliffs . . . could be difficult for the wagons. You may have to have them dismantled and carried up by mule.'

'Is that something else Intelligence did nae tell us?' Jack asked. Not expecting an answer, he passed on the lieutenant's orders to those around him. 'We'll lead the riding horses up first and form a picket line at the top of yon cliff. Meanwhile wagoneers and mule drivers, report to me over there!'

He pointed to the place where a geological fault had created a deep gully, the only possible means by which they would get off the beach.

Hamish's signals detachment had landed on the heels of the first wave of infantry, their task to set up communications with the remainder of the Australian and New Zealand forces still aboard ship outside, Suvla Bay.

As he approached the cliff path, Jack could see huge reels of cable lying piled on the shingle. The handcarts which had been used to haul them from the barges were even now on their way back down the beach to collect more equipment. Alongside the cable, two heavy wooden carts had been drawn up and the mules which had been used to haul them were being released from their harness.

'No chance of dragging these wagons up that slope, Sergeant,' Abel Peterssen, the wagon master, observed.

'Corporal Simms!' Jack shouted, bringing the corporal and his small company of men running after him.

'Dismantle the wagons, and load the parts on to the mules,' he ordered. Turning to Abel Peterssen he added, 'As soon as the first six mules are ready, take a man for every two beasts and lead them up the path.' His glance travelled up the gully, searching for places where the rocks and brush might provide some protection from enemy fire. There had been very little shooting since the major artillery posts on the two headlands had been silenced, but a few Turkish snipers were making their presence known with the occasional bullet.

'See that clump of bushes?' Jack pointed to a position about halfway up the cliff. 'That is your primary objective. Force the animals to that point, then lay low and let them rest. If all seems clear, I'll give you a signal to go on. The last hundred feet are the most exposed.' He indicated the spot where the pathway had been gouged out of a sheer rock face. A well-positioned sniper would be able to take his pick of the mule train as it tried to get to the plateau beyond.

'Simms, ask the lieutenant for a couple of marksmen to cover the mule train,' Jack ordered.

The first sappers had already gained the top of the cliff. Mounting their horses, and each leading an additional beast, they galloped across the open space and managed to reach the plateau without loss. A wild cheer rang out from those waiting below. One of the sappers raised his bush hat to wave, the signal that they were all clear. Instantly a shot rang out, echoing against the stark rock walls of the gully, and the man crumpled to his knees.

'Did you see where . . .' Jack demanded.

'Over to the right . . . up there, behind that group of gnarled willows . . . look!' He trained his binoculars on the spot and caught the brief glimpse of sunlight on steel as the sniper shifted position.

Jack called over the marksmen assigned by Hamish. He pointed out the Turkish sniper, who was in a position to shoot down every muleteer in the team.

'Can you do anything about him?'

One of the men allowed his gaze to drift to the opposite wall of the gully. He estimated angles and distances for a few seconds before declaring, 'That'll be OK, Sarge. Harris here can go up with the first mule team. I'll climb up to that overhang of rock, d'you see? Next time he shows himself . . . I'll get 'im.'

Jack twisted his head, seeking out the spot. He let out a low whistle.

'Aye – that'll do,' he agreed, 'but can you get there? The cliff is almost sheer.'

'Just leave it to me,' the man assured him. He stripped of his surplus gear and began his climb, hidden from the Turkish sniper by a wide overhang of grey rock.

Jack made his way over to where Corporal Simms headed the second group of animals to be taken to the top. Jeannie pricked her ears at her master's approach. Jack heard Simms murmuring to her, 'All right, lass, he'll be following on directly.'

'Right, Corporal, up you go.' Jack whacked the flank of the first horse in the line. 'And, Simms,' he continued, 'when you get there, dinnae bother to wave!'

He acknowledged the guarded warning with a grin. 'OK, Sarge,' he responded. 'We'll give them as little to shoot at as we can manage.'

Jack watched them climb steadily to the first way-station, the clump of rocks and bushes where the previous team had halted. As they began the next stage of the ascent, a shot was fired, the flash from the Turkish barrel glowing against the dark rocks on the opposite side of the gully. A second shot followed immediately, and a shower of rocks preceded the tumbling body of the Turkish sniper. At a point some hundred feet above their heads, the man was seen to strike a jutting boulder which flung him clear of the rock face to land with a sickening thud in the ravine below. There would be no need to check on the body, he was certainly dead.

'Now then, the mules!' Jack gave the order and the heavily laden beasts began their slow climb. The two sharpshooters kept a wary eye on the rock wall opposite, but there was no sign of further Turkish intervention.

The sun was beginning to glow red on the horizon before the Australian Third Division finally cleared the beach and set up its bridgehead on the plateau.

Jack McDougal was one of the last to clamber up the path, in company with Lieutenant McGillivray. They were nearly at the top when a worried-looking Corporal Simms came to meet them.

'Something wrong, Simms?' asked the lieutenant, as the corporal fell into step beside him.

'There certainly is, Sir,' replied the corporal. 'Search parties have been out all afternoon looking for a supply of water. There is none . . . not a single flippin' drop to be found anywhere!'

Jack ran across the open space and dropped down into the opening in the ground which allowed entry to their dugout. The bucket of water he carried was leaking from a hole made by a sniper's bullet as he had climbed the cliff from the beach. Quickly he transferred the precious liquid to another container before it was all lost.

'Anything to go with it?' he enquired, as he filled his metal canteen and placed it on the primus stove to heat. He meant tea, or even coffee, both items which could have arrived in the morning's post from home.

'Nothing but Tommy Cookers,' Tom complained. 'What wouldn't I give for a long cold pint of real beer?' He opened up the tin of solidified alcohol, stirred it into his canteen of boiled water and watched as the cloudy liquid slowly cleared. It looked horrible, it tasted of nothing, but it did leave a man with that warm alcoholic glow which, in his imagination, carried him back to the bars of Perth where the three of them had drunk their last beers as civilians.

'No post again today,' he replied to Jack's unspoken query. 'I'll bet there's piles of stuff waiting for us back in Cairo . . . plum cakes, sugar and real coffee.' He almost drooled as he thought of the delicacies which they had been denied for so long.

From Suvla beach, the ANZAC forces had driven a wedge into the countryside, establishing a front some five miles wide and about a mile deep before being ordered to dig in. Army Intelligence had neglected to tell their forces about the complete absence of water in the occupied area. Every single drop must be carried ashore from lighters, and hauled up the cliff face.

To Jack McDougal, this had been the worst blow of all. His precious mules, without water and with no feed other than that which could be brought up with the ammunition, had been doomed from the start. Without beasts to haul them, their wagons had become the roofs of dugouts. For several weeks the men ate nothing but horse meat. Any cable which had to be laid over the few miles separating their own front line from the beachhead had been laid by hand. So far they had continued to fetch water for their personal mounts from the lighters which sailed into Suvla Bay each day. Every man was responsible for his own and his mount's requirements, officers and NCOs included.

It was bitterly cold on the bare hillside. Hamish McGillivray drew his waterproof cape tighter about him and shifted his haversack to a more comfortable position. He had had softer pillows.

It had been necessary to leave their overcoats and blankets back at the base so that they could carry sufficient food and water to sustain themselves during the advance.

Through the scrubby foliage above his head he could see the stars. Sheltering beneath the branches of what looked like a holly bush, he was reminded of other chilly evenings, tracking the Factor's deer in the wild glens of Seileach Island. That life seemed centuries away.

He scratched his face on the prickly branches as he peered down the slope to where the infantry were entrenched.

The hands on his watch moved slowly, he could barely make them out by the light of a waning moon. Two more minutes and they would be on their way.

'Twenty-fifteen, sir,' Corporal Tom Pain whispered hoarsely in his ear.

With his training as an electrician, and his background of work-ing in the Keningo gold mines, where he had been obliged to turn his hand to any problem which might present itself, Hamish had been snapped up by the Royal Australian Engineers. It had soon become apparent that the ebullient young Scotsman was also a leader rather than a follower of men, and within weeks of signing on he had been offered a commission.

With no more experience of warfare than those under his command, he now found himself in charge of this special mission. Thankfully they had allowed him to pick his own men for the job.

'Now!' Hamish whispered to the sapper on his right, and the message was passed quickly around the group. The six men crept forward, using the shadows of the scattered thorn bushes for cover. Their feet made no noise on the sandy ground.

A hundred yards ahead, the Turkish lookout dozed at his post. He leaned forward over his rifle, a lighted cigarette hanging slackly from his lips. Tonight, like every other night for weeks past, was quiet following the evening exchange of artillery fire, a daily reminder to each side that hostilities continued.

Suddenly hot ash dropped on to the sentry's hand, making him start. He stared out into the empty plain before him. Was it a trick of the light or had that bush over to the right really moved? He continued to stare for several seconds . . . no, there was nothing. He shifted his position and lit another cigarette.

Corporal Tom Pain, at the lieutenant's elbow, nudged him and pointed to where the red glow indicated the position of the sentry.

Hamish turned to one of the two infantrymen assigned to his company. He indicated the glowing cigarette and the two soldiers disappeared into the night. There was a slight disturbance, a grunt from the dying Turk, and in a few moments they were back.

'All clear, Lieutenant,' one whispered.

Leaving the two squaddies to cover their approach, the sappers and their lieutenant moved forward.

Each carried a heavy haversack which he treated with extreme caution. Crawling on hands and knees, the small party approached the rampart which marked the front of the Turkish trench.

Tight up against the sandbags, each man extracted the mine he had been carrying and laid it carefully against the base of the wall. At a given signal they set the timed fuses and retreated as cautiously as they had arrived.

At a hundred yards, Hamish judged it was safe to get to their feet and run. They tore down the slope and threw themselves into the slit-trench which they had dug the previous night.

Hamish studied his watch. The little hand crept round. Three more seconds . . . two . . . one . . . The mines exploded together, creating a bright magnesium-white light which blinded them all for a few moments. When the dust cleared they could see that the wall had collapsed into the trench behind, hopefully confusing if not killing the Turkish soldiers.

Up the hill behind them came the main force of Australian infantry, howling and whooping enough to put the fear of death into the bravest heart.

The engineers, their part in the action completed, hung back in their slit-trench until the entire infantry had moved past them. Soon the night was alive with the rattle of machine-guns and the intermittent sound of rifles. For the main part the soldiers preferred to use the bayonet when charging under cover of darkness. There was less likelihood of a stray bullet killing one of their own men.

'Right,' Hamish called out, satisfied that they were free to return to base. 'Make your own way back to the line and reform.'

To the two infantrymen who had accompanied them, he said, 'You did well, thanks.'

'All part of the service, Lieutenant,' one of them replied.

'Owe you a pint,' observed Tom, patting the other on the back. The two squaddies disappeared into the gloom.

One hundred Turks were killed in that first onslaught, with the loss of eleven Australians. There were however more than seventy men wounded, many of them seriously.

Before the night was over, Tom and Hamish found themselves out on the plain again, overseeing the clearing of the dead and wounded from the site of battle before the coming of daylight and the predatory Turkish snipers.

After that single action in April, the Australian troops had maintained and strengthened their position. While elsewhere along the length of the Gallipoli Peninsula the Allied troops were struggling to avoid being swept back into the sea, here at Suvla Bay the ANZAC forces were still holding their ground.

Towards the end of July there was a tremendous increase in the amount of materials being landed from the barges and lighters. Additional troops were sent to reinforce the whole front, Hamish's engineers were hard pressed to construct sufficient emplacements to house them all. In an effort to prevent the enemy from learning about the build-up, all movement of men and materials was undertaken under cover of darkness, thereby adding to the difficulties of those in charge of the operation.

Weeks before, the last of the horses had been slaughtered and while this obviated the requirement for large quantities of water to be carried up from the beach, it also meant that everything must be dragged by hand or carried on their backs by the men. As the stocks began to pile up, boxes of food and ammunition had to be secreted in dugouts and bivouacs right across the plateau where the ANZACs were entrenched. Jokes about squaddies with long ears and tails quickly palled. The men were tired, bewildered by the prevarication of their superiors, and spoiling for a fight.

'What's this?' demanded Jack McDougal, coming upon Hamish as he inspected the latest set of dugouts and communication trenches. 'Nae more rabbit warrens, surely?' he observed dryly. 'If yon Colonel Birdwood intends to celebrate Christmas and Hogmanay up here, we might just as well build ourselves some more permanent housing!'

'We are required to provide suitable cover for a further fifteen hundred men, coming ashore the next time there is no moon,' Hamish told him. 'The idea is to get the additional troops up here and into position under cover of darkness, so that Johnny Turk has no idea we are building up to an attack.'

'Have those gold-braided wee idiots back at base no' heard of spies?' demanded Jack. 'How are we to know which of the Greek and Egyptian servants milling about camp are enemies? D'ye no' ken the Turks are ready for every move we make?'

'I don't give the orders, Jack, only carry them out!' Hamish reminded his stepbrother. 'I'll just finish checking out these dug outs while you get a work detail to start filling a few sandbags, Sergeant.'

'Aye Sir.' Jack saluted smartly and strode off to unearth Corporal Simms and his platoon.

It was several days later when Jack was summoned to his lieutenant's dugout.

'Post for your lads.' Hamish handed over a bundle of letters. 'And Headquarters Staff landed last night,' he added, watching Jack sorting through the envelopes.

He looked up, sharply. 'You mean, Birdwood himself?'

'Should be getting our orders to attack any day now,' Hamish confirmed.

Jack had found his own letters at the bottom of the pile. Breathing a sigh of relief, he extracted the one written in Jean's hand and carefully unsealed the envelope. He scanned the first few lines and let out a whoop of joy.

'I'm a father!' he cried. 'It's a wee girlie.'

'Congratulations, man.' Hamish shook him warmly by the hand, but Jack was only half concentrating on his companion's words. What was this? It seemed that there had been some complications at the birth:

. . . had it not been for Anne I might well be dead. Despite all our efforts to be scrupulously clean, I still developed puerperal fever. Anne said she thought it was probably due to flies carrying the disease. It's so difficult to keep them down. Anyway, your daughter is a 'bonny wee lassie' with red hair. I have decided to call her Ellen. Your father seems very pleased at the idea. He is absolutely besotted with his granddaughter. I can see that we shall have trouble with him spoiling her as she grows up . . .

'Any news of Granny and John McDougal?' asked Hamish. His own letter from his mother had been a rather guarded account of what was happening at the mine. Although she had tried to make it sound light-hearted there was an underlying note of anxiety. It appeared that his father was working too long hours, and Makepeace had still not come up with the necessary supplies of timber for rendering the mines absolutely safe. 'Flora has sailed for Scotland to join some special scheme run by a group of women doctors, apparently. Why she can't just be an ordinary hospital nurse, I don't know.'

Jack laughed. 'Och, wee Flora was never one to do the obvious thing,' he observed, lightly. 'Vicky has had another litter of pups by her wild dingo mate, and the flock is now over a thousand head . . .'

'Enough sheep to send anyone to sleep, counting them,' laughed Tom, ducking as he entered the dugout.

'. . . and the price of wool has gone through the roof!' Jack concluded, ignoring the corporal's interruption.

Tom, suspecting that once launched upon his favourite topic his friend would carry on with his sheep talk for hours, repaired to his own corner with his mail and sat down to read.

Hamish stood up. 'There's a strategy meeting this afternoon,' he told them. 'Things should be moving faster now.'

He envied his friends their companionship. In such a small company, the officer's life was a lonely one. Keeping his head low, he dodged through the honeycomb of dugouts to his own quarters.

For three nights they had been arriving. Smuggled ashore by the Royal Navy, the reinforcements were led up the cliff path by the seasoned veterans of Suvla Bay and packed into the trenches dug for them not two hundred yards from the Turkish lines on the summit of Mount Sari Bair.

To Hamish, who had supervised the entire operation in his sector, it seemed impossible that the Turks could be unaware of what was going on. Twice daily the lines of field artillery on both sides exchanged a few desultory shots, just to prove to each other that they still had a fighting capacity. This evening's barrage had lasted no more than fifteen minutes. For an hour since, there had been no activity from the Turkish lines.

As he waited for the signal, Hamish went over in his mind the meeting they had had with Colonel Birdwood in the ruined taverna by the shore which served as the officers' mess.

Birdwood, the English staff officer appointed to lead the ANZAC attack, had yet to gain the confidence of his colonial subordinates. His public school accent irritated them, and while his music hall antics with his monocle, legendary throughout the service, might amuse the men, his officers would have preferred less play-acting and a more informed attitude towards their operation.

'So far,' he had told the young men gathered about him in the half-light, 'you have done your job splendidly. Our intelligence is that the Turks have no information about our build-up and are not expecting any kind of attack in the near future.' He shifted his feet and screwed the monocle more firmly into his eye.

'Now then,' he barked at them, in the way they had come to expect, 'this is how it's going to be. There will be two main forces.' He turned to the wall map and began to outline the place of attack.

'As you will expect,' he concluded some time later with a wicked grin, 'we have devised our usual diversionary action.' They laughed. Birdwood's diversionary tactics were often bizarre but they usually had the desired effect of distracting the enemy from the main attack and causing him to divert troops from his line of defence.

'A detachment from the First Australian Infantry Brigade will take this post here.' His pointer rested on an outlier, a small hillock to the south-west of the great ridge of Sari Bair. 'We call it Lone Pine, for obvious reasons.' More laughter. 'There is a spring on this hill which is the main source of water used by the enemy. The attack on Lone Pine will certainly worry the Turkish commander, who will have only limited supplies of water, perched up there on the ridge!' They did not laugh now. These officers had all experienced living with a minimum of water, and knew only too well that if the Turks were short of it, then they too were going to suffer equally.

Birdwood studied a list in his hand. He raised his head, demanding, 'Lieutenant McGillivray?' Hamish rose to his feet. 'Sir?'

'Report to Colonel Ryrie afterwards, would you?'

'Sir!' Hamish sat down again, taunted from all sides by the murmured jibes of his nearest neighbours.

Birdwood concluded, 'From 1630 hours, tomorrow, the enemy will be bombarded continuously for one hour. That should make them keep their heads down while we make our last-minute preparation. At 1730 hours the main assault on the ridge will take place.'

The famous monocle, which he had been swinging in his hand as he spoke, was now thrown up and deftly caught between eyebrow and cheek to the anticipated acclaim of his officers. 'You and your men have done a splendid job in getting us to our present position. If we can sustain the same degree of commitment in battle, victory will be ours!'

He strode out, his adjutant scurrying along in his wake. The officers rose to leave, filtering out of the dark little building in twos and threes, laughing and talking just as though they had spent the night drinking and merrymaking. An enemy observer would see nothing different from any other night during the past tedious months.

Colonel Ryrie and Brigadier General Smythe of the First Australian Infantry had remained behind. Hamish hovered in the background until summoned to step forward.

'McGillivray, I have had good reports of your activities here at Suvla Bay,' Ryrie addressed him at last. 'I understand that you have led a number of successful sorties against the enemy lines.'

'Thank you, sir,' Hamish answered, shortly.

Ryrie regarded him more closely. 'You don't sound like an Australian, son,' he ventured.

'A new Australian,' Hamish replied, proudly. 'I emigrated in '13, sir.'

'And then came all the way back to join in the fight, eh? Good lad.' Hamish shuffled uncomfortably.

'Well,' Ryrie wandered over to the map on the wall, 'I have a special task for you and a company of your best men.'

Hamish joined his colonel at the wall where he was staring at the spot on the map marked 'Lone Pine'.

'We believe that Turkish fortifications here will be much like those encountered elsewhere. The trenches will be covered over, probably with whole tree-trunks if they have had sufficient time to dig themselves in properly – which they have!'

He sketched on the table top with a piece of chalk. 'The cover is almost impregnable, except for manholes which they leave deliberately for their men to enter and exit by.'

Hamish studied the sketch intently, already estimating in his head the amount of explosive likely to be required to shift tree trunks laid horizontally and, no doubt, firmly fixed into the ground at either end.

'I need a company of engineers to precede Brigadier Smythes's attack and lay explosives which will blow sufficient openings in the fortification for my men to get in amongst the Turks.' He lowered his eyes and turned away slightly, unable to face this eager young fellow directly. 'It's a job for volunteers, you understand. Every man you take with you must be given the opportunity to cry off, if he so desires.'

Hamish replaced his bush hat, saluted smartly and replied, 'My company will do the job for you, sir. I have no doubt that they will all volunteer.'

'Thank you, my boy,' the old man responded, gruffly. 'I know you can be relied upon to do your best.' He returned Hamish's salute and strode over to the map which he studied fixedly while Brigadier General smythe gave the lieutenant detailed instructions for the operation.

Dismissed at last, Hamish made his way up the cliff path to Jack's dugout. There was a deal of preparation for them to do before zero hour.

They had divided the squad into five groups of three, spread out along a line two hundred yards wide. The sappers had been dug in below the edge of the plateau, some fifty yards in advance of the main body of infantry since before first light. To lighten their load they had discarded all equipment save what they required to carry out their mission. What rations they had with them were carried in their tunic pockets: hard tack biscuits, a tin of bully beef per man and a bar of chocolate. Their water supply consisted of one water bottle each, which must last them throughout a day during which the relentless August sun would beat down upon their unprotected position.

The Turkish line was no more than one hundred and twenty yards from the edge of the plateau. Despite the continuous naval bombardment of the position for an hour each evening for the past week, it was clear from the sounds of activity amongst the enemy troops that the shells had made little impact upon the fortifications. The main function of this regular bombardment had been to encourage the enemy to take cover from the gunfire, so that when the infantry moved up to begin the process of digging themselves in on the final day before the thrust, their activity would go unheard and unnoticed. In this, at least, the bombardment had succeeded, for it was clear from the nonchalant manner in which the Turkish soldiers went about their daily routine that they were totally unaware of the attacking force lying in wait below the rim of the plateau.

Lieutenant McGillivray moved swiftly and silently from group to group, checking equipment and encouraging his men. He dropped down into the slit-trench beside Jack and Tom. Sapper Collins who, as little more than a schoolboy, had left his father's sugar cane plantation in Queensland to join the colours, crouched in his corner of the trench, white-faced and trembling despite the heat of the afternoon.

'All set, Sergeant?' Hamish whispered, glancing back along the line of dugouts from which he had just come. Not a blade of withered grass nor a dry thorn bush quivered. There was nothing to give away their position.

'Aye, sir,' Jack replied. His men knew precisely what was expected of them.

Hamish studied his watch. 'Two minutes to go.' He slumped down into the trench beside Jack and grinned at the men around him. Noting the tense expression on the face of the young sapper, he smiled. 'All right, Collins?'

The young man nodded and swallowed painfully.

'Just follow the sergeant here. And, remember – the whole of the Australian First Division is right behind you! Lay your charges and get out, that's all that's required of you.' He leant forward and tapped the boy from the sugar fields of Queensland playfully on the shoulder. The soldier smiled ruefully as he felt a sharp stone dig into his back below the shoulder blade. He was still rubbing awkwardly at the spot when the first guns began to fire.

'Five minutes to let the Turks get their heads right down,' said Hamish, 'and then we go!'

They were running now, ducking and weaving to avoid any stray rifle bullet from either of the two lookout posts situated within the Turkish line. The plan was to disable both posts simultaneously, by first cutting their communications wiring and then shooting all those within. Hopefully, the shots would be disguised by the onslaught from the Allied artillery.

'Collins, you can see the wires,' Jack whispered, pointing out where two cables left a set of porcelain insulators and snaked along the top of the sand-bagged parapet in either direction. The boy crept forward with his wire cutters at the ready. Hamish and Tom kept their rifles trained on the observation window. As Collins reached up to cut the wires, a face appeared at the opening. Jack fired as the next salvo landed some fifty feet away, along the embankment. The face in the opening became a red mass of pulped flesh and disappeared. They could hear sounds of shouting and confusion from within. Tom leapt up on to the parapet and down into the trench beyond, just as the door to the lookout post opened. His bayonet put paid to the first of the Turks to emerge, the second reeled backwards as Tom's rifle butt knocked him into the arms of the third occupant of the dugout. Before either could extricate himself, each had received a bullet in the chest. In a matter of moments, all of the Turkish guard lay dead or dying.

Tom stepped back from the doorway and gave Hamish the signal to carry on. From the far end of the line, Corporal Simms signalled the 'all clear', having gained his objective, and Hamish mounted the parapet, waving on his men. In an instant the remaining groups ran forward in threes towards the main Turkish entrenchment and threw themselves full-length upon the ground.

There was still no indication that the main force of the enemy was aware of their proximity.

The Turkish trenches were about ten feet from firing step to parados, and stretched for two hundred yards from north to south across the plateau. Behind the line, standing starkly black against the fast-disappearing sun, stood the shattered trunk of the single tall tree which had given the post its name of Lone Pine.

Across the width of the trench, pine logs had been laid so close together as to provide an almost impenetrable cover for the men below. If the advance of the engineers had been witnessed, the Turks had made no attempt to defend themselves. At intervals along the front step of the redoubt there were slots through which a rifle might be aimed, but it seemed that the troops within were relying on the lookout posts which were already rendered ineffectual, and made no effort to protect themselves from attack by ground forces. They were more concerned to take cover from the vicious onslaught of the naval guns firing from Suvla Bay.

Jack and Tom laid their explosive charges, packing them in around three of the protruding ends of the pine logs at a time. Tom completed the charge by fixing the fuse wire and held out the free end to Collins who crouched beside him. Lying full-length across the log roof, in order to avoid anyone aiming at them through the rifle slits, they crawled along a few yards and repeated the action. Within minutes, charges had been laid at intervals along the whole front. Each group of three men now fell back, sliding down the embankment of sandbags which formed the front step of the trench, and throwing themselves against the wall for protection from the fusillade of bullets from the Turkish soldiers, trapped within their earthworks.

Collins gathered up the free ends of Jack's charges and ran with them across the pine-log roof. He did not see the rifle sticking up through a gap in the logs, he only felt the bullet which penetrated his thigh and travelled up through his groin to lodge in his bowel. The pain was excruciating. He opened his mouth to call out to his companions, who were fast disappearing over the edge of the redoubt, but no sound emerged. Instead he felt a vast welling within him and a sudden desire to vomit. Blood gushed from his mouth as he fell headlong across the pine trunks. He lifted the hand which held the fuse wires, clutching them fiercely as his arm fell, lifeless, across the first of the charges they had laid.

Jack grabbed the battery from his haversack. Where was Collins? He looked round inquiringly at Tom, who shrugged and made to climb the wall once more in search of the missing man.

Along the line, charges were blowing as each of the demolition groups completed its assignment. Behind them, over the rim of the plateau, the men of the First Australian Infantry Brigade were pouring, running across the two hundred yards of open plain with bayonets fixed. The line of men checked suddenly as the Turks in their stronghold opened fire. A machine-gun cut a swathe through the advancing body of men, then another and another was brought into action, and the Australians began to drop in large numbers. Those first in the line had nearly reached the parapet by now. A few seconds more and they would be blown up by the dynamite of their own engineers!

Tom pulled himself up and saw, to his horror, that Collins was lying across the last charge they had laid, still holding the fuses. On his belly, he crawled forward towards the dead boy. He was unaware of the sniper's bullet which ripped through his sleeve. He tried to prise the fuse wires from the dead hand. They were gripped too tight. Horrified at the enormity of what he had to do, Tom broke one finger after another until the wires were freed. Gagging at the sight of so much blood, he pulled himself clear of the dead soldier and crawled back towards where Jack McDougal awaited his return with impatience.

The advancing infantrymen had nearly reached them when Jack finally completed the electric circuit and was ready to blow the charges.

'Stand back!' he cried as the troops began to swarm up the

ramparts. 'Take cover!' He thrust the plunger into the battery box. There was a second's delay before the roar of the explosion blotted out the sounds of gunfire all around them. When the dust cleared, the infantrymen continued their advance. On the roof of the trench large holes had been made through which the Australians were able to jump down amongst the terrified Turkish soldiers. Complacent in their belief that their position was impregnable, these young and unseasoned soldiers, on seeing the glint of steel and hearing the wild roars of the ANZACs as they laid about them with rifle shot and bayonet, fled – only to meet others from along the trench running towards them.

The carnage was the most horrific any of the men had witnessed before. Within fifteen minutes the fighting came to an end. Australians and Turks lay dead, bodies sprawled across one another like so much flotsam on a beach. Those Turks who remained alive cringed against the walls of their trench, hands raised above their heads, weapons thrown into heaps upon the ground. Hardly able to believe that they were the victors, the Australians stood over their captives, guns loaded, ready to shoot the first man who moved.

Outside in the open, Jack McDougal turned to his friend.

'The firing seems to have stopped, Tom,' he said. 'Shall we go up and take a look?'

There was no reply.

'Tom?' Jack shook the prone figure at his side and was relieved to hear him moan, incoherently. Only then did he notice the wound on Tom's head where a piece of shrapnel had penetrated, making a ragged incision at the base of his skull. It didn't seem to be a serious wound, there was hardly any bleeding.

'Come on, old chap.' He helped his friend to his feet. Tom was holding his hand to his face. Suddenly he drew it away and stared upwards at the sky.

'I can't see!' he cried in alarm.

Jack took hold of him, more gently now.

'You've had wee knock,' he said, soothingly. 'It's probably only concussion. I'll whack a dressing on that cut and then I'll get someone to take you back to the lines.'

Lieutenant McGillivray had summoned his party together for roll call. Apart from Collins, three other members of the company had died and two had sustained serious gunshot wounds.

'I've been directed to set up an observation post here,' he told them. 'I want three volunteers to man the post under the command of Corporal Simms.' He could have taken his pick of all those present. 'Sergeant?'

Jack named three of the men to remain behind.

'We shall need a land line and a telephone, Sergeant McDougal,' continued Hamish. Seeing Jack hesitate, his arm still tight about his friend's shoulders, he added, 'I'll see that these wounded men get back to base.'

The attack on the Lone Pine had alerted the main Turkish force to the danger to their position. As the Australian First Division waited to be relieved, Turkish forces massed at the eastern side of the plateau and prepared an attack to repossess the hill and its precious water supply. Birdwood's plan was successful in drawing off a considerable amount of the resistance which might otherwise have confronted the main ANZAC force in its attack upon Chunuk Bair Ridge.

It took no more than an hour to assemble a cable wagon which, in the absence of horses, had to be drawn by men. Jack supervised the erection of poles and the laying of a telephone line across the few hundred yards of newly gained ground to the HQ network. By the time that communications had been established, the survivors of the battle had been relieved by reserves from the Third and Fourth Battalions and the observation post had been taken over by the Brigadier himself.

Jack was able, at last, to order his men back to base. As they made their way slowly down the escarpment for which they had fought so bitterly the evening before, the sun escaped from behind the hills on the far side of the Dardenelles, throwing the landscape around them into sharp relief. There was a distant sound of firing where the battle for the Sari Bair continued, but they themselves felt divorced from the fighting now that their own part in the operation was at an end.

Jack made his way down the stony pathway behind the sappers.

He was anxious to get back to base the check on Tom. It had seemed such an insignificant wound at the time, he could not accept that his friend might be permanently blinded. He did, however, want to reassure himself that all was well before Tom was hustled off on to one of the hospital ships.

They reached their billet on the cliff top above Suvla Bay and Jack dismissed the men. They needed no urging to get into their bunks, although, tired as they were, sleep came only slowly to some. Visions of the battle and the terrible slaughter they had witnessed had made old men of boys that day.

Jack climbed down the familiar cliff path. One compensation for the day's events was that the usual Turkish snipers seemed to have left their posts, probably alarmed that they might be left behind when their own forces retreated.

As he neared the derelict village which Birdwood had made his headquarters, Jack was astonished to see that there were signs of recent shelling, and several of the tents had been burned to the ground. Worst of all the taverna, which all these months had served as the officers' mess, had been flattened.

They had set up a field hospital close to the foot of the cliff and it was here that Jack eventually found Tom. A clean white bandage covered not only the site of the wound, but also his eyes.

He knelt beside his friend, taking his hand in a firm grip.

'Here I am, Tom,' he said, cheerfully. 'I told you I'd see you before they carried you off to Blighty.'

'Jack . . . Jack . . . is it really you?' Tom's voice trembled. 'I thought you might have bought it. They said there was a counter-attack from the Turks, and when you didn't come . . .'

'Had to stay behind and lay in a telephone for the C.O.,' Jack explained, gently. 'You know how he is about ordering up his tea and crumpets.'

'Jack . . . Jack . . .' Tom was sobbing. 'I can't see!'

Jack glanced up at the medical orderly who was hovering nearby, ready to carry Tom off to the barge waiting by the shore. The man shook his head at the unspoken question.

So it was true then, Tom was blind.

God in heaven, thought Jack, what could you do with a blind

motor mechanic? He squeezed his friend's shoulder.

'Of course you can nae see,' he joked, lightly. 'They've covered you up with layers of cotton wool!'

'Do you think they'll send me home?' asked Tom.

'Wherever you go, keep your hands off yon pretty nurses.' Jack was fighting to keep his composure as they lifted the stretcher. He sank back on his heels and watched, miserably, as they carried Tom down to the shore.

Chapter 20

'Now, Miss Smith, I want you to lie back and try to relax,' Michael Brown said, helping Sally on to the examination couch. 'Perhaps you will allow me to remove your scarf?'

She glanced anxiously from one to the other of the two doctors, but as the younger one reached for the pretty piece of pink chiffon with which she had covered the lower part of her face, she drew it aside herself.

'Not a very pleasant sight, is it?' she laughed, nervously.

'We have seen worse.' David Beaton smiled encouragingly. 'And I have no doubt that Mr Brown will soon improve matters considerably.'

Seeing for the first time the unsightly carbuncle which had developed on Sally's face, Michael wished that he felt as confident. It was all very well for his father-in-law to assume a successful outcome, he was merely there to give a second opinion. It was Michael who would have to wield the scalpel should they decide to operate.

David was gazing intently at the swollen cheek. What had begun as a small red spot was now a full-blown carbuncle which had a number of angry-looking heads. The skin from mouth to orbit, and down to the angle of the jaw, was tightly stretched over the swelling, and had developed a tawny, almost purple hue.

'You were seen by a Dr Wallace at the factory?' Michael consulted the letter she had brought with her from William Whylie. 'What treatment did he prescribe?'

'Some cream to put on the spot,' she replied, adding vaguely, 'Oh, yes, and he did suggest that I use a mouthwash which he gave me.'

'And did you . . . use it I mean?' David asked intently.

She gave him a worried look. 'Well, no,' she answered, 'only a few times. It was so acid that it made the inside of my mouth sore and I couldn't eat . . . so I stopped using it.'

David was satisfied with this reply apparently. The use of a citrus wash was common practice in cases of simple parotitis. Because Dr Wallace appeared not to have recognised any association between the swollen gland and the carbuncle, valuable time had been lost. He studied William's letter carefully while Michael continued with his examination.

Taking up a small electric torch, he requested that Sally open her mouth.

'Is that as far as it will go?' he asked as she struggled to give him a clear view. 'No matter, I can manage.'

Michael swept the light over her epiglottis, her gums and the inside of her cheek. He then felt under the axillae of both sides of the lower jaw. There was a noticeable difference in the size of the two parotid glands. It might be a benign tumour, of course, in which case it would be a simple matter to excise it. Usually such things popped out as easily as shelling peas. He moved aside so that David could make a closer examination.

Dr Beaton felt for Sally's pulse. 'So you have been working with my old friend William Whylie?' he observed. 'Trust him to get himself involved with explosives . . . never used a hammer and chisel in preference to a measure of gunpowder!' He grinned across at Michael as he placed a cool hand on the girl's forehead. Then he too examined the inside of her mouth.

'I didn't know,' Sally said, trying desperately to disguise the anxiety she felt, 'that Unc—er, Mr Whylie had had anything to do with explosives. Before working at Annan, that is.'

'He operated the local slate quarries here, until a year or two ago,' David explained, signalling to Michael that they must consult outside.

'We won't keep you a moment, Miss Smith,' Michael assured the patient. 'Perhaps you would like to replace your scarf while you are waiting?'

He indicated a mirror on the wall behind him, and followed David into the anteroom.

'There's no doubt about it, I'm afraid,' said David. 'What began life as an ordinary carbuncle has been allowed to become something far more dangerous.'

'The swelling in the parotid gland could conceivably be a benign tumour,' Michael suggested. 'These things do develop, occasionally, for no apparent reason. It could be just a coincidence . . .'

'The patient is running a temperature, her pulse is rapid, and that can only mean that the cheek is seriously infected.' David, totally sure of his diagnosis, made no attempt to disguise his concern. 'According to Whylie, the girl did not report the condition for a week at least, and it has now been a further week while arrangements were made to get her here. Any normal septic macula would have come to a head and burst by now. Added to that, there is the appearance of the skin . . . that hard shiny look, and the purple colouring are unmistakable indications. I'm sorry to have to admit it, but what we are looking at is a carcinoma of the skin and probably of the parotid gland as well.'

Michael paled at David's verdict. What he had hoped would be a fairly straightforward piece of surgery, had become a major, life-threatening operation.

'There's no time to be lost if we are to save her.' David sat down at the desk and pulled forward a writing pad.

'The parotid will have to be removed, of course, as completely as possible. The ramifications of the gland are such that diseased cells may already have passed on to the pharynx, and even to the neck region. If the lymph nodes are infected, there is no hope for her.' As he spoke, Dr Beaton sketched a lateral view of her face, indicating the position of the carbuncle and the infected parotid gland.

'The main problem with the excision of the parotid will be to remove the gland without cutting any branches of the trigeminal nerve.' His pencil flew across the paper. 'As you know, the branches are numerous and delicate. A slip of the scalpel will paralyse the facial muscles.'

Michael studied the sketch for a few moments before he commented, 'Cheyne and Burghard recommend a curved incision along the anterior border of the sternomastoid, and then forwards and upwards, following the line of the jaw.' He took the pencil from David and drew a curved line to illustrate his point.

David was glad to see that his son-in-law could still find time to keep up with events in the medical world. He, himself, had not read a copy of the *Lancet* in many weeks.

'I can see how such an incision might produce a more acceptable scar,' he observed, not intending to belittle Michael's proposal, 'but I would suggest that those gentlemen were dealing with a less threatening situation than our patient presents. I'm afraid that to ensure the complete removal of all infected tissue, you are going to have to make a straightforward horizontal incision, from here . . . to here.'

He sketched a line from a point near the corner of the mouth to just below the earlobe.

'The skin in the area of the carbuncle is very close to breaking down. She will almost certainly be left with an external ulcer which will be difficult to heal. It might even be necessary to consider a skin graft on the cheek, once the carcinoma has been removed.'

Michael nodded silently, appreciating the reasoning behind his father-in-law's advice. The girl was so pretty . . . no matter how carefully he performed the operation she would be scarred for life.

'Miss Smith should be given the facts,' he said at last. 'I will not carry out surgery of so drastic a nature without telling the patient what the consequences are likely to be. She may elect to allow the disease to take its inevitable course.'

To David, the notion that their patient might prefer death to disfigurement was inconceivable. Life was precious under any circumstances. Of course the girl would wish to undergo the operation, whatever the expected outcome.

'We'll warn her that her looks will be somewhat altered,' he agreed brusquely, 'but I would advise against too graphic an explanation. There is no need to upset the patient unnecessarily at this stage. Now then . . . are we ready to tell Miss Smith what has been decided? The sooner we get on with this operation the better,' he concluded. 'If you could fit it in on Friday, I can make myself available to assist.'

> *Kerrera Station*
> *September, 1915*

My Dearest Annabel,

It seems a long time since I was able to find a moment to sit down and attend to my correspondence. Our days at Kerrera are filled with farming matters.

With only Aboriginal stockmen remaining, Jean and I are left to do a good deal of the work ourselves. John is now physically unable to help us very much, although he is a great planner and has a way of teaching the men which gets them carrying out all manner of tasks of which our neighbours would never consider them capable.

We have had news of the boys at last. Both Hamish and Jack are well, although sadly their friend, Tom Pain, who enlisted with them, was not so lucky. He was seriously injured in the raid on Lone Pine Ridge. Although we are so remote out here, I think it is no exaggeration to say that not a family in the district is unaffected by what is going on in Europe at this time. I only hope that it is worth all this terrible sacrifice.

We had a visit from Dougal and Mary last month. Doug seems to be fighting a constant battle with his superiors over allocations of men and materials. They press him to produce more gold without providing the resources to carry out the work safely . . . so similar to what used to happen at Eisdalsa! Mary is clearly worried about him working too hard, and looked so tired and dispirited when we saw her. Of course, at that time she had not had the good news about Hamish.

Flora has completed her initial training at the hospital and is on her way back to Scotland to join the Scottish Women's Hospitals. Who knows? She may soon find time to come and visit you all!

I wonder if Katherine McLean's house has become a

convalescent home yet? It is probably too much to ask, but if David could use his influence to get our friend Tom Pain transferred there, I know he would appreciate it. The poor boy has been blinded. I know that he has no family of his own left in England and it must be terrible to be so afflicted with only strangers to depend upon.

David will be interested to learn that my little friend, Taffee, has recovered well after contracting infantile paralysis. I have continued with the warm baths every day, exercising his limbs under water. The muscles of one leg are wasted, and it will probably always be very thin, but he can walk now with only the slightest limp. I think that the massage is very important. People visiting the farm, who have heard of his condition, are quite astonished not to find him shuffling about in a leg brace.

Jean is now quite recovered from Ellen's birth. What a fright we all had! I thought I knew everything about keeping things clean during childbirth and have gone over and over in my mind what could have happened to cause puerperal fever. Dr Morton took it all very calmly. He seemed quite accustomed to loosing his patients that way . . .

David laid down the letter. Anne had done well under such difficult circumstances – what a remarkable woman she was. There was still so much that they did not know about septicaemia and without any suitable drugs they seemed powerless to combat it. If an individual's own bodily defences could not cope with the infection, they were doomed to die. Statistics from France suggested that more men were being lost in the dressing stations, from gangrene, than were killed outright on the battlefields.

His thoughts strayed to his recent conversation with Michael regarding William's lassie from Annan. Was he right to insist that Michael should not tell her the truth about her disfigurement? Were she to have been offered the option not to have the operation, would she have chosen to take the inevitable consequences? The older he became, the more unsure he was that his time-worn principles were always the right ones.

The doctor knows best, he told himself, cynically. It was how he had been brought up, of course. His father would never have sought a patient's opinion about his treatment, yet Michael would . . . and Hugh? Undoubtedly.

Until now there had been no problems with Sally Smith's treatment. The operation had been entirely successful. Michael had done a splendid job in avoiding most of the tiny branches of nerves ramifying through the delicate musculature of her face. There was little movement in the cheek for the present, but there should be a complete absence of paralysis after a month or two. The skin lesions, however, had been much more extensive than either of them could have predicted. By the time that Michael had removed all the affected tissue, there had remained a gaping hole in the cheek some two inches in diameter. It was slow to heal, and as it did so the edges of the wound showed a puckering which would leave a most unsightly scar.

'Haven't you finished that letter yet?' demanded Annabel.

Startled out of his reverie, David looked up and smiled.

'It's good news about Jack and Hamish, isn't it? I wonder if they will get any leave when they reach England. It would be good to see young Hamish again.'

Lacking a grandfather, Hamish and Flora McGillivray had grown up on Eisdalsa relying upon Dr David to supply their need for an older confidant – until John McDougal had come upon the scene, anyway. David had supervised the births of each of Mary's children and they held a very special place in his heart.

'So Jack McDougal is a father,' he remarked. 'There was a time when I would have bet my shirt on his remaining a bachelor until his dying day.'

> *Oxford*
> *September, 1915*

My Dear Daniel,
As you will see from the address I have decided to carry on
with my studies for the time being in the hope that sooner
or later the Scottish Women's Hospitals will be sending for

me. I have written again to the WSPU, but it seems that for the present Dr Inglis's hospital at Royaumont is having to rely upon transport supplied by the French, and there is no place for a British ambulance driver. I have even suggested turning up there with my own vehicle, since your mother suggested that I might take the Rolls, but the authorities will not hear of it!

Dan put down the letter for a moment. Thank heavens, Heather was not going to be allowed to go to France after all. Now perhaps she would think of something less dangerous . . . He took it up again,

I have been to Overavon several times lately. Rebecca is not at all well. Her arthritis is getting her down and she worries terribly about both you and Manny. You, because she doesn't know where you are, and Manny because she does . . . and thinks he is working too hard!
Your mother is a most wonderful, remarkable woman. When she heard that I could not get the Scottish Women's Hospitals to take me on because they have no ambulances of their own, she came up with a scheme to offer them the money to build and equip three field ambulances. I am to go to Greenock shortly to deliver her message. Of course she does not say that the offer is conditional upon my being appointed, but I think they might see their way clear to having me after all . . . don't you?

Oh, no, he thought, how could Rebecca encourage her in such a foolhardy venture? If his mother knew how attached he had become to Heather, that she might be sending her prospective daughter-in-law to the front, would she be so free with her donations?

Manny is threatening to rejoin his territorial company now it has been ordered to the Western Front. It appears that many MPs are already in the services. Mind you, the

way things are going, perhaps it would be a good idea if all the politicians went off to the fighting and left a few sensible women to run the country in their stead. They could hardly make a worse mess of things!

So Manny had made up his mind to do it at last. Dan could hardly imagine his elder brother up to his armpits in mud . . . but then presumably they would give him some cushy billet well behind the lines. Supposedly it looked good in the eyes of the voters if those MPs who were young enough went off to join the fighting. Unfortunately that left the government of the country in the hands of a bunch of old men. Perhaps Heather was right, perhaps women would make a better job of it!

I have at last heard from my brother James. He has been posted to Malta, of all places, where he is supervising the despatch of the wounded from Gallipoli. He gives few details, but reading between the lines it seems that things are not going well there, either. At present he is busy shipping Australians back here to England, when anyone with half an ounce of sense would suppose them better off at home, in Australia. Do the Military believe that there are no hospitals Down Under?

Well, my dear, it is long past my bedtime so I will close now. Write soon . . . we all worry about you and Stuart when we do not hear from you for such long periods.

With much love,
Heather

Did she really worry about him? He had tried to get her to say she would marry him during those three days they had spent together in Glasgow, before the *Hampshire* sailed for Scapa Flow. She had seemed to enjoy his company. They had had a good time walking through the Botanical Gardens, visiting the art galleries, and shopping in Sauchiehall Street. They had taken in a couple of shows, and on the last evening they dined and danced until the small hours. Daniel had tried to get her to commit herself but each time Heather had neatly side-stepped the question. This was one very single-minded lady who was not to be deflected from her purpose – and now, he feared, his own mother was likely to be responsible for seeing that she fulfilled it.

He folded the letter carefully and went in search of Stuart.

The ship's doctor looked up expectantly as Dan opened the door and stepped over the combing. Glancing around the sick-bay to ensure that Stuart was alone, his friend jumped on to the examination couch and lay back, his hands behind his head.

'What, no customers at all?' he jibed. 'Lucky fellow . . . some of us have work to do, you know!'

'Just because I have no patients this morning, doesn't mean that I have nothing to do,' retorted Stuart, reproachfully.

'So I see,' said Dan, indicating the ancient Gaelic tome lying open on the desk. 'I feel sure that Their Lordships would be more than pleased to know that Surgeon Commander Beaton was practising voodoo medicine aboard one of His Majesty's battle cruisers!'

'I don't practice it,' grinned Stuart. 'Anyway, Voodoo is from Haiti, not the Hebrides.'

'What's the difference? They're all islands,' remarked Dan, knowing he could get a rise out of his friend. He was not disappointed.

'There's a world of difference between medicine which depends upon fantasy and witchcraft, and that which once used the natural materials to hand to cure common ailments. Mind you,' Stuart observed, with a wicked grin, 'I suspect that even Able Seaman Betts would pale a little at the thought of this cure. It involves the patient lying face up with his head resting on the anvil while a dextrous blacksmith pretends to smash his face in with a hammer. He is supposed to miss at the last moment!'

'Oh, a psychological remedy?' observed Dan, roaring with laughter. 'I can see Betts responding pretty quickly to that kind of treatment!'

Seaman Betts' lethargy when it came to any exercise other than eating and drinking was legendary aboard H.M.S. *Hampshire*.

'We'll have to ask the Chief which of the matelots is skilful enough with a hammer,' he continued. 'I hadn't realised all this mumbo-jumbo of yours was so practical.'

'Well, it doesn't include any fillet of fenny snake, newt's eyes of frog's toes, if that's what you mean,' laughed Stuart, showing that his scientific training had not excluded the works of Shakespeare. 'Anyway, what's the news? Are we going to get a spot of leave?'

'We are making for Rosyth, for a boiler clean. Should be good for a fourteen-day pass at least.'

'That's marvellous. I'll get a message to Annie . . . and Margaret. Maybe she'll let us borrow her cottage on Eisdalsa.' Stuart paused for a moment. 'How about you? Would you like to spend some time on the island you so disparage?'

'It's kind of you to ask, old chap,' replied Dan, noting with some amusement Stuart's look of relief at his refusal. 'But I have no wish to spend precious leave playing gooseberry to you two lovebirds! As a matter of fact, I need to go home and see how my mother is bearing up. And there's someone I'd like to see in Glasgow . . .'

Stuart looked up sharply. There was a rumour going around the family that Dan and Heather had been seeing each other. Well, good luck to them if that was the case, though he couldn't understand why they should be so secretive about it. No doubt Dan would reveal all when the time was right!

'Thanks all the same for the offer,' his friend added, hastily.

'That's all right. 'Stuart got to his feet, smiling. 'What we need is a snifter of medicinal brandy. Hand me that glass over there.'

Dan passed across the tall specimen jar.

'I hope your steriliser is working properly this time,' he observed, dryly.

Stuart completed his requisitions for restocking his dispensary, and called for a runner.

'Get this to the Number One, will you, Styles? On the double.'

The seaman saluted in the casual manner of those who have been too long at sea, and took the sheaf of papers.

'Going ashore soon, are you, sir?' he enquired.

'Yes, right away. I'll be ready to leave as soon as you get back.'
Stuart continued with his packing. He didn't need to take very
much. He would pick up some 'civvies' from Tigh na Broch. He
supposed it was time that Annie and he thought of acquiring a
home of their own but it seemed a bit pointless at present. He was
away at sea much of the time, while she was forever travelling
from one end of the British Isles to the other.

He picked up the old Gaelic manuscript rather reluctantly. It
really was a mistake to continue keeping it on board with him.
Suppose the ship foundered and he had to take to the boats?
Despite its special oiled silk wrapping, there was no guarantee it
would survive immersion in sea water.

Until now the *Hampshire* had had an uneventful war holed up
in Scapa Flow with the greater part of the British fleet. Things
could be changing, however. There was talk of a battle with the
German High Fleet, which was at present confined to the Baltic
Sea. If Admiral von Scheer chose to come out, there would be an
almighty dust-up.

Placing the Gaelic book on top of his clothes, he strapped up
the leather valise and glanced at his watch. Where on earth had
young Styles got to? He would be late meeting Annie at Queen
Street Station if they didn't get a move on.

They awoke to the sound of saws and hammers. The silence of the
night before, when they had been landed in the dark by an ancient
and decidedly inebriated ferryman, was now shattered by the
activities of Eisdalsa's one remaining industry.

'It sounds as though the boat-building business is doing well,'
Annie murmured sleepily.

Stuart groaned at being disturbed. 'Steward, where's my
morning tea?' he demanded.

'Hey, you're not on board now, you know,' she protested. 'It is
usual in these days of equality between the sexes for the man to
make the morning tea.'

'Ah, but I'm not one of your modern generation,' he chided.
'We Victorians expect our wives to see to all the domestic
arrangements.'

'Including home-making and child-rearing, no doubt?' Annie observed.

'But, of course.' Stuart put his arms around her and pulled her back down into the bed.

'Well, I don't have a home,' she remarked, 'although I am beginning to see the need for one.'

'But you would never live in it,' laughed Stuart. 'You would always be somewhere else!'

'Not if I was fulfilling that other function,' she replied, archly.

'You mean the child-rearing part?' he asked, becoming suddenly serious. 'But I thought we had agreed that this was no time to have children?'

'It's a woman's prerogative,' Annie answered, 'to be able to change her mind.'

Stuart had been meticulous in his use of contraceptives from the outset. They had joked that if a doctor didn't know how to avoid a pregnancy, who did? Annie had gone along with it because she had considered her work to be of the utmost importance, and knew that child-bearing would immediately exclude her from further participation in the war effort. Recently, however, she had seen so many young widows, and one in particular had brought home to her the importance of motherhood.

'The way I look at it,' the woman had told her, as her fingers continued the monotonous task of screwing a small component into the body of one field-telephone handset after another, 'is that it's my responsibility to see that young Billy grows up to benefit from his father's sacrifice – otherwise what was the point of his dying?'

'I know that we agreed that it was a bad thing to bring children into the world in the middle of a war,' Annie whispered, 'but I've been thinking a lot recently, about what it would be like if . . . well, if you didn't come back. It's something that we have to face.' The words came out in a rush. She had thought that she would never be able to bring herself to say them.

'I see,' said Stuart, thoughtfully. 'You feel there should be an heir to the Beaton fortunes?' He joked, but she knew he felt as deeply about it as she did.

'I would want to have a child . . . your child,' she murmured, 'someone to remind me of you. Anyway, seeing Millicent with her little boys yesterday made me long for my own baby . . . our baby.'

'Did you know that Hugh has signed on, and that he's waiting to be called up any day?' Stuart queried, thinking of the cheerful little scene they'd witnessed when they had called in on his brother's family at Tigh na Broch, to collect Stuart's things. Hugh had been supervising young Ian's mathematic's homework, while little David struggled with his first reading book at Millicent's knee. Could he himself possibly match Hugh as a father? he wondered. His brother had such an effortless rapport with the very young.

'No, I didn't know,' Annie replied. So that was what Millicent had meant when she had said that they would probably be seeing a great deal more of Dr David in the future. Was he coming back to keep an eye on the practice?

'Can you imagine what it would be like for Millicent and the children if Hugh didn't survive?' asked Stuart.

'I have no doubt that she would gain great strength from her children,' Annie responded.

Stuart stroked her hair.

'It means a lot to you, doesn't it?' he whispered.

She nodded silently, then turned to face him, her lips playing lightly over his bare chest. Her tongue found the cleft below his ear and worked its way upwards to tickle the lobe and then inside.

He grabbed her in a fierce embrace, kissing her hard upon the mouth until she was forced to pull back in order to breathe.

'All right,' he said, softly, 'we've got twelve more days . . . let's see what we can do about it.'

'I do hope this is not an inconvenient time to call,' Annie apologised, enfolding her mother's friend in a warm embrace.

'I would have been offended it you had not spared us a little of your precious leave,' laughed Katherine McLean. 'How well you are both looking. Being a professional woman certainly agrees with you, Annie,' she commented, adding as she led them into a small retreat, overlooking the park, 'I do hope you'll forgive me entertaining you in here. Nowadays we use the main withdrawing room as a common room for our patients.'

'This is a delightful room,' Annie replied, taking in at a glance the comfortable furniture, the few carefully chosen pieces of porcelain and the marble fireplace with its glowing brass dogs and log fire burning brightly despite the early hour.

'What a magnificent view,' observed Stuart, gazing out at the panorama of mountains falling away towards the sea, and the glen with its own substantial lochan fed by a dozen waterfalls, and swollen by autumnal storms.

It was indeed a fine day for late-October, but very cold. A chill north-easterly wind had swept down the glen as Stuart and Annie made their way by the shortcut through the grounds of Tigh na Broch, and up over the pass to Johnstones.

'And how are you, Martha?' Annie enquired of Jack McDougal's sister.

Martha had come to work for the McLeans long before Annie's mother had married John McDougal. The two women, related by the marriage of their respective parents, had met on only a few occasions since Annie and John had left for Australia.

This was a situation which might have been awkward in some households, but Katherine McLean did not wait upon ceremony. Her housekeeper was her friend and partner in the running of Johnstones and the distinctions of social class had no place in the McLean residence.

'No time to be anything but well, Mrs . . . Annie.' Martha had been rather too long in service to slip easily from that role, despite the fact that Annie was her stepsister.

'And what about your Iain?' demanded Stuart, a contemporary of Martha's son. Together they had attended the village school, at first under the tutelage of Elizabeth Whylie and later that of Katherine herself.

'Iain is the mainstay of the estate,' Katherine told him. 'He looks after the gardens almost single-handed, and that is an enormous task with three acres given over to growing vegetables.'

'He was turned down by the army on grounds of ill health,' Martha put in, defensively. 'He wanted to go with the others . . .'

'I'm sure that he is doing a much more useful job where he is,' said Stuart, conscious of the woman's embarrassment. 'I'll bet there are a great many fellows serving in the trenches who would be incapable of making the kind of contribution which Iain does. After all, the more food we can produce in this country, the less must be brought in by the merchant ships.'

'We noticed how much land has gone back under the plough on the shores of the lochan,' Annie declared. 'It looked just as it used to when the Johnstone family were crofters here.'

They all recalled the terrible circumstances in which the Johnstones had been evicted from their croft, and the consequences of the action taken by the quarrymen of Eisdalsa to keep out the bailiff's officers. Several of them had spent months in jail, one of their number dying of tuberculosis only weeks after his release.

'Archie manages the farm,' Katherine told them. 'I am afraid that our plans for the gardens have had to be suspended for the duration, but many of the shrubs and trees which we had already imported are now well established. By next spring we should have a good show of rhododendrons.'

Martha rose to leave them, excusing herself by saying, 'I must go and see what is happening in the kitchen. I'll have one of the girls bring you in some coffee.'

'Margaret tells me that you and Archie have opened the house as a convalescent home for wounded servicemen,' said Stuart.

Katherine smiled. 'Ever since the first mercantile marine victims of torpedoes and mines began to pass through Oban Hospital,' she responded, 'we have been opening our doors to those who need time to recuperate and are a long way from home. So many merchant seamen have no homes at all, other than the ship they are serving on at the time. For the past twelve months we have never had less than half a dozen guests in the house on any particular day. Martha has been marvellous. She was a nanny in several of the big houses in these parts when she was younger, you know. She seems to have acquired just the right skills for getting poor lonely sailormen back on their feet and, where possible, ready to return to battle.'

'I hope you are not suggesting that the men behave like children?' grinned Stuart, who was only too familiar with the dependency which some men develop upon their ship and officers.

'Let us say that they have a lot in common,' replied Katherine, 'but I was really alluding to her experience with sickness and convalescence, which has been invaluable.'

'Do you have no medically qualified staff at all then?' Stuart enquired.

'Not in residence, no. Your father and brother call in whenever they have a moment to spare, and occasionally Dr Angus Beaton comes over from Mull to spend a few days with us, when we have a particularly poorly inmate admitted. Michael retains overall responsibility for their treatment, of course. This house is merely an annexe to the hospital. If any of our guests should suffer a remission he is immediately returned to Oban.'

'If you are to gain official recognition as a convalescent home,' Stuart advised, 'you will be required to engage qualified staff to live in on the premises. Since you are principally engaged with seafarers, the Queen Alexandra's Royal Naval Nursing Service might be the best organisation to approach.'

'Or the Scottish Women's Hospitals,' suggested Annie. 'I understand that they are now seeking to establish rehabilitation centres at home for the men they treat at the front.'

The door opened to admit a young woman in a pink-striped dress and long white overall, carrying a large tray. Although she clearly wore a uniform of some kind, her hairstyle seemed quite out of keeping. Neither bobbed, nor coiled, nor pinned in any way, her blonde tresses hung down to her shoulders, covering her eye and the whole left-hand side of her face.

'Oh, Sally, thank you,' Katherine exclaimed, jumping up to relieve the girl of her burden. 'Now, my dear, I want to introduce you to Dr Stuart Beaton who is David Beaton's son and a surgeon in the Royal Navy, and this is his wife, Annie, one of my ex-pupils. The two of you should have a lot in common . . . Annie was once an active member of the Suffragist Movement, a professional lady . . . a lawyer, in fact.'

373

'Would that that were true.' Annie smiled, taking the girl's hand. 'One day, maybe.'

'Annie, Stuart,' Katherine went on, 'this is Miss Sarah Smith who is helping to care for some of our convalescents.'

Sally regarded Katherine's guests with caution, peeping at them shyly from behind the swathe of hair.

'How do you do?' she murmured, hesitantly, scarcely opening her mouth as she spoke.

Annie was sure she had met Miss Smith before. But then she met so many people in her travels.

'I believe you know Mr Whylie of the Annan Munitions Works?' said Sally, 'I was in the infirmary the day he brought you round the factory,' she explained.

Of course, that was it. The girl with the suspicious spot which might have been caused by handling the explosives.

'Mr Whylie must have sent you here for treatment,' Annie assumed. 'I do hope it was successful?'

'Oh, yes,' the young woman replied, a note of bitterness in her voice. 'Mr Brown did a splendid job in removing the tumour which had formed. He's assured me I should now live to be quite old without further trouble.'

'That's good news, surely?' observed Stuart, as he studied her more closely.

Sally turned to Katherine for reassurance. At first, it had been difficult to persuade her that she would be accepted amongst the staff at Johnstones. Indeed her appearance had disturbed some of the younger women at first, but they had all got used to it. Katherine herself barely noticed the scarred face these days. She saw no reason why her present guests should not see the extent of Sally's mutilation. Stuart was, after all, a doctor, and Annie had encountered any number of tragic sights in her life. It was an excellent opportunity for Sally to regain some of her lost confidence. She nodded encouragingly as Sally swept the lock of hair away behind her left ear.

'It rather depends on your point of view,' she observed in answer to Stuart's question.

Stuart Beaton was no stranger to the damage which could be

done by firearms and explosives, but hardened as he was, what he now witnessed appalled him.

Annie was glad that she had regained her seat because she felt that she might have fainted had she been standing. Her dismay at viewing the awful disfigurement was finally overcome by the anger which welled up inside her. How dare they expose young women to such danger without warning them of the possible consequences?

'What have you done about seeking compensation for this injury?' she demanded, fighting off nausea and looking directly at Sally.

'Nothing as yet,' came the reply. 'Mr Whylie advised that we should wait to learn the full extent of the damage before making any claim.' She was relieved that her revelation had apparently generated only clinical reactions in the two visitors.

Sally appreciated that medical etiquette prevented Stuart from commenting upon her operation, but with a gesture of bravado she advanced to where he sat and turned her head so that he could examine her more closely.

The skin of the injured cheek, although healed satisfactorily, was grossly puckered. The actual line of Michael's incision to remove the affected gland was fading nicely and would soon vanish altogether. What made her appearance so disturbing was the fact that the muscles of her cheek, those surrounding the orbit of her left eye and at the corner of her mouth, were all partially paralysed. When she spoke, or smiled, the result was a hideous grimace.

'You must not be too disappointed with this, Miss Smith.' Stuart smiled at her, reassuringly. 'I am sure that Mr Brown has told you that the paralysis in your facial muscles will probably disappear in time. As to the unsightly scar . . . it is possible nowadays to work wonders with skin grafts. Don't be too impatient. This kind of thing takes time.' Attempting to comfort her, he patted her hand. She gripped the window-sill more fiercely at his words.

For some minutes she gazed unseeing at the wintry scene outside.

Suddenly she broke the uncomfortable silence which had descended. 'You must excuse me, Dr Beaton . . . Mrs Beaton. I have my duties to attend to.' Without waiting for any response, and ignoring Stuart's belated attempt to reach the door before her, she ran from the room. Stuart returned to his place, his face suffused with anger.

'Something has to be done to prevent such a thing happening again,' he declared. He turned on Annie in his distress. 'This is what comes of you and your like, persuading lovely young girls to take a hand in this senseless fight. They should stay at home and sew shirts for soldiers if they must have a part in it!'

Annie understood Stuart's anger but could not agree with his suggestion that women should not undertake munitions work. There had to be some action which she could take to prevent such a disaster as this occurring again. She would go and talk to William about the process which had cost Sally her good looks. In the meantime, she would look into the procedure by which the girl could obtain compensation for her injury. The WSPU would surely be able to help her.

Heather had never visited Greenock before. She alighted at the railway station, wondering which direction she should take. After asking advice of a friendly porter as to the whereabouts of Port Glasgow, she joined a line of dockyard workers waiting for a tram which would carry her to the road she wanted.

'Och, you'll no' get lost,' the porter had assured her. 'The town's like a checkerboard. If you go wrong, keep turning left and you'll soon be back where you started!'

She waited somewhat uncomfortably, aware that she was quite out of place here: a well-dressed young female surrounded by so many flat-capped, muffler-clad working men. They eyed her suspiciously at first but then ignored her, returning to their pre-occupation with dogs, horses and the price of baccy.

She paid her twopenny fare to an extraordinarily pretty clippie, one of the female conductresses recently recruited to take the place of the men who had gone away to war. She wore a perky little bonnet, with a tartan ribbon to match her kilt, and a severely tailored jacket with silver-coloured buttons bearing a regulation shine.

'Dinna worrit, hen,' she answered Heather's anxious request.

'I'll sing out when we reach your stop. Goin' to the Scottish Women's, are ye?'

'The offices of the Scottish Women's Hospitals? Yes, that is where I'm going,' Heather replied.

'Nurse, are you?' the girl enquired. 'We drop a lot of nurses off at that stop.'

'Well, no, actually,' Heather explained, 'I am hoping to become an ambulance driver.'

'Fat chance,' roared a burly workman in blue dungarees. 'What? Take women to the front line, driving fifteen-hundredweight trucks?' he stuck his leg out into the aisle. 'Here,' he invited, 'pull the other one, it's got bells on!'

His companions bellowed with laughter.

The conductress stoutly defended Heather.

'Who's to say a woman canna drive a lorry as well as ony man?' she demanded. 'How many of youse has ever driven anything . . . but yer poor wee wifies mad!' Turning to Heather, she asked, 'Can ye drive, lassie?'

Grinning, Heather nodded, and taking her cue from the clippie, enquired, 'And who among you gentlemen has ever been to Brooklands race track in Surrey?'

A youth, clearly still too young for the trenches, stared at her in wonder. 'Naw . . . ye havna. Ye've not driven a racing car?'

Unable to tell a bare-faced lie, but unwilling to disappoint the lad, she gave what she considered an enigmatic smile and got to her feet as the conductress announced her stop.

As she got off, the girl called after her, 'Ye canna miss it, hen. It's the poshest house in the street. Good luck to ye!'

Heather turned to wave, and felt a pang of conscience when she saw the white face of the shipyard laddie, still overawed by the thought of anyone, least of all a woman, having raced a car at Brooklands.

The encounter with her countrymen had cheered her immensely. She realised how much she had missed such friendly banter in the medieval streets and amongst the hallowed halls of Oxford. How Dan would have laughed about this . . . she must write and tell him.

It was a long straight road with tenements to either side. The clippie had insisted that she could not miss the house, but she could see nothing resembling the girl's description. At last the tall buildings gave way to discreet villas, lying back from the pavement behind high walls. An occasional tree planted between the street-lighting standards suggested a more salubrious quarter.

At last she came to a pair of stone pillars, each topped by a Scottish lion, rampant. A wide driveway led up to an imposing portal, then curved back to rejoin the road via a second gateway, allowing carriages to arrive and depart without turning. This had to be the right house.

She glanced down at the letter in her hand to check the number, then went up two marble steps to the front door. To one side a shiny new brass plate confirmed this as her destination. On it engraved in bold letters were the words:

THE SCOTTISH WOMEN'S HOSPITALS RECRUITMENT AND FINANCE

'Good afternoon,' Heather addressed the robust woman who opened the door. She was dressed entirely in black, save for the long white apron upon which she was drying her hands.

Assuming her to be the maid, Heather continued, 'I have an appointment to see your mistress, Mrs Laurie. My name is Brown . . . Heather Brown.'

'I am Jessie Laurie,' replied the lady, hastily rearranging her untidy hair and smiling disarmingly. 'However, I can understand how you might have been misled.'

She opened the door wide.

'Won't you step inside?' she invited. 'And then you can tell me how I may help you?'

'A very good friend of mine, a Mrs Rosenstein, wrote to your Chairman, Dr Hunter . . . concerning a donation,' Heather began, hesitantly. She was not quite sure how to take this woman. Could such an apparently lackadaisical character really be in charge of the finances of so important an organisation?

'Ah, yes, of course, Nellie did mention it,' said Mrs Laurie. 'Do I take it that Mrs Rosenstein is not able to come herself?'

As she spoke she opened a door on the right-hand side of the imposing entrance hall. Heather's high-buttoned boots rang out on the black and white marble of the tiled floor. She followed the woman into what must originally have been the family's with-drawing room. It reminded her of Annabel's room at the Beaton house in Connel, the only difference being that the chaise-longue, with its Indian shawl draped carelessly across the back, and the plush-seated armchairs, with their antimacassars and frilled feet, had been pushed up tight against the walls to make way for an enormous desk in the centre of the room. Seated before this on a straight-backed dining chair, Heather felt like a sailor ship-wrecked upon an island in a sea of Victorian bric-à-brac.

'You must forgive my appearance,' Mrs Laurie apologised, 'I had taken advantage of a free hour to help Nanny turn out the children's room. You have no idea how dusty the contents of cupboards can become when they lie undisturbed for any length of time.'

'Are your children away at school then?' Heather enquired, politely.

'Bless you, no,' laughed Mrs Laurie. 'There are my babies!' She indicated a photograph in a silver frame, of two handsome young soldiers in the uniform of the Argyll and Sutherland Highlanders. 'I don't think they are likely to use their nursery again, do you?'

She smiled in friendly fashion as she seated herself in a handsome leather-upholstered office chair behind the desk.

'I was clearing out the rooms to make space for all this.' She indicated piles of documents stacked in untidy heaps against one wall. 'With operations in several parts of Europe and the Middle East now underway, the paperwork is growing rapidly. I really need an assistant, but unfortunately the funds will not run to it.'

Heather had noticed a smaller desk in one corner, upon which stood an Underwood typewriting machine. It looked as in-congruous in this setting as the swivel chair in which her hostess apparently found it difficult to remain motionless for more than a few seconds at a time.

'Speaking of funds,' Mrs Laurie rattled on, 'I believe that you have something for us?'

Heather withdrew from her handbag a cream-coloured envelope embossed on the flap with the Rosensteins' seal. Its significance was not lost upon Mrs Laurie who recognised the symbol for one which had identified garments from the most prestigious clothing stores since the turn of the century.

'Oh,' she said, as she lifted a paper knife from the desk, 'I hadn't realise it was that Rosenstein!'

She examined the letter, and the banker's draft which accompanied it. Startled by the amount of the donation, she reread the letter with closer attention.

'It is not normal for us to receive donations for specific purposes, Miss Brown,' Mrs Laurie told her. 'Do you happen to know why Mrs Rosenstein is so adamant that the money should be used to purchase field ambulances?'

'That is my doing.' Heather smiled, almost apologetically. 'I have written several times to Dr Hunter asking to be engaged as an ambulance driver, and each time I have been turned down on the grounds that in your various operations abroad you have no vehicles of your own. I have also been refused by the War Office. They will not agree to recruit women drivers, despite the fact that they are shipping hundreds of nurses to the front line.'

'It is not just a matter of owning a few vehicles, you know,' Mrs Laurie explained. 'As was pointed out to us when we raised the matter with both the French and Belgian authorities, running motor vehicles under battle conditions requires a back-up team of mechanics to keep them in working order. A War Office field ambulance unit consists of ten vehicles and more than two hundred men to operate it, including stretcher bearers, mechanics and drivers.'

'But surely there is an additional need . . . to transport patients to and from the hospitals after they have been sent back from the front-line dressing stations?' Heather urged. 'How do your people in France move their patients at present?'

'They are transported by the Army to the most convenient hospital within the district. Those ready to be sent back home have to wait until vehicles are available.' She thought for a moment. 'It is true that Dr Ivens at Royaumont has often expressed frustration at having received cases for which she has no provision, and being obliged to retain men who would have been passed on down the line but for lack of transport.'

Heather could see that she had struck a spark of interest, but wisely decided to give the lady a chance to carry forward the idea as her own. All Heather wanted was to be out there, doing the job for which she felt fully prepared.

'Mrs Rosenstein was aware of the implications of setting up a field ambulance service,' she insisted.

She recalled a discussion on the subject between her father and one of his colleagues, recently returned from Flanders. The officer had pointed out to them the faults in the present system. He had described how one pilot of the Royal Flying Corps, who had crashed his aeroplane and sustained multiple fractures, had been detained in a forward dressing station for two days before being transported to a hospital unit. When he was eventually moved, it was to a hospital which lacked an X-ray machine. The pilot died from a punctured lung, a fate which might have been avoided if he had reached a properly equipped establishment in time.

'That is why the sum offered is so large,' Heather explained. 'It should be sufficient to purchase and equip three vehicles and to set up a maintenance workshop. Mrs Rosenstein is willing to make further, regular contributions towards the wages of a good mechanic. I believe she would have gone further by paying for the drivers also, but I dissuaded her. I believe there will be others, like myself, only too willing to volunteer their services.'

Jessie Laurie was impressed by this young woman. She wondered what it was that had driven her to make such an extraordinary proposal. The Rosenstein offer was too generous to be ignored. If the lady insisted that the money be used for ambulances and nothing else, she must have a very strong reason. Clearly Miss Brown expected to be appointed as a driver if the ambulances were obtained.

'Am I right in assuming that the offer is dependent upon our allowing you to drive one of these vehicles?' she demanded.

'There is no such condition attached to the donation,' Heather was quick to reassure her. 'But since the only grounds offered to me for refusing my services has been the absence of a suitable vehicle, I trust I may assume that my application will now receive favourable consideration?' She smiled engagingly.

'There must be a great many women who have learned to drive their husbands' or their brothers' motor cars, Miss Brown,' Jessie Laurie observed. 'I suspect that handling a heavy vehicle on unmade roads would present a much greater challenge than a small motor car on a public highway.'

'I am quite prepared to give a demonstration of my driving ability to anyone you may choose to examine me,' Heather assured her confidently. She had indeed driven her Great-Uncle Angus's car over rough ground on the steep and slippery slopes of the Island of Mull. It was a heavy vehicle with a 40 h.p. engine. She did not think it would be so very different from driving a lightweight lorry.

'Do you have in mind someone who might advise us on the purchase of such vehicles?' Jessie asked. She was hard pushed to find any other obstacle which might dissuade this insistent young woman. Unfortunately her colleagues on the committee might not find Miss Brown's argument so persuasive.

Heather was quite ready for this question.

'I have here a specification for the type of vehicle which would be required,' she replied, placing a neatly typed sheet on the desk in front of Jessica Laurie. 'I approached the Morris Motor Company when I was last in Oxford. One of their engineers was kind enough to draw up a specification. As you will see, he recommended that we approach the Albion works at Scotstoun. I understand that they make the sturdiest of chassis.'

This young woman has thought of everything, Jessie thought. Nothing has been left to chance. What an asset such a mind would be, here in the office.

'I make no promises,' she said, 'but I will put your proposals to the committee at their next meeting. Meanwhile, I will send my thanks to Mrs Rosenstein, explaining the reasons for the short delay in implementing her wishes.'

'Thank you.' Heather rose to leave.

'We have your address?' queried Mrs Laurie. 'So that you may be advised as to the outcome of our discussion.'

'I am on my way home to Oban,' Heather explained. 'Doctor Hunter has the address. I have just completed my studies at Oxford University, and will be staying with my parents until I find a way of helping with the war effort.'

'Tell me,' Mrs Laurie asked, tentatively, 'did you type this specification yourself?'

'Why, yes,' Heather replied, somewhat surprised at the question. 'I taught myself to use a typewriter while I was studying. My handwriting is not very legible, you see.' She smiled, ruefully.

'I just wondered . . .' Jessie was not sure how this educated young woman would react to her suggestion, '. . . if you might care to help out here in the office for the time being? We are in need of someone who can manage that thing.' She indicated the shining new Underwood. 'It was donated by a firm of stationers in Glasgow, but I have no idea how to use it!'

Heather was not at all sure that she wanted to act as secretary to this apparently disorganised lady, particularly if she was expected to work in the midst of chaos. The suggestion did, however, offer an opportunity to gain insight into the working of the organisation, and it could mean that her presence constantly reminded Mrs Laurie of her real aim.

'I am certainly prepared to consider it,' she replied. 'The only problem is that I would have nowhere to stay. I have no wish to be a further burden upon my parents who have supported me for so long at university.'

'That is a difficulty which is easily resolved.' Jessie was effusive. 'I knew when I began turning out the old nursery this morning that a good reason for doing so would occur to me eventually. If you will accept the position on a temporary basis, you shall have the rooms to yourself. I think you will find them comfortable and quite self-contained.'

Heather, feeling she was being pushed into a position from which it would be difficult to extricate herself, drew back cautiously.

'I really must take time to visit my parents,' she temporised. 'Perhaps you will let me know how your committee reacts to Mrs Rosenstein's proposal first? Then I shall be in a better position to consider your suggestion.'

As she rose to take her leave, Heather glanced once more around the cluttered room. One thing was certain: if she did come here to work, there would have to be a few changes made.

Part 3

1916–1918

Chapter 21

⌐

On the morning of 5 June, 1916, vessels of the Grand Fleet of His Majesty's Royal Navy lay in Scapa Flow, licking their wounds after one of the greatest battles in naval history, off the Jutland peninsular.

Apart from the devastating loss of battleships like the *Queen Mary* and the *Indefatigable*, the most severe damage had been caused to the little ships, the destroyers and light cruisers, which had been responsible for drawing out Admiral Hipper's fleet into the path of the big guns of the mighty British battleships. Some, like the destroyer H.M.S. *Onslow*, had gallantly placed themselves between the guns of the dangerously fast German light cruisers and their less manoeuvrable British opponents, and had sustained severe damage.

Daniel Rosenstein, as officer of the deck, stood with his hands upon the bridge rail, looking down on to the mutilated superstructure of the *Onslow*. The maintenance crew had made remarkable progress in restoring the damaged vessel to some semblance of normality. Holed as she was below the water line, it had been necessary to make temporary repairs immediately, before she could make the trip south to the naval shipyards in the Clyde.

Hampshire's own part in the battle had appeared at one time to be of little significance. She had been on the van, leading the flagship H.M.S. *Iron Duke*, with Admiral Jellicoe aboard.

Since the Admiral's vessel was unlikely to find itself in the thick of the fray, *Hampshire*'s duties had been restricted to those of a sheepdog, ensuring that her charge kept clear of danger.

It was only after the main protagonists had exchanged fire and

Hampshire was steaming off Horn Reef, while leading the flagship's change of course to the north-north-west, that she encountered the enemy for the first time. With only the loss of her observation aeroplane and its pilot, and with nothing but minor injuries amongst her crew, *Hampshire*'s shells had sunk a German light cruiser and two submarines.

Dan reflected upon his good fortune in not having been duty pilot on that day. He had been less than honest with his mother and Heather about those six weeks spent in Oxford at the Morris Motor Works. While there he had certainly learned to maintain the engine of the observation biplane carried aboard *Hampshire*. What he had not told them was that he had also learned to fly the machine.

He could see a number of his own men helping to sort out the mess on *Onslow*'s deck. Her superstructure, which had appeared to be a mangled heap of metal when she first hauled alongside, now bore some semblance of order. Down below, Stuart Beaton would be attending to the wounded. The destroyer's casualties had been very heavy.

The voice-pipe interrupted Daniel's brief moment of relaxation.

'Mr Rosenstein to report to the captain's cabin, immediately!'

Dan acknowledged the order, and made his way swiftly to the main deck.

The door was wedged open and seamen were frantically removing filing cabinets and furniture. Amidst the chaos, Captain Savill sat at his desk, furiously signing chitties which he handed, one at a time, to the first officer. Keeping half an eye on the activities of those around him as he worked, he barked out orders. 'Leave that . . . move this . . . take that to my quarters . . .' He glanced up as Dan stepped over the combing.

'Ah, there you are, Rosenstein. New sailing orders. We're expecting the lighters to come alongside at any moment, bunkering to proceed as soon as possible – have to make ready for sea by 1700 hours. Number One will be tied up with getting our requisitions organised ashore. I want you to ensure that everything is Bristol fashion on deck. The Admiral is bringing aboard some very important passengers and he is to find nothing to complain about, understand?'

'Aye, aye, sir.' Dan was manoeuvring a passage for himself out of the crowded cabin when he heard the first officer mention those members of the crew who were aboard other ships in the harbour.

'Better send out a general order to report on board immediately,' said Savill. 'You will need all hands to provision ship when the lighters come alongside.'

Dan interrupted, 'The doc is still aboard *Onslow*, sir. Shall I have him brought back?'

'Still there, is he?' Savill responded. 'Well, there's no need to recall him just yet. Have the SBA get hold of his list of stores, and tell Beaton to be back on board not later than 1630 hours, will you?'

In the sick bay Dan discovered Stuart's sick berth attendant busily checking stocks of pharmaceuticals.

'Did Commander Beaton complete his requisitions list before he went over to *Onslow*, Hemmings?' he demanded.

'On the desk, sir,' the rating replied, indicating a pile of forms completed in Stuart's hand.

Dan picked up the sheets and found lying beneath them an envelope addressed to Annie. By the time Stuart was back on board, the last mail collection would have gone ashore. He tucked the letter into his inside pocket with the intention of slipping it into the bag when he had an opportunity.

'We're sailing at 1700 hours, Hemmings,' Dan told the SBA. 'You'd better get started battening down for leaving harbour . . . the doc won't be coming aboard until the last minute.'

'Aye, aye, sir,' Hemmings acknowledged. He had already begun replacing bottles and instruments in their carefully allotted places.

Like many of the smaller vessels in His Majesty's Royal Navy, *Onslow* carried no doctor. Medical emergencies were attended to by the second officer, who was qualified in First Aid, and a sick berth attendant. Considering the enormity of the task set them, these two had done a remarkable job in tending their comrades' wounds.

As the SBA removed yet another bloody dressing for Stuart's inspection, he staggered with weariness. The poor lad must have been on his feet for hours.

'Look, you go and turn in for a while, Poulson,' Stuart ordered him. 'I can manage this alone. No point in having another sick man on our hands.'

'The fleet tender should be here in an hour to collect the seriously wounded, sir,' said the younger man. 'You'll need help to identify them as they are carried off.'

'I'll send for you when the boat arrives,' Stuart assured him, and turned back to his patient.

The boy on the table could not have been more than eighteen. He had been carrying ammunition from the magazine when he was struck by the blast from a German shell. He had managed to drop his lethal burden, but the explosion had left him with a chest laid open to the rib bones. His face was pot-marked with powder burns and quite devoid of eyelashes and brows. A burn blister across his forehead showed every sign of going septic. It was amazing to Stuart that with so much injury the lad could still be breathing.

The SBA had made a fair job of cleaning the chest wound before binding it up to relieve the pain from several broken ribs. Stuart swabbed the area of dried blood and searched for fragments of shrapnel. Finding nothing, he replaced lint and cotton wool over the area and held it in place with sticking plaster.

'I'm afraid you're going to have to help me out, old boy,' he said gently to the young matelot. 'I'm going to have to ask you to sit up whilst I get this bandage around your chest.'

The boy, weak as he was, managed a smile. 'OK, doc. anything you say.'

He used his hands for leverage as Stuart supported his shoulders. The movement to a sitting position caused him to cry out in pain, and the doctor paused for him to recover.

'Sorry about that, doc,' muttered the sailor. 'Shall we try again?'

They did, and eventually Stuart had the rib cage firmly bandaged and his patient comfortably flat on the pillows.

As he cleaned the scorched forehead, Stuart recalled the condition of Sally Smith's face and wondered, not for the first time, just what it was all for. Here were two innocent young people, both scarred for life for no apparent reason. If Sally Smith did not make the shells for Ordinary Seaman Phillips to fire, and if Gretchen in the Rühr Valley did not do the same for Wolfgang on the *Bremen*, no one would be in this awful predicament. Politicians had a great deal to answer for. Maybe Annie and her pals had it right when they said that the country would be better governed by women. The idea that the problems of the world might be solved without aggression was one of Annie's strongest arguments for a woman's voice in politics. Remembering the violence engendered by the Women's Suffrage campaign, however, Stuart smiled ruefully and turned back to his patient.

'Now, old chap, I'm just going to give you a shot of morphine to dull the pain,' he explained. 'The tender will be here quite soon to carry you to the arms of some beautiful QARNS nurse ashore.'

The sailor smiled wanly, and as the morphine took effect, he dozed off into an untroubled sleep.

On the arrival of the fleet tender, Poulson was recalled from his hammock to oversee the disembarkation of the wounded, while Stuart made his way to the main deck to report to the officer on duty. He was accosted by a wireless rating who saluted smartly.

'Commander Beaton, sir?'

'Yes, I'm Commander Beaton.'

'Message from the Admiral, sir.'

Stuart looked at the man askance. Admirals did not normally send personal messages to officers aboard ship, except via their captains. Mystified, he took the flimsy message and read:

**TO SURGEON LT CMDR STUART BEATON RN STOP
REPORT ABOARD MERCHANTMAN DELORES
OF MONTEVIDEO MOST URGENT STOP
C IN C SCAPA STOP**

'Thank you.' Stuart dismissed the man and went to seek out the officer of the deck. It was an unusual request to be made in port, where civilian doctors were usually called upon to deal with merchantmen. It must be a matter of some importance however, since the order was issued from the Admiral's office.

'Would you happen to know a merchantman called *Dolores* of Montevideo?'

Surprised by the question, the number one nodded. 'She's holed below the waterline and has been grounded on a mudbank near Scrabster Bay,' he replied. 'Came limping in ahead of us when we retired from Jutland. Looked as though she had been shot up quite badly – caught by a sub, I shouldn't wonder.'

'Isn't it a bit odd to bring a merchantman in here?' Stuart asked.

'Oh, I don't know,' was the reply. 'Any port in a storm, I suppose.'

'How can I get over to her?' he demanded, showing the first officer the message.

'This tender'll probably drop you off. She will pass alongside as she makes for harbour. Wait here a minute, I'll go and have a word with the skipper.'

As the fleet tender approached the merchantman, the extent of the damage to *Dolores*'s hull became more clear. A gaping hole near her bows appeared to have been ripped open by a giant tin-opener. The vessel lay heeled over on the mud bank with welders operating from harnesses suspended over the side of the ship. They appeared to be cutting away the damaged metal. Even as one set of plates was removed, new sections of sheet metal were hauled into place and the riveters got to work.

'I'd have thought that was a dry-dock job, meself,' observed the leading hand at the wheel of the tender.

'Yeah, well, they wouldn't want 'er exposed to public view down at Rosyth, would they?' observed his mate, then, seeing Stuart's look of interest, the man cautioned his companion, with a hand covering his mouth.

Stuart regarded the vessel with interest. There was something familiar about her. He racked his brains, trying to remember where he had seen the ship before. Of course! It had been in Portsmouth roads, during the visit of the Grand Fleet. Dan had remarked on the delivery of large-calibre guns to what appeared to be an insignificant, elderly merchant vessel. He recollected an exchange between Daniel and his brother, the Minister, about some wild idea of Churchill's . . .

The tender's skipper wandered over towards him.

'She's had a nasty encounter with a submarine, doc,' he explained. 'I believe they have some serious casualties on board, too bad to be moved ashore until a surgeon has had a go at them.'

That would be the reason for his orders then, Stuart decided, although he didn't understand why someone from the hospital on shore could not have gone out to her.

The angle at which the ship was lying made Stuart's boarding from the fleet tender difficult. The tide was beginning to rise, and with it the current seemed to have gained pace. As he leapt aboard the *Dolores,* two scruffy-looking fellows grabbed him by either arm and hauled him on to the companion ladder which, like the ship itself, was tilted at a crazy angle.

Stuart turned back for his medical bag, but one of the seamen, who was still clinging firmly to his right arm, said, 'OK, sir, we'll look after that. The skipper's waiting for you at the head of the gangway.'

It was a crisp voice with a public-school accent. He might look like a pirate, but he certainly did not sound like one!

At the head of the gangplank Stuart was met by a tall, gangling figure who looked a little cleaner than the two ruffians below but was just as casually dressed. His dark trousers and navy blue reefer jacket, which was worn over a natural wool Aran sweater, were clean and well-brushed. His black cap, faded by long exposure to the sea air, bore neither decoration nor insignia, yet Stuart was well aware that he was in the presence of a senior naval officer.

'Thank God you've come, doc,' he exclaimed, and his relief was manifest as he shook Stuart warmly by the hand. 'Your patient is this way.'

Annie Beaton settled back in the chair set aside for witnesses and regarded the scene from this vantage point.

The room chosen for the tribunal hearing the case of Sarah Smith against His Majesty's Munitions Works at Annan, was one of those attached to the city chambers. It was small, holding no more than thirty people in all.

At one end of the room a long table had been placed, facing the main body of seating, and behind this sat the members of the panel.

The chairman, by statute, had to be the Sheriff of the District of Dumfries or his deputy. In these days of total employment due to the war effort, the number of industrial disputes was rising. At the same time, the number of persons qualified to adjudicate diminished, as more and more lawyers volunteered for the services. Principal Sheriff Sir Reginald Howard found himself, more often than not, the only person available to take the chair.

On Sir Reginald's left sat Major Peppard, RAMC, supposedly an expert in the effect of explosives materials upon the human skin. The retired doctor had clearly practised his medicine in another century, and even Annie had recognised his confusion when faced with the medical evidence submitted by David Beaton. She caught David's eye where he sat beside William Whylie to the rear of the room, and smiled. Her new father-in-law was still the tall, confident figure she had always known. The bright auburn hair had dulled to a mousy-grey, but his eyebrows and moustache still held their gingery tints – although, she suspected, the hue might be due more to nicotine than natural colouring. Even now he was fiddling with his empty pipe and no doubt dying to escape outdoors, where he could have a quiet smoke.

William Whylie was as smartly dressed as ever. His suit might be a little outdated and perhaps it hung more loosely from his shrunken frame than on the day that it was made, but he was still the best dressed man in the room. She was gratified to see that he wore her favourite of all his famous waistcoats. Its careful blend of blues, crimson and purple, glimpsed from beneath his lightweight grey jacket, was enhanced by the spotless linen at his throat.

There was a shuffling of seats as Wakefield Harcross rejoined the panel. Like so many of these powerful industrialists, Annie thought, he must show his importance by being called at least once to the telephone during a meeting. She suspected that more often than not the matter could easily have waited until later. Before seating himself, Harcross passed a written message along to the chairman. A look of concern flitted across the face of that gentleman as he passed the paper on to others of his team. He whispered to his immediate neighbour as the note was returned to him, nodded in agreement with what was said, and laid the paper aside. Whatever information the note contained, quite obviously had no relevance to the present case and must wait until later.

When Mr Harcross had been obliged to excuse himself, the chairman had decided to call a halt to the proceedings for a short while. It was a warm afternoon, and everyone was grateful for a few moments in which to stretch their legs, exchange a few words with their neighbours, and relax.

Wakefield Harcross was a man without pity when it came to industrial matters. He had successfully set up, and still directed, four factories in the north of England, and two in southern Scotland, but not by being soft on people. He had grilled William mercilessly on his safety policies, clearly believing that the Annan works mollycoddled its female employees.

'No wonder,' he had suggested, 'that they had the impertinence to bring this kind of action against their employers.'

Annie would have gained a great deal of satisfaction from inspecting one of his establishments. His attitude today made clear just how little regard he paid to the new statutes regarding the health and safety of factory workers. She would have enjoyed being able to bring the full weight of legislation to bear upon this obnoxious, self-opinionated gentleman. She placed a hand on her belly, and smiled. Just one more little thing you have to answer for, young Beaton, she told her unborn baby.

'Ahem.' Sir Reginald cleared his throat and tapped with his gavel for silence. 'Now then, Mr Elleridge, I think we may resume. In view of Mrs Beaton's, ahem . . . condition . . .' the condescension in his smile made Annie cringe '. . . I trust that we shall not need to detain her for too long.'

He glanced for confirmation at the one woman present on the panel.

Annie could not make out what Mrs Aubury-Blythe was doing there. A statutory woman member, perhaps? How she had been chosen, for what expertise or from what representative body, it was impossible to say. She had advanced into the room like a galleon in full sail, her magenta afternoon gown in glowing silk lending a certain air of summer garden parties to the otherwise sombre proceedings. Despite the temperature, she appeared to remain cool under her huge cartwheel of a hat, bedecked with artificial roses.

'Mrs Beaton, in your capacity as His Majesty's Inspector for Factory Welfare, you visited the Annan works in . . . May of 1915?' The bulbous Mr Elleridge, in his ill-fitting frock coat, stuck a thumb into each armhole of his food-stained waistcoat and peered at her over the top of his steel-framed spectacles.

'On May the eighteenth,' Annie affirmed, in a clear voice.

'You reported your findings on that occasion in the regulation manner?' he asked.

'I did.'

'Will you be kind enough to tell the tribunal, as briefly as possible, what was the gist of your report?'

Briefly Annie described what she had found at the Annan works, praising the efforts of the management in ensuring the health and safety of employees. 'In view of your remarks, Mrs Beaton,' Elleridge prompted, 'am I to understand that you saw no evidence of workers either ill-equipped to carry out their work effectively, or without protective garments?'

'That is so,' she replied.

'And from your observations, would you say that operatives had every opportunity to seek first aid, should they receive some minor injury in the course of their work?'

'I found the factory's infirmary to be of a high standard, and a qualified nurse was in attendance,' Annie agreed.

'In the course of your inspection,' Elleridge continued, 'were you able to observe the women working at the bench?'

'Yes.'

'And were you aware of any pressure upon them to cut corners, where the safety regulations were concerned?'

'Not at the time, no,' Annie replied, 'but my discussions with some of the workers later, revealed a somewhat different story . . .'

'Thank you, Mrs Beaton,' the sheriff interrupted her. 'The panel does not wish to listen to hearsay . . . we are interested only in what you yourself witnessed.' Turning to Elleridge, Sir Reginald Howard, Sheriff for the District of Dumfries, asked: 'Do you have any further questions for Mrs Beaton?'

'No, My Lord,' Elleridge replied, mopping his brow as he resumed his seat.

'Mr Swanson?' The sheriff invited Sally Smith's legal representative to question Annie.

Despite the fact that she was appearing at the tribunal as a witness for the employer's side, Annie Beaton had, at William Whylie's request, been instrumental in obtaining for Sally the very best lawyer she could find.

Martin Swanson, Q.C. had been recommended by the Scottish Federation of Women's Suffrage Societies as one who had given good service to the movement during the heady days of 1912 and 1913, where there had been several court cases brought against the Scottish Suffragists. He was an elderly man, slim in build and white-haired, but he spoke with authority, his gentlemanly manner in pleasing contrast to the self-satisfied and overbearing Mr Elleridge.

'Thank you, My Lord Sheriff.' Swanson approached Annie. Smiling benignly, he asked: 'Mrs Beaton, in answer to a previous question of Mr Elleridge's, you indicated that you thought that regulations on the factory floor might not always be as scrupulously observed as you found them to be on that particular day. Is my assumption correct?'

'Yes,' Annie replied. 'The shift in question boasted record production figures for the previous week, but when I was watching, my impression was that the speed of operation was only average for that kind of work.'

'Was any explanation given for this apparent discrepancy in output figures?' Swanson asked.

'The women assured me that they could work much faster when not wearing protective gloves,' she answered.

'And from this explanation, you understood that the gloves were being worn that day for the benefit of the inspection only?' He asked the question with eyebrows raised in mock surprise.

'That is what I was led to believe, yes,' replied Annie.

'Thank you, Mrs Beaton,' Swanson concluded. 'You may step down.'

Elleridge was on his feet instantly. 'I would like to call Ralph Dickson to the witness stand,' he declared.

Dickson looked most uncomfortable in his thick tweed suit, so inappropriate on this fine June day. He thrust a finger between his stiffly starched collar and his neck, in a vain attempt to relieve the pressure, as Elleridge led him through his evidence. Ralph described how he had instructed Sally Smith to seek medical attention for the eruption on her cheek.

'Tell me, Mr Dickson,' continued Elleridge, smoothly, 'at the time when Miss Smith reported to you, was she correctly dressed in her protective uniform?'

'As far as I can recall, yes.' Dickson hesitated. 'Except for her gloves. As I remember it, she was not wearing any gloves.'

'Thank you, Mr Dickson.' Entirely satisfied, Elleridge gave way to Mr Swanson.

Swanson consulted his notes for a few moments before addressing the next question to Dickson. The foreman was clearly uncomfortable, and Swanson had no intention of making matters easier for him.

'Mr Dickson,' he began, at last, 'for the benefit of the members of the panel, will you be so kind as to take us through the operation of filling the shell cases with explosives – the operation which, I believe, Miss Smith was engaged in at the time of her injury?'

Dickson gave a long explanation about the method used to fill the shell cases, suggesting that no matter how careful the girls were, they could not avoid getting powder on their hands. 'And, presumably, that is why the women are required to wear gloves?' Swanson suggested.

'Yes.'

'Can you then explain, Mr Dickson, why any young lady would wish *not* to wear gloves in such circumstances?'

'Too slippery,' he murmured.

'Would you kindly speak up?' Swanson asked politely.

'I said, the cases, with powder on them, are too slippery to hold while wearing gloves, especially when the work is going quickly.

As the shell case is tapped on the bench, it may slip out of the hand, and then a shower of powder comes up into the girl's face.'

'Is it correct to say then, Mr Dickson, that when production is speeded up, there is a fair chance that the women will have discarded their gloves . . . for their own safety?'

'That is correct.' Dickson cast an apologetic glance in the direction of Elleridge who, red-faced and perspiring freely, looked as though he might have an apoplexy at any minute.

'Thank you, Mr Dickson, that will be all.' Swanson took his seat next to his client and whispered a few words to her.

Elleridge was on his feet in an instant.

'That concludes the evidence for the employers, My Lord,' he said. The sighs of relief from all around the room were clearly audible.

'Mr Swanson,' the sheriff called, 'do you have anything further to add before the panel makes its decision in this case?'

'Yes, My Lord, I would like to make a short statement, if the tribunal will bear with me for a moment longer. We have heard from her doctors how Miss Smith developed a carcinoma of the skin which required surgery so drastic that it has left her permanently disfigured. From this same very eminent and experienced source, you have heard that there is every reason to suppose that the initial cause of the carcinoma was the chemical substances used as explosives in the Annan factory.

'Much has been made of the careful attention paid to the welfare of those working in the factory. Mr Whylie has instituted standards of hygiene and safe practices which would be envied by workers in other factories of the kind. There comes a moment, however, when no matter what care is taken, what legislation is put into effect, only the workers on the spot can decide what is the best step to take.

'One witness after another has been questioned as to whether or not Miss Smith was obeying the rules at the work bench. Was she wearing gloves on the days prior to her first noticing the eruption on her face? Did she touch the spot with hands contaminated with chemicals? The factory foreman was forced to admit, albeit reluctantly that when production was speeded up, it was more dangerous to be wearing gloves than not.

'We are not here, My Lord, to decide whether or not Miss Smith scratched a spot on her face, or whether she was or was not wearing gloves at the time. It appears to me that had she touched her face, while wearing gloves, they too would have contaminated the spot. We are here to decide whether Miss Smith's disfigurement is due to the fact that she worked for several months during 1915 in a factory manufacturing weapons for the war effort. We have to decide whether she would be unblemished, as she appears in this photograph taken only weeks before she began working at the factory, had she not offered her services in this way.'

Swanson placed before the sheriff a studio portrait of Sally which, even allowing for the photographer's art, displayed a remarkably pretty face. The picture was handed along the line of panel members and back to the sheriff.

Absorbed in the minutiae of question and answer, more than one member of the group was forced to admit that the real purpose of their presence here had somehow become overlooked in the struggle to prove the guilt or innocence of either party in the dispute.

'Seeing that portrait, My Lord, I submit that the only thing which changed in Miss Smith's lifestyle in 1915 was her handling of dangerous chemicals. It was this daily exposure over a period of several months that was the cause of her condition. Who can say that, even had she obeyed every rule in the book, she would not have suffered the same fate?'

Swanson looked around the assembled witnesses, taking many of them with him as he continued, 'We are also here to decide what recompense should be made for the loss of youth and beauty. How much money can compensate for a disfigurement so horrific as to prevent my client from living a normal life ever again?'

He moved to join Sally, who was seated at a table a little to the front of the assembled witnesses. 'I have persuaded Miss Smith to unveil, in order that the panel may see for themselves the extent of her injuries and make their assessment accordingly.'

At his signal, Sally removed her hat, and with it the chiffon veiling which had so skilfully obscured the right side of her face.

There was a moment of shocked silence. One woman in the body of the hall gave a strangled sob, while Mrs Aubury-Blythe was observed to recoil in disgust. Several men were moved to mutter oaths. If any member of the tribunal had thought the matter trivial before, they did not think it so now.

'Thank you, Miss Smith,' said the sheriff. 'That took a great deal of courage.'

Swanson sat down beside Sally, entirely satisfied with his performance. She replaced her hat with trembling fingers.

The sheriff conferred for some moments with the members of his panel. While he did so the room erupted in a buzz of conversation. At last the gavel was again employed to restore order.

'Ladies and gentlemen,' Sir Reginald began, 'the panel has heard all the evidence in this case and,' with a nod in the direction of Sally's lawyer, 'taken particular note of the sentiments expressed in his summing up by Mr Swanson.

'We shall now repair to discuss these matters in private. The outcome of our deliberations will be made public in due course, and those parties having a particular interest in the case will receive written confirmation at a date no later than three calendar months from today.'

As the assembly began to stir, anxious now to quit the gloomy confines of the chamber, he tapped once more on the table.

'I have during the course of these proceedings received information of the gravest nature which I feel I must share with you all.' He took up the piece of paper with which Wakefield Harcross had returned after the recess, and read: ' "Two days ago a vessel of the Royal Navy, carrying the Secretary of State for War to a meeting with the Russians, foundered off the Orkney Islands and everyone on board, with the exception of a handful of seamen, perished." ' He laid down the paper. 'Ladies and gentlemen, Lord Kitchener is dead. I will ask you to join with me in a minute's silent tribute to an outstanding soldier, and a great patriot.'

With a scraping of chairs they got to their feet. Silence hung over the room like a funeral pall. The one man upon whom an entire nation had hung its hopes of a glorious victory was dead.

Annie Beaton could think only of all those poor men, struggling in the water, gasping a last breath before the cruel waves overcame them. As she shuddered at the frightful vision, a sudden stirring in her abdomen, so fierce as to take the breath from her body, caused her to grasp the back of a chair for support. David, noticing her discomfort, gave her an anxious glance. She smiled at him, and placed her hand over the spot where the child's foot had made itself felt.

'Just a wee protest from your grandson,' she murmured.

'Sit down for a moment and rest,' he instructed her, solicitously. 'You know, Annie, it is high time that you gave up this sort of thing. It is too much for you . . . in your condition.'

As the tiny foot gave her another blow under the ribs, she felt inclined to agree with him.

Outside in the street people were strangely silent, overawed by the enormity of the nation's loss. At a time when every day brought news of further tragedy and disaster there had always been the firm conviction that Kitchener would see them through. At the news stands queues had formed, everyone eager to read for himself about the death of a hero.

As David and Sally assisted Annie to the waiting car, William Whylie went to collect a newspaper. He returned looking extremely grave, carrying the paper carefully folded to obscure the headline. Only when the women had been safely installed on the back seat did he show David the words printed in letters an inch high:

HMS HAMPSHIRE LOST WITH ALL HANDS
KITCHENER DEAD

Annie did not believe that Stuart was dead. They had said that a handful of seamen had escaped; he would assuredly be amongst them. Both Sally and William had been very kind and gentle towards her but there was really no need. She just wished that she could convince poor David that Stuart was alive.

David Beaton drove his powerful Argyll Tourer as fast as the poor road surface would allow. The quickest route to Oban had been by way of the ferry to Rothsay from Weemys, and from there to Inverary. Once they joined the road from Glasgow, the going would be easier.

He wished now that they had elected to take the train to Dumfries, but mindful of the embarrassment felt by Sally Smith in public places, he had deferred to Annie's arguments and agreed to the long car journey.

Annabel must surely have heard the news by now. She would need him as never before. No doubt Margaret would go to her immediately, but he wanted to be there himself.

The front offside wheel struck a loose rock and the car shifted to a position precariously near the edge, where the road fell away into the glen, five hundred feet below. The sudden fright was enough to shake him out of his reverie, and force him to concentrate on what he was doing.

He was concerned for Annie. She seemed unable to understand that Stuart must be dead, and seemed to be clinging to the hope that somehow he had escaped. Her baby was not due for another month at least, but the shock of accepting that she was a widow might very well bring on her labour. He pulled on to a wider verge which had been left to allow two vehicles to pass, and stopped the engine.

The two women in the back of the car looked up, startled.

'What is it?' demanded Annie, thinking there might be something wrong with the motor.

'I thought you might like an opportunity to stretch your legs, and enjoy the view,' he replied. 'The engine is running a little hot. I think the radiator needs topping up.'

He withdrew from the tool box on the running board a can kept for the purpose and began to climb down off the road to where a small burn, emerging from a culvert beneath the road, fell in a series of spectacular waterfalls to the valley floor.

Annie had spent a sleepless night in the hotel after reading the full details of the sinking of H.M.S. *Hampshire*. William had complained that news of this kind should be withheld until the next-of-kin of the victims could be informed privately, but Annie had reminded him that the nation deserved to know of the death of its great war hero. Suffering now from lack of sleep, she had been dozing in the car throughout the journey. Startled into wakefulness, she realised that she was indeed cramped and her bladder uncomfortably full. Appreciating David's thoughtfulness in calling a halt, she told Sally she was going off to relieve herself. She stepped out of the car into the sunshine, and gazed down into the green valley.

At this height, the gentle summer breeze bore the snap of a winter chill from higher up the mountains, where snow still lingered in the corries.

The silence was broken only by the trickle of water in the burn, and the murmur of bees, busy among the miniature wild flowers which clothed every small patch of upland pasture in the bright hues of early summer. She crept behind a convenient boulder and crouched down; when she stood up she noticed a small amount of fresh blood on the turf.

Stuart had mentioned this as a precursor to labour . . . but she had another month to go yet. She could not have her baby now. As if to confirm her misgivings, a dull pain asserted itself in her lower back. Cautiously, she rearranged her clothing, and walked slowly back to the car. She knew that it would be some hours before the child was born. There was no point in adding to David's anxieties too soon. Maybe she could wait until they reached Connel. Regaining the spot where the car was parked, she sat down on a moss-covered boulder to wait for her father-in-law to finish his task.

After a few minutes Sally came to stand beside her. Used to the softer contours of the Border country, she was unaccustomed to this craggy scenery. Where Annie felt comforted by the presence of the high peaks, Sally felt threatened. She shuddered when she realised how sheer was the drop into the glen.

'It's all right,' Annie told her. 'The road is really quite safe. Many vehicles climb over this pass, every day of the week.'

'I would rather not have seen the drop, that's all,' said Sally, and hurried away to resettle herself in the vehicle where she felt more secure.

Annie watched as David, having struggled back up the slope to the car, undid the radiator cap and poured in the water. There was a sharp hiss of steam which quickly subsided as the cold water mixed with hot. He replaced the brass cap and, wiping his hands on an oily rag, came and sat beside her on the rock.

'What's the matter with Sally?' he asked.

'I think she is a little overwhelmed by the altitude,' Annie replied, smiling at his surprised expression. 'Not everyone finds mountains so engaging as we Beatons do.'

'I like that,' he said, taking her hand as he spoke. 'I like to hear you call yourself a Beaton. Somehow I have always thought of you as one of the family.'

'Which is more than can be said of Stuart,' she smiled wanly. 'He spent the first thirty years of his life escaping from me.'

David continued to hold her hand as he said, quietly, 'He may have been blinded by the light of ambition in his youth, but when it came to choosing a wife, he thought of no one else but you. I have never seen him so happy as on his wedding day. He glowed with his love for you.'

He placed his hand on her abdomen, feeling the tiny movements within.

'It means so much to Annabel and myself that he will live on in this child.'

'I am relying upon you both to set me on the right road to parenthood,' she replied. 'I am going to need a great deal of tutoring.'

David knew very well that Annie was more than capable of taking care of her baby. She was inviting himself and Annabel to share in the upbringing of Stuart's child for their sake, not her own.

'Thank you,' he murmured, as he stood to help her to her feet. Before they reached the car, he paused once more. 'I fear that Annabel will be very distressed when we arrive home. You must leave Margaret and me to cope with her . . . for the baby's sake.'

Still totally convinced that Stuart would be back to claim his newborn child, Annie took David's arm as she insisted, 'I will do whatever I can to help.'

When the doctor had settled his daughter-in-law in the car, he went to the front to swing the starter handle. To everyone's relief, the engine coughed instantly into life.

In the rear compartment, Sally turned to her companion. 'If I have been quiet all this while, Mrs Beaton, it is because I have had a great deal to think about. I do hope you don't think me rude.'

Annie nodded, understanding.

'We are none of us in the mood for conversation,' she replied.

Sally continued, shyly, 'I want you to know that whatever happens about the tribunal, I shall be eternally grateful to you and to other members of your family for what has been done for me. I came to Oban as a stranger, and no one could have been made more welcome. If I can repay the kindness in any way at all, if there is anything that I can do to help you in your trouble, you will tell me?'

Annie smiled at her, but the expression on her face was one of defiance.

'That is very good of you,' she replied, 'and much appreciated, but really there will be no need. Everything is all right, I know it is!'

In the driver's seat, David, overhearing Annie's response, frowned. How was he to convince her that there really was scant hope of Stuart's survival?

Of Annie's companions, only Sally Smith had refrained from insisting that Stuart must be dead. Sally had remained stoical throughout her own time of trial, and the strength which she had displayed then seemed now to have been passed to Annie. The two young women stared ahead as the car rounded a bend in the pass and began to negotiate the steep slope downwards towards the shores of Loch Fyne. To stop Annie from lurching forwards and injuring herself, Sally grasped her firmly about the shoulders. Comforted by this sisterly gesture, Annie leant her head against Sally's, and slept.

The long June afternoon was drawing to a close and a crimson sun, setting over the island of Mull, had drawn the intricacies of the ironwork of the Connel railway bridge into a black silhouette by the time that David turned in to the entrance to Creag an Tuirc, beside Loch Etive. For the last few miles of the journey, as they had driven alongside the peaceful waters of Loch Awe and through the lowering Pass of Brander, Annie had felt more and more the urgency of her condition. After once crying out involuntarily, when they had hit a rutted part of the roadway, she had been forced to admit to David that she was in labour. He had stopped the car somewhere near Dalmally and made a cursory examination.

'Why did you not tell me?' he had remonstrated with her. 'We could have found a bed for you in Inverary.'

'But we must get home to Annabel,' she had insisted.

They had continued on their journey, with Sally sitting up front beside David so that Annie could lie flat on the rear seat. Not wishing to disturb David while he was driving, Annie suppressed the urge to cry out as the labour pains increased in strength, and the time between them lessened noticeably.

David pulled up outside the house, switched off the engine and bolted inside, calling out as he went, 'Don't try to move, Annie, I'll be back in a minute.'

Within the house there was a strangely gloomy air. In his anxiety to reach home he had almost forgotten his concern for Annabel, and any grieving of his own for his son must be set aside in the interests of his grandchild.

He stood in the hall and cried out, 'Mrs Murchieson, Margaret, Annabel! Where is everybody?'

From the kitchen, the housekeeper emerged, her expression full of compassion.

'Oh, Dr David, sir, it is terrible news. I am so sorry.'

He barely took time to acknowledge her condolences.

'Mrs Stuart is outside in the car, Mrs Murchieson. She is about to give birth. I shall not be able to get her upstairs so I want you to make up the day bed in Mrs Beaton's sitting room. Is my daughter here?'

'Mrs Brown is upstairs with her mother, Doctor. I'll call her immediately.' She flew up the stairs while David returned to the car where Sally was helping Annie to ease herself up into a sitting position.

'I don't think she can walk,' said David. 'Miss Smith, can you make a hand-chair with me so that we can carry her between us?'

Under instruction from David, Sally Smith linked her hands with his so that Annie could sit between them. Thus they carried her into the house and settled her in Annabel's pretty room overlooking the loch.

Sally had never witnessed the birth of a child. Having helped Mrs Murchieson to relieve Annie of her clothing and make her comfortable on the narrow bed, she could only stand by nervously, anxious to help but not knowing what to do. The housekeeper took her by the arm and led her into the kitchen.

'Why don't you make everyone a nice cup of tea, miss?' she suggested. 'While I make sure the doctor has all the linen and hot water that he needs.' Without waiting for a response, Mrs Murchieson busied herself with heating up water in the great copper which stood just inside the scullery.

Sally filled a kettle from the tap and stood it on the range. The fire had been allowed to die down low on this warm afternoon. She opened the door to the firebox and added coal and a few pieces of wood to get it going strongly.

Mrs Murchieson, coming in from outside, satisfied herself that the young woman was at home in a kitchen and left her to her task.

All afternoon Margaret had sat at her mother's bedside while Annabel either sobbed or lay silent – which was worse. At times she spoke quite coherently, recalling moments from the lives of the boys and Margaret when they were children.

Every now and again she would stop, lift her head and listen.

'Is that David's car?' she would ask, and as the approaching vehicle changed gear on the bend, and continued on past the end of the driveway, she would revert to her doleful wanderings.

When, at long last, a car turned in to the drive and stopped below her bedroom window, with much shouting and banging of doors, she showed concern that David should see her looking so dishevelled and insisted that Margaret fetch her a hand mirror and hairbrush, so that she could make herself presentable. When he did not come bounding up the stairs immediately, she began to fret again.

'Where is your father . . . does he know I am up here? Go and fetch him, Margaret,' she demanded plaintively.

Meanwhile, Mrs Murchieson, having taken the staircase at a

rush, had stopped to straighten her pinafore and calm herself before entering the bedroom of her poor grieving mistress. Quietly, she opened the door and beckoned to Margaret.

'The doctor is here, Mrs Brown,' she whispered, 'but he can't come up just yet. Mrs Stuart is having her baby . . . we are going to put her into madam's sitting room.'

'All right, Mrs Murchieson,' Margaret murmured, 'I'll come down directly.'

She closed the door behind the retreating housekeeper and turned back to her mother. Taking Annabel's hand, praying she would understand, she said, 'Mother, Pa is rather busy just now . . . it seems that Annie has gone into labour. I shall have to go and help him.'

'But it's too soon!' Annabel exclaimed, eyes filling with horror at the prospect of a stillborn child to add to her loss.

Margaret, torn between her mother and what was going on down below, knelt beside the bed and stroked Annabel's grey hair.

'Don't worry, Mother, Pa will do his best for Annie and the baby. They'll be all right, you'll see.'

Annabel understood. She squeezed Margaret's hand.

'You go along, dear. David needs you more than I do at this moment.'

Margaret hesitated for an instant only. She stood up and moved towards the door. Suddenly the air was rent by a shriek of pain from Annie. With one final glance back at her mother where she lay, face vacant, hands listless upon the counterpane, Margaret closed the door and ran downstairs.

Another sharp cry from below penetrated Annabel's consciousness. Margaret's words came suddenly into sharp focus. Stuart's child was about to be born . . . Stuart's flesh and blood, his final gift to them! She swung her legs over the side of the bed and dressed speedily. Then she rifled through a drawer, pulling out a long white apron such as she had worn in the days when she used to help David in the surgery at Tigh na Broch. For a moment she paused to view herself in the mirror on her dressing-table, then wringing out a face-cloth lying in the unemptied wash basin, wiped her eyes, which were red and swollen with weeping. She scraped a comb through her hair and tied it back with a piece of ribbon.

Margaret hurried down the stairs and into the sitting room. David, on his knees beside Annie, was urging her through the last stages of labour. He did not look up as his daughter came into the room.

'Here, come and give a hand,' he ordered. 'She needs some encouragement. Now then, Annie, with the next contraction . . . that's it, . . . wait for it . . . now push! Go on . . . push!'

'I am bloody well pushing,' yelled Annie, angrily, forcing her bottom down into the bed. David, inured to the language of childbed, did not turn a hair. Margaret was too busy obeying her father's instructions to take any notice of the tirade.

'Nearly there,' said David. 'It's a redhead, of course.' He smiled at Annie as he and Margaret held on tight for the next push down.

'Steady now,' said David. 'Pant . . . little breaths . . . like a steam train . . . that's a good girl . . . you're doing fine . . . steady now. One last push and we're there . . .'

David, busy with the process of tying off the cord, took an anxious look at the tiny form. The baby had not yet cried which was a bad sign. He picked it up, took a handful of cotton and wiped the mouth free of mucus. He held the child by the ankles, and while Margaret and Annie watched, horrified, swung it in a wide arc above his shoulder. Suddenly, with a gasp and a gurgle, the infant began to breathe and then to roar its protest at so unorthodox an introduction to the world.

Satisfied that the baby would now continue to breathe, David wrapped it in a towel and handed it, still squalling, into the arms of the nearest person.

'It's a boy!' Annabel said, her voice full of wonder as she loosened the towel and laid the baby on a low table. 'A beautiful, red-headed Beaton boy!'

Margaret, who had been busy attending to Annie, looked up, startled to hear Annabel's voice. When she saw that her mother was totally absorbed in her task of sponging clean the little body, she heaved a sigh of relief. It was the first time Annabel had appeared to be herself since they had heard the terrible news about the loss of the *Hampshire*.

David returned to Annie. The baby was clearly premature, a downy covering of long villus hair indicated that he was more than four weeks too soon arriving, but nevertheless he was a good weight. Lucky for Annie, David reflected, as he repaired a small tear created in that final push, that the child was born early, for he would surely have been nine or ten pounds had he gone to full term!

Annabel had sent Mrs Murchieson off to the room occupied by Annie in recent weeks. She soon returned with a pile of napkins and tiny garments prepared by Annabel and Annie herself, whilst sitting together in this very room during the lengthening days of spring and summer. With deft fingers, Annabel completed her task of dressing the baby in his first suit of clothes by wrapping him tightly in the fine woollen shawl completed only days before.

'There, I knew I had to get it finished quickly,' she said, smiling at Annie, 'but I wasn't expecting it to be quite so soon.'

'Is he all right?' Annie asked, wary but triumphant.

David undid the shawl a little and made great play of examining the baby's feet for the correct number of digits. 'All there,' he declared, smiling.

Annie cuddled the little body to her. If only Stuart could have been here to welcome his son, everything would be perfect. Nevertheless she felt a surge of contentment, and was at ease with the world. Stuart's son, an island child, brought into the world by his own grandfather . . . what better start in life could anyone have?

'Who would like a cup of tea?'

Sally Smith had come into the room unobserved and laid her tray on the low table by the window. When she had handed round the cups, she approached the bed and Annie lifted the baby for her to hold.

The veiling, without which she never appeared in company, had slipped to Sally's shoulders during her battle with the kitchen range. Her poor disfigured face was fully exposed. The tiny child in her arms chose that moment to open his eyes for the first time.

What he saw seemed to please him, for his face relaxed, the wrinkles disappeared and Sally swore that he smiled at her. It was a simple enough little incident, experienced by many who hold a newborn child in their arms for the first time, but for Sally, who had come to expect only revulsion from those who looked upon her face, this was a unique moment. The child knew nothing of her disfigurement. His senses were otherwise stimulated, and they told him that this was someone whom he could trust.

There had been squalls of rain, and a strong wind had blown from the south-west for nearly a week after Annie's baby was born. At last the day came when the skies cleared and a warm sun sparkled on the water where the Falls of Lora emptied Loch Etive into the sea. David agreed that his daughter-in-law might venture outside to enjoy Annabel's beautiful garden which had, indeed, fulfilled all her expectations of the previous autumn.

The two women sat in the sunshine on the little wooden terrace outside the summer-house, halfway up the cliff. Baby Stephen lay in his bassinet, sleeping soundly.

'I am afraid that Stephen and I have been disrupting your comfortable existence for far too long,' said Annie, hesitating to bring up the subject which had been very much on her mind as she lay sleepless throughout the long nights.

'Oh, what nonsense you do talk, dear,' protested Annabel. 'I don't know what David and I would have done without the two of you to keep us occupied during recent days.'

'Nevertheless,' Annie persevered, 'the time is coming when I must make a move to set up home alone, with my baby. It is not fair to Dr David to have his household so dominated by an infant.'

'But he loves to have you here,' said Annabel, suddenly terrified that this little child, in whom she had now invested all that love which she had borne for her favourite son, might be snatched from her too.

'We shall only be going to Eisdalsa,' Annie protested. 'Margaret says that we may use her cottage for as long as we wish.' She paused. Not wishing to disturb Annabel with her own conviction that Eisdalsa would be where Stuart would come to find her, she argued, lamely, 'Stuart would expect us to live there.'

'But you would be almost alone on the island now,' Annabel objected. 'It will be very lonely for you in the winter months with just the McPhersons for neighbours.'

'There are a great many of them,' laughed Annie. 'I hear there are twenty children in the Seileach school, eighteen of whom are called McPherson! With all those young people on the island, and with Hugh and Millicent just across the water, I shall hardly find it lonely. If the winter months begin to drag, I can always come back here for a visit.'

Annabel could see that her daughter-in-law had made up her mind.

Although she and David had been disturbed night after night when the baby cried, he had never once complained, and even if his work was suffering from his lack of sleep he would never dream of mentioning it to Annie. David was working far too hard for one who should already be retired, and Annie was quite right in suggesting that he could ill afford to lose the few hours of rest which he *was* able to snatch.

Annabel sighed deeply, giving in at last to the inevitable.

'Well, my dear, if you insist,' she agreed. 'We had best begin to make plans for your move. The cottage is fully furnished, so it is only your own personal things, and the baby's, which will have to go. You will need to make a list of provisions – you know how uncertain the supplies are from the village shop these days. With so few people living in the district, the provision of some food-stuffs is very meagre.'

'If I am to be a permanent resident,' Annie replied, patiently, 'they will be given an additional allocation.'

Annabel had found it difficult to come to terms with the food shortages. Her recipes came from the affluent days of the Victorian era, and she could no more consider baking a cake with fewer than six eggs, than she could use margarine rather than butter in creamed potatoes.

'Well, anyway,' she continued, unheeding, 'I suppose Millicent will be able to supply you with eggs and vegetables.'

'I am sure that I shall manage very well,' said Annie, 'and I shall expect both you and Dr David to come and visit us often.'

David's Argyll Tourer followed the winding road south across the island of Seileach, taking the final slope upwards past the Kilbride township with consummate ease. When they reached the summit of the pass, he pulled his vehicle on to a wide grass verge so that they could look down upon the panorama which stretched before them. On impulse, he opened the car door and, reaching across for his grandson, lifted him gently from his mother's arms and walked with him the last few yards to the top.

'There you are, Stephen,' he said, holding the infant up as though presenting an heir apparent to his subjects. 'That is the house where your grandfather was born, and your great-grandfather before him! And it is where your dear father spent the best part of his life.' He gazed down upon the old house with a curious longing, something he had not experienced even on the day when he and Annabel had finally vacated Tigh na Broch, in favour of Hugh and Millicent and their growing family.

The house lay in a wide valley which separated the volcanic cliffs of Caisteal an Spuilleadair above Seileach village from the hills which formed the spine of the island of Seileach. This fertile glen had sustained the Beaton family for many generations, providing cereal crops and fodder for a small herd of cattle and a few sheep. The doctoring, which had in every generation been the main occupation of the Beaton menfolk, had always been subsidised by the croft, which provided additional resources to raise a family and educate its sons.

Behind the main house were the sheilings, farm buildings where David and his brothers had romped as children . . . in time little Stephen would no doubt join his cousins in their play, discovering the secret places and reinventing the timeworn games.

David turned seawards to where the tiny island of Eisdalsa nestled in the bay, some four or five hundred yards offshore. Stretching out towards the island was the great wooden pier, built by the steamship company to accommodate the steamers which in peacetime had sailed daily between Fort William and Crinan.

The pier was deserted now, the steamer service fallen victim to intimidation by German submarines.

A tiny rowing boat cut a swathe through the still waters of the sound. It was the ferry, plying its course between Eisdalsa and Seileach, the only link between the islanders in their white-washed cottages and the village on the main island.

David looked down at the little bundle in his arms.

'You're going home, Stephen,' he whispered, and the bright blue eyes stared back at him in apparent comprehension.

David allowed his gaze to wander out to sea, where a string of triangular rocky islands stretched westwards into the Atlantic Ocean: the Islands of the Sea. To the south-west were the remaining low-lying slate islands, dotting the sea to the west of Lunga, from behind which rose the mountainous peak of the mysterious almost uninhabited island of Scarba. In the far distance, shrouded in sea mist even on this bright summer's day, was the outline of Colonsay.

What a marvellous day for a sail, he reflected. His thoughts were suddenly filled with memories of other such days when, aboard the *Saucy Nancy*, with William Whylie at the helm, they had negotiated those treacherous waters where whirlpools appeared and disappeared without warning, and where a tranquil sea could turn into a maelstrom within an hour.

He returned the baby to his mother and started the engine. Looking somewhat shamefacedly at Annabel, who was seated beside him, he explained, 'I just wanted to be the one to show it to him, for the first time.'

Annabel allowed her hand to rest on his knee for a second. She understood, better than he knew.

They had settled Annie into Margaret's cottage with little ceremony and a minimum of fuss. David had lit a fire in the range to make sure there would be sufficient hot water for the baby's bath. Annabel had busied herself organising the stores in the kitchen, while Annie carried her son around the house, admiring once again the beautiful old furnishings and the lovely porcelain which Margaret so treasured.

'I will have to pack some of this china away before His Lordship begins to crawl,' she laughed, as she watched the baby stretch a tiny hand towards the ruby-coloured bowl of a brass oil-lamp, sparkling in the bright sunshine which poured through the little window.

'I have just spoken with Mairie McPherson,' said Annabel, bursting back into the room from outside. 'She has promised to call in as often as you like, to give a hand with the housework, and she says that if you have any problems within the house, repairs that need doing, coal to carry . . . anything heavy to be lifted . . . you have only to ask, and one of her boys will see to it.'

'Thank you, Mama,' Annie said, wishing she had been left to make her own arrangements. Dear Annabel, she was only trying to help.

David had brought in more wood and coal for the range. He piled it beside the grate and stood up, regarding his hands somewhat ruefully.

'I'll just wash,' he commented, 'and then we must be getting on our way.' He turned to Annie who was still standing in the middle of the room, holding the baby.

'You look tired,' he said, solicitously. 'Are you sure you can manage?'

'Yes,' she replied, firmly, willing them to be gone. Now that the move had been made, she just wanted to be left alone.

She stood at the door of the cottage and watched Stuart's parents rounding the head of the harbour, nearly empty now but for a few small fishing boats. They reached the ferryman's bothy and she waved until he had rowed them out of sight. Then, turning back into the house, she began to prepare Stephen for his evening feed and bath.

As she worked, tears of weariness and relief overflowed. She sat in the old armchair beside the grate and undid her blouse. Stephen nuzzled in and at his insistence the milk began to flow. A feeling of peace and contentment, greater than anything she had ever known, now consumed her. She wondered about Stuart. Where could he be all this time? On some desolate Hebridean island, unable to reach civilisation? Of one thing she was absolutely certain. He was alive . . . somewhere, he was still alive.

It was more than a week before a letter addressed to Annie at the
Connel house eventually reached the cottage on Eisdalsa.

Meg Roberts, postmistress and proprietor of the Seileach
Village Stores for more than twenty-five years, seldom had letters
to bring to the island these days. She remembered when it would
have taken her a couple of hours to deliver all the mail, stopping
for a wee crack here, a cup of tea there. Nowadays, Donnie
McPherson collected the business mail himself from Seileach,
while the remaining members of the family scarcely ever received
correspondence, for the majority of those with whom they might
wish to communicate were living beside them on the island!

'It is a large letter, so it is,' commented Meg, as she watched
Annie examine the outside of the envelope curiously. It had been
posted in Orkney, and was written in an ill-educated hand, one
which she did not recognise. She looked up, feeling Meg's
inquisitive eyes upon her. Tucking the letter into her apron
pocket, she opened the door wider for the postmistress to enter.

'Do step inside, Mrs Roberts,' she invited, 'you must take a cup
of tea, now you are here.'

While Annie bustled about in the tiny kitchen, Meg went to
look at Stephen, wide awake and gurgling contentedly in his
cradle beside the range.

'Och,' she exclaimed, 'he's a braw wee laddie. I mind when
young Master Stuart was no bigger than that. There is no
mistaking that hair and the determined frown. This is a young
man who will have a mind of his own, no question about it.'

'I sincerely hope so,' said Annie, returning with the tea.

Meg knew just about everything there was to know about the
folks who had populated the island when Annie was a girl. She
tried to listen politely to all the postie's gossip but her mind kept
wandering to the letter in her pocket. Oh, dear, would Mrs
Roberts never go?

At last, realising that Annie had no intention of revealing the
contents of her correspondence, Meg stood up and chucked baby
Stephen under his chin to make him smile.

'Now remember, Miss Annie,' she insisted, kindly, ignoring the married status of this woman whom she had known as a school-girl, 'if there is anything you need, just tell one of the McPherson children, and I will send it over to you when they come home from school.'

'That is very kind of you, Mrs Roberts,' she replied.

'Och,' said the woman, 'you must call me Meg – everyone else does – and if you have no objection, I shall continue to call you Annie, for I cannot think of you in any other way!'

Left to herself at last, Annie withdrew the envelope from her pocket and again examined the postmark. Who could be writing to her from the Orkneys? She tore open the envelope and with-drew a thick wad of sheets covered in familiar handwriting. An additional single page slipped to the floor. She bent to retrieve it.

The covering letter was written in the same illegible hand which had appeared on the envelope.

Westray
16 June, 1916

Dear Madam,
Walking along the shore one day I found washed up a naval officer's jacket. Most of the papers in its pockets were destroyed by seawater but this envelope addressed to you survived. The jacket was handed in to the police as they are collecting all evidence of the wreck of the cruiser Hampshire *off this coast, but I have taken it upon myself to send this directly to you.*

I am sorry to say that no body has been recovered which could be associated with the coat. My condolences for your loss. I hope the receipt of this letter from your late husband will give you some comfort . . .

Annie's hand dropped to her side. Her fingers, suddenly limp, let slip the sheets of Stuart's letter to her as she collapsed, unconscious, beside the baby's cot.

Chapter 22

Annie had no idea how long she had been here in her bed. She could not remember getting into it. In fact all the events of the past few days seemed to be a meaningless blur.

She could hear the sound of activity in the kitchen. Vaguely she wondered who it might be. Then she heard a piercing cry, which brought her instantly to full consciousness. Her baby . . . what was happening to her baby?

She threw back the covers and staggered to the door, wrenching it open with the last of her strength.

In the low armchair beside the range, Sally Smith, having gathered up the hungry baby, had begun to feed him from a glass bottle.

'What . . . ?'

Sally looked up, startled, and seeing Annie clinging to the doorpost, she exclaimed: 'Oh, lor' Mrs Beaton, you did give me a fright! Now you just slip back into your bed this instant. I'll finish feeding the wee one, and then I'll make you a cup of tea.'

Annie needed not further bidding. Her legs seemed to be made of rubber. She turned back into the bedroom and collapsed on the bed. After a few moments she found the strength to creep beneath the covers, and was again fast asleep when Sally appeared with the promised drink.

The next time Annie awoke, it was to find her brother-in-law, Hugh Beaton, bending over her.

'What is it, Hugh?' she demanded weakly. 'What is the matter with me?'

'A case of delayed reaction, I suspect,' he replied, gently. 'It's the body's way of telling you to slow down and give yourself a chance to recover.'

He seemed satisfied with her pulse, for he laid her arm on the covers and settled down on the fragile bentwood chair beside the bed.

'You gave us all a bit of a fright,' he explained. 'I was obliged to knock you out with opiates for a day or two. I expect you have a headache.' Without waiting for her confirmation, he produced two tablets of aspirin and a glass of water. 'Take these,' he urged, 'they will help.'

Obediently she swallowed the pills and lay back upon the pillows.

'I don't remember anything,' Annie told him. She had a faint recollection of talking with Meg Roberts, then there had been the letter . . .

She put a hand to her lips to stifle a cry. The letter . . . Stuart's letter. Her hands wandered over the counterpane and beneath the pillows.

Hugh understood the reason for her searching. He opened the drawer of the little night stand, and placed in her restless hand the letter which had been delivered by Mrs Roberts three days before.

'This is what you are looking for,' he said.

Annie touched it as though it were made of red hot steel. She had tried to tell herself that it was not real, that the letter had not come to her from some deserted shore on a remote western island. An officer's coat, the man had said. If a coat, why not a body? Stuart had signed the letter and sealed the envelope. If the *Hampshire* was headed out on some new voyage, why had it not been posted before she sailed? These had been the questions tormenting her more lucid moments these past days.

As though reading her thoughts, Hugh said, 'Stuart wrote this after the sea battle.' He turned over a page. 'Look, he says here: "*Fortunately I have not been too busy on board, but it looks as though some of our sister ships may need some help*". The newspapers have been full of the sea battle off Jutland,' he continued, 'and they make particular mention of the fact that H.M.S. *Hampshire* was not damaged. That was why she had been selected to carry Lord Kitchener to Russia. Stuart makes no mention of the forthcoming voyage, although of course he would not have been allowed to say where they were going anyway. He must have written this as soon as they dropped anchor in Scapa Flow.' He looked up then to find Annie regarding him quizzically, and hurried on apologetically: 'I'm sorry about reading the letter, but I needed to know what it was that had caused you to react so alarmingly. I skipped the very personal bits.'

Remembering some of the loving expressions with which her husband normally laced his correspondence, Annie was forced to smile at Hugh's discomfiture. She squeezed her brother-in-law's hand as she murmured, 'Of course you had to read it. I do understand.'

'Annie,' Hugh went on, 'this has to be said . . . cruel as it may seem. You have been deluding yourself, thinking that by some miracle Stuart is still alive. That is a very natural reaction, but it is one which, if you persist, will eventually cause you to lose your sanity. You have to accept that he went down with his ship, and that along with hundreds of others, including Lord Kitchener himself, his body will never be recovered.'

She looked so lost and helpless lying there, her face white as the pillows beneath her head, he was filled with the desire to take her in his arms and kiss away her tears just as he would have done all those years ago when, as children, Hugh had been Annie's champion and her stalwart protector.

'For the sake of the baby, Annie . . . for Stuart's son . . . you must accept the truth and make a new beginning.'

'If there is no hope of his coming back,' she said quietly. 'I have no wish to go on living.'

Hugh choked back his own emotion. Filled with that old yearning which had once caused him to risk his career and his impending marriage for the chance to be with Annie McGillivray, he put his arm around her shoulders and kissed her on the brow.

'You have to fight this, Annie,' he said. 'Mama has accepted the inevitable, but in so doing, she has with the very best of intentions focused upon little Stephen. You must not allow her to usurp your position with your own child. That would not be good – either for her or for you.'

'Dear Hugh.' Annie stroked his hand. 'I could always rely upon you to do or say the sensible thing.' She drifted off into reminiscence of faraway days. 'Do you remember when we found poor Ellen McDougal's baby in the cave? I was so frightened, until you came and took charge . . .'

'You were just a baby yourself then.' He smiled.

'But Dr David praised you for the way you dealt with things,' she insisted, 'and so did the Procurator Fiscal.' She could remember how she had struggled to read the account of the inquest in the newspaper. It had been difficult to get her tongue around *Procurator Fiscal*, but it had sounded so well that she went on to learn other legal terms with increasing interest. 'Do you know,' she confided, 'I think that as early as that, I knew I wanted to be a lawyer.'

'You were always well able to talk your way into and out of everything!' he teased, and was gratified to see her eyes light up with something of their old intensity, as a smile spread across her tear-stained face.

It was only now that Annie looked properly at Hugh, taking in for the first time the khaki field dress which he was wearing.

'Hugh,' she exclaimed, 'you're in uniform!'

'Yes,' he replied, 'I came over this morning to say goodbye, although I must admit I had little hope of finding you lucid.'

'I have caused everyone a great deal of bother,' she said.

'No, you haven't,' he urged. 'In little Stephen, you have given Ma and Pa something to hope for. They will look forward to watching him grow to manhood. When the time comes that they are no longer with us, I hope you will allow me to help. Stephen belongs to a great tradition you know. I only hope he likes the idea of becoming a doctor!'

'I don't doubt,' Annie smiled, 'that Dr David will see to that.'

There was a gentle tap on the door. Hugh got to his feet and went to open it. Sally, with the baby in her arms, looked past him into the bedroom and was clearly relieved to see Annie looking so much better.

Remembering vaguely that she had seen Sally in the house before, feeding Stephen, she asked, 'How long have you been here, Sally?'

'When Dr Hugh came to Johnstones with the news that you were ill,' the girl answered, 'Mrs McLean suggested that I might come and take care of things here for a while. I do hope you don't mind?' she added anxiously.

Hugh chipped in. 'Mother stayed overnight for two days, but in the end Father and I persuaded her that Miss Smith was quite capable of looking after the two of you by herself. I have no doubt that she will be back again as soon as Pa agrees to it.'

Annie turned her attention to Sally.

'Does Mrs McLean not need you at the nursing home?'

'Since we had the Queen Alexandra's nurses allocated,' Sally explained, 'there has not been so much for the rest of us to do. Mrs McLean is quite happy for me to stay here for as long as you need me.'

Hugh, who had remained standing, chose this moment to take his leave.

'Remember what I said, Annie. Stuart would expect you to carry on playing his part as well as your own in bringing up his son. It is a daunting responsibility, but I'm confident that you will cope admirably.'

'I will try,' Annie said, as he kissed her lightly on the cheek.

'Morag will be home for the summer holidays at the end of the week,' he went on, 'and she will be across here to see you, I have no doubt.' He paused as he reached the door, and turning back for one last look at her, pleaded, 'Keep an eye on Millicent and the children for me, Annie.' He ducked under the low-slung lintel. 'I hope you will keep an old soldier informed of what is going on in your world from time to time.'

'I will do my best.' Annie waved limply from the bed, and then stretched out her arms to receive her infant son.

Reluctant to leave her like this, Hugh set off along the path to the harbour. Poor Annie, had he been too rough on her, so soon after her collapse? He thought not. Annie was made of stern stuff and could be relied upon to pull herself together. Anyway, it would be up to Pa now to see that she was all right.

The loose slate shifted beneath his feet as he strode purposefully around the head of the harbour, waving to Donnie

McPherson seated outside his workshop, enjoying the bright noonday sunshine. By this time next week, Hugh told himself, the island would be ringing again with the voices of children, released from the bonds of academe for six whole weeks.

He wished that he could be here to enjoy the summer break with his family. He had not seen Morag since Easter, and now all he could hope for was a strained conversation with his daughter in some crowded Glasgow tearoom after he had met her from the train. Would she accept his going away without question? he wondered.

Millicent had pleaded with him to remain, declaring that someone had to stay at home to take care of the sick – and how could he expect his father and his uncle to undertake the work of the practice, she had demanded, when it so often entailed driving long distances over treacherous roads, even walking across rough ground where access was denied to motor vehicles, and taking hazardous boat trips to the more remote islands, in calm weather or rough, day or night? She had remained unconvinced by his argument that his skills were needed at the front, and that his membership of the Territorials obliged him to go when required. This was not strictly true of course. As a married man with three children and necessary work to perform, he could have pleaded exemption.

Stuart's death had somehow clinched matters for him. Some member of the family must be out there doing his bit for the war effort.

As for his patients . . . well, he mused, the housewives of Eisdalsa would just have to turn to the nursing skills which their grandmothers should have taught them. He thought of the remedies he had been browsing through only an hour ago, while he waited hopefully for Annie to regain consciousness. Stuart had done a fine job with his translation of the old Beaton manuscript. In it, he had left a lasting memorial to himself, and to all those medical men who had preceded him. The work must be published, Hugh decided. It would be one of the first tasks to be undertaken once things got back to normal.

He approached the bothy where Baldie Campbell had said he

would be waiting. The ferryman laid down his pipe when he heard the doctor's step, and drew on his bonnet as he emerged into the sunshine. No one had ever seen old Baldie rowing his boat with his bonnet!

Hugh remembered the days when there were so many people living and working on the island that the ferry plied constantly across the narrow strait between Eisdalsa and Seileach. Now, it was wise to make a firm appointment with the ferryman if one wanted to get across promptly. Otherwise it might be necessary to seek him out, digging in his plot of ground, beside the flooded Camas quarry, or crouched over the fire in one or other of the half dozen houses on the island which were still occupied, sharing a pot of tea or a bottle of whisky with one of his few remaining cronies.

To the elderly folk left behind by the younger members of their family when the quarries closed, like his sister, Meg Roberts the postie, Baldie was a link with the civilised world. He brought their coal and carried their messages from the village store. Once the steamers from Crinan would have brought goods ordered from Glasgow right to the pier. Now larger parcels must wait for the bus to transport them from the train station in Oban. Three times a week Wullie Mackey backed his charabanc out of the long tin shed on the pier and drove the villagers into Oban for their supplies. Otherwise members of the depleted community must rely upon their feet or some accommodating neighbour with his own form of transport to take them into town.

'And how iss the young lady this morning, Doctor?' the man enquired in the soft, sibilant tones of the Western Highlander.

'A little better, Baldie,' Hugh responded, stepping lightly into the small sturdy boat and seating himself aft, facing the rower, so that they could continue to converse as Baldie plied his oars.

'Och, this war iss hard on the lassies, Doctor, and no mistake,' the ferryman observed, mildly. 'Now there's yourself away to the fighting and Mistress Beaton left alone with her wee boys.' He shook his head, accusingly. 'These are bad times, Doctor, and no mistake.'

'Morag will be home tomorrow,' Hugh told him. 'She will be

coming and going to see my sister-in-law,' he added. 'Will you take care to see she crosses safely?'

'Need you ask, Doctor?' replied the other, a broad smile suffusing the wrinkled old face, with its wind-reddened cheeks and bushy grey beard. 'Miss Morag and I are old friends.'

The rowing boat sidled up to the disused steamer pier and Baldie made fast. Hugh grasped the ladder and hauled himself out of the boat. It was a fair climb when the tide was as low as this.

'Dr Hugh,' the ferryman called after him.

Hugh looked down into the kindly eyes of the islander.

'Don't you be worrying yourself about the ladies now, they will be well cared for.'

Hugh, too overwhelmed by his emotions, could only nod in acknowledgement. He was leaving his family in good hands.

The news of the sinking of the *Hampshire* had left Heather grieving silently and alone. For days she remained in a state of shock, and although her mother noted her long silences, her eyes reddened by weeping and sleepless nights, Margaret assumed that Heather's grief, like her own, was for the loss of Stuart.

Although there had been no plans for the future, Heather had come to rely upon the knowledge that Daniel was out there somewhere, and would come back one day to claim her. Now there was an empty void in her life which she tried desperately to fill by working long hours at the sailors' canteen, and driving convalescent patients back and forth between Johnstones and Oban.

At her insistence, they had kept their liaison secret. Now she felt that it was pointless to distress her own family with the revelation that she and Dan had been sweethearts. Margaret and Annabel had enough to do coping with Stuart's widow and orphaned son, while her father and Dr David were totally committed to their own work. So irrational had her thinking become that she decided she could not go to Rebecca Rosenstein, because she might be suspected of exaggerating the relationship for financial gain.

After weeks of deliberation, the Scottish Women's Hospitals

committee at last made up its mind to purchase a fleet of ambulances. In July of 1916, Heather, relieved to be able to engage in something purposeful at last, agreed to move into the accommodation in Jessie Laurie's Greenock house, to assist with the operation of the finance and personnel office while arrangements were made to get the ambulances purchased and equipped, ready for the war in France.

The nursery suite, which Jessie had been clearing on the day that Heather had visited her, turned out to be much more suitable than she could possibly have imagined. It consisted of two rooms on the second floor of the imposing villa, but in addition there was a small kitchen, and, wonder of wonders, the suite had its own bathroom.

Jessie had moved some of the furniture from the ground-floor room, which had become the administrative centre of the organisation, so that Heather's living-room now contained the plush-covered armchairs and the large mahogany occasional table which had so cluttered the office.

Heather created order out of chaos in a matter of weeks; so much so that by the time that the Albion Works had the first vehicle ready for inspection, she felt confident that anyone could follow her into that office and take over the reins of administration.

Although she had at first appeared to be completely disorganised, Jessie Laurie turned out to be very astute when it came to finances. Not only did she read a set of figures as a musician might study a piece of music, but her knowledge of the intricacies of finance and banking was phenomenal in a woman of that time. Heather once asked her how she had acquired her skill.

'My father was a banker,' Jessie had replied, 'and I was the oldest of three daughters. There were no sons to pursue the family business. Papa had me trained to follow in his footsteps. Unfortunately he had not reckoned with the female urge to marry and have a family. I kept on working in the bank until I was nearly thirty, but Cupid had his way with me in the end!' she concluded, with that infectious laugh which endeared her to all who met her.

Jessie's other great talent was an unfailing instinct for selecting the right people for any particular task. As she pointed out to Heather, on more than one occasion, 'I picked you, didn't I?'

This ability stood them in good stead on the day they visited the Albion Motor Works at Scotstoun, on the north bank of the Clyde.

The works manager, having shown them the factory floor where chassis in various stages of completion were assembled, ready to receive customised bodywork, introduced them to the chief design engineer to whom they were asked to explain their requirements.

Jessie took a back seat while negotiations proceeded.

Armed with the specification which she had acquired from her engineering friends at the Morris factory, Heather was able to describe precisely what was wanted. The chief engineer was a smooth-talking, smartly suited, grey-haired gentleman, who tried to give the impression that there was nothing he did not know about motor vehicles. There were times, however, when during the course of their conversation, Heather was surprised by certain discrepancies in the man's explanations about the engines and their capacity to meet the required standards of performance. She referred often to her advisor's notes and this seemed to cause him some disquiet. Heather suspected that had she not been prepared in this way, she would have been putty in the hands of this man. As it was, she felt competent to insist on the specification as laid down. She was not to be fobbed off with less than the best that their money could buy.

Standing at the designer's elbow throughout their discussion, and taking careful note of Heather's instructions, there was a young man of perhaps twenty-five or thirty years. Heather wondered vaguely how he could be there at all, since most men of his age were now being conscripted into the services. He had been introduced as Malcolm Hendry, and his knowledge of engines became apparent when, from time to time, he slipped in a whispered correction to something his superior said concerning the operation of the vehicles, or manufacturing techniques employed.

They shook hands on an order for three ambulances, and Malcolm Hendry was instructed to conduct them to their taxi. As they made their way out into the yard, Jessie stopped abruptly and turned to him.

'How is it that you are not in uniform, young man?' she demanded in a tone which both surprised and shocked Heather.

He looked at her coldly, and answered in a voice from which all emotion had been carefully expunged. 'My work here is considered of national importance.'

'No other reason?' she asked, less harshly.

'I am a Quaker, Madam. I am not able to take up arms.'

'Ah, I see,' Jessie replied, thoughtfully. After a moment's pause she asked him, 'Suppose I were to offer to employ you to organise the maintenance of transport used by the Scottish Women's Hospitals? Would you be prepared to go to France in such circumstances?'

'Ask me again, madam,' he replied, 'when the vehicles are ready for you.'

The Albion leapt from one pothole to the next like a bucking bronco while Heather clung to the wheel, which seemed to have come alive under her hand. They had been quite right at the Clydeside factory . . . this had to be the sturdiest chassis ever made. The vehicle would ride more smoothly with a load on board, she told herself, but it would need to. Wounded men could not be subjected to the tossing and bruising which she had endured these past two hours!

As she drove along the deserted road, the dawn chorus of artillery fire began in the east. The road ahead stretched between the stumps of shattered poplar trees to where the early-morning glow of the sunrise was enhanced by a white glare of marker flares and the red and yellow flashes of exploding shells. The sky was dotted suddenly by puffs of black smoke, and Heather moved her gaze from the road for an instant, to see if she could spot the patrol plane which was receiving so much attention from anti-aircraft guns.

It was one second too many. The truck lurched into a large pothole, from which even the powerful 30 h.p. Albion engine could not pull free.

Heather put her foot down hard and felt the rear wheel spinning without effect. She shut off the engine and climbed down out of the cab. There had been rain the night before, and a considerable pool had gathered in the bottom of the shallow crater into which she had driven. No amount of gunning the engine was going to get her out of this. She unhitched the shovel which was strapped to the side of the vehicle for just such an event, and began to scrape gravel and mud down into the hole to provide a grip for the tyres.

'Need a hand, girlie?'

The voice, with its cheerful colonial twang, startled her.

She turned around to discover three soldiers wearing the distinctive Australian bush hats which had become a familiar sight in France since the spring of 1916.

'Yes, I could do with some help, thanks!' she replied, smiling as one of the three Australians took the shovel out of her hands and turned to his companions.

'C'mon then, fellers. What we want here is some of those branches.' He indicated the shattered trees lying alongside the causeway upon which the road ran straight ahead towards the horizon.

Heather was brushed aside as the three of them went to work. After a few moments, the biggest of the men, who had spoken first, stripped off his tunic to reveal broad shoulders and strong sinewy arms.

'Let's get some of those pieces of wood right under the wheel. I'll jack her up, Marty, while you shove in the stuff, OK?'

Marty and his friend armed themselves with handfuls of twigs and stood by.

With his back against the side of the vehicle, the huge fellow took a grip of the chassis just to the front of the wheel arch and tensed himself for the lift. Heather, fascinated, watched his muscles ripple and bulge, as with one almighty heave he had the side of the lorry a foot off the ground. He had performed the lift with such consummate ease that it might have been a child's toy rather than a fifteen-hundredweight truck that he was shifting.

Quick as lightning, first Marty and then the other man thrust their bundles of material beneath the tyre and stepped back with alacrity before the big man could let go. The wheel sank down into the hole once more, but this time it was resting firmly on the mattress they had made for it.

'OK, miss, in you get. We'll start her up, then when I give the word, you engage second gear.'

The third soldier, who had remained silent throughout, now moved to the front of the vehicle and took hold of the starting handle.

Heather climbed back into the cab and opened the throttle to its fullest extent. 'Ready!' she called. The man swung the handle and the engine fired instantly. 'Now, let her in easy and keep the revs low,' came the instructions from the rear. She closed the throttle cautiously, until the motor was just ticking over, then shifted the gear lever. The ambulance crept forward, taking a grip on the hastily manufactured mattress, and began to climb out of the hole.

'Now,' shouted the soldier, 'give her some gun!'

Heather opened the throttle and the heavy vehicle shot out of the hole and advanced several yards along the roadway before she was able to bring it to a halt.

Leaning out of the cab, she looked back to where her three gallant knights of the road stood, arms akimbo, watching her progress.

'Can I give you a lift?' she called.

They needed no second bidding. In a few moments, her burly saviour had climbed up beside her, while his two companions piled in over the tailboard at the rear of the truck.

'I'm making for the field hospital at Noyon,' she told her passenger.

'That's beaut!' he replied. 'We're joining our company at the next place to Noyon . . . we had a few days' stand down and hitched a lift into Paris,' he went on, 'but getting transport back to the lines isn't so easy when your journey is unofficial. We've hoofed it the last ten miles, hoping to catch a wagon.'

'Lucky for me you didn't,' she observed. 'I must say I was

surprised when you came up to me like that. I had seen no sign of you on the road as I was driving along.'

'Well, no.' He hesitated. 'We were keeping cave, you see . . . in case you were the MPs.'

'Ah, now I understand,' she exclaimed. 'You three are AWOL, is that it?'

'Not exactly absent without leave,' he insisted, 'but the Sarge didn't give us permission to go as far as Paris . . . that kind of happened by accident.'

'Well,' she laughed, 'you'd better let me do the talking when we get to any check point, that accent is a clear give-away. And perhaps you'd better put your hat under the seat. They might just mistake you for my Tommy co-driver if you keep mum.'

'Aw, gee, miss, you're a sport,' he announced. 'My name's Bluey, by the way. Bluey Jackson.' With his massive paw, which was black with grease from handling the lorry, he swept a fringe of bright red curls out of his eyes. Without the bush hat to keep them under control, they had tumbled forward on to his brow. She could see, now, that despite his huge frame, he was just a boy, no more than eighteen or nineteen years at the most.

'You handled that problem back there as though you had done the same thing many times before,' she remarked. 'Have you been in France for long?'

'Oh, the Froggies aren't the only people with potholes in their roads.' He grinned. 'My old man, back in Kellerberrin where I come from, he makes a fair living out of a pothole no bigger than that one. It lies just outside the boundary of our property. By rights the old man should fill it in and make good the road surface. Not on your life, mate! He keeps a pair of Suffolk Punches stabled close by, and every time some unsuspecting farmer gets his cart or motor stuck in the mud-hole, he charges a quid to haul 'im out. Reckons it beats farming as a way of making a bob or two!'

Heather laughed.

'Excuse me saying so, miss,' Bluey continued, unabashed, 'but you have a really beaut accent there. You sound just like our Sarge. He's a Scot, like yourself.'

'I come from Argyllshire,' she confessed.

'A girl as pretty as you has got to have a pretty name,' he persisted.

'It's Heather . . . Heather Brown,' she told him, not knowing quite why she had done so. It was just that his super-confident manner impelled her to give him an answer.

For many miles the road had led them across flat marshy land, drained by innumerable canals, but now the landscape was beginning to change. They were approaching a low escarpment with a town sprawled at its base. The houses had been shattered by shell fire, and the rusting headframes of a dozen idle coal-mines merely served to compound the overall impression of dereliction and decay.

On the approach road, a barrier had been erected to control the passage of civilians and military personnel into the town.

Heather drew the ambulance to a halt and was immediately addressed by a British sentry with the distinctive red hatband of a military policeman. He demanded to see her movement order. She handed over the papers, while Bluey, his bush hat wedged firmly beneath the seat, tried hard not to look like an Australian soldier getting a ride in an ambulance where he had no right to be.

The policeman glanced at her passenger and lifted one eyebrow in query.

'Stretcher bearer,' Heather replied sharply. The MP nodded and waved her through.

As Heather picked a way along the main street, which had been only partially cleared of the rubble of buildings destroyed in the shelling, a head appeared through the window behind the driver's seat.

'That was close!' observed Marty. 'Geoff and me got on to the stretchers back here so they'd think we was wounded.' He laughed, and added, gratefully, 'You're a real dinkum sheila, ma'am, and no mistake.'

Heather hoped it would be the only journey that these cheerful young men would take in an ambulance. She pulled into a side road where they would not be too closely observed, and stopped the lorry.

'You'd better get out here,' she said. 'It wouldn't do for me to be carrying stowaways when I arrive at the hospital.'

Bluey slid down to the road, as his two companions joined him from the rear of the truck.

'Any time you need a strong arm . . .' he laughed. 'Goodbye, Heather Brown!'

She thrust the ambulance into gear and manoeuvred it back on to the main thoroughfare. Gathering speed as the road opened up before her, she was soon out again in the countryside, travelling north westwards below the escarpment of Vimy Ridge.

In the town which she had just left, three somewhat subdued young men were facing their officer.

'Sappers Jackson, Martin and Jones, sir . . . overstayed leave!' Sergeant Major Jack McDougal barked at them. 'Hats off!'

Smartly, they removed their bush hats and tucked them under their arms. As they stood stiffly to attention, Bluey's eyes were level with the top of his officer's head, despite the fact that Captain Hamish McGillivray, M.C., was himself more than six feet tall.

The wind blew strongly across the headland as they lowered the last of the coffins into the ground. There was a fluttering of white ensigns as the flags were withdrawn and folded by the bearer party. Now nothing moved but the black ribbons on the sailors' caps.

In the small Orkney town of Kirkwall the church bells had tolled mournfully all morning. Now they too were silent as across the acres of open moorland the strains of the last post were swallowed up on the wind.

Manny Rosenstein brushed his hand across his eyes, and bowed his head. It was such a meagre number of coffins which had been needed, only a handful of bodies had been washed ashore, and such a small gathering of mourners to bid farewell to the many hundreds of men lost.

Rebecca had begged him to come in the hope that he might obtain a little more information about her son's last hours.

There was no doubt about the fate of Daniel Rosenstein. He had managed to launch one of the lifeboats and navigate her to a landfall on Westray Island, only to be drowned within sight of land when the boat broke up on the rocks.

Manny introduced himself to members of the boat's crew who had managed to scramble ashore. They were full of praise for their second officer, talking of how he had kept them alive during their long cold vigil at sea, even draping his jacket over one badly burnt stoker who had jumped overboard clad only in his singlet. The last they had seen of Dan was the white sleeve of his shirt, as he raised one despairing arm above the waves before sinking out of sight. It would be some comfort to Rebecca to know that her son had died a hero.

To the sounds of reveille the company came to attention and those in uniform saluted. The ceremony, moving in its simplicity, came to an end at last. Senior naval officers and local dignitaries climbed into their vehicles, but Manny chose to walk the short distance into town with the bulk of the mourners. His enquiries led him to the local police station where he was introduced to the sergeant in charge of the *Hampshire* incident.

The sergeant led Manny Rosenstein into a small hall behind the Kirkwall police station where, laid out on a series of trestle tables, was a pathetically small collection of personal effects; all that remained of a splendid fighting ship and her crew of hundreds.

'Items such as these have been coming ashore for the past week,' the sergeant explained. 'It is all we have to identify those members of the crew who drowned.'

Manny studied the items laid out for inspection, seeing nothing that he recognised as belonging to his brother. At the far end of the table a uniform jacket was neatly folded. Although the garment was clearly the worse for a wetting, someone had carefully dried and pressed it before handing it in. The coat bore the insignia of a Lieutenant R.N.

Manny picked it up and examined it. Discretely hidden in a fold in the lining, he found a label he recognised and gave a start. The label read: H. Schwartz, London. Tailors to H.R.H. Prince of Wales.

Haime Schwartz had been a tailor of gentlemen's fine suitings for half a century, in Potsdam at first, the town where he was born, and later in London where Joseph Rosenstein had befriended him and set him up in his own business in Savile Row. The Rosenstein boys had always had their suits made for them by Haime and this was undoubtedly Daniel's jacket.

Manny pointed out the label to the bemused sergeant.

'Ah, now,' he said, cautiously, 'we thought that we had already identified the owner of that coat. There was a letter you see, just one that was still readable. Thinking that he was doing the right thing, Ewan McGregor posted it before turning the coat over to us.'

'A letter . . . to whom?' Manny asked.

'Would you know if your brother was acquainted with a gentleman called Stuart whose wife is a Mrs Beaton of Connel in Argyll?'

'Stuart Beaton was the surgeon aboard H.M.S. *Hampshire*,' Manny explained. 'He and my brother were good friends. I suppose it is possible that Dan might have been carrying a letter for Stuart . . . maybe he had been asked to post it, and forgotten.'

The sergeant sighed. They already had all the proof they needed that Lieutenant Rosenstein was dead. Now they could not be sure about Commander Beaton. He made an adjustment to the meticulous record he was compiling before following Manny out into the yard.

Manny waited impatiently while Harry Wilberforce searched through the piles of paper spread across his desk.

'The problem is, you see,' explained the young naval lieutenant, 'that *Hampshire* received her orders to sail at very short notice. Although she herself was undamaged at Jutland, several of her crew had been sent to other vessels to help out in the clearing up operation and a number of them had not returned on board before she sailed. In several cases there were no written orders. We have to depend on reports from the individual ships to which men were assigned.'

'But surely one would expect the *Hampshire*'s men to report in when they heard what had happened?' Manny suggested.

'Not necessarily.' Wilberforce grinned at the politician's

naïvety. 'What a perfect way of disappearing if one didn't want to go back to sea!'

'And this is the reason why no official notices have as yet been sent to next-of-kin?' Manny found the explanation quite unacceptable.

'What fools we would look if we reported a man dead to his family, only for him to turn up on the doorstep the next day,' the lieutenant suggested. 'But that's only part of the problem,' he added. 'Normally when a ship goes down the news of the sinking is not released until all the next-of-kin have been informed. Unfortunately, in view of the importance of the passengers aboard *Hampshire*, the matter could not be kept secret. It takes time to sift through the details of several hundred men, so the delay is inevitable.'

'You know now that Commander Beaton cannot be identified by the jacket found washed ashore on Westray?' Manny got to the point of his visit to the Admiralty.

'Yes, we have been informed.'

'Is there any doubt that the doctor was on board *Hampshire* when she sailed?' Manny enquired.

'As far as I am aware, there is nothing known to the contrary,' Wilberforce replied. 'Now, sir, if you will forgive me, I do have work to do.' This man Rosenstein might be a member of the Cabinet but it did not give him the right to come throwing his weight about at Admiralty House! He took up the next file on the heap in front of him and waited for Manny to leave.

With the Minister out of the way, the lieutenant searched frantically through the files awaiting processing. Beaton must be somewhere near the beginning of the list . . .

Commander Reginald Shepherd leaned back in his chair and, placing his fingertips together thoughtfully, stared at Harry Wilberforce over the top of his steel-framed spectacles.

Harry had laid out on the desk before him copies of the signals sent to Commander Beaton prior to the *Hampshire*'s sailing on 5 June.

'This last,' Harry explained, 'recalling Beaton to the

Hampshire, was never received by the doctor. He was already on board the *Dolores* when it was acknowledged by *Onslow*'s signals officer. I think we must assume that he was still aboard the merchantman when she sailed, some hours after *Hampshire*'s departure. Which means that he is probably still alive.'

'Yes,' drawled the Commander, 'I do see that you have a problem.'

'May I have your permission to write to Mrs Beaton to tell her that her husband did not go down in the *Hampshire*?'

'No, I don't think that will be necessary.' The senior officer showed no emotion whatsoever as he added, 'The *Dolores* is what our friends in Fleet Street euphemistically call a Q-ship. She is on a suicide mission; out of touch with the Admiralty, until her next scheduled meeting with her supply ship. The fact is, she is probably already at the bottom of the Atlantic. I would suggest that the chances of Commander Beaton's ever being restored to the bosom of his family are too remote to be considered.'

Harry was flabbergasted. 'Are you suggesting that Mrs Beaton should not be told that her husband is still alive?' he demanded.

'I am insisting upon it,' Shepherd retorted. 'The *Dolores* of Montevideo has no connection with this department.' He leant forward to give emphasis to his next comment. 'Do we understand one another, Wilberforce?'

Harry nodded, glumly.

'Good.' His commanding officer nodded a curt dismissal and as the lieutenant opened the door, added, 'Incidentally, Wilberforce, if that fellow Rosenstein comes poking around again, refer him to me, will you?'

Chapter 23

*I have at last heard from the Scottish Women's Hospital,
that I may join their staff at Royaumont, about twenty
miles from Paris. I realise that this will give you yet
another worry, but I hope you understand that it is
something I just have to do. Every day I see the boys who
have been shipped back home having lost limbs, or
suffering terrible internal problems, often through neglect
of their injuries after the fighting, and I realise how
important it is to have proper nursing care as near to the
front as possible. At Royaumont the wounded are received
straight from the clearing stations.*

*The thought that Hamish and his friends might end up
in the condition of some of the boys I have nursed here
recently, is enough to convince me that I am making the
right decision.*

*Please don't think that this is just some ploy to get back
to Scotland. Australia is now my home, and I look forward
to the day when we are all together again. Until this awful
war is over, I feel that I have as much of an obligation as
the boys themselves to use my talents to the best advantage.*

*I have a passage on a boat leaving Sydney on 15 July.
Would you believe . . . it is the old Geraldtown! I don't
suppose that it will be such fun as we had on our outward
voyage, and I expect that the crew will have changed, but I
am looking forward to being aboard ship once more!*

*Please try not to worry. I will write whenever possible,
and will make every effort to meet up with Hamish.*

Please give my regards to Madge and old McKenzie. I

*often think about you all, sprawled in your wicker chairs
on the veranda, in the cool of the evening . . .*

Mary laid down the letter, unable to read further with her eyes
filled with tears. It was bad enough knowing that Hamish was in
France but to have her daughter on her way there also . . . so far
away and so close to the fighting. Surely she had made enough
sacrifices already in her life?

She tried to convince herself that Hamish led a charmed life.
Had he not come through the Gallipoli campaign without a
scratch? Dougal had been so pleased when he heard about the
Military Cross and his son's promotion to Captain that he had
Walt open up the bar for a celebration drink even though it was
the middle of the week!

She glanced at the clock. It would soon be time for school.

Gathering up the exercise books she had been marking the
night before, Marty Mallacoota's fell open at the essay for which
she had awarded ten marks out of ten, a rare occurrence for work
produced by any of the children.

She had read in the paper that some philanthropist in
Melbourne wanted to endow a university for the Aborigines. She
thought she might write to him and tell him about Marty. There
could not be many children receiving the level of education that
she gave her Aboriginal pupils. She had extended the curriculum
for the most able, and a small group of high-flyers was even now
making its way through the writings of authors such as Jane
Austen, Thomas Hardy and Charles Dickens. She regretted the
scarcity of good literature about their own country, and had
already approached the library in Perth for suggestions for
suitable books by Australian writers.

Marty wrote about the history of his own people and about
everyday life in the tribal encampment where he lived. He had a
clear, descriptive manner of telling his stories which made one
see and feel exactly what he himself experienced. How
wonderful it would be if he were to become a recognised writer.
What marvellous strides could be made for his people if they had
their own educated, erudite spokesman working on their behalf.

Thrusting aside her daydream, she gathered the pile of books and hurried off down the dusty road to the schoolhouse.

McKenzie added a column of figures, checked it and completed the total with something of a flourish.

'I canna think that Head Office will be too unhappy about these results,' he declared with some satisfaction. Since his return to the mine, albeit in the capacity of book-keeper and clerk, he had shed a few years and with them his excessive craving for the bottle. The war had given them all a sense of purpose, and Doug McGillivray was an inspiration, even to one as cynical and long in the tooth as the mine's retired manager.

Doug looked over his shoulder and whistled appreciatively. 'That looks like bonuses all round,' he said, squeezing the older man's shoulder sufficiently hard to make McKenzie wince.

Doug picked up his miner's helmet and the geological hammer he carried with him at all times.

'Och, ye'll no be going down yersel this forenoon?' McKenzie chided. 'You spend far too much time underground.'

'I can't leave Jones to get on with it until I'm satisfied that that last piece of shoring is holding adequately. Yesterday we encountered an area of softer feldspar rich clay which looks rather unstable. I'm not convinced that the timber sent up from the coast is strong enough for the job.'

'Och, all this eucalyptus wood is the same,' McKenzie observed, 'fibrous and flexible. It may bend a little but it'll no snap!'

'We'll see.' Unconvinced, Doug made for the door. 'I'll be back in an hour,' he declared, and was gone.

McKenzie sighed, then pulled out a new sheet of paper and headed his letter to the company's agent.

There had been far too many injuries of late, Doug reflected as he made his way to the main shaft. Only a week ago two men had been trapped when an insecure shoring had given way in the approach tunnel to the new seam which they were opening up. One had suffered a crushed pelvis, the other a compound fracture of both legs. Despite the arrival of another group of immigrant workers from the Balkan States, he was running short of experienced people. It was a situation in which he could not win. With fewer men those remaining were forced to work harder and their resulting fatigue led to even more accidents.

His approach to the new exposure was accompanied by sounds of drilling together with the intermittent noise of broken rock falling and shovels scraping on bare stone.

'Anything?' he enquired, as he bent his head slightly in order to negotiate the final approach tunnel.

As he emerged into the cavern where Jones's men were working, the foreman handed him a lump of quartz rock.

'Half an hour ago I was ready to pack up and get out,' his foreman confessed. 'Then Charlie started digging out this stuff. It's hard to tell whether that's gold or pyrites at first glance, but my hunch is that it's gold.'

Doug took the specimen which Jones had handed to him and examined it closely with his jeweller's lens.

'Could be,' he replied cautiously, trying hard to suppress his rising excitement. He thrust the lump of quartz into his pocket. 'I'll need a proper assay to be absolutely certain it's worth going on. Has any more of that soft material come to light?'

'Not where Charlie is drilling at present,' Jones assured him. He had withdrawn the men from the suspect area and set them to work on the opposite wall of the cave.

'It seemed possible that the original seam stretched right across this space and continued in that direction.' He indicated where the Aboriginal driller was working. The cave was about fifteen feet across and perhaps ten high, the size of a small room. It was likely that in past millennia water had penetrated these strata, gouging out the system of caverns which had led men to discover the gold contained within its walls.

Doug examined the new drilling site for any sign of movement in the surrounding rock. In the glare of the electric lighting any tell-tale cracks would show up immediately. The cavern had been considerably enlarged by the operation to exploit a gold-rich quartz vein on the north side. After tunnelling into the wall of the cave for twenty yards, extracting high quality ore, they had encountered the feldspar rich clay which caused Doug so much concern. With the driller continuing with his task on the opposite wall, Doug stumbled along the now abandoned north passage, in semi-darkness. Since the electric lighting equipment had been removed, he was obliged to rely on the torch on his helmet. As he penetrated deeper into the tunnel, he began to regret not having checked the battery before he started. The light, though feeble, was sufficient to show him that he had reached the end of the tunnel and the barrier of soft clay.

He rubbed a little of it between his fingers. There was no doubt about it: it was damp. Promising himself a new battery for his torch, he returned to the main cave.

Doug had worked at Keningo long enough to know that the presence of moisture at this depth could mean only one thing: they had penetrated close to a natural artesian basin.

In the normal course of events the discovery of a new source of water in this barren land would be cause for rejoicing. When the basin was this close to the mine, however, there was a very real danger that the water, under enormous pressure so far underground, would force its way through the rock and flood the whole mine. If, as he feared, the recent drilling operation had weakened the rock structure, the water might break through at any time.

Doug wasted no time on further inspection. He ordered the men to pick up their gear and get out.

Surprised to be dismissed before their shift was over, the men voiced their dissent and were slow to respond to his order. They were paid on a piecework basis; an early finish meant less money for all of them.

Doug had no wish to cause panic but there was no time to argue. 'Humour me in this, will you?' he pleaded. 'I'll guarantee that you receive normal payment despite the lack of production – just hurry it up!'

Dai Jones, surprised by Doug's order to stop work, had himself taken another look at the northern workings.

At his shout, Doug left Charlie to deal with his workmates, and hurried back to the face.

Jones pointed to a small pool of water at the base of the rock.

'It's got deeper while you were talking,' he observed. 'I don't like the look of it at all!'

Doug needed no further urging. He shouted to the men: 'Leave everything and make your way up to the second level as fast as you can. Clear the galleries as you go . . . no one is to be left behind on this level, understand?'

He turned to the foreman.

'If we seal off the entrance to the cavern we might have a chance of containing the water in here. As it bursts out into the larger space its advance should be slowed sufficiently to give us time to escape.'

In response, Jones collected a supply of dynamite and together they began to plant bundles of the explosive along the fifteen-foot tunnel which linked the cavern to their escape route to the main shaft. Each took a section of the tunnel, intent upon ensuring that the rock fall would be sufficient to stem the advancing flood water.

Neither man heard the approach of Alfie Mallacoota who stood silently by ready to help. He gathered up the remaining bundles of dynamite and the fuse wires and handed them to the engineers as required. Their combined effort had the job completed in remarkably short time, and Doug thanked his men for remaining to help him. Without them he could not possibly have finished in time.

Doug worked his way along the narrow corridor checking the charges while Jones connected up the fuses. Retrieving the battery from his foreman, Doug indicated that the other two should take cover and crouched behind a substantial baulk of timber. He lifted the plunger and thrust it down with all the force at his command.

Nothing happened.

They waited a full minute in case the charge had been delayed in its transmission, but no explosion occurred.

At that moment, Mallacoota spotted a thin trickle of water advancing towards them along the tunnel.

At his cry of alarm, Doug looked in the direction of his pointing finger and knew that they were doomed if the dynamite refused to blow.

'I'm going back in,' he called to Jones, 'there must be a loose connection somewhere. If the water bursts through . . . try to blow the charges, and get out as fast as you can.'

As Doug moved back along the narrow tunnel he realised that the floor was already awash. Water was streaming down the walls and gathering into a rapidly widening pool in the centre of the cave. He reached up to examine the first of the charges. The fuse was firmly attached.

He tried another and another, acutely aware that a small water-fall was now coursing down the rock face behind him.

Suddenly the lights failed.

'Damn!' he cried out. 'The water's caused a short. There should be a flashlight in my haversack.'

In the darkness, Jones was loath to let go of the plunger lest he could not find it again in time.

Mallacoota grunted as he searched for the bag; he had been holding on to it only moments before. Suddenly his hand landed upon it and he gave a little cry of triumph.

The torch gave a strong beam, sufficient to reach the length of the tunnel and into the cave beyond. Doug, working only by the dimming light on his helmet, had discovered the loose connection and was hurriedly rewiring it.

'Here, boss, I'll hold the torch for you.' Alfie approached him, casting the light into the depths of the cavern behind him. The wall was beginning to crumble under the force of water behind it. As Doug gave a final twist to the wire, a small section of rock fell away and water spouted out horizontally as if from a giant fire hose. Doug barely had time to call out before being bowled over by the force of it.

'FIRE!'

Jones acted instinctively. Had he taken time to think he might have disobeyed. He forced down the plunger and with a roar sufficient to burst the Welshman's eardrums, the rock shattered, filling the tunnel between himself and the other two men with ton upon ton of rubble.

As the dust settled and an eerie silence descended, he knelt beside the rockfall, hoping to hear something to indicate that the trapped men were still alive, but he knew in his heart that they must be dead.

Dazed and deafened by the blast, he waited for the first trickle which would indicate that Doug's sacrifice had been in vain. The floor at his feet remained dry.

The dam would hold.

Sorrowfully, the foreman made his way to the foot of the shaft and climbed the ladder to join the remainder of the men. He was greeted by a sea of solemn, ashen faces. No one needed to enquire. Dai Jones's expression was sufficient to tell them that their boss would not be following after.

In the schoolroom the children were packing away their books when the siren sounded. Three sharp blasts on the whistle: the signal for a disaster in the mine. Mary's hand went to her throat. Doug had said he would be going down today. Suddenly she felt faint and would have keeled over had not Marty grabbed hold of her.

'You OK, missus?' he asked anxiously leading her towards a chair.

She thrust him aside, adrenaline beginning to course through her veins. 'I have to go . . . he may be hurt,' she cried frantically, darting out into the yard with the boy at her heels. A small crowd had already gathered around the open shaft when Mary arrived. McKenzie, seeing her, stepped forward and prevented her going closer to the edge. 'All right, Mrs McGillivray . . . ma'am,' he tried to calm her, 'they're coming up now. We'll know soon enough what has happened.'

The cage arrived at the surface and the first man to step out was Dai Jones. Seeing both Mary and the Mallacoota child standing together he walked up to them, eyes staring, the sound of the explosion still ringing in his head.

'I'm sorry,' he stammered. 'His orders . . . I had to do what he said . . . to save the mine and the rest of the men . . .' He staggered towards an upended oil drum and sank down, burying his head in his hands.

Mary stared past him at the men walking towards her, heads bent, unable to look her in the eye. Where was Dougal? What had they done with him?

Marty stood silently beside her, waiting patiently for Alfie to appear. His father would be able to tell them what had happened.

They all wondered at the calm manner in which the manager's wife made arrangements for the funeral service. How could they know of the tragedy that had dogged Mary throughout her life and hardened her to the exigencies of fate?

Thirty years before she had supported her ageing father in his ministerial duties while one after another of her friends and neighbours had died of cholera, and had endured the grief of her mother's death and that of her best friend, Kirsty McGillivray. Soon afterwards, her cousin Peter Lugas, who had been like a brother to her, had drowned in Loch Fyne. She had passed through the barriers of grief before, and knew that life must go on.

Because there was no hope of recovering the bodies of the dead men, Mary could take time to make her arrangements. She wrote to Anne to tell her of the tragedy and suggested that she might come to the funeral service which Mary was arranging.

She summoned the preacher from Kalgoorlie, a man whose parish consisted of a hundred square miles of bush country surrounding the town, and engaged masons to fashion a memorial stone to be erected over the spot beneath which her husband had died.

Under the laws of Western Australia, all Aborigines were placed in the charge of a responsible white citizen. Like all the Aborigines associated with the Keningo gold mine, Alfie's family was subject to the protection of the mine's manager who, as the company's senior member of staff, had been nominated their Chief Protector. Doug had found it difficult to come to terms with the notion that he had the power to command every aspect of the lives of these people. It seemed that he was expected to treat them as slaves, an idea which was utterly abhorrent to him. Consequently he had left the Aboriginal families largely to themselves apart from administering the fair distribution of food and clothing provided by the State. He had contributed what medical care he could, and had ensured that his charges were properly housed, while Mary had fulfilled the requirement to provide education for the children.

Both Dougal and Mary had taken these paternal duties very seriously, ensuring that the white population of the district did not exploit the Aborigines in any way. The example set by the beneficent couple had encouraged the Mallacootas and several other families to join the Christian faith, and on the rare occasions when the settlement was visited by the local preacher, the Mallacootas always turned out in force.

On the day before the service was to be held, Mary visited the one-room shack in which Marty and his numerous brothers and sisters had been raised. Seated in the shade of the wide veranda which was formed by the extended iron roof, she found Alfie's widow, silent and empty-eyed, surrounded by her female relations. They made way for the manager's wife as she approached, and Mary sat down beside Mrs Mallacoota while the women began a mourning chant, a rhythmical low murmuring which seemed to seep into Mary's brain and calm her tortured mind.

Children of every age darted about the compound or sat in the shade playing five-stones. An infant at the breast suddenly stopped sucking to open its eyes and roar a protest. Its mother quickly raised her discarded nipple to the child's mouth and the noise ceased as suddenly as it had begun.

At last the chanting stopped and while some of the women drifted away, others busied themselves with the preparation of the evening meal. At this moment Marty appeared and came and stood beside his teacher.

'Does your mother speak English, Marty?' Mary asked.

'Jus a little bit, missus,' replied the boy. 'You tell me what you wanna say . . . I tell it to her,' he continued helpfully.

'Tomorrow, the preacher from Kalgoorlie is coming to say prayers over our men,' Mary explained. 'I have had a commemorative stone made, to stand above the spot where they died, with words written on it . . . so that they will be remembered.'

The boy regarded her solemnly for a moment. Then he spoke to his mother in his native tongue. She made little sign of understanding but when he had finished translating she mumbled a few words.

'My mother, she say she will remember here,' he touched his head, 'and here,' tapping his chest above the heart. 'She does not need a stone to remember.'

'Would she come to the service?' Mary asked. 'You always came as a family when the preacher visited.'

'It was my father made us go to church because the boss expected it,' Marty explained. 'Mama never understood the words.'

'Ask her, will she come? I would like her to be there.'

The boy turned once again to his mother. Their exchange was short. The black woman shook her head, turned away from Mary and wiped tears from her eyes. She reached for her youngest child, an infant of just a few weeks which was being nursed by an elder daughter. The baby was taken to the woman's breast and held there as though its very presence gave her comfort. Silently, Mary leant across and touched the hand which held the baby. She rose to leave.

The woman muttered again, and Marty's countenance brightened at her words.

'She say, she think about it, missus,' he told her.

Jean McDougal settled herself in the dusty carriage, and as the transcontinental express pulled out of the station, she waved to young Taffee who had driven her into Southern Cross that morning and now waited by the level crossing to see the train pass. The boy waved back from his seat on the buggy, a broad smile lighting up his face. It was good to see him looking so well and walking normally.

She withdrew a book from her small valise and resigned herself to the discomforts of a second-class railway carriage. The journey to Kalgoorlie was less than a hundred miles. She should arrive in under three hours.

By the miracle of the telegraph, the news of Doug McGillivray's death had reached Kerrera Station only hours after the accident.

Anne had received the terrible news in the same stoical manner displayed by her daughter-in-law. John had looked on helplessly while his wife sat silent throughout the night. Towards dawn, in the hope of comforting her, he had reached for his bible and began to read in a quiet voice: ' "For all flesh is as grass and all the glory of man as the flower of grass. The grass withereth and the flower thereof falleth away: but the word of the Lord endureth forever." '

He had closed the book when he saw that she was weeping. Enfolding her in his arms, he had rocked her gently until she went to sleep.

The next morning Anne had woken early and was crashing about in the dairy when Jean found her. They worked silently side by side for some time before Anne slammed down a steel basin with extra force, slopping milk which she was separating for butter-making.

'Would Wee Ellen stay with me and her granda while you went on an errand for a few days?' she had demanded of a startled Jean.

'I can't see why not,' she had replied hesitantly, not knowing if her mother-in-law was yet in proper charge of her senses.

'I should go to the funeral service,' Anne explained, 'but I cannot leave John. I don't trust him to stay away from the heavy lifting if I'm not here to keep an eye on him. But someone must go and fetch Mary out of that hell-hole in the desert,' she had cried despairingly, choosing uncharacteristically coarse language to express her rage. 'She is more likely to listen to you who are of her own generation. There is to be no nonsense about keeping a home going for Hamish and Flora – there will be places a-plenty for them here, once John has his way about developing the township. We have talked about his plans often enough . . . now it is up to you to convince Mary that she has a part to play in them!'

Finally, exhausted by her tirade, Anne had set her work down quite suddenly and wandered off across the yard, leaving Jean to direct the activities of the two dairy maids.

* * *

Jean McDougal thought that she had already experienced the worst that the Australian outback had to offer when she had arrived at Kerrera Station nearly three years before. Nothing in all her reading about the continent was to prepare her for the desolate wasteland which surrounded Keningo settlement. Why anyone should require persuading to leave such a place, she could not understand.

The weekly delivery lorry from Kalgoorlie had left, conveniently so it had seemed at the time, within an hour of her alighting at Kalgoorlie railway station. As the rattletrap vehicle crested the rim of the Keningo basin, she wondered whether it might have been advisable to remain in town overnight. She was bruised in so many unmentionable places, she felt as though she had not bathed for a week and her flimsy white muslin dress was red with dust. The prospect of there being a bath, or even a shower in the miserable little settlement which she could see in the distance, seemed very remote.

In a cloud of red dust, the van drew up before Walt Wilson's store.

'McGillivrays' is the place at the end of the row, missus.'

Jeanie thanked her chauffeur, thrusting into his hand the half a crown fare upon which they had agreed.

'I shall be leaving tomorrow around noon,' he told her. 'Let me know if you want a lift back into town.'

'I fancy my business will take a little longer,' she replied, 'but thanks all the same.'

The house at the end of the row looked well cared for. The little wicket fence was painted white, as were the barge boards and the elaborately carved finials on the gently pitched iron roof. In the shade of a generous veranda, Jeanie spotted Mary, dozing on a long cane chair. She pushed open the little gate and began to walk up the path.

'G'day.'

Jeanie looked towards where the sound had come from and found a round pink face peering at her through the spindly branches of a frangipane tree.

'How do you do?' she responded.

'Was you callin' upon Mrs McGillivray?' Madge Bowler demanded.

'Why, yes, I'm her sister-in-law from Southern Cross,' Jean explained, guardedly.

'Mary's resting,' whispered Madge. 'It's the first sleep she has had since . . . it would be a shame to disturb her now.'

'It's OK, I'll just slip through into the house and wait for her to wake up.' Jean picked up her valise and would have continued down the path had Madge not thrust her bulk through the sparse hedging and stood, arms akimbo, blocking her way.

'Won't you come into my place and have a cup of tea?' It was a command rather than an invitation.

Jean decided there was nothing to be gained by a confrontation. Placing her bag on the veranda step, she followed Madge through the hedge into the neighbouring yard.

They sat in her dimly lit parlour, its blinds drawn down against the afternoon sun. The clinking of china and the constant murmur of insects were the only sounds to be heard as the two women eyed one another over the rims of their teacups.

At last Madge could contain her curiosity no longer.

'Funny thing,' she observed, 'how people can live for years in a spot like this without any visitors from the outside world until someone dies . . . then suddenly the place is swarming with relatives. They seem to come up out of the woodwork!'

'Surely it is a sign of true family solidarity?' Jean replied, catching the unpleasant drift of Madge's observation.

'Or a desire to see what might be gained from it!' she said, triumphantly. 'Most folks out here,' she continued, 'have come to get away from their families . . . if they had wanted them all flocking round, they would never have left home in the first place.'

'Who other than myself has come flocking around, as you put it?' Jean was trying very hard to control her temper.

'Oh, you're just the first,' said Madge, nodding her head, knowingly.

'Look,' Jean retorted, 'I don't know who you are, or what gives you the right to speak to me in this manner, but I will tell you this:

I have been sent by Doug's mother to persuade Mary to return with me to the family farm where she will be well looked after. Thank you for the tea. I think it will now be in order to announce my presence to my sister-in-law, don't you?'

Without waiting for a reply, she marched out of the house and down the path to Madge's front gate. She did not turn her head when she heard a chuckle from the porch.

Will McKenzie, who had been snoozing in the shade beneath the parlour window, had overhead the exchange. When Madge, red-faced and angry, followed the retreating figure of her visitor out on to the porch, he called out sharply: 'It's nothing to do with you, girl. Let it go.'

'What am I gonna do if Mary leaves?' she demanded, desperately. 'There's only a few illiterate farm wives and a bunch of Abos left in Keningo now. Who'm I gonna' talk to when she's gone?'

'There's always me.' The old man grinned through his bush of iron-grey whiskers.

The woman turned and looked at him, noted the sparkle in his bright eyes and caught his infectious good humour.

'Why, you silly old bugger,' she laughed, 'you're no substitute for Mary McGillivray!'

She gave him a quick peck on the forehead and as she turned away he slapped her bottom, hard.

'There,' he called after her, 'one of those is worth a whole parcel of women's talk!'

Strangely elated, Madge hummed to herself as she gathered the tea things and carried them into the kitchen.

Mary appeared pleased to welcome her visitor.

'Jean, my dear, it's good to see you.' She pecked her on the cheek and led the way into the house.

'Anne wanted to come herself,' Jean explained, placing her valise in the middle of the living-room floor, 'but John has not been so well lately and I think she is afraid to leave him too long alone.'

'Of course,' Mary replied. 'I understand.' She turned her back as she continued, 'It's not as though it will be a proper funeral . . . poor Dougal. I wish I might have seen him once more . . . to say goodbye.' The tears which had been bottled up for days suddenly and inexplicably flooded out. Jean ran to Mary, gathering her in her arms, and led her gently through into the bedroom.

Mary sat down on the bed as Jean chafed her hands, ice cold despite the heat of the day.

'Why don't you lie down for a while?' she suggested presently. 'Can I make you a cup of tea?'

Mary, still blinded by her tears, nodded bleakly and allowed Jean to remove her shoes and help her to slide on to the bed.

'I have tried so hard not to let go,' she sobbed. 'Doug hated any display of emotion. It would have been easier with someone to talk to . . .' she tailed off. In that moment she became fully aware that she was now alone. With a chill calm she continued, 'He and I discussed everything . . . what we had done during the day . . . all the gossip of the village. We talked about the children and our plans for the future. We were going to Adelaide next month to see Flora . . .' She stopped for a moment, despairing at the memory of yet another tribulation. 'She has already sailed for France by now.' Again the tears flowed freely. Shoulders shaking with her sobbing, Mary buried her face in the pillows and wept until, drained of all emotion at last, she fell into a fitful sleep.

Jean was impressed by the degree of comfort which the McGillivrays had managed to achieve during their time at Keningo. The house was lined, walls and ceilings, with planks of jarrah wood, which had been planed smooth and polished with beeswax until they glowed. Neatly embroidered cloths covered tables and mantleshelf, and bright rag rugs were strewn over the floorboards. Pretty cushions in a variety of hues gave an air of cheefulness to the heavy furniture, which had seen better days.

She had made some tea and sat for a long time on the veranda where she could enjoy the delightful garden which Mary had created out of a dusty yard. The afternoon was hot. Perspiration was coursing down her face, the scent attracting myriads of flies. She got up and went inside, pulling the screen door to behind her.

What she really wanted was a proper wash.

She had discovered the second bedroom, where Flora's childhood possessions were much in evidence, and unpacked her few belongings. Now she looked around for a towel.

'There is a shower out on the back porch.'

Startled, Jean turned to find Mary standing in the doorway. Her eyes were red and swollen but she was smiling a watery smile and had clearly recovered her composure. 'I expect you would like a wash after your journey,' she added.

Jean required no second invitation. As she stood beneath the cistern and pulled the cord which released a fine spray of warm water, she realised that she had underestimated Keningo. This was as civilised an arrangement as she had seen, even in the house of Mrs Savery.

As the water washed away her travel stains, Jeanie thought about her confrontation with the strange woman next door. Perhaps she was right in suggesting that Mary might not wish to be dragged away from her home? It was obvious that she and Doug had put a great deal of effort into making the house comfortable. The best memories were made of such endeavours. Mary might prefer to remain where she had been happy. She resolved not to be in too much of a hurry to pass on the message from Anne; Mary should be encouraged to make decisions about her future only after she had rested properly.

Jean could see that although Mary was doing everything required of a good hostess, her mind was constantly elsewhere. Conversation was difficult because to every one of her queries Mary's answers were monosyllabic. Finally Jean gave up all idea of holding a conversation, continuing to talk without expecting any response from her companion.

'We have had a record yield from the last shearing,' she recalled. 'Considering that John had only a half dozen roustabouts and about the same number of Aborigines to do the work, they have done wonders. Anne's dairy products are selling well in Southern Cross, and once we can get in a proper refrigeration plant at the station, there's no knowing where that will lead. What we need now is a good electrician to build the plant and keep it operating for us and to equip the dairy with an electric milking machine.' She glanced up, hoping to see some sign that Mary had been listening, but she was sitting motionless staring into the fire-box, whose embers had died to a dull red glow.

Hoping to elicit some more positive action, Jean jumped to her feet. 'Shall I stoke up the fire?' she asked. 'We could have a cup of tea.'

Wordlessly, Mary went to the sink to fill the iron kettle. As Jean placed the coals and wood, and watched yellow flames spring up from the embers beneath, she smiled to herself. Her sister-in-law might not appear to be hearing what was said, but she was listening all the same.

'John has such ambitious plans for Kerrera once the boys come home after the war. He sees a whole lot of young men and their families coming out to Australia to find a new life, now that they have experienced the excitement of travelling to other lands.' Jean paused to sip her tea, and glanced up to see that Mary's face was at last showing some expression.

'He is planning a proper little town, with its own church and a hospital. If the government carries out its promises to provide returning soldiers with a parcel of land and a house, that is how we shall get our community. A larger population will require shopkeepers, builders, engineers, every kind of trade you can think of. It is all so exciting.'

'You will have to have a school.' The words were whispered, but Jean heard them, clearly.

'The school is the first priority,' she confirmed. 'In fact, if there was someone suitable to set it up, we could find at least thirty children to fill it, even today.'

'Were you not a governess yourself?' Mary asked.

'There is a world of difference between keeping a couple of unruly girls under some kind of control, and fully educating the young people of a whole community,' Jean declared. 'Anyway, my place is on the farm, keeping things going for Jack so that everything is in order when he comes home . . .' She realised she had made an unpardonable gaffe. After all, Mary's husband would never come home – what a cruel thing to have said! She continued, hurriedly.

'I was born a farm girl, and I love the work. Besides, John is no longer fit enough to do more than oversee the men, and Anne cannot shoulder the whole burden of the work at home on her own.'

'How is little Ellen?'

For the first time Mary was showing an interest in their conversation. Eagerly, Jean pounced upon her favourite subject.

'She is walking very well now – in fact she gets about far too easily for her own safety. Sometimes we are obliged to tie her to the veranda rail, just to make sure she doesn't wander off across the stockyard on her own. If it wasn't for her bodyguard, we would never be able to take our eyes off her.'

'Bodyguard?' Mary raised her eyebrows, questioningly.

'Vicky . . . Jack's old sheep-dog. She is partially blind in one eye, and far too rheumaticky to go after the mob, but she won't let anything or anybody near her treasure, and when the baby is toddling about, she herds her into the safe places as though she was a sheep!'

At the vision of Vicky herding babies, Mary had to smile.

'Let's hope Jack gets home soon,' she observed. 'A child needs brothers and sisters.'

'Yes,' Jean agreed, allowing her thoughts to wander to her little house under the gum trees beside the creek. She yawned and stretched her arms. 'I think I shall just have to go to bed,' she said. 'What about you? Do you think you will sleep tonight?'

'I hope so.' Mary smiled up at her. 'I feel more relaxed now than I have for days.'

Jean stood up, gathering the cups and carrying them into the kitchen.

'Good night, Jean,' Mary called after her, 'and . . . thank you for coming. You don't know how much it means to me to have you here.'

'We'll talk some more tomorrow,' Jean replied. 'Good night!'

Mary sat staring into the embers for a long time before turning in. She had been to Kerrera and could easily envisage the farm, the buildings and the acres of land stretching away to the horizon. It was a little greener than Keningo. John had found water enough on his territory to grow sufficient fodder for cattle as well as sheep; even his hopes of growing the Scottish strain of barley had begun to be fulfilled. Each year the yield had been improved slightly, as John saved seed only from the strongest plants. The crop grew very much more sparsely than in Scotland, and the stems produced only short straw for which they could find little use, but the grains were improving.

She remembered how Doug had told her of John's ambition to brew his own ale from the barley, and how he hesitated to put the proposition to Anne in case she disapproved. Doug had assured him that his mother would almost certainly go along with the idea. Like many Scottish matrons of the day, she knew more than a little about brewing herself. Mary thought that maybe she would be able to help them with that enterprise. Although of strictly Presbyterian upbringing, she herself knew something of the art.

She tried to picture the little town which Jean had described, imagining its buildings standing either side of the highway on the edge of John's land. As the population grew and the area became prosperous, she could imagine the building of more prestigious houses and municipal offices, perhaps a library and a sports stadium. The perfect place for her children to raise their families. A place where they would be happy to remain. There would be parks and gardens, she thought, and suddenly realised that she was herself immersed in the dream and wanted, more than anything, to be a part of it.

'This school,' Mary raised the subject, as they sat over their breakfast the following day, 'is there a suitable building which might be used . . . just for a start?'

Jean had not expected quite such a rapid response to her suggestion of the previous evening.

'I don't know.' She floundered a little. 'We could very probably clear one of the barns, but there are no desks or anything to make it into a schoolroom.'

'That's not really a problem,' said Mary. 'I brought with me from Scotland a couple of crates of equipment which were given me by the slate quarrying company, from the schoolroom on Eisdalsa. Furniture is easily manufactured. The people here managed desks and benches without any difficulty and I have everything else that would be needed. All we would want would be some kind of a building.'

For some time during the long night, she had given thought to her Keningo school. It had been made very clear that the State was not going to agree to a mixed race school. If her application to the Education Board had done anything at all, it was to alert the authorities to the need for a properly established reservation for the Aboriginal tribes of the area. This would of course include a school and a clinic, both of which would have to be organised under the aegis of the Aboriginal Welfare Board. Mary, with no knowledge of Aboriginal culture and unable to speak the language of the tribes, would not be a suitable candidate to run such a school. At the same time, it was clear that the few white children remaining at the settlement did not warrant the establishment of a proper white school. These children would be expected to learn by correspondence course, until they were old enough to go away to the city to finish their education. Mary could see that her equipment, brought with so much enthusiasm from Eisdalsa, might serve a better function at Kerrera Station.

'Do you think that they would allow me to run the school for them?' she asked anxiously.

'Anne sent me to fetch you,' Jeanie confessed at last, 'but only if it is your wish to come and join us.' She was thinking about what Madge Bowler had said the previous day.

'There is nothing to keep me here,' Mary said, in hollow tones. 'Everywhere I turn I'm reminded of the mine which has robbed me of my husband. I believe that Doug would have wanted me to join his mother, and I'm sure that Hamish and Flora are more likely to want to settle at Kerrera than here.'

'When would you like to leave?' Jeanie asked, missing her little daughter and excited now at the prospect of returning to her.

'I'd like to leave as soon as possible,' was Mary's reply.

* * *

The memorial service was a simple affair, held in the open on the ridge of high ground beneath which Dougal McGillivray and Alfie Mallacoota were entombed.

They sang the twenty-third psalm, and because it was Dougal's favourite, the Old Hundredth. As the ceremony drew to its close, Mary stepped forward and unveiled the commemorative stone.

DOUGAL JAMES MCGILLIVRAY
1868–1916
ALFRED MALLACOOTA
1875–1916
In saving the Keningo Gold Mine from flooding, they gave
their lives.

As the large congregation began to break up, many filed past the stone to read the inscription. Mary, with Jean at her side, acknowledged the condolences bravely, trying hard to fight back the tears. Nearly everyone had gone when she was surprised to find Alfie Mallacoota's widow standing before her, solemn-faced. The black woman stepped forward and placed her arms about Mary.

'Thank you,' she said, haltingly, 'for putting my man on the stone with yours. They all right together.'

Mary was so astonished to hear the woman speaking in English that she found no words to reply.

Marty, standing at his mother's elbow, smiled. 'My mother . . . she is shy about talking in English . . . she don't try very often.'

They turned to go. On impulse Mary called the boy back.

'Marty,' she said, 'I have to go away from Keningo, but there will be a school here for you, very soon. I expect you to work very hard and complete your studies. Will you try?'

'Oh, yes, missus,' he replied, his eyes filling with tears, 'but I wish you weren't going.'

She handed him the small bible she had carried with her to the service.

'Take this,' she said, 'read a short passage every day . . . it will help you with your studies. Keep on writing your stories.'

The little face lit up with pleasure. 'Thank you, missus, I will!' he replied, and ran to catch up with the others. Almost out of sight he turned to give one last wave. Mary waved back then smiled, an embarrassed little smile. 'One is not supposed to have favourites,' she told Jean, 'but he is rather special.'

Jean made no comment. She slipped her arm through Mary's and together they took the path back into town.

They had had one of the workmen from the mine make up new packing cases for the schoolroom equipment. These had been strapped firmly into place on the huge dray which one of the farmers used to transport his produce and livestock into town. Beside them stood Mary's harmonium, the double bed which she and Doug had brought from Eisdalsa, and a few of the lighter pieces of furniture which he had either made or bought for her. The remainder of the items in the house belonged to the company, having been left behind by various former tenants, including old McKenzie himself. The battered oak bureau, in which Doug had kept his business papers, remained to be cleared. Otherwise, they were ready to set out at first light in hope of catching the Perth-bound express.

'What on earth am I going to do with all this?' Mary began to rummage in the bureau, viewing with dismay the multitude of papers stuffed into every available cubby hole and drawer. 'Most of these documents relate to the mine . . . I suppose I should leave them here for the next manager.'

There had been a message of condolence from Makepeace, but nothing had been said about what was to happen next. Mary assumed that for the time being Mr Jones would be in charge. She would tell him about the papers when she handed over the keys.

As she idly turned over the top layers of documents, her gaze fell upon a letter which had been sent by Hamish, early in his career as a soldier. Fearing that there might be other personal papers, she began to sort the material into separate piles.

It took some time to sift through the catalogues, official reports and personal documents accumulated by Doug during the past three years. At last she was able to close the lid on the material relating to the mine and concentrate on the personal papers. Apart from further letters from Anne and the children, there were two official-looking papers which required her attention.

The first was a will, written by Doug, witnessed by Dai Jones and McKenzie, leaving his entire estate to his wife. Mary was startled to find that Doug had made the will without telling her. Well aware of the dangers he was facing every day in the mine, he had left his affairs in order. Not wanting to give her cause for alarm, however, he had said nothing to Mary.

The second envelope contained a number of statements from the Bank of Western Australia in Perth. When Mary saw the amounts quoted, she gasped in surprise. An initial deposit had been quite modest, but to this had been added, from time to time, the bonuses accrued from Doug's carefully negotiated contract with the company. Australian share prices were running at record levels as a result of the prosperity engendered by the war in Europe. Sales of meat, wool and wheat on the world markets were at an all time high. Doug's investment was now worth far more than when he had started the account. Although she could hardly be described as a rich woman, Mary McGillivray could live very comfortably on what her husband had provided.

By the time that Jean had cleared away the supper things and brought in their bedtime drink, Mary was ready to tuck the documents into her valise.

'All that remains is to hand over the keys to Mr Jones and say my goodbyes to Madge Bowler and old McKenzie.' Mary cast a glance about her. 'At least it looks a sight cleaner than the day we arrived!'

She was still relating the details of her first day in Keningo when they heard the kitchen door open, disturbing the windchimes in the hall.

'Only me,' called Madge, picking her way around the packing cases which littered the hall, and baskets of crockery scattered about the living room.

'Thought I'd just pop in to say cheerio. I expect you'll be making an early start in the morning.' This was a very different Madge from the cantankerous person whom Jean had met two days before. There was a confident glow about her, something that even Mary had never witnessed in the past.

'There's also my own little piece of news.' She blushed coyly. Jean and Mary looked up, expectantly.

'Me and Will have decided to get spliced!' she cried, triumphantly. 'He's a drunken old sod at times, but there's plenty of good in him . . . anyway, there's no point in the two of us going through life alone when we could be keeping each other company, if you know what I mean.' She grinned and her good humour was contagious.

'We shall have to drink your health before we leave,' said Mary, searching through the remaining hampers. 'There was a bottle of whisky . . . ah, here it is.' She studied the label absently for a moment and explained quietly, 'Dougal put this aside so that we could toast the children at Hogmanay.' Jean, taking the bottle from her, squeezed her hand gently in a simple gesture of understanding.

'Madge, go and fetch Will,' Mary said, regaining her composure, 'I'll find some glasses.'

Jean, looking somewhat perplexed, watched Madge close the door behind her before she commented, 'You know, Mrs Bowler doesn't think much of me. She as good as suggested that I had only turned up here for what I could get out of it.'

'She was only trying to protect me in her own curious fashion,' Mary said, generously. 'She has had some hard knocks in her own life – cannot bear to see anyone put upon when they are too weak to take care of themselves. She may be a bit rough and ready but she's a kind-hearted soul. Salt of the earth is Madge Bowler, believe me. I could not have had a better friend.'

When Madge Bowler returned with her future husband, the four of them stood amongst the packing cases feeling somewhat uncomfortable: Madge and Will because they felt that their own happiness was inappropriate in the presence of their widowed friend, and Mary because she had no wish to mar their happiness with her own misfortune.

It was Jean who raised her glass in a toast.

'I hope you will both be very happy,' she said, 'and I am sure that Doug's parents would want me to invite you to visit Kerrera Station whenever you wish to come.'

Mary took a sip of whisky. The smooth spirit coursing through her veins warmed her, and suffused her with a strange feeling of well-being.

'Doug should have been here to wish you both well,' she said, and toasted them a second time on his behalf.

Chapter 24

'There.' Margaret Brown took a step back and admired the result of her labours. She wiped a hand across her forehead, leaving a smear of distemper.

'I thought it was the walls you were trying to paint white, not yourself,' laughed Millicent, returning from the scullery with a pail of water.

There was a scream of anger from outside the window. Annie, who had been putting the final touches to the blackleading of the grate, ran to the door, wiping her fingers as she did so.

'What is it, my precious?' she called. She rounded the corner of the house to see baby Stephen about to launch a little wooden boat from his perambulator, in the wake of the toy engine which already lay, missing one of its wheels, on the path.

'Oh, you are a silly little monkey,' she scolded, gathering up the child and carrying him under her arm in the way which seemed to please him most. 'If you throw away your toys, you will soon have nothing left to play with!'

She sat down upon *clach an t'seabhdail*, the stone seat beside the cottage door, and dandled him on her knee.

'You're a canny boy, Stephen.' She cuddled him affectionately. 'You know we are all excited about Aunt Elizabeth coming to see us, and you feel neglected!'

The child was clearly satisfied with the diversion which he had caused, because he now began to gurgle with pleasure at the sight of Meg Roberts's white terrier trotting along the path towards them. He stretched out a pudgy hand and the wee dog licked it, furiously.

'Hallo, Whisky,' Annie greeted him, and looked up, smiling, as

Meg herself appeared around the corner of the building.

'Here you are, Annie,' she called, puffing slightly from the climb. She settled herself down beside them on the stone bench.

'What's all the activity about?' demanded the postie once she had regained her breath. 'I saw the children playing by the harbour and they said you were up here.'

'Elizabeth and William Whylie are coming to Eisdalsa for the month of July, and they have asked me to find them a house on the island where they might stay. I decided that it was as good a reason as any to start tidying up our old home,' Annie explained. 'This is really Dougal's cottage, but I'm sure he won't mind us fixing it up. Robbie McPherson replaced a few slates where the water was getting in, but otherwise the roof is quite sound.'

There was a clanking of iron pails, a burst of laughter, and Margaret and Millicent emerged into the bright sunshine of the summer's day.

'It seems to be time for elevenses,' said Annie, placing Stephen on the grass. There had been a shower of rain earlier, but the morning sun had dried the surface of the ground and now only the occasional muddy puddle remained in low-lying places. The infant immediately turned on to his knees and took off across the grass after the retreating terrier. His Aunt Millicent, following quickly upon his heels, collected him and returned, taking Annie's seat by the door.

Soon she had Stephen contentedly searching for sea shells amongst the stones on the path.

'I don't know how you do it, Millicent,' Margaret commented, genuinely impressed. 'Little children absolutely terrify me. I have no idea how to speak to them until they are at least Wee Davy's age.'

As though on cue, Millicent's two boys, Ian and Wee Davy, came running into view across the green. The meadow grass was already long; tall thistles and the occasional bramble bush blocked their route, but no male member of the Beaton line would take the normal path when there was a more hazardous method of approach available!

Ian arrived first, his knees plastered with the uniquely black

Eisdalsa mud, while seven-year-old Davy followed behind, looking as though he had been swimming fully clothed in the harbour.

It was a good job that it was a warm day, Millicent thought. She had no spare clothes for her children.

'What on earth have you been doing?' she demanded, trying not to laugh at her little son's bedraggled appearance.

'We were building rafts,' Ian explained, casually. 'Davy's sank!'

'How many times have I told you not to play near the water when there is no one with you?' Millicent scolded, genuinely alarmed at the thought that they might have been drowned.

'We weren't alone,' Davy replied, with an injured expression, 'Baldie was helping us.'

'He got wet, too!' added Ian, triumphantly.

They were still laughing at the thought of the submerged ferryman when Annie returned with tea and scones for everyone.

When Margaret and Annabel had begun looking for suitable accommodation for the Whylies, Annie had suggested the house which had been occupied by the McGillivrays. The last of several generations of their family to live there, Dougal and Mary McGillivray had renewed the lease on their cottage before setting sail for Australia. On the closure of the slate quarries, William Whylie had negotiated a deal with the Estate of the Marquis of Stirling, by which tenants of the quarrymen's houses might purchase a long-term lease on their homes. As insurance against the failure of the Australian adventure, Dougal McGillivray had thought it prudent to pay the token sum of twelve shillings and sixpence for a thirty-year lease on the property even though it would probably remain unoccupied. The house provided a base to which the family might return if things did not work out abroad.

Knowing that Dougal would be only too pleased to have the cottage opened up and occupied for a spell, Annie with Margaret's help, had taken it upon herself to get the house cleaned and redecorated, while Millicent and Annabel supplied sufficient odds and ends of furniture to make it into a comfortable holiday retreat.

'I think that once we have put up the curtains and lit the fire, we can call it a day,' said Margaret, more than satisfied with their efforts.

'It's funny to think how the positions have been reversed,' mused Annie as they bundled the cups into the sink, and she began to wash them. 'Here am I, living in the house which Gordon McKintyre had built for Elizabeth, and here she is, about to take up residence in the cottage where I was born.'

Margaret smiled. 'It's just an example of the strange bonds which link us all,' she said. 'There is something magnetic about this island, which attracts the people who have once lived here . . . I suspect that the Beatons and the McGillivrays will not be the only families to return, even if it is only to restore themselves from time to time.

Meg Roberts popped her head inside the scullery.

'I nearly forgot to give you your letter,' she said, handing Annie an important-looking envelope.

Annie gave it a cursory glance before thrusting it, unopened, into her pocket. Manny Rosenstein's letter would have to wait until she was alone.

After the first few letters had been delivered from this source, Meg had come to accept as normal Annie's personal correspondence with some important figure in the Government, and no longer commented up the House of Commons stationery. Millicent and Margaret, on the other hand, exchanged knowing looks, but neither made any comment.

Meg bade them goodbye and continued on her way to Donnie McPherson's boat shed, while Margaret turned to close the door behind her.

'I've left the key on the mantleshelf,' she said to Annie, 'in case Elizabeth wants to use it.'

There seemed little point in locking doors on Eisdalsa . . . there was no likelihood of intruders.

'Knowing we would be busy all morning, I packed up a picnic lunch for us all,' said Annie. 'Why don't we take it to the shore? If you will push Stephen in his pram, Millicent, Ian and I will go back to the house and fetch the hamper.'

The most extensive quarrying had taken place on the western side of the island. Here the deep pits had been gouged out of the ground to depths approaching two hundred feet. A mighty wall, built of vertically placed slate blocks, had once held back the sea from the deep workings, and steam pumps had operated night and day to keep the floor of each quarry free from water.

Once the pumping had ceased it had not been very long before the water took over. Rainwater, streaming off the high ridge which bisected the island from north-east to south-west, had combined with sea water washing over the walls at the highest tides to fill the quarries. The lashing gales of five winters had, in the absence of careful maintenance by the Eisdalsa masons, succeeded in destroying parts of the sea wall, thereby increasing the volume of water entering the pits. Today, under a cloudless summer sky, the quarries were limpid pools of deepest blue, their surfaces reflecting the fluffy white clouds which scurried by in the upper atmosphere.

Along the edges of the workings, where once the constant activity of men and machinery had made a wide bare surface upon which nothing could grow, natural rock-gardens of wild thyme, stonecrop, lady's slipper and harebell had established themselves, while closer to the sea, the pink sea thrift had managed to secure a tenuous foothold even on parts of the decaying sea wall.

Below the escarpment, in the lee of a protective outcrop of whinstone, grass had begun to grow, interspersed by dense bushes of wild fuchsia, blackthorn and gorse. It was the most recent of the quarries, one which had been well away from the sea, that had succumbed most rapidly to the encroachment of natural growth. Perhaps because the mining here had been less aggressive, and because the poorer quality rock crumbled more easily, a soil deep enough to sustain heather and bracken had developed quickly, and plants grew strongly in the warm moist air. Steel tools, and anonymous piles of cast iron equipment left to rust where they lay, were camouflaged by a luscious growth of bramble and nettles, angelica and wild carrot.

The picnic party found a patch of ground where thick

hummocks of wild thyme, now in full bloom, scattered the springy rabbit-cropped turf, and provided a sweet-scented carpet on which to lie. While the woman reclined in the warm sunshine, the two older boys scrambled amongst the rocks, playing their age-old game of hide-and-seek while Baby Stephen, full of milk and rusks, slept soundly in his perambulator.

'Coo . . . eee!'

Annie started up, and Millicent shaded her eyes to see who was coming.

'They must be here already, and we're not at home to greet them!' cried Margaret, dismayed.

She scrambled to her feet and hurried towards the sound.

Morag Beaton came racing along the path. Her bright auburn hair, released the moment she had landed from the ferry and discarded her prim school hat, streamed out behind her as she ran.

Elizabeth Whylie followed, trying unsuccessfully to keep up with the child. Tall and thin, her hair now more grey than red, she wore her sixty-three years with ease. Her step was firm, and her skin glowed with health. She too had discarded her hat, and her travelling coat was slung carelessly over one shoulder. She caught Margaret in her arms and the two women hugged one another, delightedly.

'We did not expect you as soon as this!' cried Margaret.

'I know!' Elizabeth laughed lightheartedly. 'It was this little minx who had us up at such an early hour that we were able to catch the first train.' She put her arm affectionately around Morag's shoulders, as she continued, 'We pulled into Connel at twelve noon. Annabel gave us a quick luncheon and David drove us straight here by the back road.'

'Where is William?' demanded Annie.

'He and David are bringing up the luggage. Knowing how difficult things can be, we have brought with us pretty well everything we shall need by way of food.' Elizabeth accepted the glass of lukewarm lemonade which Annie handed her.

'There's not much left of our picnic, I'm afraid, and the drink has been standing in the sun,' she apologised.

Millicent had been preoccupied with greeting her daughter.

She now shook hands with Elizabeth, her greeting formal. Unlike both Margaret and Annie, she had not received her schooling at the hands of Elizabeth Whylie. To her, the schoolteacher was almost a stranger.

'Was the train very crowded?' she enquired politely. 'There must have been quite a few people coming home for the holiday.'

'One might have expected it,' said Elizabeth, 'but apart from the children returning from boarding school, I wouldn't say that there were many holiday-makers. I don't suppose that people are finding the time, or the inclination, to travel just at present.'

'There were lots of servicemen,' volunteered Morag, excitedly. A smart uniform had begun to hold a particular fascination for her. 'There were some Australian soldiers in hospital blue, travelling to Johnstones. It was very sad. Some had lost limbs and two of them were blind. Do you think Mrs McLean would let me visit them while I'm home ... or even go up there to help sometimes?' she demanded, eagerly.

'We'll see, dear,' Millicent replied, non-committally. She was not at all sure if it would be a suitable environment for her quickly maturing daughter.

Stephen, disturbed by all the renewed activity, began to whimper. Nothing would suffice but that he should be picked up, and introduced to Morag and Elizabeth.

At last Annie set him on his feet, and proudly displayed his latest talent, which was to stagger a few steps before hesitating momentarily, and then collapsing into a sitting position with a howl of disgust. Elizabeth, noting the red cheeks and the scowling expression, began to giggle.

'He looks so like David,' she exclaimed.

The younger women gazed at Stephen, unable to see the likeness themselves, while Morag's wee brother piped up, 'He doesn't look like me, Mummy ... I don't look like that, do I?'

'Not you, ninny,' scoffed his sister. 'Mrs Whylie thinks he looks like Granddad.'

Annie, who saw no one but Stuart in her son's features, chose not to join in this light-hearted argument. Such reflections were still too painful for her.

The boys had wandered a little away from the remainder of the party.

'Are you going to show Morag our secret now?' enquired Davy, in his penetrating, piping little voice.

'Not now,' Ian scowled at his brother. He had wanted to show Morag when they were alone – after all, it was he who had found it. Now Davy had gone and spoiled his surprise.

'Show me what?' demanded Morag, coming upon them suddenly.

'Oh, nothing much . . . just a new plant I discovered while we were playing.' Ian tried to keep the excitement out of his voice.

Their grandfather had instilled in the children his deep interest in the wild flowers which grew on the island. From the time that they had each taken their first faltering steps, it had been David who guided their walks and taught them the names of the plants. As they had grown older and Morag, in particular, had begun to show an interest in becoming a physician, he had informed them of the medicinal properties in the species he described.

One sophisticated game which these children enjoyed was to see how many species they could find in flower in a specified square of turf. Such training had made keen observers of them all.

Upon Morag's insistence, Ian now led the way along a narrow path between the boulders to where one of the old engine houses, stripped of its machinery, its door and windows gone, stood gazing forlorn and sightless across the ocean.

'It's somewhere here,' Ian announced, 'I'm not going to tell you any more.'

'But what am I looking for?' his sister demanded querulously.

'Just look,' was the boy's reply, as he heaved himself on to one of the boulders and settled down to watch her.

Wee Davy would have taken his sister by the hand and led her to the spot, but Ian's commanding voice prevented it.

'You come and stand by me, little 'un,' he ordered. 'It's more fun for her to find it for herself.'

Accepting that her brother was not going to help her, Morag walked cautiously across the open ground beside the old shed, quartering the turf with keen attention. Nestling in a clump of tall grasses and hiding discreetly beneath the spreading leaves of a thick clump of pignut, she found it.

It was a single spike of reddish-purple flowers, each individual blossom a miniature replica of those exotic blooms which Mrs McLean grew in her conservatory at Johnstones. The long, strap-like leaves were faintly spotted and yellowish, in contrast with the vivid green of the surrounding grasses and freshly sprouted heather. The firm stem, tinged with the magenta colouring of the florets, confirmed the identification.

Morag experienced a moment of sheer delight as she breathed, 'An Early Purple.' She crouched down close to the wild orchid plant, knowing that it was too precious to be picked, examining every facet of the bold intruder.

'Granddad said that it would be years before we would see any orchids on the island,' observed Ian, with satisfaction. 'They never grow where people and animals will disturb them.'

'Who is there to disturb them now?' Morag observed. She turned to her younger brother. 'Now don't you go showing this to any of the McPherson children, Davy,' she instructed him. 'They will only pick it. If we leave it alone to make new corms, in a year or two it will become a clump of plants.'

They scurried back down the path to where their mother awaited them with Stephen, his perambulator stacked with the remnants of the feast.

'If you will push the pram, Morag,' suggested Millicent, 'I'll carry Stephen.'

'Where are the others?' she asked as she grabbed hold of the wooden handle and began to trundle the cumbersome baby carriage across the stony ground. Her brothers had scampered on ahead, making sure that they would not be asked to carry anything.

'Aunt Annie and Aunt Margaret have taken Mrs McIntyre to show her the cottage. I offered to take care of Stephen until they have finished explaining everything.'

'Mother, how is Aunt Annie now? Is it all right for me to talk to her about Uncle Stuart?' Morag looked back over her shoulder, noting the little frown which clouded her mother's brow.

'She seems able to cope when his name comes up in the course of an ordinary conversation,' Millicent replied, 'but I think you must rely upon your instincts as to when to mention him yourself.'

The girl remained silent and thoughtful. That she was tussling with a problem was apparent, because the next obstruction in the path was tackled with undue force. The wheels of the perambulator suddenly shot over the stone and nearly carried Morag and the pram over the edge into a small quarry to one side of the path.

'You must be more careful,' warned Millicent, catching up with her and grasping the handle, while holding the baby on the other arm, 'or you'll have it over.'

Shaken by the possibility of what might have happened, Morag pushed more cautiously until they were well clear of the diggings, and eventually the open meadow behind the McGillivrays' cottage came into view.

Once on level ground the way was easier and Morag could drop back to walk beside her mother.

'What would you do if Daddy didn't come back?' she queried, suddenly.

Millicent stopped in her tracks. So that was it. The child was worried about her father.

'Daddy will come back,' she assured her daughter. 'After all, he isn't in the front line of the fighting. The wounded soldiers are brought back behind the lines for treatment, and the doctors and nurses are kept well away from the battle.'

'Three of my best friends have lost their fathers this term,' Morag told her, in subdued tones. 'Every day I wonder, is this going to be the day that they call me into the study to tell me?' She could not suppress a little sob, and suddenly, to her dismay, Millicent realised that the girl was weeping.

Hampered as she was by Stephen, she tried to comfort her daughter by cuddling her with her free arm. Stephen, annoyed at being squeezed, thrust out a tiny fist to force his cousin away, and said something which sounded very much like, 'No!'

Morag, seeing his determined scowl, could not help smiling, even through her tears.

'Daddy will come home soon, Morag,' Millicent assured her. She wanted to believe it, herself . . . oh, how she wanted him home!

Margaret, Millicent and the children had gone away on the ferry, Elizabeth and William were settling into the McGillivray house, and Stephen had at last given up the battle against weariness, and lay sleeping in his cot. Taking the opportunity of a little peace at last, Annie withdrew Manny Rosenstein's letter from her pocket.

Unlike most of his previous communications, this was one confined to a single sheet.

. . . I fear that Daniel's death was sufficient to break the spirit even of a tough old lady like Rebecca. My mother finally succumbed to what the doctors described as a combination of grief, and heart failure brought on by her arthritis. She passed away in her sleep a month ago. Forgive me for not informing you earlier but I fear that these days there is too little time for observing the normal conventions.

Now that Overavon is without a mistress, I beseech you to reconsider my proposal, which I now acknowledge to have been too precipitate.

Having business in Fort William on the fourth of this month, I shall take the opportunity to call upon you at around noon on the fifth. My visit can be for a few hours only. I beg you to provide me with an answer this time, and pray that it will be in the affirmative . . .

Poor Rebecca, she had been a good friend to Annie and would be sorely missed. Despite her sadness, she could not help smiling at the tone of Manny Rosenstein's letter, so businesslike, so unemotional. He was not good at love letters, that was for sure.

Soon after the sinking of the *Hampshire* Manny had suggested that they should marry when a decent period of time had elapsed. A year ago Annie had been certain that Stuart had escaped drowning and would be home very soon; the suggestion that she

475

might remarry had appalled her but, wishing to spare his feelings, she had begged Manny to give her more time to consider his proposal.

What he offered her was an affection which he found difficult to express, financial security, and a chance to use her talents in whatever manner she chose. She knew that her sister-in-law thought her foolish to hesitate any longer. Manny Rosenstein could give her so much . . . a secure future for herself, excellent schooling for Stephen, a beautiful home, and even, if she so wished, the opportunity to take over from Rebecca the organisation of a business empire renowned throughout the world.

Annie cast her eyes over the room which still bore witness to the recent visit from her little nephews. Books, paper and pencils, a small collection of Davy's pebbles and several pieces of slate rock, gleaming with the iron pyrites crystals which so fascinated the children, all these lay scattered about. It would be a matter of minutes to tidy them away in the morning, but why should she bother? Manny should see for himself what it was like to have a small child in the house! If he thought that her baby was going to be confined to a nursery on the second floor of Overavon House, he was mistaken! Her sudden indignation was quite unreasonable. She had no idea how Manny would react to Stephen; she had never seen him in a normal domestic environment. In fact, she hardly knew him at all. He said that he loved her, yet whenever he had kissed her it was with the same deference he had showed to his mother. Never had there been any sign of the passion which she had come to expect from a lover.

That was grossly unfair! How could he have expressed his true feelings to a woman so recently widowed? Even Manny was not so insensitive as to display his passion when she was still in mourning.

There had been a period before her betrothal to Stuart when Manny might have considered himself the only candidate for her affections . . . why had he not made more of his opportunity then? She had always believed that his aloofness was a mask to cover his true feelings. Was she wrong? Was he in fact as dispassionate as he appeared? If so, why had he asked her to marry him? He needed a mistress for Overavon . . . someone to act as hostess in his household . . . would she become just another of his possessions? Many women would put up with such a position for the sake of the lifestyle he could offer, but not her – not Annie Beaton.

Quite determined not to make any over-zealous effort to prepare for her visitor, she strode to the door and stepped outside. It was past eleven o'clock, but at this time of the year there was hardly any real night. It was still possible to see clearly the rows of abandoned cottages nestling beside the harbour. Close by the old school room, where she and Margaret had spent so many happy days, one of the cottages was obviously occupied. No doubt the McPherson children had gone to bed late, for beams of light pierced the gloom from two small skylights in the roof. Annie thought of the reaction such a display of light would cause in the darkened streets of London or Edinburgh. Thank God there was no chance of enemy aircraft penetrating this far to the west.

On the opposite side of the green, on a raised piece of ground overlooking both the harbour and the western ocean, the McGillivray cottage was also showing a shaft of light from the open doorway. It gave Annie a warm feeling of contentment to see that particular house occupied once more. It held so many memories for her. Now it was habitable again she wondered if she should offer to move in there herself. Margaret had been most generous with her cottage, but perhaps it was time that Annie made more permanent arrangements of her own.

Shining more brightly now that the light from the setting sun had faded behind the hill, the moon rose high above the island of Lunga to the south.

What if Stuart was still alive? The old question posed itself again, as it did whenever she had a quiet moment to herself. What if somewhere out there he too was looking at that same moon and wondering about her? How could she possibly consider marriage to Manny Rosenstein when she was not convinced, even after all this time, that Stuart was dead?

'Not in bed yet, Annie?'

Elizabeth Whylie had come up beside her without her noticing.

'I would have thought you would be too weary to be wandering about at this time of night,' observed Annie. 'You have had a tiring day.'

'So have you,' was Elizabeth's rejoinder, 'you must all have worked like Trojans to get the house so spick and span. It is very comfortable . . . thank you for all your efforts.'

'It's wonderful to have you both back on the island,' said Annie. 'Much as I love it here, there are times when I yearn for some intellectual conversation.'

'How did you manage through the winter months?' Elizabeth enquired, squatting on the low stone wall which surrounded the cottage.

'It was no problem, because Stephen was so tiny. He was quite content to eat and sleep most of the time. Next winter it will be more difficult . . . I can see that he will either be constantly muddy and soaking wet or screeching with boredom because he can't get out of the house!'

'Do you see yourself living anywhere else in the future?' Elizabeth asked. 'Have you thought, for instance, of resuming your career?'

'Oh, yes, I have thought about it.' Annie's short laugh had a ring of cynicism about it. 'Can you imagine any lawyer's chambers accepting as a member of their staff a widow with a toddler to support?'

'There will be a shortage of experienced lawyers when the war is over,' Elizabeth assured her. 'Who knows to what lengths employers will be forced to go in order to get staff?'

Annie felt that here was the one person in whom she could confide.

'I have had a proposal of marriage,' she said, quietly.

Elizabeth turned to look at her. She did not, as would Millicent or even Margaret, express surprise or pleasure at the news.

'I don't know what to do.' Annie was glad of the gloom for she felt a familiar prickling behind the eyes and did not want Elizabeth to think that she could not control her emotions.

'I understand.'

Elizabeth was the one person Annie knew who would appreciate her dilemma. Her first husband, Gordon McIntyre, had drowned at sea during a storm thirty-six years before. She had remained a widow for thirty of those years, only agreeing to marry William Whylie when they were both about to leave Eisdalsa.

'Do you regret all those long years of widowhood now?' asked Annie.

'I found fulfilment in my work,' Elizabeth explained, 'and I thought that there could never be another love as intense as that which I had felt for Gordon. I did not think it fair to anyone else to offer them second best. William has shown me that it is possible to love more than once, deeply and even passionately. Yes, looking back, I can see that there were many wasted years. I was lucky to have a very patient suitor.'

Annie gazed into the night sky, making no further comment. What Elizabeth had said had explained her reasons for keeping William waiting for so long, but it did not help Annie with her own dilemma. She knew that she was irrational on the subject of Stuart's death, and had long ago ceased to express her belief that he was still alive for fear that the family would think her unhinged. Surely she should have experienced some feeling of loss, of separation? But she had felt nothing – other than the conviction that one day he would return.

'I had almost forgotten what the nights were like up here,' Elizabeth sighed. 'I don't know how we ever managed to tear ourselves away.'

'I am sure that Mother would be happy for you to come and stay any time,' Annie told her.

'William is feeling the effects of his work more and more these days,' Elizabeth said, and Annie noted the hint of anxiety in her tone. 'He is really too old to continue with his responsibilities at the Munitions Works. The result of Miss Smith's tribunal hearing upset him greatly. He seems to feel in some way responsible for the outcome.'

Three months after Stephen's birth, Sally Smith had been notified that the tribunal did not accept that the Annan Munitions Works was in any way responsible for her injury, and that she was not therefore entitled to a disability pension. Annie could see the words on that document even now:

In view of the fact that the injury occurred in the course of work on behalf of His Majesty's Government, however, the Committee has agreed to award an exgratia payment of fifty pounds (£50). This sum is not negotiable. No right of appeal exists in these circumstances . . .

Fifty pounds! For how long was Sally expected to live on such a paltry sum? Had it not been for the generosity of the Beatons, and Mr Brown at the Oban Hospital, it might all have been swallowed up in medical fees.

William had written letters of protest, of course. Annie had pursued the matter through the WSPU, but it seemed that nothing could be done.

For as long as Johnstones remained a convalescent home, Sally would have a job with Katherine McLean, but it provided no more than a roof over her head and a few shillings in her pocket. The war would end one day, and then jobs would be much more difficult to come by. Without hope of normal employment, and knowing that no one was likely to propose marriage, Sally's prospects for the future were grim.

'She was very kind to me when I was ill,' observed Annie, thoughtfully. 'She still comes over to the island whenever she has any free time. Stephen adores her. I just wish that I could afford to employ her as a nursemaid, but as it is I have barely enough to live on myself.'

The Admiralty had continued to pay Annie a married woman's allowance rather than a widow's pension. David had made enquiries, and it had been suggested that since there was little difference in the amounts payable, and since there was no absolute proof of her husband's death, Annie would do best to continue to accept the money she was given without pursuing the matter. It was strange advice, and had they not all been so distraught at the time, perhaps David would have made further representations, but he did not. Naturally, he and Annabel would never allow their daughter-in-law to go short, but Annie was an independent creature. She would have to make proper provision for herself before long. Manny Rosenstein would be one solution, of course, but financial security did not seem to Annie sufficient justification for forsaking her dedication to Stuart's memory.

Seeing William standing at the door of their cottage, peering into the gloom for a sight of his wife, Elizabeth bade Annie good night and made her way up the hill.

The lifeboat stood off on the lee side of the burning vessel. At a signal from the bridge, the helmsman leaned on the tiller while four of the more able bodied of the men bent to the oars, pulling the boat away past the stern until they were in full view of the German submarine. Its occupants might be the most severely wounded and least combative members of the *Dolores*'s crew, but they were all part of the skipper's plan.

Despite the cloak of secrecy, the British Q-ships, armed merchantmen equipped with the means to blow a submarine clean out of the water, had become legendary on the high seas. The Commander of U-171 was a veteran of the war in the South Atlantic and had good cause to be suspicious of any merchant ship sailing unescorted in these waters. No longer did he surface before approaching within artillery range of such a cargo vessel, for experience had taught him to fire his torpedoes first, no matter how harmless his target might appear.

The torpedoes had struck without warning, killing half the *Dolores*'s crew and injuring many more. She had begun to take in water at once and was already sinking steadily by the head.

On ordering the wounded into the lifeboat, the skipper had initiated one of a number of well-rehearsed plans. They had to convince the U-boat's captain that they were abandoning ship in order to lure him within range of their guns.

He was drawing closer, perhaps with the intention of boarding his prize in search of water and much-needed food supplies. There was not much time left. *Dolores*'s main deck was already awash . . .

The conning tower of the submarine loomed large in the sights of the high-velocity cannon mounted aft of the bridge. Able-seaman Charlie Naughton lifted his head for an instant, wiped away a trickle of blood from the deep gash above his right eye and returned his attention to the enemy vessel. Behind him, Chalky White craned his head to catch a glimpse of the skipper's signal from the smoking bridge. There it was, an almost imperceptible flutter of the old man's yellow bandanna. He leant forward and tapped Charlie on the shoulder while at the same time releasing the canvas awning which disguised their weapon.

The first shell landed at the foot of the submarine's conning tower at the very moment when her folding dinghy was being launched over the side. It tore into a group of German sailors preparing to go overboard, and blew a hole in the superstructure. A bloody rosette burst across the side of the conning tower as one sailor disintegrated where he stood and the remainder were hurled into the water. At close range Charlie continued to fire round after round until the submarine's hull, torn open like a can of beans, was burning from end to end.

Dolore's final shell landed upon the forward hull of the submarine, tearing a huge black gaping hole in her deck and scattering the crew of the German's only artillery weapon, but not before they had managed to get off one round themselves. Charlie's moment of glory ended abruptly as the German's shell landed with devastating accuracy, consigning the *Dolores*'s one remaining weapon, Charlie Naughton and Chalky White to oblivion.

The remaining German sailors poured from every hatchway on to the deck of the sinking submarine, leaping into the sea in their blind panic. Some were seen to swim away from her side as the hull upended, her single screw pointing heavenwards for an instant before she slipped under the waves. The shouts of men in the water gradually subsided as one by one they gave up the struggle to survive.

The skipper of the *Dolores* slumped down below the bridge canvas. The wound in his side had caused him to lose a great quantity of blood and he was fast losing consciousness. The bodies of his crew members lay strewn about the deck. His own guns had ceased firing, but he was too weak to find out for himself what had happened to them. The deck was listing at a crazy angle, making it difficult for him to struggle even into a sitting position. Agonising shafts of pain shot through his body as he moved. Mercifully the effort caused him to faint away. When he came to he found that he was staring at the familiar features of his navigation officer.

The dead man's hair was thrown back, revealing a lurid scar where during an earlier skirmish a piece of shrapnel had torn into his skull, missing his brain by a whisker. The doc had saved his life on that occasion, but even he could do nothing for the poor beggar this time.

With a concerted effort he stretched out his hand and closed his friend's sightless eyes.

It seemed strange to hear water sloshing about right up here on the bridge. Waves were lapping at the rail and the deck beneath him was awash . . .

The occupants of the lifeboat felt no remorse as they watched the submarine go down. Without doubt she had sent many defence-less British mariners to their death, and there was not a man on board her who did not deserve to die.

As the merchantman prepared to follow her enemy to the sea bed, they watched in vain for any sign of their comrades still on board. When she finally disappeared beneath the waves not a soul was seen to leave the vessel.

Of the fifteen men in the lifeboat only three were not seriously wounded. The bo's'n was the only experienced seaman. The other fit rating was a sick berth attendant whose responsibility it had been to muster the wounded on the after deck of the *Dolores* and supervise their disembarkation. Of the *Dolores*'s officers the only one to have escaped injury was the ship's doctor.

Chapter 25

Towards the end of March 1918 the German spring offensive in France and the Low Countries had caused the armies of the Western Allies to retreat eastwards until the Channel ports themselves were threatened. Valuable ground, hard won the previous year, had been swallowed up by Ludendorff's crack battalions. Even Cambrai, won by the shock advance of Britain's first offensive employing tanks, in November 1917, had fallen once more into enemy hands.

With the Americans poised to enter the fray, Earl Haig was convinced that now was the time to make a final stand against the advancing tide. He set up his defences on a line from Arras in the north to Noyon, sixty miles to the south.

The British forces, comprising a mixture of Commonwealth and UK troops, were to defend the northern section, while the French and the as yet untried US regiments took the south of the line.

The fourth Australian Division had moved north from Noyon to a position on the south bank of the River Scarpe, while on the north bank, a division of the Argyll and Sutherland Highlanders was entrenched.

Settling his burden into the most comfortable position, Captain Hamish McGillivray moved swiftly to the water's edge and slipped into the reeds. Once clear of the bank he began to swim, long strong strokes, his movements only partially hampered by the extra weight.

Once in midstream, the strong current tugged at the unwieldy shape made by their combined bodies and Hamish could feel himself being carried further and further down stream.

There was a shout from the bank behind them: '*Halten*!'

Hamish paid no attention. He concentrated on the far side of the river, and kept on swimming.

A shot rang out and the bullet landed in the water, close enough to splash him in the face. He ducked instinctively, surfacing almost immediately with the realisation that if anyone was going to get hit it would be Jack rather than himself. He had no way of shielding his stepbrother.

The next fusillade was answered miraculously from the opposite bank. Rifles and then a field gun opened fire from somewhere to the north of him. He heard the shells whistling overhead and landing among the German troops and prayed that the rest of his men had got well away downriver by now. It would be an ignominious death for them to be slaughtered by the shellfire of their allies.

The exchange of gunfire had become more desultory now as the current carried them out of range of the southern bank. Shells continued to travel overhead from the British guns but the Germans had ceased firing, engaged no doubt in clearing up the mayhem left behind by Hamish's Australian mine-laying section.

In an interval between shots he thought he heard shouting and paused briefly to see a row of soldiers, lining the river bank and cheering him on.

When he was no more than ten yards from the shore, several figures leapt into the water and their arms relieved him of his burden.

'C'mon, son . . . you can do it!' The Scottish voice was like music to his ears. He felt himself grabbed by strong arms and hauled up the muddy bank and on to the grass. As he lay panting, trying to get his breath, he looked up into a smiling face which was crowned by the familiar black bonnet of the Argyll and Sutherland Highlanders.

Hugh Beaton took off his mask and threw it disconsolately into the bin. Another precious life lost. This one looked as though he was still too young to have left his school playing field. The orderly gave a signal and two stretcher bearers stepped forward to remove the corpse.

'Next!'

On the table before him was laid a soldier wearing the uniform of an Australian Sergeant Major.

Orderlies struggled to remove the soldier's soaking wet clothing, cutting away one trouser leg to reveal a badly shattered tibia and fibula. The foot was missing.

Hugh loosened the tourniquet hastily applied on the river bank. The lower leg was already turning a sickly grey colour, while higher up there were definite lines of reddening following the course of the major vessels, an unmistakable indication that gangrene was setting it. 'How long has this man been waiting?' Hugh demanded, angrily. Had the sergeant been brought in earlier, it would have been a matter of cleaning off the stump and leaving it to the prosthesis people to build him a new foot. Now there was nothing for it but to take the whole lower leg.

He tilted the light to shine directly on to the wounded man's face. Beneath the grime and blood he recognised his old school friend.

'Good God!' Hugh exclaimed. 'I know this man . . . he comes from my home village in Argyll . . . where's his tag?'

They fished about amongst the sodden undergarments and found the little metal disc on which was stamped the sergeant's name and number.

85972
Sgt. MAJOR JOHN McDOUGAL

'That's him right enough,' Hugh confirmed. 'Jack McDougal . . . what a coincidence!'

At the sound of his own name, Jack opened his eyes. He seemed puzzled.

'What's happening?' he demanded. 'Did we send them about their business?'

'I don't know, old son,' Hugh replied, calmly. 'You have been brought to a casualty clearing station on the north bank of the

River Scarpe. This is an attachment of the Second Division, Argyll and Sutherland Highlanders.'

'The Argylls . . .' Jack closed his eyes content with that.

'I'm afraid you have already lost your foot, Jack,' Hugh persisted, 'and the infection has gone too far to save the lower leg. I shall have to amputate.'

The realisation of what Hugh had said stung his patient into full consciousness. Jack's eyes opened abruptly.

'Christ, Doc,' he cried out, 'how do I ride a horse with only one leg?'

'You might surprise yourself,' Hugh replied, noncommittally. He nodded to the orderly who lowered the ether mask over Jack's face.

'It seems that there is a big flap on, all along the front.' Dr Frances Ivens spiked the flimsy telegraph form and surveyed her team with a worried expression. 'The High Command are insisting upon clearing all front-line hospital units in preparation for a major assault. We are going to have to empty as many beds as possible, at a moment's notice.'

Shortages of supplies, staff and transport had caused Dr Ivens great concern for many months past. There seemed to be no way in which she could disengage herself from the quagmire of military bureaucracy. It was not that there was any lack of support for the Scottish Women's Hospital scheme. Reporters from the national press had found, in units such as this at Royaumont in northern France, a source of endless interest. At times their high praise for the work of the women doctors, nurses, orderlies and drivers was an embarrassment, for it began to cause friction with the committees at home, both in London and Glasgow. The staff at Royaumont were accused of courting publicity at the expense of their more immediate obligations, and while the press reports increased the flow of financial support from the public, the funds raised were, Dr Ivens believed, being deliberately channelled to other spheres of operation.

She turned now to her senior driver. 'Heather, how many serviceable ambulances can we put on the road at half an hour's notice?'

Heather Brown had come to this meeting armed with a number of arguments for additional drivers and vehicles; she had not expected to be involved in another major offensive without receiving considerable additional resources.

'Despite the fact that Malcolm Hendry has been working without a break for the last fourteen hours, there are only five vehicles which are in a fit condition to be sent to the front line. Three others are suffering various forms of damage from the fearful road surfaces, and a fourth has been pierced by shrapnel and is awaiting a replacement radiator from Glasgow.'

'Only five serviceable vehicles?' Frances Ivens was dismayed to hear Heather's response.

'Are you sure that Malcolm cannot make some of the others roadworthy, even if it is only temporarily?' she demanded.

'Our biggest problem is spares,' Heather explained. 'There's a consignment waiting on the dock at Calais, but the army transport division insists that our deliveries have no priority.'

'It's a pity some of those clerks down at the docks are not made to stand in the trenches for a day or two,' observed Elizabeth Courtauld, sourly. 'They'd soon appreciate the degree of our priority then!'

Despairing, Frances could only accept her driver's assessment of the situation. 'Well, Heather, you must tell Malcolm to do his best.' Frances was reluctant to push these dedicated people any further, the strain had begun to tell upon them all. 'You are to report to the Second Argyll and Sutherland Highlanders Division headquarters at Roeux. Your convoy will leave at 1800 hours. The casualty clearing station is very close to the front line but, with luck, the last part of your journey will be under cover of darkness. Colonel Leekie has agreed to post men on the road about five miles from the camp, to guide your vehicles in.'

As Heather prepared to leave, Elizabeth Courtauld placed a hand on her arm. 'Good luck, Brownie,' she whispered. 'We'll be waiting for your safe return.' Heather gave her an appreciative grin. 'See you in the morning,' she replied.

At the garage, she found Malcolm stretched out beneath the chassis of her own vehicle.

'Don't tell me you've found something wrong with Emmeline now?' she cried, exasperated.

He emerged, rubbing the perspiration from his brow with a greasy hand.

'You need a new clutch,' he replied. Heather's look of concern disturbed him. She was overtired, as were they all, but there was more than weariness in her strained face. 'Do you know what to do if she fails on a steep hill?'

'Turn her round and go up backwards?' Heather responded automatically.

'Oh . . . you'll do!' The dour Scotsman found himself grinning, too. He had never met a woman like Heather Brown for knowing about motoring. The other girls were good enough drivers, but Heather always had the edge.

'I need every serviceable vehicle ready for operation by 1800 hours,' she told him. 'How many will that be?'

Before Malcolm had time to reply, they were interrupted by the arrival of another of the drivers.

'Malcolm, is Christobel ready for her test run now?' Lavinia Beauchamp demanded as she sailed into the workshop. Although all the drivers wore uniform of a singularly unflattering nature, Lavinia still managed to look as though she were on the catwalk at a Parisian fashion show. At the neck of her dark green tweed jacket she wore a silk scarf of rainbow colours, which was draped fetchingly across one shoulder. Her hat, which owed something to the style of the ANZACs bush hats, had its brim curved upwards to one side and held in place by a brooch which Heather knew to be set with real diamonds. Lavinia's driving had been learned in her father's 45 h.p. Daimler, travelling around his Perthshire estates.

There was no doubt that the conditions at Royaumont had come as something of a culture shock to this pampered daughter of a Scottish textile baron. Miss Beauchamp had made no attempt to adjust to her surroundings; on the contrary, she made very effort to adjust her surroundings to suit herself. Her fond parent seemed to be influential enough to be able to keep her supplied with the most extraordinary luxuries. Hampers appeared regularly from

Jenner's of Princes Street, containing fine wines and items of food which many of the girls had never even heard of, let alone tasted. She might be obliged to sleep on a cot constructed of canvas and wood like the rest of them, but Miss Beauchamp did so between silk sheets!

Strangely this flamboyant character, who might well have been the cause of sharp divisions between the girls, created quite the opposite effect. For Lavinia was not in the least bit selfish with her little luxuries. She made every delivery of mail an excuse for a party, and life for the ambulance drivers of Royaumont would have been a pretty miserable affair had it not been for her and her food hampers.

Malcolm indicated Lavinia's vehicle, its bonnet propped open, its radiator stripped out so that it looked like a toothless whale.

'Oh, poor Christobel,' she cried, 'what have you done to her?'

The naming of the ambulances after prominent Suffragettes had been Heather's idea. Lavinia's own particular Pankhurst was going nowhere that day.

'You caught some shrapnel on your last trip,' explained Malcolm, 'her radiator just won't hold water. I have a new one coming, but it seems to have been held up on the way.'

'Oh, you silly boy,' she exclaimed, making the young man blush to the roots of his hair, 'you should have told me. Daddy would have seen that it had priority.' She sat on an upturned oil drum, swinging her leg so as to reveal not only a dainty ankle but the full extent of her elegantly booted calf. 'I'll tell you what,' she exclaimed at last, 'I'll send the old Daddykins a wire . . . I bet that'll get things moving.'

'I don't think that would be a good idea at all,' Heather decided, firmly. 'Mrs Jack is responsible for all requisitions. I think it best if we leave it to her, don't you?' Her exasperated expression caused Malcolm to smile.

'What you *can* do, Lavinia,' she continued, 'is to muster all the drivers in the mess hall, right away. We have an hour to prepare for a big evacuation of wounded from the front line.'

'But I haven't got anything to drive,' Miss Beauchamp complained.

'Sophia over there will make the trip if you treat her gently,' Malcolm assured her. 'The brakes are a bit dodgy, but if you use your gearbox for slowing down, you should be fine.' The vehicle's usual driver, Susan Forsyth, had been wounded by shrapnel the week before but there had been no replacement driver sent from headquarters in Glasgow.

'Oh, you are a dear,' Lavinia enthused, grabbing the young mechanic by the shoulders and landing a kiss on his greasy brow.

'Do remember, miss, the slower you are travelling, the easier it is to stop!'

Only Lavinia had ever been able to coax more than thirty miles an hour out of any of the Albions. Unfortunately, she was inclined to do just that, on every possible occasion.

'We shall be driving in convoy,' Heather assured him, 'and I will be taking the lead vehicle.' Lavinia looked a trifle disconcerted, but the mechanic was obviously relieved. If any of the girls ran into trouble in one of his vehicles, he could not help holding himself responsible.

There had been a distinct change in the weather. The sky had become overcast during the period of their preparation for departure, and dusk had turned to darkness before Heather, in the lead ambulance, spotted a weak torch light waving from up ahead of her. Her own acetylene headlamps were carefully shielded from the night sky in the hope that the convoy would not be spotted by enemy aircraft on a late patrol. She drew to a halt.

A British soldier, wearing the familiar bonnet of the Argylls, stepped out into the thin beam from her headlights, holding up his hands. He approached the cab uncertainly, clearly disconcerted to discover that the driver was a woman.

'Convoy of ambulances from the British hospital at Royaumont, bound for the dressing station at Roeux,' said Heather, crisply.

'Colonel Leekie's compliments, ma'am,' was the reply. 'I have been instructed to allocate one man to each of your drivers, to act as guard.'

'Thank you, Corporal.' Heather smiled disarmingly, pleased to see the worried expression on the man's face dissolve into a smile.

The corporal turned to address his men, who had by now emerged from the dark shadows at the edge of the road.

'All right then,' he barked, 'the first six men, one to each vehicle. Devlin, watch your bloody language in front of the young lady!'

The squaddie so addressed responded with a loud, 'Yes, Corp,' and swung himself into the cab of the second ambulance, settling himself beside Lavinia Beauchamp. She had, as usual, managed to stall her engine in coming to an abrupt halt. Smiling sweetly at the young squaddie, she said, 'Would you be a darling, and give her a little turn on the handle?'

Melting completely under her gaze, the soldier jumped down on to the road and ran to do her bidding.

No sooner had the ambulances drawn up in a line outside the dressing station than bearers began to carry out the wounded while the orderly medical officer allocated places in the ambulances.

'Two stretchers to a wagon, and four men sitting,' he bellowed. 'Have a care there,' he shouted, as a pair of over-enthusiastic bearers nearly tipped their patient off the stretcher.

Heather climbed stiffly from her vehicle. 'My drivers need a cup of tea and a wash and brush-up, Lieutenant,' she advised him. 'It's a twenty-mile drive back to Royaumont, you know.'

'Yes, ma'am,' the officer replied, a worried expression on his face. Tony Pierce had been at Roeux only a few weeks. Fresh out of medical school, he was still feeling his way through the daily routines of front-line surgery. No one had ever told him to expect to have to deal with women in such circumstances. Anyway, there were no suitable facilities for females in the camp. 'If you'll wait there a moment,' he stammered, embarrassed by her request, 'I'll enquire of the senior medical officer.'

He disappeared, leaving one of the orderlies in charge of loading the wounded.

The officer returned in a few moments with a masked and gowned figure, his clothing spattered in blood, obviously straight from the operating theatre. He strode towards Heather, clearly annoyed at being disturbed in his work. Tearing off his mask he demanded, 'What is the problem here?'

For an instant they stared at each other, unbelieving. Then Heather exclaimed, 'Hugh!'

'Heather? What on earth are you doing here?'

The nervous lieutenant was so startled by Hugh's sudden change of manner that he dropped his notes in confusion and the entire company of bearers, and those of the wounded who were sufficiently conscious to take an interest, were amused to see the young woman throw her arms around Major Beaton and kiss him full on the lips. There was a roar of approval from all quarters which quickly died away under Hugh's icy glare.

A moment of silence followed in which his soured, weary expression was transformed into one of genuine pleasure.

His greeting was effusive. 'Heather, my dear, what a marvellous surprise!'

Heather was shocked to see how thin he was, and the deep shadows under his eyes were evidence of the low ebb to which he had fallen.

'Margaret wrote that you were in this sector,' she told him.

'I can't believe they are sending women so far forward,' declared Hugh.

'We go where we're needed,' she replied, smiling up at him.

At that moment he caught sight of the lieutenant's expression, and noted the smirks on the faces of some of the men. In a tone loud enough to carry to all those about him, he introduced Heather to his colleague.

'Lieutenant Tony Pierce, this is my niece, Miss Heather Brown,' he explained. There was a snort of disbelief from somewhere in the shadows. 'Her father is the superintendent of Oban Hospital, maybe you know of him?' That would shut them up, he thought. Many of the men came from the Oban area and Michael Brown was a noted figure in the town.

'Delighted to meet you, Miss Brown.' The lieutenant shook her hand solemnly, and excused himself to continue with his duties.

'I really am very pleased to see your convoy,' Hugh told her. 'We have two hundred men to ship out, and as you can imagine, not a lot of time to do it in.'

Even as he spoke the sound of gunfire, which until now had been a distant background accompaniment to the rumbling of her vehicle's engine, broke upon Heather's ears with a deafening roar.

'Don't worry,' he reassured her. 'Those are our guns. We are actually on the offensive at last.'

'Now,' he continued, taking her gently by the arm and leading her towards the lighted doorway of the hospital tent, 'I'll show you where your drivers can get a cup of tea and a rest while the sergeant here makes suitable arrangements for their other needs.'

He stood back to allow Heather to precede him inside, and as she did so, she was amused to hear the sergeant issuing his orders: 'Two men, at the double! Round the back of the officers' mess, one latrine, needed yesterday . . . understand? Oh, and McPhail . . . tell the quartermaster it will want a *new* canvas!'

Having settled her drivers in the canteen, with mugs of tea and plates of sandwiches, Hugh led Heather to a ward where a small section had been partitioned off for the superintendent's office. He motioned her to take the single chair, and turned up the lamp so that he could see her more clearly.

Shocked to see how much older and thinner she looked, he demanded, 'How long has your unit been in this part of France?'

'About six months,' she answered. 'We arrived just in time to participate in the November offensive, although on that occasion no one would even have considered sending us to the forward dressing stations. I suppose they have become accustomed to the idea of women drivers now . . . or maybe they are simply desperate for more ambulances. We are all of us well aware of the possible consequences, but some of us have good reason to want to make our contribution.'

He squeezed her shoulder, sympathetically. He had heard from Stuart about her association with young Rosenstein, and suspected that it had involved something more than friendship.

'You look very tired,' Heather remarked, deliberately diverting attention from herself.

'It's not so much the long hours which drag one down,' he

replied, 'but the sheer hopelessness of our task. If only I could see some good reason for all the carnage. So many enthusiastic, intelligent young men cut down . . . so many gross mutilations. They are the worst. I sometimes wonder if the boys without limbs, and those who have lost their sight or their minds, will thank me for having saved their lives. Perhaps it is kinder to let them die.'

'That cannot be right,' Heather protested. 'Nothing can be worse than losing one's life!' She thought of Dan. She would have welcomed him back, no matter what his injuries. 'Think of the wives and mothers,' she protested. 'Don't you believe that they are grateful for what you are doing to save their boys?'

'Forgive me,' he apologised, abruptly. 'A moment of inexcusable self-indulgence. I know you have very little time before you return to the hospital, and you must have a few moments' rest.' He hesitated a moment before adding, 'There is a matter that you might attend to for me. The Royaumont patients are often sent back to convalesce in Scotland, is that not so?'

'The SWH has a number of hospitals both north and south of the border,' she affirmed. 'In fact, since you left, Johnstones has become one of them.'

'I have very recently performed an amputation on an Australian engineer – not a young man. His return to normal life will depend largely upon the quality of care he receives in these next crucial weeks. The thing is . . .' He hesitated to plead a special case when so many were in dire need. 'He's an old school friend of ours from Eisdalsa . . . Jack McDougal. Perhaps you know him too?'

'Anne McDougal's stepson,' she confirmed. 'I never met him myself, but I know of him naturally. Anne often mentions him in her letters to your mother. My old boss, Mrs Laurie, is responsible for organising the distribution of patients. I will certainly see that your message is passed on to her.'

'Bless you, my dear,' he murmured, and kissed her gently on the brow. 'Take care.'

Further admonitions would be pointless, they both knew. She slipped out into the empty ward while Hugh slumped down in his chair. Reaching into an open box beside the desk, he pulled out a glass and a bottle of whisky. He poured a generous measure, and swallowed it straight down.

By the time that the Royaumont ambulances had completed their third run to Roeux it was broad daylight, and the escort to the five-mile perimeter seemed scarcely necessary. Heather dropped off the corporal who during the past few hours had become an old friend.

'Good luck, miss,' he said as he stood back away from the cab. 'Now, remember what I said. There are rumours that the Germans have broken through, somewhere near Albert. If so, it will only be a small force that far to the east. If you should find your road blocked, take a route to the north rather than the south.'

'Thanks, Ronnie.' She shook him by the hand. 'Maybe we'll meet again, in more pleasant circumstances?'

'I hope so, miss. Good luck!' He waved her on and watched as the six vehicles followed one another along the narrow, rutted road.

They had been going for nearly half an hour when Heather became aware of smoke and gunfire ahead. She drew her vehicle to a halt and went to the back of the wagon to consult the wounded sergeant who had been placed in charge of her patients.

'Do you think you could come and have a look at this, Sergeant?' she asked, putting out a hand to assist his descent over the backboard. His right arm was held rigid at shoulder height by an uncomfortable-looking splint.

'I'm sorry to disturb you,' she apologised, 'you must be very uncomfortable.'

'Glad of the exercise, miss,' he assured her. 'Now what seems to be the trouble?'

She pointed up the road. In those few minutes, a thick pall of black smoke had formed above the village, obliterating its red roofs and the elegant church spire.

'What do you think?' she asked.

The sergeant did not appear too concerned. 'Might be anything,' he said. 'We must be a long way from the German lines here. Maybe it was bombardment from the air.'

'Do you think we should carry on along this road?' she asked anxiously. She produced a map and together they pored over it, while several of the other drivers gathered round.

'There's this other road here.' He pointed out a right-hand fork, a mile or so before the village. 'If things look suspicious when we get closer, we could do a quick get away along it. One thing is certain: the Bosch won't have entered the village from the north!'

What was it the corporal had said? If in doubt, keep to the north.

'What would an army convoy do in similar circumstances?' she demanded.

'Well, for one thing, I'd do a recce,' he replied, hesitantly.

'Go on,' Heather urged him.

'Well, miss, if it was left to me, I would send a vehicle on ahead and see what happens. Then the most we are likely to lose is the one ambulance. The rest will have a chance to escape by the other road.'

Heather considered carefully what the sergeant had said. It made sense to her.

'We will distribute the wounded from one ambulance among the others,' she thought aloud. 'That way if there is any trouble, only one driver will be in danger.'

'An empty truck will be able to skedaddle out of there faster than one that's fully laden,' the sergeant agreed. 'I suggest that we drive in convoy as far as this bit of woodland here.' He pointed out a belt of trees a few hundred yards wide, bordering the road. A short distance beyond where the trees ended, the road divided with the major highway taking the left fork, straight through the village.

The convoy could remain shielded by the trees until the first wagon had approached the village in safety. If all was well, a signal would be given to the trucks behind. If not, the driver was to reverse to the fork and drive as fast as possible, taking the northern route, where once clear of the enemy she could wait for the rest of the ambulances to catch up.

'Very well,' said Heather, 'start unloading Emmeline right away.'

'Just a minute, darling,' Lavinia Beauchamp intervened, 'don't you mean Sophia?'

'I'm in charge of this convoy,' said Heather. 'I go first!'

'Well, that's really it, Heather old dear,' Lavinia drawled. 'You have the responsibility of seeing that the wounded get back to Royaumont. Besides, I'm the fastest driver!'

There was no denying that!

Heather was the first to admit that what Lavinia had said about her own responsibilities was true and was forced, for the first time, to make that most difficult of all decisions of leadership: to send another into certain danger.

When they had unloaded Sophia, and the wounded men had been redistributed, the convoy continued towards the belt of trees, reversing the vehicles in amongst the bushes at the side of the road. It was not a total camouflage, but sufficient to obscure them from a distant observation post.

Heather and the sergeant, keeping under the cover of the trees, walked to the edge of the wood to watch Lavinia's progress.

She drove at a steady twenty-five miles an hour as far as the fork. Without slackening speed or hesitating in the least, she continued on towards the village. The ambulance was nearly out of sight when the first shot rang out. They saw the flashes of gunfire before they heard the firing. Heather watched, numbed with horror, as Lavinia slammed into reverse gear and hurtled backwards along the road towards the fork. She turned at such speed that Heather, sure that she would overturn the vehicle, closed her eyes and waited for the crash. Miraculously, when she opened them again it was to see Sophia belting along the northern road, enveloped in a cloud of dust.

'What now?' Heather turned to the sergeant.

'We'll give it a few minutes . . . see if there's any sign of a pursuit. Then we'll go after her.'

They caught up with Lavinia's ambulance some miles north of the village.

By taking the right-hand fork and travelling at speed, they had managed to avoid the guns. The occupying troops were probably nothing more than a small patrol, cut off from its main body and terrified of capture by the British. Why else would soldiers of either side have fired on an ambulance which was clearly marked with the red cross?

Sophia was rear end down in the ditch, her bonnet raised to heaven as though in salute.

Heather, elated with their successful escape, was inclined to be lenient.

She approached Lavinia, who had remained in the driving seat. Unable to shift the vehicle by herself, she had presumably chosen to wait in comfort. Heather leant through the window.

'What happened?' she enquired.

'I took that last bend rather faster than I should,' Lavinia replied, bluntly.

Heather thought her friend was looking rather white and strained. 'What you did back there,' she began, 'it was bloody marvellous!' Then, when there was no response, 'OK,' she continued, 'let's see if we can get you out of here.'

In a matter of moments they had a tow rope attaching Heather's vehicle to Lavinia's front axle. Heather engaged first gear and began to move forward across the road. As the rope tightened and she opened the throttle wider there was a tremendous roar but unfortunately even the most powerful engine was useless with a slipping clutch.

Sophia remained firmly embedded in the ditch.

Heather switched off. Angus Beaton's long-ago instruction came back to her. *Backwards ... if in trouble use the reverse gear*.

She jumped down from the cab and began to wrestle with the rope attached to her rear bumper.

By now, the remainder of the drivers had gathered round and several of the more mobile soldiers had joined them, all giving their advice. Ignoring them, Heather turned Emmeline around in the road until she faced Sophia. She leant out of the truck.

'Now attach the tow rope to the front,' she instructed, selecting reverse gear. The engine roared, the clutch held without slipping, and slowly but surely Lavinia's vehicle was hauled out of the ditch.

There was a mild cheer from the onlookers and a tendency to stand around discussing the events of the past hour.

'Come on,' Heather called out. 'Let's get Lavinia's passengers back on board. It's time we were going . . .'

In a matter of moments the wounded men had been redistributed, and Lavinia, strangely silent, waited patiently for someone else to swing her engine. It was a job she rarely did for herself.

The remainder of the journey was taken at a steady twenty miles an hour, and they arrived at Royaumont without further incident in the early-evening. The girls had been on the road for twenty-four hours without rest.

Nurses and orderlies unloaded the ambulances, while drivers reported their various problems to a very relieved Malcolm.

'How did Sophia perform?' he enquired. Lavinia was usually the first to come forward with her list of complaints. Heather turned to where Sophia was parked behind Emmeline. Lavinia was still in her seat.

Sensing that something was terribly wrong, Heather ran to the door and flung it open.

Lavinia slipped sideways out of the cab into her arms.

Gently she laid the girl down in the roadway and unbuttoned her green uniform tunic. The rainbow-coloured scarf was soaked in blood.

They called for Dr Ivens, but there was nothing that she could do. Lavinia Beauchamp, shot during those few minutes outside the village, had driven for a further two hours until her task was completed. All the while she had been quietly bleeding to death.

Sally Smith had gained greatly in self-assurance in recent months. Her looks had hardly improved, despite a number of attempts by Michael Brown to graft new skin, but her kind and thoughtful nature, and her natural cheerfulness, endeared her to all who worked with her. As for the patients, once they had overcome the initial shock of her appearance, they appeared to forget about it and treated her to the same bantering and teasing as all the other girls.

One reason for her continuing improvement was her blossoming relationship with Tom Pain, the blind Australian engineer.

Unable to come to terms with his blindness, Tom had refused all attempts to help him. He rejected suggestions that he be sent to a school to learn Braille and perhaps some means of earning a living. He was equally uncooperative when they tried to teach him the basic skills of leading a normal life without sight.

Matters came to a head on the day when Sally nicked him while she shaved his face. Angrily he thrust her aside and hurled the basin of soapy water across the ward.

Sally turned on him.

'Who do you think you are to behave so childishly, Tom Pain?' she demanded. 'There are men here with missing limbs, shattered bodies and no hope of ever living a full life again. So you can't see . . . but you can hear, can't you? And you can smell and feel. Think how bad it would be if you could do none of these, and then tell me about your troubles!'

There was a shocked silence in the ward. Nurses and other patients waited with bated breath to hear his reply. They were treated to the rare sound of Tom laughing. He stretched out his hand, feeling for her own.

'Bravo, Smithy,' he said, 'I deserved that!'

From that time on, he had cooperated with Sally, and as time went on he became more responsive to the others. But it was the little girl from the munitions factory to whom he appealed when there was a letter to be written, or one from his friends at the front which must be read to him.

One morning Sally came upon Katherine McLean enjoying a moment of quiet solitude in the conservatory. It was May, and the valley lay shimmering in the early-morning haze which heralded another warm sunny day.

'Just look up there,' said Katherine as Sally approached. 'Have you ever seen the rhododendrons looking so wonderful?' Along both sides of the valley, the giant blossoms, purple, pink and yellow, ruby red and brilliant crimson, glowed like jewels against their dark foliage.

Sally drank in the scene. A lowlander born and bred, it had

taken her some time to get used to this wild and unpredictable countryside. At first the mountains had seemed to her like prison walls. The wind and rain were a constant torment and the mist hanging low on the hills filled her with deep depression. Recently, however, she had begun to come to terms with her disfigurement. She was no longer afraid to venture out alone, and with Tom occupying so much of her free time, she had come to view her surroundings in a different light. On this lovely May morning she could see nothing but beauty in the valley and the mountains beyond.

'The gardens are absolutely glorious,' she agreed. 'And it looks as though it is going to be a lovely day.'

'I don't suppose you would care to run down to Eisdalsa for me, in the Ford?' Katherine suggested. 'There are a few things I need from the village store.'

She knew how much Sally appreciated an opportunity of driving the car. Although travel on public vehicles was still a trial to her, she enjoyed the sense of freedom which she had when driving alone along the country roads, and while the possibility of an encounter with strangers still disturbed her, ever since the time when she had lived on the island with Annie Beaton, the villagers had made her welcome.

Out in the stable yard she swung the handle of the neat little vehicle. The engine coughed into life, juddered a little and subsided into silence.

'Try a little more choke.'

She turned suddenly, startled by his silent approach, and hit her head on the front of the radiator as she came up.

'Ouch!' she exclaimed involuntarily.

'I'm sorry,' Tom apologised, 'did I startle you? Have you hurt yourself?'

He stepped towards her, his white stick held in front of him, feeling his way.

She straightened up and held out her hand to guide him towards the bonnet of the car.

'It's all right,' she assured him. 'I just can't get the wretched thing to start, that's all.'

He felt his way along the bonnet to the windscreen. His hands wandered over the door and the driver's seat. Squeezing the leather, he relished the familiar scent . . . a mixture of polish and petroleum.

'A Model T,' he breathed. 'They were just beginning to import them down under when the war started.'

'Have you ever driven one?' she asked. The encounter with the machine seemed to give him immense pleasure.

He had his hand on the handle now. He pulled it down and opened the door. Feeling his way, he sat behind the wheel and fingered the various levers. He put his foot down on the clutch and shifted the gears about for a few minutes. Then he adjusted the lever of the accelerator.

'Now swing her,' he called out.

The car came to life instantly, and with only the smallest further adjustment he had the engine purring in a most satisfactory manner.

'Move over,' Sally said, waiting while Tom felt his way with some difficulty into the passenger seat.'

'You must show me how you did that,' she told him, letting the clutch and steering the car down the drive.

'Gladly,' he replied. 'What's this . . . are we going somewhere?'

'Mrs McLean wants some messages from the village store, and I thought we might pop over to Eisdalsa Island and visit my friend Annie Beaton.'

She felt confident, driving with Tom beside her. If anything went wrong with the car, he would know how to fix it. They drove in silence for some time until they reached the top of the brae where she pulled over on to the grass verge.

For a few minutes they sat in silence, enjoying the heavy scent of gorse mingled with the tang of salt sea breezes.

Suddenly, Tom leant towards her and groped for her hand.

'You and I would make such a good team, Sally. You could be my eyes, I'd tell you what had to be done.'

'What, in the motor business?' She looked at him in disbelief. For a moment she suspected he was making one of his usual cynical jokes, but she could see from his expression that he was absolutely serious.

'What are you suggesting, Tom?' she asked.

'I was wondering if you would come out to Australia with me, and help me to get my business going again?'

'Oh, I don't know . . .'

'We get on so well together,' he said. 'At first I used to wonder why any young woman should want to settle down with a blind man who would be absolutely dependent on her for the rest of her life. But then . . . well, you seemed to be so good at handling that side of things that I thought you might possibly come to care for me sufficiently . . .'

Sally touched his cheek very gently. It had become her most intimate means of communicating with him.

'Don't you know that I am probably the most hideous-looking woman in the whole of Argyll?' Her words were light, almost flippant, but he sensed the underlying despair behind them.

'To me you are the most beautiful woman in the world, Sally.' His fingers wandered over her face. Crossing her forehead, they began to travel down over the scar tissue on the right-hand side. She flinched away but he held her firmly with his other hand and continued his exploration. Then he leant forward and kissed her on the poor, wounded cheek.

'There,' he said softly, 'now I know it all.'

'Oh, Tom,' she breathed.

'Will you marry me, Sally?'

For answer she flung her arms about him and kissed him softly on the lips. He drew her closer and kissed her again and again.

For a while they sat in comfortable silence, while the sunlight danced on the waves. The sun disappeared for a moment behind a bank of cloud and instantly the sea was changed from deepest blue to a dark slatey grey.

Sally shivered. 'Best be getting along,' she said. 'Mrs McLean will wonder what we've been up to!'

She started the engine without any difficulty this time, and steered the car slowly down the steep hillside. In the green meadows at the foot of the brae, sheep grazed while their lambs gambolled in the spring sunshine and across the valley the cluster of white buildings that is Tigh na Broch stood out boldly against the craggy cliffs of Caisteal an Spuilleadair.

Tom could see nothing, but he caught the warm pungent smell of the animals they passed on the road, and the fresh smell of new bracken below the escarpment and all the while Sally's voice rose above the noise of the engine, describing what she saw in the minutest detail.

Chapter 26

~

The British Consulate
Lisbon
16 December, 1917

My Darling Annie,
I hardly know where to begin, for during the year or more
that has passed since I last got word to you, my adventures
would read as though straight from a tale in a schoolboy's
annual. Please believe me when I tell you that in all this
time I have been unable to communicate with anyone, and
have been utterly miserable knowing how worried you
must be.

I was transferred from the Hampshire *at a moment's*
notice, when the fleet was licking its wounds after the
affair at Jutland. The old Hampshire *sailed without me and*
I was virtually kidnapped to act as surgeon on a special-
service vessel, about which I am not allowed to say
anything . . .

Annie laid down the letter with a trembling hand, and took the
glass of brandy which David had poured out for her.

'He still does not know that we believed him dead,' explained
her father-in-law. 'It appears that no one has yet told him of the
sinking of the *Hampshire*, for in his note to me he mentions his
concern for his personal possessions.'

The bulky package, addressed to himself in Stuart's handwriting, had arrived at the Connel house that morning.

At first David had supposed that his correspondent was
someone with a hand remarkably similar to Stuart's. Even this

realisation had given him a start and set his pulse racing. He had opened the package, still unsuspecting, and read the first few words before the full impact of the communication hit him. Mrs Murchieson, alarmed by his shocked reaction, had run to fetch Annabel. David rallied meanwhile, poured himself a stiff whisky and was feverishly going over the contents of the letter by the time his wife burst into the room.

'What is it, David?' she asked, anxiously. 'Mrs Murchieson said you had had some bad news.' She sank down beside him on the couch, her mind full of ghastly possibilities. 'What is it . . . is it Hugh?'

He turned to her, slowly.

'It is a letter posted in Lisbon, Annabel.' He allowed her a moment to recognise the handwriting and then continued, 'A letter from Stuart.'

He watched her anxiously, and reached across for the whisky decanter.

'Here, have a sip of this,' he said, handing her a generous dram. Obediently she swallowed half the measure, spluttered a little because she normally took her spirits with some water, and whispered, 'Let me see it.'

He held out the precious document and she looked at it, afraid to touch it in case it might suddenly disappear, as happened so often in her dreams.

'Then Annie was right after all,' she murmured, envious that Stuart's wife had had more faith than she.

Without taking the letter, she emptied her glass and set it down.

'You read it,' she said, 'from the beginning.'

Stuart had sent a two-page letter to his parents, and a thicker envelope addressed to Annie. Dated in January, the package had been four months on its journey from Lisbon.

During their drive from Connel to Eisdalsa, David was racked by indecision. How was he to put it to Annie that her husband was not dead without causing her distress? Despite having denied the fact for so long, recently even she had begun to accept what they had all believed to be the truth. Why, she had even discussed with him the possibility of a second marriage. 'Thank Heaven she refused Manny Rosenstein's offer,' he blurted out, suddenly forgetting that, to spare her feelings, Annabel had been kept in the dark over the matter.

She looked at him, startled by the revelation, but made no comment. She had always suspected that Mr Rosenstein's interest in Stuart's fate had been more than the kindly gesture of a family friend. There had been a period when he was visiting Admiralty offices in Whitehall almost daily, trying to determine what had become of Annie's husband.

When David had crashed the gears several times, and nearly driven them into a stone wall on the approach to the Clachan Bridge, Annabel insisted that he draw the car to the side of the road while they discussed the matter sensibly.

'You have told me often enough what a strong personality we have in our daughter-in-law,' she declared. 'I cannot see any reason why Annie should not take this news in her stride. She will be overwhelmed with joy, as we were . . . any shock she feels will be quickly dispelled.'

'But what if she should blame Stuart for not letting her know where he was all this time?'

Annabel found it difficult to believe that this was the same man whom she had married forty years before. That David had been eager, resourceful, imbued with energy and enterprise and, if a little pompous in his attitude, always ready to leap into any situation which provided a challenge. Age had made him cautious, anxious not to cause injury by his words or actions, inclined to put to one side all the more difficult decisions. He was getting old.

Realising that nothing she said was going to help him to resolve his own problems, she patted his knee and said briskly: 'She will understand, David. Annie is not a foolish girl. Like us, she will just be glad of his safe return . . . you'll see.'

Calmer now, Annie picked up her letter once again.

Our ship went down somewhere north of the Cape Verde

Islands, but thinking that we might have better treatment at the hands of the Portuguese Governor of Madeira, we decided upon a course which would take us some six hundred miles to the north-east.

Our craft was, thankfully, a cut above most ship's emergency boats, with two sets of oars, a mast and sails. How glad I was to have done all that sailing with the fishing boats around the islands back home! None of the crew had any knowledge of sailing under canvas. (It's amazing, isn't it, to think that what were once considered the essential skills of seamanship are now no longer taught?) Fortunately we had a splendid bo's'n aboard, and the men were quick to get the hang of things – those who were not too badly injured that is. We soon got into a good routine which brought us into the safe haven of Funchal Harbour in the early dawn of a December day.

Oh, the tales I could tell you about that voyage, and the men who accompanied me. I shall save them for our own fireside. How I long to be beside you in some cosy room, you in my arms and our child at play upon the rug at our feet. The baby must be nearly eighteen months old already. I am sorry to have missed so much of its little life but determined to make up for this by having others . . . lots of them! Why, I don't even know whether we have a son or a daughter.

We found Madeira to be the most beautiful of islands. It is volcanic, which means that the mountains are precipitous, with deep, heavily wooded gullies separating one section of the land from the next. The hillsides are terraced to retain the soil which appears to be very fertile, since vines cover the higher slopes while on the valley floors there are fields of sugar cane. It is a very green island, and the most glorious flowers bloom there throughout the year. One day I will take you to see it for yourself.

No matter what fine sights I may have experienced on Madeira and elsewhere, nothing can match the beauty of

our own Eisdalsa, and although I am sending this letter by
way of the Connel house, I hope that it will find you on the
island. I like to picture you carrying our infant to the top
of the hill, wading through the fresh green bracken and
heather a foot high – oh, I can smell the wild thyme even
as I write – and showing him or her the Islands of the
Sea . . .

Annie looked up suddenly, brushing a hand across her face to
wipe away the tears.

'He makes no mention of how he will get home,' she said,
anxiously. 'Did he say anything to you?'

David withdrew his own letter from his inside pocket. 'He
explains that as Portugal is a neutral country, he and his crew may
well be interned until the end of the war. He asks that I approach
the Admiralty and the Foreign Office, to see what can be done.'

'I wonder how the package got to Britain?' Annabel asked.
She had remained silent all this time, allowing David to do the
talking.

'I imagine it would have been sent in the Diplomatic Bag,' he
observed. 'A stamp was affixed in London. Anyway, whatever the
means employed, I am glad that the letters have not been
scrutinised by the censor. It is a pleasure to receive something
from abroad which does not have half the writing blocked
out!'

Annie returned to her reading.

After some considerable negotiation I managed to
persuade the Governor to arrange a passage for all of us
aboard a boat bound for Lisbon. Here we sojourn in
relative comfort, but with a gnawing desire to get home.
We are allowed to wander around the town and the
surrounding countryside at will during daylight hours,
and are in constant touch with the British Consul, a
delightful fellow who does his best to make life tolerable. He
believes that a certain amount of pressure in the right
places might secure our release, so I have asked Pa to make

some overtures to the Admiralty. Dan Rosenstein may be able to pull a few strings through his brother's influence in Government circles . . .

She gave an involuntary sob when she realised that Stuart was unaware of Dan's death. He was right about Emmanuel Rosenstein, however, he was certainly the man to approach. Could she really place herself under yet another obligation to him after the way she had treated him?

He had taken her final refusal very hard. She had heard nothing from him since that day last summer when she had walked with him to the headland, and told him that she could never marry a man she did not love. She had begged him to continue to be her friend, but he had stumped off in such a rage that she thought she would never hear from him again. By the time she had reached the cottage, Manny had already left. A curt note lay upon the table.

Should you need me at any time, you know where to find me.

Well, she needed him now, and had no compunction about getting in touch with him.

'I shall write to Mr Rosenstein,' she told David. 'He must know people in the Diplomatic Service. Perhaps you will make contact with someone in the Admiralty? There has to be a way of getting word to Stuart . . . someone we can approach to arrange for his release.'

She pushed back her hair, smoothed her fingers over her damp cheeks and began to move purposefully about the room, tidying the debris of Stephen's ceaseless activity.

'What we need,' she announced, at last, 'is a nice cup of tea.'

Annabel regarded her daughter-in-law with a mixture of admiration and compassion. As she had suspected, Annie was made of sterner stuff than David had given her credit for. Leaving Stephen to his bricks, she joined Annie in the kitchen. Placing an arm about her thin shoulders, Annabel stroked the raven tresses which were prematurely streaked with grey.

'Stuart is very fortunate to have you for his wife,' she murmured.

Annie smiled happily through her tears, then throwing back

her head in a defiant gesture, exclaimed: 'What foolish creatures we women are. We weep when we are sad, and when something as wonderful as this happens, what do we do? Again, we weep!'

Flora McGillivray looked anxiously at her watch. The train was an hour late already; by the time they reached Oban it would be almost dark. She prayed that the transport they had been promised would still be waiting. Some of her charges were looking very poorly.

When Matron had suggested that she might escort the contingent of wounded soldiers from Royaumont to the new convalescent home in Argyll, she had jumped at the chance.

The two days' journey had certainly taken its toll of them all. They had travelled by way of the Hook to Harwich, and then by a network of interminably slow local trains to Peterborough and the main line north. There had been voluntary services along the route, ready to provide hot drinks and sandwiches at every station where they had stopped, but the walking wounded were uncomfortably seated in the second-class carriages, and had had no proper sleep now for forty-eight hours.

Those still confined to stretchers had a better time of it. At least they were lying down. The jolting, and the constant stopping and starting on this last stretch of the line, however, had caused them all great discomfort.

There was an air of excitement now amongst the men. The line had joined a road running alongside the River Awe as it flowed north-westwards through the Pass of Brander, linking Loch Awe to Loch Etive and the open sea.

For many of the men, wounded in that recent stand against the Germans' spring advance along the banks of the River Scarpe, this was home territory. Noses were pressed to windows as their eyes drank in the sight of the high peaks and wooded valleys of Argyll. Expressions of delight were heard from every quarter as the track rounded a bend and Lock Etive came into view. At Taynuilt and Connel stations, groups of villagers waved them on. Word must have got out that some of the boys were coming home.

Flora moved along the corridor, stopping at each compartment to see that her patients were as comfortable as possible. The last compartment had been stripped out and four bunks fitted, two to each side. These were occupied by the worst cases.

She looked intently at the young man on the top bunk, felt for a pulse and glanced anxiously at the mass of bandages which covered the stumps of each of his severed legs. He had told her that he was a fisherman before the war. She doubted he would ever go to sea again.

On the bottom tier, the occupant stared, sightless, at the underside of the bunk above. His internal injuries had been so severe that for many days Dr Ivens had declared him a hopeless case, and had instructed her staff to keep him warm and comfortable while he waited to die. In the circumstances, the fact that he had also lost his sight had seemed of little consequence. Contrary to all prognoses, the man had continued to live and was at last declared fit enough to be shipped home. Now, his impaired lungs and destroyed digestive function were as nothing to the despair he felt for his loss of sight.

Flora squeezed his hand, comfortingly.

'We'll soon be there, Callum,' she said, cheerfully. 'In no time at all they will have you tucked up in your bed, all washed and brushed. What a corker you'll look by the time your girl comes to see you!'

He tried to smile, but she knew only too well that it was this very encounter which worried him the most. What would his Mairi want with a blind husband . . . half his insides shot away?

The soldier on the other top bunk was sleeping. It was a good job they were nearing Oban. She had run out of supplies of morphine.

She crouched down to place her hand on the forehead of the Australian sergeant on the lower bunk.

While trying not to provoke accusations of favouritism, over the past few weeks she had taken extra special care of Jack McDougal, determined to nurse him back to health before he sailed to join his Jean at Kerrera Station.

When he had first arrived at Royaumont, brought in by Heather Brown's convoy of ambulances from the forward dressing station at Roeux, Jack had seemed very down, unable to view the future with anything but despair. It had been Flora who had explained about false legs, now so sophisticated by comparison with the old wooden stumps which he had seen on veterans of earlier conflicts. She it had been who had pointed out that since the surgeons had saved his knee, he would still be able to sit a horse and, if he could ride, he could herd sheep.

From that point on, he had begun to plan once more.

He talked endlessly about the new breed he had begun to develop, of the way in which he intended to extend the water supply to his land, and most of all about the new town which he and his father had planned together in those heady days after their first good wool cheque had arrived.

And this new optimism had not only furthered his own recovery. Flora remembered Jack as a quiet, thoughtful man, dour to those who did not know him. Now he had become the life and soul of the party, bringing a cheerfulness and a positive approach to the future which enthused everyone who had contact with him, putting heart into even the most despondent of men.

'I hope the transport has been held at Oban.' She was worried that there might be difficulty moving her patients out to Johnstones. It was a long drive for sick and weary men.

'Sure to be,' he said. 'And if they haven't waited, no doubt people in the town will work something out. They'll not let us want for a meal and a bed for the night.'

'I don't want my patients lined up on the platform, exposed to an Oban gale, even if it is nearly June.'

'Well, you'll soon know what's been arranged,' he assured her. 'If I'm not mistaken, that's the electric light station we have just passed. We shall be arriving at any minute!'

The train drew in to the station and decamped its passengers on to the draughty platform. Chill though the breeze might be, there was not a man among them who was not pleased to look up through the Victorian glass canopy at the massing clouds, and to hear the station clock striking the half-hour, a perpetual tribute to the old Queen's reign.

Striding along the platform, intent upon being the first to greet the returning warriors, was Dr David Beaton. He had been her grandfather's friend in the days when Jamie McGillivray had fought his own particular battle against injury and despair; he had been instrumental in obtaining for her father, Dougal, a university education so that he could become a mining engineer; and he had been a friend and support to her grandmother in her widowhood. There was no aspect of the McGillivray's fortunes in which the kindly doctor had not played a significant part, for forty years or more. As for Flora, he had brought her and her brother Hamish into the world and, did he but know it, was responsible for initiating her own interest in a medical career.

Abandoning all decorum, and heedless of the curious glances of the two junior nurses and the twenty wounded men in her charge, Flora flew into his arms.

'Dr David!' she cried. 'How marvellous of you to be here to greet us. I hoped all along it would be you!'

He allowed her to hug him for a few moments longer than was absolutely necessary, enjoying the envious looks from those about them. Then, holding her at arm's length, he surveyed her from top to toe, registering his approval with a little nod of the head. He turned to his companion, a younger man whom Flora scarcely remembered.

'I was told to expect a Sister Flora McGillivray, Michael,' David explained. 'Annabel and I have been speculating for the past three days as to whether it could possibly be Mary McGillivray's girl.' He turned back to Flora. 'Annabel was beside herself with delight at the prospect of your return to Eisdalsa. She will be so relieved, for Mary's sake, to know you are safely back in Argyll.' He glanced now from one to the other, suddenly appreciating that these two were almost strangers.

'Michael, let me introduce Sister McGillivray . . . Wee Annie's niece. Flora, this is my daughter Margaret's husband, Michael Brown.'

'I'm afraid the train was very late leaving Queen Street, Dr Brown.' Flora shook hands with Michael, and continued apologetically, 'I wondered if perhaps our transport might have been dismissed?'

'The trains are so unreliable these days,' Michael responded, 'that I had the station master call me up on the telephone when the train left Connel.'

'Some of my patients are very poorly,' Flora explained. 'It has been a long and tiring journey.'

'Michael has everything under control,' David assured her. 'There are two ambulances standing by for the stretcher cases, and a number of volunteers with private cars have been summoned to take the walking wounded.'

Michael had taken an instant liking to this efficient young woman whom he remembered as the pretty little teenager who had acted as bridesmaid at her grandmother's marriage to John McDougal.

She waved a sheaf of papers which she had been holding tightly in her left hand.

'I need to check with the station master about the travel warrants,' she said.

'Oh, give me those.' Michael took command. 'You must get your men under cover while we allocate transport. My wife has arranged for them to be given refreshment in the Seamen's Mission, just along the pier.'

While they had been speaking, a small army of civilians, mostly ladies, had appeared as if by magic, and were shepherding the soldiers into the Mission Hall. Fishermen who moments before had been busy with their catch had come to handle the stretchers. As one of these was carried past, Flora signalled to the men to halt for a moment.

'See here, Dr David,' she said, 'another old friend for you to greet.'

Jack McDougal stretched out his hand, and David, surprised and delighted to see him, gripped it with such fervour that the sergeant was forced to beg for mercy.

'Hold on, Doc,' he cried, his voice sounding strangely colonial in this setting. 'If you want to grab anything that tight, make it my left leg!'

David glanced down to where the missing limb left a flat space beneath the blanket.

'I'm sorry, Jack,' he murmured.

'Think nothing of it, Doc,' came the reply. 'I don't. Flora assures me that you people are going to give me a nice new tin one that I can use to kick the 'roos without stubbing my toe!'

Laughing at the thought of Jack chasing after the kangaroos, Flora took David's arm while Michael Brown went to report to the station master's office.

Annie went about her life during that summer of 1918 in a state of quiet expectancy. She knew that it would take time for the powers that be to agree upon a date for Stuart's repatriation. Manny Rosenstein, as good as his word, had moved heaven and earth in order to have Annie's husband restored to her.

Their Lordships at the Admiralty, clearly embarrassed by Stuart's reappearance, had proved reluctant to make any effort to have either him or his comrades returned. Their replies to David's repeated exhortations to do something about the matter had been evasive. No one was prepared to admit to any responsibility for the fact that Annie had not been informed that her husband was alive.

As week followed week, she became more and more certain that something must happen soon. Whenever she spotted the postie alighting from the ferry boat, she would grab Stephen, and no matter how much he protested at being disturbed in his play, would hurry to meet her.

On a sunny morning in June, while Annie was passing the time of day with her neighbour, Edith McPherson, they looked up to see Meg Roberts, official postbag banging on her back, hurrying towards them across the green. There was an urgency in her movements which alerted Annie at once. The whole village was by now aware that Annie was waiting to receive word from Portugal. Perhaps this was it . . . a letter from Stuart.

'You get along, dear,' Mrs McPherson, suggested. 'I'll keep an eye on the wee one until you get back.'

Annie needed no second bidding.

She flew down the path, meeting Meg outside the old school-house.

'Well,' cried the postie, smiling as the younger woman rushed towards her, 'you must have known I had something special today! There's one from Australia and one from London.'

'Oh, thank you, Meg.' Breathlessly, Annie accepted the two envelopes. Her mother's hand she recognised immediately, and thrust that letter into her pocket to be read later. While Meg waited expectantly, she tore open the other.

The packet contained a second envelope, and a thick sheet of expensive-looking notepaper bearing the official letter head of the Foreign Office.

She scanned it rapidly, read the contents twice to be sure that she understood what it said, and threw her arms around Meg, delightedly.

'He's on his way home, Meg. Isn't it wonderful? He has already left Lisbon by train. He could be here any day!'

She examined the second envelope. The writing was Stuart's. Presumably it had been sent in the Diplomatic Bag like the first letter. Thanking Meg a second time, she turned to go.

'Will ye no' be getting in touch with the doctor?' Meg called after her. Despite the fact that Hugh Beaton and his wife Millicent had occupied Tigh na Broch for the past six years, to those of Meg's generation there was still only one doctor in the district, and that was David Beaton.

'I will cross over later and make a telephone call,' Annie replied. She would also have to tell Millicent the good news.

Anxious now to read her letter from Stuart, she hurried back to where Edith was waiting outside the cottage door.

She dropped down beside her neighbour on the stone seat, exhausted by all the running.

'Will I go inside and make a wee cup o' tea, hen?' demanded Mrs McPherson, seeing how anxious Annie was to read her letter in private. Annie nodded, thankfully. When Mrs McPherson had gone she tore open the envelope.

At first the Portuguese authorities seemed reluctant to do anything about arranging for us to get home. I think they must have been waiting to see the outcome of the German offensive in March, because as soon as news began to filter through about the Allied counter-attack, and the advances being made by our side all along the front, attitudes began to change towards us. I suppose it's understandable really, a neutral country cannot afford to antagonise either side, and despite their obvious preference for the British, Portugal is a very small country which could easily be swallowed up by a victorious German Army.

Negotiations for our release have gone on at the highest level. I am told by the Consul here that the prime mover seems to have been Dan's brother, Emmanuel. As you know, he is still an MP, despite being a Major in the Hampshire Regiment. I knew it was a good idea of mine to get Dan to help you!

I am told that we should be issued with our travel warrants any day now. It could be that we shall be back in Blighty within days of this letter reaching you. I can't wait to see you both. Little Stephen sounds like a chip off the old block. I can just imagine Pa in miniature. By the way, I like the name Stephen. It makes a refreshing change from all the usual family names.

Edith had returned with cups of tea, and a drink of milk for the baby.

'Stuart will be home any day,' Annie told her, bubbling over with happiness. 'I must get word to his father. When I have finished this, I'll have to go across and make a telephone call.'

'I knew there was something I wanted to tell you,' Edith exclaimed. 'Did ye know that we're to get a telephone box, here on the island?'

'Never!' cried Annie, incredulous. 'Whatever next!' She was prepared to be amazed and delighted at everything on this wonderful day.

At Tigh na Broch, Annie found that Millicent was entertaining some of the staff from Johnstones. Katherine McLean's car was parked in the drive, and as she approached the house, Annie could see that the visitors were taking advantage of the fine spring day and having their tea in the garden.

While Millicent rose to greet her sister-in-law, Stephen was taken in tow by his cousins, Ian and Wee Davy. He toddled off, leaving his mother to explain her unexpected visit.

'Stuart is on his way home!' she announced, unable to keep the good news bottled up for another instant.

'Oh, Annie,' Millicent hugged her, 'how wonderful. I'm so happy for you.' If only it could be Hugh also, she thought, wistfully. Nevertheless, she showed her delight at Annie's good news by announcing it to her visitors.

Katherine and Sally Smith crowded round, eager to hear the full story. Then Millicent remembered that she had another guest.

'Oh, whatever can I be thinking of?' she exclaimed. 'Your news has put it right out of my head . . . we have such a surprise for you!'

As she was speaking a figure appeared at the French window. Annie stared in disbelief at the newcomer.

'Daisy was having her usual moan about eating out of doors,' laughed Flora, 'so I said I would carry the tea things!'

She placed the heavily laden tray on a sturdy wooden garden table, and straightened up.

Annie stepped forward and flung her arms about her niece.

'Flora? Can it really be you? Oh, what a day for miracles!' She was laughing and crying together.

The rest of the company now busied themselves pouring and handing round the tea, leaving Annie and Flora alone to talk.

'Have you heard from Hamish?' Annie asked.

'Better than that, I actually met him for a short while . . . in France.' Flora led her aunt across the lawn to where a bench had been set conveniently beneath the branches of an ancient sycamore tree.

'He came to Royaumont, looking for his sergeant who had been wounded,' she explained. 'And you are never going to believe who the sergeant is – Jack McDougal! He's convalescing at Johnstones at this very minute. I was placed in charge of the contingent of wounded which arrived here a week ago. I've been waiting for an opportunity to get in touch with you, to let you know that we are here.'

'Is Jack badly wounded?' Annie asked, anxiously.

'His left leg was amputated below the knee,' her niece explained. 'He is here to recuperate, and to be fitted with a false leg before being shipped back to Australia.'

'Oh, the poor man,' gasped Annie. 'And what of Mary and Dougal, have you heard from them lately?'

'Not for six months at least,' said Flora. 'I was supposed to go straight to Royaumont when I left Australia, but when we arrived at Cape Town there had been some submarine attacks upon convoys off the coast of East Africa, and we were obliged to wait several weeks in port. Because of the confusion caused by our delayed journey, my post must still be wandering around the globe.'

Annie remembered the second letter she had received that morning and withdrew it from her jacket pocket.

'Maybe your grandmother will have something to tell us about Mary and Dougal,' she said, showing Flora the unopened envelope. 'In all the excitement I forgot to read it.'

'Will you open it now?' Flora pleaded, anxious to hear any news from home.

The letter was dated in early January, it had been nearly five months in transit. Annie began to read, her happy expression altering as she absorbed the full impact of her mother's words.

> *Kerrera Station*
> *Southern Cross*
> *West Australia*

My Dearest Annie,
I hardly know how to write the sad tidings which I must convey to you. Dougal died in a mining accident in December. It seems that to prevent flooding the whole mine, he sacrificed his own life, and that of one of his Aboriginal workers, by blowing up a tunnel to stem the flow of underground water.

Mary could not bear to remain at Keningo without him,

and she has now made her home with us at Kerrera Station. It is going to take time for her to adjust to her loss, but John has persuaded her to open a school for the local children. The challenge is just what she needs at present, and although she is still very silent around the house, and obviously grieving bitterly, when she is with the children she seems to be a different person altogether. I hope the time will soon come when we have our real Mary back again.

One thing which would help to hasten that day would be news of Hamish and Flora. If you should hear anything at all, please write immediately – the poor girl has nothing to live for without them. We all trust that they too will make their home at Kerrera when they return. John and Jack have been planning to build a proper town here and there will be plenty of opportunities for them to make a living for themselves.

I have had only one letter from you this past year, telling of the birth of baby Stephen. I wonder if you have written more? The post is so erratic. Letters from the front line seem to have priority, Jack's to Jean were coming regularly up to a few weeks ago. Mary has had a long letter from Hamish filled with his plans for going into business as an electrical installations consultant – he anticipates electric power will reach even remote homesteads in the next few years!

Well, my dearest Annie, you are now the only baby I have left. Try not to be too sad about Dougal's passing. He had a good life, and achieved as much as many men who live out their full span. I know that your father would have been proud of him.

I long so very much to see you and my new grandson. What a gathering it would be if we could all get together when this dreadful war is over. Perhaps you will be able to come for a visit some day, before little Stephen is quite grown up.

Let us pray that the rest of our chickens will come safely home to roost.

Give my regards to Annabel and Dr David, and tell them I will write soon.

When Annie had finished reading, she sat silent for a few minutes, her thoughts in turmoil. It had been such a wonderful day and now she was filled with gloom. Her brother was dead.

Dougal had been away from home for many of the early years of her life. He had always been a shadowy figure in those days, coming home occasionally and causing her mother extra work in rearranging the house to accommodate him and getting the place all spruced up before his arrival. As a little girl she had sometimes resented the attention which he received, although she had always been pleased to accept the little gifts he brought her from London. By the time he returned to Eisdalsa to work, she was already away at boarding school. No, she really had not known her brother very well. Her feelings now were of remorse rather than grief . . . regret that she had not taken the trouble to get to know him when she had the chance. She looked up through her brimming tears to find her niece gazing at her, anxiously.

'Flora, your grandmother has terrible news.' Annie paused, praying for the strength to continue. 'Your father is dead.'

Flora had known that it was something very bad. She'd expected Annie to say that something had happened to John, he was an old man and her grandmother always said that he worked too hard. But how could her father be dead?

Annie handed her the letter and she read her grandmother's words in stony silence. How like him to have died so bravely. Flora had become used to the sacrifices that men made, but that was on the battlefield. Why should her father have given his life to save the mine? What a dreadful waste for a pot of gold.

She became suddenly aware of her aunt and she saw her strained and sorrowful expression. She understood the pain which Annie must have experienced in telling her the news. There was no easy way to say it.

'Poor Mother,' she said quietly. 'Having to bear such grief all on her own.'

She handed back the letter and Annie accepted it with a trembling hand.

Flora found herself blinded by the tears welling in her eyes. She had loved her father as dearly as any daughter could do. She regretted now the past two years during which she had made no effort to go home and visit her parents. At a time when her mother had needed her most, she had been far away. She cried quietly for a little while and Annie, powerless to assuage her grief, looked on helplessly.

'I am so glad that Mother is at Kerrera,' Flora said, wiping away the tears at last. 'I hate Keningo. It is the worst place in all the world!' So vehement was her outburst that Annie wondered again about their life in Australia. Dougal's letters to her, though frequent, had always implied a comfortable existence and good prospects for the future. Flora's attitude suggested that things had not been quite so marvellous as he would have had her believe. Well, it hardly mattered now. There was no reason for any of them to return to Keningo.

'Yes, Sister, I think you are right . . . it's time this patient was measured for his new leg.' An amused glance was exchanged above the head of the far from patient Sergeant Major Jack McDougal.

Sister McGillivray supervised the rebandaging of the stump, which had lost its raw redness and had faded to a healthy pink colour.

'Well, it's about time too, Doc,' declared Jack McDougal. 'God knows what they're doing with my farm while I'm stuck here, wiling away the days!'

'You won't be going far, even when you do get your leg,' warned Michael Brown. 'It's not exactly a case of simply strapping it on and walking out of here, you know.' He made a note on the patient's chart.

'How long then, Doc?' Jack demanded.

'You'll require a number of fittings to begin with. The stump will continue to shrink for a time, but hopefully it will shape itself to the contours of the prosthesis to some extent and make a good, comfortable fit. Then, and only then, we can start to practise some walking.'

'Just let me get going with my tin leg,' said Jack. 'I'll soon get it licked into shape.'

'You'll take it very easily at first,' Michael insisted. 'If you are too hasty, he stump will rub raw and you'll put your progress back by weeks.'

Flora, who knew her uncle better than Michael, realised that whatever his medical advisor suggested, Jack would attack this problem with the same determination he applied to everything else. Once he had made up his mind to walk on his new leg, nothing would deter him.

Sister Flora accompanied the surgeon to the door of the ward, listening carefully to all Michael's instructions, making the occasional note on her starched cuff, just to remind herself.

When they reached the front door, Michael turned to her, a look of concern clouding his usually cheerful countenance.

'Margaret told me the sad news of your father's death,' he said, quietly. 'You have my deepest sympathy.'

Flora acknowledged his words with a grateful smile.

'I still find it difficult to believe that he is dead,' she replied. 'So far away from home, the reality of the situation is hard to accept. My greatest concern is for my mother who is left to bear the entire burden on her own.'

'I could arrange to have you shipped home on compassionate grounds, if that is what you wish?' he suggested.

'Oh, no! I feel that I am doing something useful here at present,' she insisted. 'When the Australian boys are due to be repatriated, I would like to escort them, if that can be arranged?'

'I can see no reason why you should not be transferred at the same time. Transhipments are in the hands of the Glasgow office of the Scottish Women's Hospitals. I will write to them as soon as we have a release date for the men.'

Flora stood watching while Michael reversed his car in the driveway and drove away towards the narrow pass through the hills. She turned, thoughtfully, making her way back to the ward. Dougal McGillivray had been Jack's contemporary during their school days on Eisdalsa, and they had been good friends all their lives. Jack would have to know about her father's death sometime. Now seemed as good a time as any to tell him.

When she returned to the dayroom, she found that Jack had been joined by another of the patients. Tom Pain, his white stick held over his shoulder like a rifle at the slope, was standing in the doorway, demanding, 'All right then, you old bugger, you. They tell me you're in here somewhere, Jack McDougal. Just give me a shout and I'll home in on your voice!'

Jack, seated at the window in a wheelchair, spun the wheels expertly and turned to face the newcomer. 'Tom, you old reprobate, I'm over here!'

When he saw Tom lower his white stick and approach, swinging it delicately in order to locate any obstacles in his path, Jack felt a lump come into his throat. These days he could not look at his friend without remembering the scene of devastation on the day he was loaded on to a barge full of wounded, at Suvla Bay.

When Tom was within touching distance, Jack reached out to him, caught his hand and guided him to the chair at his side. Tom sat, allowing his cane to drop to the floor with a clatter.

Flora held back, not wishing to intrude. She too had been surprised and delighted to learn that Tom was here at Johnstones. She had visited his ward late on the night of her arrival, and studied him as he slept. A fine white line across his temple was the only indication of scarring on his otherwise unblemished face. It was hard to believe that he was so severely disabled. Looking down upon him in the half-light she had remembered those happy times aboard the *Geraldtown*. She had loved him then, with all the passion of a sixteen-year-old experiencing romance for the first time. She understood now that his kindness towards her had been in friendship alone; there had never been any serious romantic intentions other than those conjured up by her own lively imagination. She had smiled, embarrassed at her girlish memories, and kissed him lightly on the brow, hoping not to disturb him. He had turned over with something between a groan and a murmur. She listened intently to what he said. It sounded like 'Sally'.

She approached the two men with a light step. Taking a firm grasp of Tom's arm, she greeted them both with, 'Well, here's a wild Colonial trio.' Tom's expression altered from one of bewilderment to sudden recognition.

'Flora? Little Flora McGillivray?' he queried, unable to believe the evidence of his own ears.

'Sister McGillivray to you, Corporal Pain,' she replied pertly, just like the old Flora.

'Where did you spring from?' he asked, fingers wandering over her features, reminding himself of how she used to look. He found furrows on her brow and above her nose, and a few tell-tale crow's feet at the corners of her eyes. Too much studying or too much worrying, what was it?

'We are none of us quite the same as we were,' she said, softly, and he let his hand fall.

The men would have taken up the banter again, but Jack sensed from her expression that all was not well with Flora. He quieted Tom with a touch of his hand and asked her, 'What is it, love?'

'I heard yesterday . . . Annie received a letter from Grandmother . . .' she faltered, anxious not to distress him yet knowing that she must. 'I knew that you would want to know. It's my father . . . Dougal . . . he's dead.'

Her voice had a hollow quality, as though by the telling of it she at last believed it to be the truth.

'How? When?' Jack demanded, bewildered. Dougal had shown no inclination to enlist when he himself had joined the younger men in that first major recruitment drive.

'It happened in the mine at Keningo . . . an explosion.' Her explanation died on her lips.

Jack grasped her hand.

'Oh, my dear, I'm sorry. Poor old Doug.' For a moment he recalled his friend, remembering their boyhood together on the island and those other times, when things had gone so badly wrong for the McDougals and the McGillivrays had given them so much support. 'What about Mary?' he demanded, suddenly. 'Surely she will not wish to stay at Keningo on her own?'

'She is already at Kerrera. John has had a schoolhouse built and

Granny says that Mother seems quite content to run the school.'

'What of the rest of them at Kerrera?' he asked, anxious for news of his own family. 'Did Anne mention Jean and Ellen?'

'They are well, and longing for you to get back home,' she told him. In truth she could remember nothing of what followed after the news of her father's death, but she knew that her grandmother would not have neglected to mention Jack's little family.

'It seems that there are plans afoot to build a new town at Kerrera,' ventured Tom. 'I'm told that ex-servicemen are to be allocated a plot of ground on which to build a house and a business. Any viable proposition will be considered. My girl and I are going to set up in the motor trade.'

Flora and Jack exchanged glances. How could Tom pursue his infatuation with the internal combustion engine when he was blind? What girl was he talking about? As if in answer to their unspoken question, Sally Smith appeared.

'Here you are, Sapper Pain,' she admonished, sounding like a governess. 'I have been scouring the whole hospital looking for you.'

She stopped abruptly on seeing Flora. She had not yet been introduced to the new Australian sister who had arrived with the latest contingent from France.

'I'm sorry, Sister,' she stammered, blushing. Subconsciously, she pulled her hair forward to cover her face. It was an action she made before strangers.

Tom, recognising Sally's voice, stretched out his hand and grasped hers.

'No need to stand on ceremony here, love,' he told her. 'These are two of my greatest friends. You had better get used to them, because we are all going back to Kerrera together!'

Every day now, Annie took Wee Stephen by the hand and led him up the steep path to the top of the hill. In his lisping little voice he would recite the names of the islands which stood out in sharp silhouette against a cloudless blue sky.

The breeze was a little stronger today. Annie regretted having left her jacket in the house. Stevie did not seem to notice the cold. She cuddled him to her, feeling his vibrant little body passing its heat through the thin material of her blouse.

There were several small fishing boats in the bay. The threat of submarines in these waters seemed to have passed, and there was even talk of restoring a regular steamer service from Glasgow.

She found a sheltered cleft in the rocks where a bed of wild thyme provided a soft and fragrant seat upon which to rest and watch the activities of the local fishermen in their small boats. From here she had a good view right across the bay towards the green island of Lunga which crouched below the dark and menacing cliffs of nearby Scarba. Stephen began to search out the flowers which grew in every sheltered cranny, struggling to exist against all odds. Protected by the boulder, the grass grew long and cinquefoil and vetches entwined themselves around its slender stems. The child's little fingers made to grab the blooms, but Annie restrained them.

'No, Stevie,' she admonished, gently, 'the flowers have struggled hard to grow and bloom in this place. Leave them be.'

The little boy pouted, but knew better than to disobey. He searched amongst the tall grasses, parting the blades more carefully now, aware of his mother's eyes upon him. 'Pretty!' he exclaimed.

Annie, whose attention had wandered because she had caught sight of a column of smoke in the gap between the islands of Lunga and Scarba, turned to see what he had found.

'Why, Stevie,' she cried, delightedly. 'You have found an orchid.' She reached into the satchel which she always brought along on these expeditions. It contained a bannock or two, some apples, and today a bottle of lemonade as a special treat for Stephen. In addition, a separate compartment housed a copy of Stuart's book which Annie carried with her always.

It had been Margaret's idea to have his translation of the old Celtic manuscript published in his memory. Annie had been reluctant at first, considering that such a gesture would be an admission that he was truly dead. Confident that Annie's resistance would eventually be worn down, Margaret had pursued the idea, persuading Katherine McLean to illustrate the book with pictures of the medicinal plants which medieval physicians had used. Katherine's flower drawings were famous in the botanical circles in which she and her husband moved. Not only would her illustrations enhance Stuart's work but they would be certain to ensure the success of the book.

To advise her on aspects of the actual text, Margaret had approached her Uncle Angus. David's brother, now a septuagenarian, had retired to his house on Mull, emerging only very occasionally to help in some medical emergency.

When she had seen the illustrations, and witnessed the delight with which both David and Angus viewed the project, Annie relented and the publication had gone ahead. Now that Stuart was on his way home, she was again filled with apprehension lest he might disapprove of what had been done.

She turned the pages, seeking the entry which she knew was there. Yes, here it was, the Wild Orchid . . .

. . . They are hot and moist and under the dominion of Venus. The roots, bruised and applied to the place, heal the King's evil. An infusion may be used against worms in children. Applied outwardly as a cataplasm they dissolve hard tumours and swellings . . .

Annie remembered that last year, at this time, the children had found an orchid on the lower slopes and was glad to note that the plants were spreading. She remembered Morag had looked up the flower in the old manuscript, and enquired of David what was the King's evil?

Taken aback by the child's question, he had answered bluntly: 'Scrofula,' but then, seeing the girl's puzzled expression, had gone on to explain. 'These days, we know that a form of tuberculosis in the glands of the neck is responsible for what is sometimes a really huge swelling. A modern surgeon would have little hesitation in cutting out the offending gland but there are certain dangers. The main blood vessels run close by, and a complex system of spinal nerves must be avoided . . .'

He was giving her a serious lecture, and Morag drank in every word.

'But why "the King's evil"?' she demanded.

'Because,' David replied, straight-faced, 'King Edward the Confessor was said to have cured his subjects of the condition by laying on his hands.'

Despite Millicent's insistence that her daughter was just going through a childish phase and would soon change her mind about wanting to study medicine, Annie was convinced that her little niece was as determined as any male member of the family to carry on the tradition of healing.

Annie bent down to show the book to Stephen.

'Look,' she said, 'there is your pretty flower . . . a Wild Orchid.'

'Orchid,' the infant repeated, solemnly.

She looked up to see what had happened to that puff of smoke she had observed. It was now a column, white like a cumulus cloud, pouring forth from a tall funnel. The paddle wheels were clearly visible, white water cascading from them like waterfalls down a mountainside.

Annie stood up, gathering Stephen in her arms.

'Look, Stevie,' she cried, 'the steamer!'

The child chuckled with delight.

Gathering up her belongings and thrusting the book into her haversack, Annie carried her little boy down the hill. If they were quick they would reach the harbour before the vessel tied up at the pier on Seileach.

Others on the island now rallied to the unfamiliar call of the whistle from the steam engine. Several cottages were occupied for the summer: factory workers needing a little respite after three and a half years of war, servicemen snatching a few days' leave before going back to fight. But there was an air of certainty about, a conviction that the war would not last much longer, that by the end of the year it would all be over.

Annie arrived breathless at the ferry landing to find that Baldie Campbell had already rowed to the entrance of the harbour, expecting to be called to take off passengers for the island. She set Stephen down on his feet and together they watched, hand in hand, as the steamer drew in to the pier and the crew hastened about their task of securing her, to allow the passengers to disembark.

The *Maid of Lorn* looked tired and shabby. She had fought her own war, carrying supplies to the more remote communities, shipping troops back and forth to outposts on the Western Islands. She had come under fire on occasion, and bore her scars proudly. Her comings and goings had at all times been subject to the threat of mines and torpedoes, but like the men who manned her, and those who now disembarked to join their waiting kinsfolk, she had survived.

Annie lifted her eyes to where the sun, reflecting from the windows of the bridge, blinded her for an instant. Could she be deluding herself or was there really something familiar about that figure in naval uniform leaning upon the bridge rail, shielding his eyes against the glare?

He began to wave, frantically, as though he had recognised someone. She waved back, certain now that she was not mistaken. Lifting Stephen in her arms so that Stuart would see him, she waited impatiently while Baldie collected his passengers and began the slow pull back to the island.